THE JEWISH PEOPLE IN AMERICA

THE JEWISH PEOPLE IN AMERICA

A Series Sponsored by the American Jewish Historical Society

Henry L. Feingold, General Editor

Volume I
A Time for Planting
The First Migration, 1654–1820
Eli Faber

Volume II
A Time for Gathering
The Second Migration, 1820–1880
Hasia R. Diner

Volume III
A Time for Building
The Third Migration, 1880–1920
Gerald Sorin

Volume IV
A Time for Searching
Entering the Mainstream, 1920–1945
Henry L. Feingold

Volume V
A Time for Healing
American Jewry since World War II
Edward S. Shapiro

A Time for Gathering
The Second Migration

THE JEWISH PEOPLE IN AMERICA

A TIME FOR GATHERING
The Second Migration
1820–1880

Hasia R. Diner

The Johns Hopkins University Press

Baltimore and London

The Johns Hopkins University Press
701 West 40th Street
Baltimore, Maryland 21211-2190
The Johns Hopkins Press Ltd., London

Library of Congress Cataloging-in-Publication Data

Diner, Hasia R.
A time for gathering : the second migration, 1820–1880 /
Hasia R. Diner.
p.   cm. — (The Jewish People in America ; v. 2)
Includes bibliographical references.
ISBN 0-8018-4344-8 (alk. paper)
1. Jews—United States—History—19th century.
2. Jews, German—United States—History—19th
century. 3. Judaism—United States—History—19th
century. 4. Jews—United States—Social conditions.
5. United States—Ethnic relations. I. Title. II. Series.
E184.J5D493   1992
973'.04924—dc20   91-45368

*In Loving Memory
of Hannah Ticktin,
My Dear Friend*

CONTENTS

Contents

Illustrations follow page 140.

SERIES EDITOR'S FOREWORD

OVER the generations, there has been much change in the content of Jewish culture. Some writers argue that in the benevolent and absorbent atmosphere of America, Jewish culture has been thinned beyond recognition. But one ingredient of that culture—a deep appreciation of history—continues to receive the highest priority. The motto on the seal of the American Jewish Historical Society enjoins us, "Remember the Days of Old." It is taken from the Pentateuch, itself a historical chronicle.

Indeed, the Jewish community boasts almost one hundred local historical societies and two professional archives for preserving source material. The cherishing of its history goes beyond any biblical or cultural injunction. History is especially important for Diaspora communities because corporate memory rather than territorial space ultimately ensures their survival. That is what Bal Shem Tov, founder of the Hasidic movement, may have meant when centuries ago he counseled his followers that "memory is the key to redemption."

The American Jewish Historical Society offers this history of the Jews in America to both the Jewish community and the general reading public as a repository of memory. For Jewish readers this series provides an opportunity to enrich their self-understanding, quickening Jewry's energies and enhancing its potential for survival. We hope to remind the general reading public that, at a time when the American dream may be found wanting, the American Jewish experience is evidence that the promise of America can still be realized. Without the opportunities, freedom, and openness found in this land, American Jewry would not have been able to realize its energies and talents and become what it is today.

How that has happened over the generations is a story the American Jewish Historical Society is committed to tell. In fact, the society could think of no better way to honor its historical task and its rich hundred-year history than by recounting that story through this series. No single volume by a single historian can do justice to the multilevel historical experience of American Jewry. Drawing on the talents of five historians with a common vision and purpose, this series offers a historical synthesis at once comprehensible to the intelligent lay reader and useful to the professional historian. Each of these volumes integrates common themes: the origins of Jewish immigrants, their experience of settling in America, their economic and social life, their religious and educational efforts, their political involvement, and the change the American Jewish community experienced over time.

Predictably, the project encountered many conceptual problems. One of the most vexing stemmed from the difficulty of classifying American Jewry. To treat American Jews solely as members of a religious denomination, as was once the practice of the Reform branch, was a distortion, because most American Jews are not religious in the sectarian sense. And though some sociologists have classified Jews as a race, clearly that category does not adequately describe how they differ from other Americans. More than other ethnic communities, American Jewry is influenced by two separate historical streams: the American and the Jewish. To be sure, American Jewry is but one of the many ethnic groups woven into the American national fabric. Yet it is something beyond that as well. It is part of an evolving religious civilization that has persisted for millennia. This persistent tension between assimilation and group survival—the will to remain part of the universal community of Israel—is well evinced in the volumes of this series.

In this second volume, Hasia Diner details the tension between accommodation and survival, in the process revising the prevailing view that holds that German Jews in America tipped too far toward accommodation. Rather than finding sharp divisions in the way German Jews came to terms with their Jewishness and the conflicting demands of the American culture, she notes many continuities with the Jews of east Europe who succeeded them and had in fact already begun to make their debut in America.

On behalf of the society, I thank the many participants of this venture, which had its beginnings over fifteen years ago as a way of commemorating the society's 1992 centennial. Dr. Abram Kanof, Rosemary E. Krensky, and the late David Lubart provided initial support for the project. Dr. Kanof has been repeatedly generous in his financial contributions over the years, while the Sherman and Jill Starr Foundation and the Max and Dora Starr Foundation have provided additional welcome assistance. The authors, Eli Faber, Hasia R. Diner, Gerald Sorin, and Edward S. Shapiro, deserve special thanks. In addition, we are grateful to Ruth B. Fein and the late Phil Fine for their efforts on behalf of the project. For their technical and legal expertise in making publishing arrangements for the series, Robert L. Weinberg and Franklin Feldman need to be singled out. Words of thanks also go to Henry Y. K. Tom, executive editor of the Johns Hopkins University Press and to his colleagues for their dedication and professionalism in bringing the society's dream to realization. Last, a special appreciation is in order for the society's untiring staff, particularly Bernard Wax and the late Nathan M. Kaganoff, for their administrative support.

Henry L. Feingold
General Editor

ACKNOWLEDGMENTS

Acknowledgments take many forms. First, as is fashionable today, they are a public statement of the baggage one brings to a project. I had always taken on face value the "truth" that mid-nineteenth-century American Jews were largely the economically successful, Reform-oriented, acculturated Germans depicted in the literature. As the child of eastern European Jewish immigrants, I subscribed to the notion of "us" and "them." "They" were stiff and formal, afraid to assert their ethnic identity, and their primary goal, apart from achieving economic wealth, was to be accepted and to blend into America. The task of writing about a group of people I basically did not like was not easy.

Importantly, plunging into the sources and looking at these women and men on the community level changed my mind and ultimately shook up the "truths" about American Jewish history that had seemed so self-evident. What came across was not so much how different they were from the later immigrants, whom I knew, but rather how similar.

Secondly, I want to acknowledge that placing one's book in a series can be a tricky matter. A good team player should strive to create a work that fits into the themes, goals, and visions of the whole set. Yet for most scholars, writing is an individualistic process. One follows one's own instincts, leads, research orientation, and style. This may produce something that upsets the balance between volumes and pushes the line of thinking in a direction different from that which came before it and that which follows. Henry Feingold, the editor of this series, and Bernard Wax, of the American Jewish Historical Society, helped me in this dilemma. Their belief in me and my book helped me steer my course between these two shores, and they did not interfere with my tendency to tilt toward the latter. For this and all sorts of other help, I thank them warmly.

Acknowledgments

Stephen Whitfield and Harold Wechsler are among the best editors and critics around. Their comments were insightful and useful, and most of all they challenged and encouraged me throughout the years of thinking, researching, and writing about nineteenth-century American Jewry. Their ideas and insights sustained me. Paula Hyman commented on a paper derived from this book at the Berkshire Conference on Women's History, and I benefited greatly from her words. In addition, conversations with Benny Kraut, James Gilbert, Mary Corbin Seis, Lee Shai Weissbach, Mechal Sobel, and many others made a difference as I approached the mountain of notes I had collected. Dale Dowling, then a graduate student at the University of Maryland, always kept her eye out for references on synagogue architecture and she shared insights with me on the history of architecture.

Many other people and institutions helped make this book possible. First, I would like to thank the General Research Board of the University of Maryland for its support in the form of a summer and then a semester leave that enabled me to concentrate full time on this enterprise. Secondly, the American Jewish Archives in Cincinnati gave me a generous fellowship to use their rich holdings, whose surface I could only scratch. Dean Robert Griffith of the College of Arts and Humanities helped me in numerous ways. Finally, the University of Maryland's Department of American Studies and its chair, R. Gordon Kelly, granted me a sabbatical leave to help get this manuscript ready for publication.

Jenny Tringali and Kathy Price, of the Department of American Studies, taught me how to use WordPerfect over the telephone. They put up with an endless series of questions and never made me feel inadequate. They provided much needed support for this project, and without them I would truly have been lost. Marcia Goldberg was the perfect proofreader for this project—meticulous in attention to detail and well-versed in the lexicon of Jewish life and history. Dabrina Taylor provided excellent editorial services, making my life easier. Henry Tom and others on the staff of the Johns Hopkins University Press helped see this book come to life.

I would further like to thank several librarians and archivists for helping me in the search for illustrations. Hannah Sinauer, of the B'nai B'rith Archives in Washington, D.C.; Mary Isen, at the Library of Congress; and Elizabeth Kessin Berman and Virginia North, of the Jewish Historical Society of Maryland; gave me their time and expertise. In addition, I want to thank Susan Myers of the Smithsonian Institution's Museum of American History for helping with some photographs and reproductions. Peggy Pearlstein and Michael Grunberger at the Library of Congress in the Hebraic Section facilitated my research and trusted me with valuable photographs.

A few more people, in a very select group, deserve some special mention. Joshua Greenberg served as an able and enthusiastic assistant. I hope that the experience he had digging for me in the Library of Congress whetted his appetite for the enterprise of history. If he should choose to become a historian, I will take a lot of delight and a small bit of responsibility for it. My daughter, Shira, worked off many debts to me by laboring on the book, making cards, alphabetizing, and organizing notes. My own debt to her for her cheerfulness and company can never be really paid off. My son, Eli, never ceased to encourage me and take pride in my work.

I have derived immeasurable benefit from the insights, comments, support, and friendship of two historians who make up my own special community of scholars: Marsha Rozenblit and Pamela Nadell. Their help and encouragement was boundless, and if they tired of hearing about the project and if they minded marking up my manuscript, they never complained. Instead, they made me always feel like I was pursuing the right path.

Finally, saving the best for last, Steve Diner listened endlessly to my talking about this project, asked penetrating questions, read and edited the text in its crudest form, and expressed tremendous excitement for what I was doing. I could not have finished this book without his help as critic, editor, husband, and friend.

A Time for Gathering
The Second Migration

INTRODUCTION:
AMERICAN JEWS, 1820–1880

LIKE CAESAR'S Gaul, American Jewish history has been divided into three parts. Historians of the American Jewish experience have clung to the idea of a Sephardic era (1654–1820), a German era (1820–80), and an age dominated by eastern European immigrants beginning in 1880. But Jewish migration and community building in the United States followed a pattern more complex and uneven than this tripartite conceptualization that has dominated historical and popular thinking.

This book focuses on the "German" period of the middle decades of the nineteenth century. It challenges this simplifying label and questions some of the images that pervade the history—and hagiography—of these years. The familiar figure of the mid-nineteenth-century American Jew portrayed a successful man of German origin who, devoted to German language and culture, participated fully in German American life. His connection to Judaism and the Jewish people eroded dramatically as he became integrated into the staid comfort of Victorian America. Collectively, American Jews of this sixty-year period have been depicted as a homogeneous group sharing their Germanness, their affluence, their Reform Judaism, and their striving for acceptance in America.

The fact is that "Germans" made up perhaps a slim majority of the Jewish immigrants of this period. They arrived together with other Jews from Poland, Bohemia, Moravia, Galicia, Alsace, and even parts of Russia and Lithuania. Moreover, historians of central European Jewry have significantly refined the meaning of the adjective "German" as applied to the thousands of village Jews, peddlers, horse traders, artisans, domestic servants, and petty merchants of Bavaria, Posen, and Württemberg, and the young women from those regions and classes, who made up the bulk of the immigrants from what became unified Germany in 1871. What did "Germanness" mean to them? How much of what they brought with them to America can truly be considered "German" and how much of German culture influenced the choices they made in America?

We also need to look more closely at the class structure of American Jews of nineteenth-century America. This book concerns itself less with the fabulously successful because "our crowd," as they called themselves, made up but a tiny stratum of the Jewish population. Instead, it explores the nature of the family economy in communities of peddlers and petty merchants who constituted the vast majority. Additionally, religious adaptation offered a more complex and variegated pattern than a straight-line move from European piety to abandonment of tradition in America.

Historians of American Jewry, being largely the children and grandchildren of the eastern European immigrants themselves, have painted a stilted portrait of these earlier American Jews. They said repeatedly that these Jews earnestly sought to integrate into America, usually at the expense of their Judaism and Jewishness. Most of the institutions created by these "German" Jews have been viewed as compromises with modernity, devoid of Jewish content and shallow in a larger meaning. Their charities, social clubs, and synagogues have been presented as slavish imitations of the Christian models around them rather than as serious efforts to transplant traditional forms into new terrain. Historians have contrasted the immigrants of the early part of the century with the Russian and Polish newcomers at the century's end, who emerge as more interesting, more Jewish, and more willing to confront and criticize the demands of mainstream American culture. I postulate instead that the differences between the two waves of Jewish immigrants were less pronounced than previously assumed and that the concept of immigration waves oversimplifies the history of Jewish migration and adjustment.

This book asks questions about the culture and social structure of American Jews. As such, it fits into the broad category of cultural history that assumes that what people did—how they made a living, how they spent their leisure time, where they lived, and whom they lived with—are as much indices of values as formal belief systems. Although these mundane activities reflected the pressures of the marketplace, the impact of geography, and the practicalities of family life, they also demonstrated the ways in which Jews coped with their environment and blended traditional values and contemporary needs. These activities of ordinary life cannot be dismissed as trivial because, for the most part, they were not conscious. Mass behavior was indeed a key to identity.

For example, in just about every American Jewish community of this period, the vast majority of families made a livelihood in small business, especially clothing and the closely related field of dry goods. Choices of work grew out of a variety of factors, not incidental to Jewish history and identity. Petty merchandising had been the mainstay of the Jewish economy for centuries. After coming to America, Jews opted for familiar work despite a range of other possibilities in an expanding economy. In America, as in Europe, a kind of Jewish subeconomy existed in the interstices of the larger one, in which Jews dispensed interest-free loans to one another; family and kin networks were linked by small stores and peddling routes; rival businessmen in the same trades clustered in the same congregations. Business connections made up part of the history of the Jewish people and confirmed patterns of identity and meaning.

For these men and women, Jewishness involved little systematic thought, philosophical speculation, or even traditional study of sacred texts. Judaism as a formal body of knowledge, a vast corpus of law, and a tradition of textual analysis and commentary played little or no role in their lives. Those classes of European Jews who were involved in the study of Judaism did not come to America. The few rabbis who migrated to America in the years 1820 to 1880 came later than the masses, and rather than shape the communities, they usually, and unhappily, served institutions founded by the laity. Of the rabbis who migrated, those most smitten by the winds of Reform found America most attractive, while the more traditional ones knew that America was a place where congregations were the domain of the laity who accepted or rejected traditions as they wanted.

But even the modern rabbis eager to innovate found themselves stymied by ordinary members who in their synagogues acted as Americans, asserting the right of citizens to determine policy and operating on the principle of "no taxation without representation." Their dues built the synagogues and paid the rabbis; therefore, they believed they had as much voice in decisions over ritual practice as did the rabbinate, whether ordained or not. What characterized American Judaism of these years was the widespread belief on the part of the laity that it had the right to change tradition as it saw fit and that American Jewish life derived its power from the "consent of the governed" as did the machinery of the American political system.

It is then to the ordinary Jewish women and men of these years that this book looks most closely for answers to questions about the creation of an American Jewish culture. Leaders actually played a small part in founding and shaping communal life. Indeed, the absence of educated leaders acknowledged by the masses as their representatives or as authoritative voices of tradition provided one of the most distinctive characteristics of American Jewish history of this era. The rabbis, many of whom also published newspapers and lectured widely across the country, defined positions and argued points about a variety of subjects, namely, religious practice, participation in politics, education, and philanthropy. But the masses of Jews in their communities did not defer to them, asserting that rabbinic status did not confer the right to structure communal life.

In the main, the Jewish men and women who came to the United States had little formal education, and philosophical and theological issues made little difference to them. These "average" Jews, however, built institutions, decided what they should look like and how they would function. Ultimately, they—and not rabbis or other communal leaders—decided what the character of American Jewry would be.

In their actions they never lost consciousness of the fact that they were Jews—heirs to a centuries-old tradition, elements of which some or another group of them considered nonnegotiable and unchangeable. They believed that Jews *did* certain things. They lived in a Jewish community that provided services to its people. Jews passed on to their children a sense of ethnic and religious identity.

Yet they expressed these general convictions in distinctly American ways. They did not particularly stand out as outsiders because immigrants bringing in a wide range of other cultures were arriving in America at precisely the same time. While Jewishness offered them no privileges, it also meted out to them few liabilities: the state played no role in the internal affairs of their community, and American Jews could freely mold their institutions and religious practices without outside pressure.

The Jewish immigrants who left central Europe in the 1820s, found little of a Jewish world awaiting them on the other side of the ocean. Before the 1820s a half dozen congregations existed, one each in New York, Philadelphia, Richmond, Charleston, Savannah, and Newport, Rhode Island. Founded and led by the descendants of Spanish-Portuguese Jews who had begun to make their way to the New World in the seventeenth century, the early congregations served as the sole institutions of communal life. Although Ashkenazim (German and Polish Jews) actually made up a majority of the miniscule Jewish population of America at the time of the American Revolution, the small knot of Sephardic leaders in congregations like Philadelphia's Mikveh Israel and New York's Shearith Israel exercised monopolistic control over synagogue affairs. By extension, these gatekeepers controlled access to all Jewish services, including marriage, burial, circumcision, charity, education, and the provision of kosher food.

Tightly bound to these synagogues and relatively invisible in public life *as* Jews, American Jews in the pre-1820s era created little in the way of a distinctively American Jewish culture. As Jews they lived in a transatlantic outpost of European Jewry; they relied on European rabbinic authorities to decide thorny legal problems and imported prayer books and other texts since they did not produce their own. As Americans they drew little attention to the differences between themselves and their Christian neighbors other than in matters of faith. In the increasingly heterogeneous American religious landscape, the pre-1820s Jews emphasized that they were a religious faith rather than a distinct community.

The new arrivals of the nineteenth century broke apart the mold set by the earlier Jews. Geographically, they pushed far beyond the six-city complex and spread out all over America, founding communities in every region and in almost every state. Within the older cities, they defied the single synagogue structure and splintered into many individual congregations, each a reflection of diverse national origins, petty squabbling over personality, and eventually disagreements over questions of religious reform. Institutionally, they created agencies of education, philanthropy, group defense, recreation, and religion outside the synagogue orbit. They published newspapers, wrote books, and founded schools and societies that asserted that Jews did more than pray differently than other Americans.

They founded most of the Jewish communities that exist to this day and created the vast panoply of American Jewish religious, philanthropic, educational, and political institutions that, more than a century later, still live. Rather than criticizing these women and men for compromises or celebrating them for pioneering efforts, I hope to demonstrate how the fluidity of American culture interacted with the dictates of traditional Jewish life to create an American Jewish experience that was in some ways sui generis, yet in others followed the lines of experience of all Diaspora Jews, continuing the old and responding to the new.

CHAPTER ONE

IN EUROPE'S HEARTLAND

We are not immigrants, we are born in Germany and, therefore . . . have no other claim to a home; we are either Germans or homeless.

There is only one expedient to remove this nuisance, namely not to give permission from now on to any Jew to trade, until out of the number of their coreligionists the number of individuals in other crafts, services, and labors will be in the same proportion to those Jews still in trade as exists among other groups in the nation in which they wish to be accepted.

EUROPE'S Jews had long constituted a special case in the Christian societies in which they lived, and the tumultuous years from 1820 to 1880 were no exception. In these decades, Jews became "normal" citizens; they moved from their collective medieval outcast status to a modern one of individuals. The Jewish community as a legally recognized, state-empowered entity lost much of its authority to enforce its will as the governments in France, Germany, Austria, and elsewhere took over many of its previous functions. At the era's beginning, religious culture unified the Jewish people; at the end, with the rise of Reform and the Orthodox reactions to it, the faith of their ancestors divided them. At the inception, Judaism and Jewish life differed little from place to place. A solid phalanx of Jewish culture and life-style linked the Jews of Russia with those of Alsace. By the era's end, a variety of Judaisms existed, often in conflict with one another.

These years brought Europe's Jews into emancipation, citizenship, the bourgeoisie, the cities, and modernity. They went through what one scholar has labeled an "encounter with emancipation," witnessed what another has dubbed "the origins of the modern Jew," while yet another moved them "out of the ghetto" and into confrontation with the "ordeal of civility." These processes engulfed the Jews of Europe, including those who at some point in the century chose to emigrate to the United States. Patterns of migration, settlement, and adjustment to America were shaped by these European experiences.[1]

Historians of modern Jewish history have crafted an enormous body of literature focusing on this era. They have sought to delineate the national differences in the process of emancipation and enfranchisement. In the countries of western Europe—England, France, and the Netherlands—Jews experienced full emancipation. In much of central Europe, particularly in Germany with its patchwork quilt of small states, the Jews' legal disabilities were lifted with fits and starts, and they experienced sporadic emancipation. Historians have further plotted out the various reactions and roles of the different classes and factions—the peasantry, the clergy, the Left, the Right, the bureaucrats, the crown—in each country to the "normalization" of the Jews' status. They have probed how emancipation affected classical Christian-based anti-Semitism. Did it mitigate or exacerbate it? Did it create a new form of the old hatred?

The literature has equally focused on the Jews, not just as passive recipients of citizenship rights, but as actors, and on their political, social, economic, and cultural responses to the debate swarming around them. What role did the Jews play in their own emancipation? Did some Jews fear emancipation and its impact on the Jewish community? What price did the Jews feel they must—and would—pay to accept membership in the French, German, and Austrian polity? What came first: Jewish emancipation or the "modernization" of the Jews? How did the Jews of nineteenth-century Europe respond to the complex rise of nationalism in many of the polyglot states in which they lived? Did, for example, the Jews of Poznań, a Polish enclave annexed by Prussia, share the stirring of Polish nationalism with their neighbors, or did they turn their attention westward to Berlin? What about the Jews of Moravia, Bohemia, or Galicia? How did the debate over the Jews and the erratic emancipation emerge as a factor in the migration of Jews within Europe and to America?[2]

Mid-nineteenth century Europe, from which tens of thousands of young men and women left to try their luck in America, defies easy categorization. Political emancipation and economic modernization occurred over a vast continent, from democratic England in the west to the borders of czarist Russia in the east. Many of Europe's regions included multiple ethnic-linguistic groups of Christians, each of which constituted a separate category and received different treatment in public policy. The heterogeneous nature of Prussia, Hungary, or Austria, for example, touched the political and cultural lives of Jews and complicated their responses to the new challenges. Thus Jews in the Hapsburg monarchy had to accommodate to a different situation if they lived in Bohemia than if they lived in Slovakia, if they resided in Vienna as opposed to Lemberg, and the simple category "Austrian" Jew meant little then. Furthermore, "Germany" did not emerge as a single state until the completion of unification under Bismarck in 1871. Jews in Bavaria experienced the years 1820–80 differently than those in Prussia or, say, Silesia, Pomerania, or Westphalia. They all responded to different local developments, policies, and pressures.

Therefore, emancipation, acculturation, anti-Semitism, and migration—internal and external—can only be understood in the context of local developments. The experience of Jews varied widely, making it impossible to speak meaningfully about "German" or "Austrian" Jews. Surely then we cannot generalize about the experience of all "western European" Jews.

Germany's Jews or German Jews?

In 1820, most Jews in what would become a unified Germany lived in scattered, small towns. Heavily concentrated in the southern and western regions, these *Dorfjuden,* village Jews, lived their lives as petty merchants and peddlers. Special laws about where they could live and how many of them could marry, how they should keep their business records and what kind of taxes they had to pay governed their relationship to the states. They spoke Yiddish and meticulously observed traditional Judaism. By 1880, however, most German Jews lived in cities. Many had moved into the middle classes through commerce and, in the next generation, the professions. They spoke mostly German, as befitted the "equal" citizens of a modern nation, and for a sizable portion of them, the reform of their religion fit their new stations in life.[3]

While in these and other ways the world of German Jews of 1880 differed radically from that of their parents and grandparents of 1820, certain elements of their social and cultural lives remained stable. For one thing, they continued to live primarily in proximity to other Jews. For another, they still tended to opt for commercial occupations, albeit at the higher rungs, far out of proportion to their numbers. Thus their "otherness" persisted despite seeming acculturation and integration.

Each transition represented an important stage in the transformation of German Jewry and played a role in propelling outward the migration of tens of thousands of these Jews across the Atlantic. Essentially the same forces that would send rural Jews from hamlets in Swabia, Bavaria, and Württemberg to Berlin, Hamburg, and Frankfurt also sent them to New York, Cincinnati, and Chicago. The more modern village Jews of the nineteenth century, those with more means and greater rights, stayed in Germany, moving to cities there, while the least modern and those with the fewest rights set out for America.

Contrary to the claims of Judeophobes of both the nineteenth and twentieth centuries, Jews had never constituted a large percentage of the population of Germany or the earlier German states. However, in the nineteenth century, it appeared that the number of Jews was steadily rising, despite the outward migration. Increased Jewish fertility in the first part of the century, linked with a drop in mortality rates, helped push up the number. Additionally, the annexation of areas of heavy Jewish concentration, like Poznań in the east, and a fairly steady in-migration of *Ostjuden* (eastern Jews) increased the Jewish presence in Germany. Still, Jews in Germany never added up to more than 1.3 percent of the population. In 1820, their numbers stood at about 270,000 and by 1850 reached the half-million mark.[4]

Unevenly spread through the Germanic states, Jews did not live in all towns or regions in proportion to their number in the population as a whole. They rarely lived in Saxony and the Ruhr region but were concentrated in Bavaria, Hesse, Baden, Swabia, and in towns lining the Rhine Valley, that is, in the southwest of Germany, as well as in the east, on the Polish fringe, particularly Poznań and Silesia, which Prussia annexed from Poland.

Prussia, the center of what would become the unified Germany of 1871, was also home for many Jews, who essentially fell into two categories. Approximately one-third hailed from former Polish territories, while the rest lived in the rural villages and small towns of West Prussia. As of 1816, just under half of all Jews in "Germany" found themselves in Prussia, while by the key year of 1871, almost 70 percent lived there. Bavaria housed the second densest concentration of Germany's Jews, and in 1818 approximately 25 percent of all German Jews lived in this state.

Within any of these regions, Jews clustered in some provinces and towns. Of the 1,550 settlements in Baden in 1825, for example, Jews could be found in only 173, whereas in the Bavarian state, 40 percent of all Jews

9

lived in one province, Lower Franconia. In Württemberg, according to the 1846 census, Jews lived primarily in the Jagst region, with further clusterings in the Künzelsau and Mergentheim district, while vast sections of the state had virtually no Jews. In short, German Jews in the nineteenth century lived primarily among other Jews and not integrated into the "German" society around them.[5]

Within these regions, throughout the period 1820–80, Jews lived in small towns, although the urban-rural balance changed. As of 1840, for example, 88 percent of Bavarian Jews lived in villages and rural towns, whereas by 1910, 78 percent made their homes in the larger cities. In Württemberg, which had the largest concentration of rural Jews, 93 percent lived in hamlets in 1832, but by 1864 that number had dwindled down to 60 percent. As of the early nineteenth century, less than 20 percent of Baden's Jews lived in towns of more than five thousand inhabitants, even though they were absent from the tiniest of villages. In Hesse in 1871, approximately half of the Jews still lived in communities of fewer than two thousand. By 1882, however, only 27 percent dwelled in villages of fewer than two thousand, although higher rural concentrations persisted to the century's end in Bavaria and Württemberg.[6]

Within German towns, Jews lived together in family knots, forming their own communities and interacting with their non-Jewish neighbors only for business and in formal dealings with the state. Jews rarely lived apart from one another. In these towns, Jews sometimes made up almost half the residents, although *somewhat* smaller proportions were more typical. One Baden village, for instance, registered that in 1825, 36 percent of its population were Jews, and, interestingly, despite the emigration, the number jumped to 45 percent by 1875. According to historian Steven Lowenstein, while Jews lived in a minority of towns, where they dwelled, they were thickly concentrated. In southern and western Germany, Jews comprised 10–25 percent of the population of the fewer than one thousand villages where they resided. On a personal rather than census-based note, Joseph Austrian, an immigrant to America from Whittelshofen, Bavaria, remembered his home town of 500 to have been equally divided between Jews and Christians.[7]

Jews lived together in small towns in relatively densely clustered units. They depended upon one another for basic needs, through a *kahal,* a legally structured Jewish community. Religious piety prevailed in their public and private lives, and its myriad regulations of behavior distinguished them from their fellow townspeople. Certainly, at the beginning of the era of emancipation, these Jewish women and men differed little one from another, but there was a marked difference between them and the non-Jews in whose midst they lived.

Everything in their lives bespoke homogeneity—religion, language, family structure—and yet, no aspect of the German Jewish experience announced that sameness more dramatically than their economic profile, which can be summarized in one word: trade. Involvement in buying and selling functioned as a powerful homogenizing agent within the German Jewish communities. One study has asserted that between 80 and 90 percent of all German Jewish families at the beginning of the nineteenth century made a living in some form of petty trade. Another concluded that for Bavaria in 1821, that figure stood at a staggering 96 percent. Overall, historian Bernard Weinryb noted, "the great majority was employed in sectors of the economy that were directly connected with the market," and, therefore, "the market psychology affected the activities of the greatest majority."[8]

Trade in all forms was a Jewish province; Jews peddled in the countryside, selling all kinds of wares to the isolated households and returning to their villages and homes for the Sabbath. The Jewish peddler, the *Hausierer,* played a crucial role in the rural economy of the German provinces, despite the fact that in some areas, in the preemancipation era, the law forbade Jews to trade with non-Jews. They ran small shops, particularly dry goods and hardware, and mediated between peasants on the land and urban markets for agricultural goods. They dealt in cattle and horses. They bought up excess grapes to sell to wine makers; they bought flax for the textile manufacturers. They handled grains in exchange for goods.

The "betweenness" of the Jews' economic position made them unique and indispensable but—more often than not—despised by the peasants and indeed by other classes in the German economic structure. For example, Jews acted as agents who shuttled back and forth between farmers and government agents in search of horses for the cavalry, and between the growers and the millers in need of grain or the textile manufacturers looking for flax. Each part of the Jewish trade network sustained the other. Shop owners often provided merchandise for itinerant peddlers, and former peddlers, knowledgeable about the countryside, often shifted over, permanently or temporarily, to cattle dealing or horse trading.[9]

These merchants lived economically marginal lives. Most Jews barely eked out a living wage from their shops or peddling routes. Beggars,

Betteljuden, were hardly uncommon. Some Jewish women went into domestic service, while many of their brothers, who could not even get a foothold in the lowest rungs of business like peddling, hired themselves out as day laborers. Historian George Mosse asserted that "most Jews were poor . . . and others lacked a steady source of income," while an 1811 report in Baden, commenting on Jewish poverty in that state, conjectured that "their forefathers could not have been poorer when they were slaves in Egypt than are these depraved people in their wretched huts."[10]

Jewish life in Germany derived many of its characteristics from the way in which most Jews earned their living. This kind of economic life of necessity forced men and women to flexibility and improvisation. They chose new routes and products if they thought such changes would make a difference. They shifted back and forth between peddling and shopkeeping, between selling grains and selling horses. They moved, when they could, to areas that offered a greater margin of hope. They journeyed far to make a sale. According to one study of Baden, Jews dominated cattle dealing there because of "their knowledge of broad geographic areas of Baden," their network of personal acquaintances, and "their willingness to travel considerable distances to participate in cattle fairs." They took economic risks, in part because they had little to lose.

The labor of all family members spelled the difference between economic ruin and survival. Until well into the middle of the nineteenth century, Jewish women participated alongside men in the functioning of the family economy. Jewish women, as wives of peddlers, played a central role in that endeavor, and since most men could not earn enough to keep the family afloat, daughters and wives traded themselves, not to supplement the family's larder but to put something in it. One Jew, reminiscing about his family life in Obernheit, Bavaria, remembered not only how his family juggled a variety of goods and activities—wine, flannel, shopkeeping—but that his "Mother [was] always accompanying Father as his main clerk, riding on top of one of the goods cases on the wagon. . . . Mother was a valuable assistant and a hard worker at the home"[11]

Throughout the years 1820–80, non-Jews of a variety of political persuasions wanted to wean the Jews from their concentration in trade, which, the argument ran, produced nothing, and so neither did the Jews. Many Jews themselves, reformers and advocates of self-emancipation, concurred and believed that Jewish prospects for economic and civic betterment would accompany a shift from trade to skilled crafts. The Society for

Fostering Industry among the Jews was founded in Prussia in 1812 and worked primarily with orphan boys in the cities. The various Societies for the Promotion of Handicrafts among Jews hoped to instill in young Jews a positive orientation toward productive occupations shunned by their elders "to overcome courageously through common spirit and perseverance the prevailing prejudice that we supposedly have an exclusive inclination toward trade."[12]

Jews did show up infrequently in statistics on crafts and other kinds of "productive" enterprises, but agriculture attracted almost no Jews. German Jews participated in a limited number of handicrafts. Jews did, of course, bake bread, butcher meat, and produce wine for their own consumption as required by Jewish law. Jews also established a toehold in such crafts as tailoring, shoemaking, and weaving. For example, figures from the Kissingen district of Bavaria in 1844 found that of 249 Jewish craftsmen, 75 percent fell into the ranks of either butchers, weavers, shoemakers or tailors.[13]

Ironically, Jews began to achieve economic mobility not by moving into crafts but because of the burgeoning of trade that ushered in and accompanied Germany's emergence into industrialization. In fact, *had* Jews taken to heart the calls for "productivization" through crafts, they might have found themselves in a worse economic position on the eve of the industrial take-off than the one they occupied.

By the century's end, the Jews' economic situation had been reversed. Jews as a class experienced a tremendous move upward in a short span of years. There had always been some class stratification within the Jewish villages, and Jewish city dwellers, pioneers in the urban migration, constituted an early economic elite. But in the second half of the nineteenth century, upward economic mobility became something of a mass phenomenon for German Jews. As early as 1874, according to historian Marion Kaplan, 60 percent of German Jews found themselves in the upper tax brackets. The 1850s and 1860s saw the rise of Jews as railway builders, textile magnates, garment manufacturers, bankers, shippers, department store owners, and exporters and importers. By the 1880s, German Jews had become solidly middle class, typified by the comfortable *Kaufmann,* the tradesman. Drawing upon their long history as merchants, Jews responded to the destruction of the traditional peasant economy by moving to the cities and becoming once again middlemen, this time between the factories and the purchasing public. With industrialization and urbanization, Jews, not tied down to the land or outdated crafts, used their mercantile skills, communal networks for credit, literacy, willingness to try new ventures, and "outsiderness" to take advantage of revolutionary opportunities.[14]

Not all Jews partook in the economic transformation that accompanied German industrialization. Vast numbers of young German Jews, primarily from the lower classes, left. They simply vanished from the communal rolls by moving to America, thus removing the bottom layers of the poor and, statistically, pushing upward the economic profile of those who stayed behind.

Yet the story of Germany's Jews and movement into the middle class—as well as their movement to America—makes no sense without understanding the process of civil and political emancipation and the complex relationship between the Jews and their Christian neighbors. Jews could participate in capitalism's expansion because emancipation involved the lifting of civil disabilities and emancipation was fueled by the progress of capitalism.

The emancipation of the Jews of Germany occurred over a long span of time, beginning in the early nineteenth century with the Napoleonic invasions of the Germanic states on the left bank of the Rhine, and continuing until 1871 when, through the newly created German Reich under Bismarck, the last civil and political disabilities were removed. Each state within Germany handled the problem of its Jews differently varying over time. Even within states, districts and towns maintained idiosyncratic policies. Historian Jacob Toury has asserted that much of the real process of civil improvement for the Jews took place on the local level and that "municipal emancipation" provided the real context of the process. Furthermore, the map of "Germany" underwent significant modifications in the nineteenth century, and states with one set of policies concerning the rights and responsibilities of the Jews annexed or merged with other states with different policies. Part of the process of political integration thus involved coming to a compromise as to which policies would prevail.[15]

Despite the regional hodgepodge and lack of a unitary "German" experience, a few generalizations can be sustained. Before emancipation, the Jew as an individual did not exist in the eyes of the state. The authorities decided where the Jews lived and how they worked, what kind of taxes they paid, and how many could dwell in the region or town. The authorities could give and the authorities could take away. According to Jacob Katz, "the Jew had no legal claim to acceptance or toleration, and if he was admitted, it happened on the basis of a contract between the Jewish community and the relevant political authority." Formally constituted Jewish communities and their leaders mediated between the individual Jews and non-Jewish political powers.[16]

Secondly, the process of emancipation that ended this legal, corporate status of the Jews came from without and was by and large imposed upon the German "people" and the Jews by various external sources. In some regions, such as Württemberg and Baden, Jews in the 1810s were granted rights by the invading and conquering French armies. With the collapse of French forces, German states generally returned to the status quo ante, although they continued to debate the Jews' future. Ultimately, the consolidation of Prussian hegemony brought in its wake final changes in Jewish rights, and Jewish emancipation derived from the triumph of the centralized, bureaucratic state. Prussia had emancipated its own Jews (although it did not lift a disallowance of Jewish office holding) except those who lived in Poznań in 1812, and as Prussia gobbled up the other states, it imposed its Jewish policy on them.

The process of Jewish emancipation rode on the wings of political liberalism—for liberals, changing the status of Jews represented an important part of their agenda. When liberal policies succeeded, the Jews gained greater rights. Conversely, with the failure of liberalism, Jewish rights were curtailed. Thus, in the 1840s, the liberal-minded Frankfurt Parliament voted to remove Jewish civil disabilities. But within a few years, this same representative body rescinded some of its emancipatory largess in response to anti-Jewish popular sentiment. While individual bureaucrats, policymakers, and representatives may have genuinely believed that Jews deserved equal rights, the emancipation of the Jews grew from a larger political agenda, not out of philo-Semitic or humanitarian sentiments.[17]

State by state, region by region, various disabilities were lifted from the Jews over the course of the fifty-year period between 1820 and 1871. Not all elements of the Jewish policy were addressed at the same time, but issue by issue, the fate of Germany's Jews remained a constant matter of political debate and discussion. Emancipation did not follow a straight path from marginality to mainstream.

Few issues had as direct an impact on the lives of the Jews as restrictions on their rights of residence. An 1813 law in Bavaria, for example, stated that Jews could not change residence within the state, and individual Bavarian municipalities could fix the number of Jews who might officially reside there. That law remained valid until 1861 when Jews were granted the right of *Freizügigkeit,* literally "freedom of movement." Bavaria and states like Hesse-Kassel and Württemberg also limited the number of Jewish marriages, variously for all Jews or for Jews in specific occupations, such as peddling and shopkeeping, thus hoping to limit the total number of Jews. This notorious law stated that each Jewish community had to maintain a list, the *Matrikel,* of all legally permitted Jewish families. No others could live there. No Jewish marriages could take place unless a space came free, through death, on the much wanted list. A Jewish newspaper noted that "the register makes it little short of impossible for young Israelites to set up housekeeping in Bavaria; often their head is adorned with gray hair before they receive the permission to set up house and can, therefore, think of marriage." Many young Jewish men and women had to emigrate to avoid the law's onerous impact.[18]

Emancipation came with a price tag. The various edicts and acts granting Jews fuller rights and greater civic equality presumed that Jews would go through the process of *Bildung,* "improvement" of their character, transforming themselves into "Germans" and shedding much that was Jewish and hence considered odious. Jews could become citizens when they ceased, as much as possible, to be different. Emancipationists put tremendous faith in education to create Germans out of Jews, and states linked increased rights to the creation of secular schools where Jews would learn German and useful subjects, as opposed to Hebrew and Judaica. Most states based increased rights on edicts that banned the use of Yiddish in business records and that insisted that Jews take German surnames. Furthermore, to wean the Jews away from the "noxious" trades, many German states connected increased rights of citizenship with Jewish entry into "productive" fields. In 1816 and again in 1833, Hesse-Kassel denied emancipation to Jewish cattle dealers, pawnbrokers, dealers in used goods, and peddlers. Similar legislation arose in the other states as well and made the emancipatory process double edged.[19]

Policymakers in Germany not only made *Bildung* a precondition for emancipation but also insisted on restructuring the Jewish community, again as a prerequisite for the admission of the Jewish people into the German polity. First, states insisted that all rabbis speak German and hold German university degrees. Intended partly to weed out foreign rabbis, since Poland supplied many rabbis for the German-speaking regions, this edict sought to make rabbis agents in the Jewish transformation. Legislation and edicts also tried to control internal synagogue matters. In the 1830s, a Prussian ordinance forbade vernacular, that is, Yiddish sermons. In 1823, the Grand Duke of Sachsen-Weimar-Eisenach declared that all prayers had to be in German. He furthermore forbade moving around during the service and banned Purim festivities and the wearing of shrouds on Yom Kippur. Another law, the *Gemeindezwang,* obliged all Jews to belong to the Jewish community unless they converted to Christianity. Similarly, during these years, state authorities took a role in the election of Jewish community officials and in the handling of communal finances. In Hamburg and elsewhere, the state banned the use of the *herem,* the rabbinic ban of excommunication. These regulations were designed to control, acculturate, and regulate the lives of the Jews. The various states actually seesawed back and forth on Jewish religious matters, sometimes attempting to change them, other times supporting traditional practices. In either case, the fate of the Jews and Judaism could not be determined by the Jews themselves.[20]

The period 1820–80 encompassed the entire emancipation process. In 1820, this process had just begun, and Jews—dwellers in small towns, marginal tradespeople, and peddlers—enjoyed only those meager rights that the Jewish community as a whole had been granted. By 1880, the completed process was a decade old, and Jews, now primarily middle-class urbanites, had access to most rewards of citizenship in the German Reich.

Yet, despite this massive change in civil status, the Jews remained distinguishable in German consciousness, and antipathy to them remained in place. The very process of emancipation added fuel to the ancient animosity.

Negative feelings towards the Jews in Germany cut across political and class lines. Peasants and upholders of the preindustrial order blamed Jews for destroying traditional agrarian life by fostering modernity. Conservatives, regardless of religious denomination, believed strongly that Germany was a Christian state and a priori had no room for nonbelievers. Ultranationalists doubted that Jews could shed longings for their promised homeland of Zion and become German. They knew that the Jews innately differed from the Germans and could never assimilate into the Volk. Liberals and intellectuals chafed at the persistence of Judaism and Jewishness despite the emancipation's largess and saw persistent Jewish difference as a barrier to the ultimate triumph of the state and the "unity of the German spirit." Conservative churchmen and liberal philosophers alike lambasted Judaism as a religion. Both the Left and the Right condemned the Jews' economic power. In 1878, the Christian Socialists became the first political party founded expressly to promote anti-Semitism. As one historian has succinctly noted, "the German-Jewish coexistence was never idyllic or anything approaching it. The eye of friendship was perhaps never entirely closed, but the eye of hatred was always open."[21]

Thus, in the middle decades of the nineteenth century, Germany's Jews found themselves in a new, baffling position. On the one hand, their political and economic future looked better than ever before. They looked forward to better lives and full German citizenship. On the other hand, to achieve modernity's blessings, they had to give up much that had held them together for centuries. Furthermore, amidst the prospects of emancipation always loomed the clouds of anti-Semitism. Even in good years, halls of parliaments and corridors of bureaucracies echoed with debates about the Jews: What to do with them? How to change them? Under what terms to accept them?

How did German Jews respond to emancipation's opportunities and crises? While their reactions varied widely, in the main Germany's Jews greeted emancipation positively and, both consciously and unconsciously, responded to their critics and did become more "German."

Among the traditionalists, however, some rabbis feared emancipation and opposed the unfolding of citizenship. In 1846, rabbis in Baden actively campaigned against complete emancipation. In general, the rabbinate was, according to Jacob Katz, "shocked into passivity." Their passivity had tremendous implications for them, because in the process they yielded authority to the state over civil matters and over numerous religious questions as well. It did not really matter if the rabbis—or the Jews as a group—wanted emancipation; the state thrust it upon them.[22]

Jews did not organize as a political entity or bloc and refrained from efforts that would draw attention to them and to a specifically Jewish political agenda. They did not band together to set the terms for their own emancipation, founding no political organizations for their defense until 1869. Even then, the Deutsch-Israelitischer Gemeindebund declared itself avowedly apolitical. Generally, Jews turned to the state for defense rather than confront the bursts of anti-Semitism directly.[23]

Jewish leaders and intellectuals argued that the Jews deserved emancipation and that Judaism did not jar with Germanness. According to them, Judaism constituted a religion, not a separate nationality, and Jews would, if they could, leave the hated trades and become productive. One writer for the newspaper *Shulamith* promised that "the people of Abraham, fighting against obstacles of all kinds, are working their way up to humanity." The Jewish press called upon its readers to demonstrate their cleanliness, self-control, orderliness, restraint, reasonableness, and ability to defer pleasure—traits that Germans believed Jews lacked. Polemical literature written by traditionalists as well as modernizers of Judaism stressed the ritualistic and cultic nature of Judaism and downplayed the concept of Jewish "peoplehood."[24]

This emphasis on the compatibility between Jewishness and Germanness emerged in much of Jewish literary and artistic output of this period. The sentimental paintings of Moritz Oppenheim, full of nostalgia and sweetness, blended the imagery of the two parts of the German Jew's culture. In one of his paintings of the 1830s, *The Bar Mitzvah Discourse,* a picture of King Frederick the Great of Prussia hangs on the wall in an old-style house of prayer, while another one, *The Return of the Volunteer,* demonstrates how patriotism—symbolized by a handsome soldier bedecked with medals—meshes organically with Jewishness, personified by an old father at home, enjoying a Sabbath. Oppenheim offered Jews—the major consumers of his art—and non-Jews alike a portrait of the ideal harmonization. Jewish writers also used their writings to project a Jewry comfortable with German culture. The popular Berthold Auerbach, author of Schwarzwalder (Black Forest) tales of German peasant life, excelled at this. He purposely shied away from Jewish themes and characters and, as such, declared that a Jew could understand the essence of German culture. He indeed boasted that, "it gives me special pleasure that it was I, a Jew, who happened to succeed in revealing something of the innermost aspect of the German *Volksgeist.*"[25]

Jewish life changed in fact as well as in rhetoric between 1820 and 1880. Jews began to speak and write in German rather than Yiddish, probably not so much because of the law but because of the demands of urban life and economic integration. In 1820, most Jews in Germany, particularly in Bavaria, spoke Yiddish and functioned in a Yiddish-based culture. A Yiddish literature of devotional materials, for example, developed in Germany, and Yiddish publishing houses could be found in cities like Leipzig. By the 1880s, pockets of Yiddish still existed. Many continued to speak a recognizably Jewish German, derided and mocked by some Gentiles, and a few continued to write in Judeo-German, that is, actual German with Hebrew characters. But most Jews, particularly the young, the educated, and the urban, increasingly opted for German as the language of choice.[26]

Following the terms set by the advocates of emancipation with Bildung,

Jews dropped their distinctive dress, began to stream to German schools, and, with a particular zest, entered the ranks of university students.[27] Jews sought admission to lodges of the Freemasons, a fraternal organization that claimed the brotherhood of all and drew deeply on biblical sources and Hebraic imagery and codes.[28] They gradually shifted away from naming their children Aaron or Abraham and Rachel or Leah in favor of Heinrich and Sigmund, Rika and Babette. Under pressure they adopted German surnames.[29]

Integration changed Jewish lives on an even more intimate level. In order to seize the opportunities dangling before them, German Jews began to marry later and bear fewer children, although such changes did not become universal until after the 1880s. (In this, Jews differed from German non-Jews. Jewish fertility dropped significantly earlier and more precipitously than did that of Gentiles.)[30] The Jewish family structure changed as well. With the Jewish entry into the bourgeoisie, Jewish women became separated from the production of goods and services, and were divorced from the active economic lives of their family.[31]

The Germanization of Jews and their social integration were *never* total and did not proceed smoothly or evenly. Historian Deborah Hertz has, in fact, asserted that even into the early twentieth century, few Jews, including the wealthy and accomplished, ever socialized comfortably with Christians.[32] The anguish of individual Jews—able, refined, German by every measure save ancestry—emerged in the tortured writings of poet Heinrich Heine and others like him, who despite converting to Christianity still found themselves outsiders stigmatized by their Jewishness.[33]

This persistence of "otherness" despite the Jewish move toward the middle class led to a number of developments. Some Jews were pushed to the baptismal font, and most of them opted for a political identification with liberalism as an ideology that de-emphasized race and *Volk* in favor of social progress. A few questioned the possibility that integration could never occur, and one German Jewish writer, Moses Hess, offered what was essentially the first call for the reestablishment of a Jewish state in his 1862 book, *Rome and Jerusalem*. Hess, the product of an intensive traditional Jewish education as well as a secular one at the University of Bonn, became a mentor and socialist compatriot of Karl Marx. Yet, Hess became disillusioned with socialism and decided that "the race struggle is primary, the class struggle secondary." His experiences with German socialists convinced him that Jews remained different and outside. He wrote, "I have experienced it [anti-Semitism] personally . . . even with my own party members. . . . I have made it easy for them to use this weapon by adopting my Old Testament name, Moses." Thus, for Hess, the price for integration was not just too high; it was unpayable.[34]

The most profound and permanent response to incomplete emancipation involved Reform Judaism, which had its roots in the preemancipation era of the late eighteenth century and derived its earliest intellectual authority from the *Haskalah,* the Enlightenment as embodied in Moses Mendelssohn. A devout Jew himself, Mendelssohn strove to "modernize" Judaism by restructuring Jewish education and making the Bible accessible to all. He stressed the compatibility of Judaism with modern German culture and emphasized the ritualistic-ethical nature of Judaism. In his *Jerusalem* (1783), he admonished the Jews of Germany to "adopt the mores and constitutions of the country in which you find yourself, but be steadfast in upholding the religion of your fathers, too." Judaism, he told his many non-Jewish acquaintances, constituted a religion of reason. "True" Judaism did not give rabbis power of communal governance, and when rabbis criticized his German translation of the Pentateuch, the five books of Moses, he wrote:[35]

> Oh, my brothers. You have until now all too severely felt the oppressive yoke of intolerance and perhaps thought to find a kind of compensation in the power granted you to impose an equally severe yoke upon your people. . . . If you want to be cherished, tolerated and spared by others, then cherish, tolerate and spare one another.

Mendelssohn's reforms, however much they challenged rabbinic hegemony, rested on a bedrock of tradition based on Jewish law that strictly regulated personal behavior and insisted on the immutability of Jewish religious practice. The situation was completely different with the accumulation of reforms that became Reform Judaism. Over the course of the nineteenth century, these reforms would gradually change the face of Jewish religion by altering the ritual, declaring the laws regarding diet, Sabbath, family, and personal status inoperative in the modern world, and articulating the idea that Judaism could—as it always had—adapt to new circumstances.

Although much of the fuel for reform came from the laity, particularly from the urban economic elite of German Jewry in the 1810s and 1820s, most innovations emanated from rabbis themselves, then filtering from the top down. Probably no state decision during the long-drawn-out process of emancipation had as enduring an impact as the requirement that rabbis receive a university education. Young Jewish men, primarily from small towns, steeped in Jewish learning and dedicated to lives of service to the Jewish people, entered universities to receive their training and encountered new ideas and intellectual debates that shook to the core their identities and beliefs. While they may have known in advance what lay in store for them when they left their villages and made their way to Bonn, Berlin, or the other centers of higher learning, for many, the university experience destroyed the bedrock of faith. Universities taught philosophy and philology, biblical criticism and history, all of which rested on intellectual assumptions at variance with traditional Jewish learning. Rabbi Kaufmann Kohler, for example, was born in Furth in 1843 and entered the University of Munich as a devout follower of Samson Raphael Hirsch, the founder of Neoorthodoxy. He learned there that his teacher, his mentor, and his intellectual-religious idol, Hirsch, had erred. In his study of philology, Kohler discovered, with the aid of his university teachers, that Hebrew was not the oldest human language; it had not been spoken by the earliest of mankind or by God at Creation. Receiving no intellectual comfort from Hirsch, already a university-trained rabbi himself, Kohler embraced the growing reform impetus. Apocryphal though the story may have been, it was also paradigmatic.[36]

The rabbis who opted for Reform—in their congregations and at Reform synods and conferences held in Braunschweig (1844), Frankfurt (1845), Breslau (1846), Leipzig (1869), and Augsburg (1871)—did so to preserve Judaism. They feared that the same jolting experiences, both intellectual and personal, they had undergone when confronted by modern German culture and society would propel other young Jews into Christianity. Reform Judaism thus offered not just an alternative to traditional, "orthodox" Judaism but an antidote to Christianity.

The Reformers, clerical and lay, feared the seemingly skyrocketing number of conversions and hoped to create a modern, enhanced place for women, the largest group of defectors, in new, Reform synagogues. Traditional Judaism carved up the world in two. The synagogue and its ancillary public institutions provided male space, while women fulfilled their crucial roles in the home. Traditional Judaism mandated no education for women, and in civil matters, Jewish women, particularly married ones, had few rights. Reform rabbis hoped to change that picture and keep women rooted in the Jewish community. A prominent Reform rabbi, Abraham Geiger, asserted that only by ameliorating her status "will the Jewish girl and . . . woman [become] conscious of the significance of our faith and . . . fervently attached to it."[37]

Other Reform-minded rabbis and the growing number of lay people in Berlin, Hamburg, Frankfurt, and the other German cities agreed. They felt obliged, and free, to tamper with the synagogue service to make it more aesthetically appealing and spiritually uplifting. Reformers adopted modern European aesthetic standards that were typical of churches and considered congregational singing, inspiring sermons, and polite, hushed behavior religiously appropriate. They hoped that enhancing the service would weaken the appeal of churches to the Jews already uncomfortable and alienated from traditional rites. They added resonant organ chords, shortened the prayers, and inserted German sermons and hymns. They admonished Jews to behave decorously in synagogues and built lofty buildings to reflect their affluence. They moved the Jewish wedding from out of doors into the synagogue, and draped the rabbi in the austere garb of the *Prediger* (preacher), the Protestant minister.

Much of Reform focused on style, but it also tackled serious matters of belief. First, the Reformers questioned the binding nature of *halakah,* Jewish law, and asserted the right of Jews to mold the law to fit their environment. Samuel Holdheim asserted that since the traditional texts—the Bible and the Talmud—were human invention, they had no authority. If, for example, modern Jews found halakic practices governing marriage and divorce unacceptable, then they could freely remove such matters from Jewish control and rely upon the state instead.[38]

The modernizers also rejected the concept of Judaism as a national entity and emphasized the Jewish community's religious nature. That is why they needed to alter the liturgy, removing passages and prayers calling for the restoration of Zion as a Jewish homeland into which the scattered people of Israel would be gathered. Instead, they proved through revised prayers that Jews constituted a religious group of loyal German citizens.

The Reformers offered not just a lure back to Judaism, but they also hoped to gain ammunition in the ongoing struggle to prove the worth of the Jews to Germany. If some Jews felt embarassed by distinctive Jewish ritual, it was because Christian society never let them forget that "real" Germans considered Judaism a retrograde religion, out of character with the German soul. Crucially, the many critics and opponents of the Jews, who occupied formidable places in German society, never let the Jews—Reformers or others—forget that Judaism had to be on the defensive, that Jews *did* have to prove themselves, and that Judaism could not be considered natural to German culture.

Reform Judaism offered the most palpable Jewish reaction to emancipation's discontents. Jews did not want to cease being Jews. They did not want to become Christians, nor did they harbor antipathy to the faith of their ancestors. Rather, they believed that they could, and had to, tinker with that faith as befitted their rising status in German society. Judaism's outward symbols and public manifestations, they argued, could be shorn of elements that jarred with German culture. They asserted that Judaism had always molded itself to respond to the civilizations around it, slowly evolving under new circumstances. Thus, they asserted, those aspects of Jewish life that did not fit, creating a barrier between Jews and Germans, must be rethought to harmonize with the *Geist* of modernity.[39]

Ultimately, the absence of that harmony plagued many German Jews of the mid-nineteenth century. The discomfort, the feeling of being on the "edge," ran through their literature. It emerged in autobiographical details of those who tried to opt out of Jewishness by embracing Christianity. It ran through the autobiographies of those who chose to remain Jews but lacked models of blending Jewish and German identities. It surfaced in the intellectual movements that had their roots in this critical era in Jewish history, including Marxism and Zionism, both of which wanted to smooth that edge, to make the Jews a normal people. At their core, the Jews of nineteenth-century Germany, however much they may have wanted to be German Jews, remained primarily Germany's Jews.[40]

To add to their disjunction, precisely during these decades of emancipation, urbanization, economic ascendance, and Reform, there loomed the spectre of the "eastern" Jew. Masses of Polish Jews, who either migrated into Germany or who, by virtue of European geopolitics in the years 1793–1807, had been incorporated into it, became an issue for the German Jews and for their non-Jewish fellow citizens as well. The problem of Polish Jews indeed complicated the already bumpy process of political integration.

Beyond Germany

Traditionally, historians of the Jewish experience have created their own "Iron Curtain" and analyzed the experiences of the Jews of Poland and the "east" as quite separate from those of German Jews and others in the "west." This artificial division has not only skewed our understanding of the process of nineteenth-century Jewish immigration to the United States but also ignored the fact that until the middle of the century, a fairly unified Jewish culture existed throughout much of Europe. Obviously, differences existed. Hasidism, for example, made no inroads in Germany, whereas it dominated vast areas of Galicia, Poland, and Russia. However, until the middle decades of the nineteenth century, when the Jews of Germany became caught up in modernization and emancipation, uniformity rather than difference prevailed. All European Jews (with the important exception of the Sephardic world of Italy, southern France, and the Balkans) spoke the same language, Yiddish, regional dialects notwithstanding. Hebrew or Yiddish books printed in Warsaw were read in Bavaria or Baden. The literary output of German Jews and their presses found its way into the hands of readers in the east. One study of the *ze'enah u-re'enah* literature, Yiddish devotionals for women, asserted that until the 1830s, editions published in Germany dominated the eastern European markets.[41]

The forces of modernization and change that swept through German Jewry, whipped through eastern European Jewry as well, much slower and later, for sure, and meeting more stringent Orthodox resistance. Michael Meyer, in his definitive history of Reform Judaism, has demonstrated how in Hungary, Galicia, Poland, and even czarist Russia, some Jews, small in number, began to experiment with new forms of Jewish expression. For example, reform-style congregations existed in the mid-nineteenth century in Odessa, Warsaw, Lemberg, Riga, and Vilna. Similarly, Salo Baron's study of the crisis of Jewish communal authority during the 1848 revolutions has detailed how political change shook up not only Jews in Hamburg or Berlin but also those in Poland, Hungary, and even in parts of Moravia and Galicia.[42]

East-west connections in nineteenth-century European Jewish history appeared repeatedly. Jews from Poland and even further east had migrated into the German states for decades before emancipation. Young Jews from Poland and Lithuania studied at German universities as early as the eighteenth century, thus coming under the influence of the Haskalah and bringing elements of it back home. In the mid-nineteenth century, itinerant Russian cantors brought to the Pale new synagogue music composed by Solomon Sulzer and Louis Lewandowski from Berlin and Vienna. The biographies of the early generation of Reform rabbis, those who stayed in

Germany and those who made their way to the United States, abound with references to pious young Polish rabbinical students who went to Germany to round out their education and ended up in the Reform camp.[43]

From the seventeenth century on, Polish, Russian, and Galician Jews served as Hebrew instructors on the elementary level, heads of *yeshivot*, institutions of advanced Judaic learning, and rabbis in hundreds of German communities. In 1787, David Friedlaender, a disciple of Mendelssohn, claimed that the German rabbinate lay in the hands of Polish Jews, while Russian Jews often worked as tailors in German villages, living among their fellow Jews. Many of the schnorrers or *Betteljuden*, itinerant beggars who roamed from town to town, also hailed from Poland and Russia. By the early nineteenth century, and certainly after the massive emigration out of small towns, the stereotypical *Schacherjude*, the "haggling Jew," and the *Trödeljude*, the Jew who dealt in second-hand goods in Prussia, were more often than not newcomers from eastern Europe. Among nineteenth-century Pomeranian Jewish craftsmen, the majority had migrated from Russia and settled in the small Jewish villages there, and—like the Polish teachers, rabbis, and beggars—bridged "German" Jewish culture with that of the "east."[44]

Contacts between Jews in Germany and "eastern" Jews were tightly twined by two broad phenomena: the Prussian annexation of the Polish province of Poznań at the end of the eighteenth century and the constant Jewish migration from there and other parts of Poland, from Lithuania, and even Russia into Germany. Indeed, as a result of the political annexation, by 1816, up to 40 percent of Prussian Jewry, two-fifths of those women and men who might have been considered German or who listed themselves as hailing from "Germany," actually lived in the former Polish territory, among Polish-speaking people.[45]

Just when that large number of Polish Jews "became German" in a geographic and, eventually, in a linguistic and cultural sense, waves of other eastern Jews moved into Germany as well. Gentiles noticed this phenomenon. The anti-Semitic historian Heinrich von Treitschke exaggerated ominously in 1879: "Over our eastern borders presses year after year, from the bottomless Polish cradle, a herd of pushy pants-selling youngsters," making tailoring and garment-making synonymous with Polish Jewry. Jews from the east were making their way into Germany, and he had justified the growing anti-Semitism in Germany by citing "a natural reaction of Germanic folk consciousness against foreign elements."[46]

According to historian Moses Shulvass, the process of Jewish migration into Germany from Poland and elsewhere in eastern Europe began as early as the eighteenth century. These eastern Europeans filled the ranks of the *Betteljuden* in the south of Germany, but others settled permanently in northern German towns and cities, such as Anhalt, Hamburg, Hanover, Hildesheim, while other Polish Jews opted for western provinces in Germany, judging by the number of Polish names found among the Jews in Offenbach, Paderborn, Hanau, and Düsseldorf. Polish, Lithuanian, Galician, and even Ukrainian Jews, according to Shulvass, all found their way into eighteenth-century Germany and complicated the meaning of "German Jew." In the nineteenth century, the influx of eastern European Jews into Germany increased markedly and posed a serious problem for their coreligionists undergoing *Bildung*.

Eastern European Jewish migration into Germany represented a complex process. Poznań's Jews migrated in droves into Prussian cities and into other provinces, while Russian and Polish Jews in the 1860s and beyond moved into Poznań and other parts of Prussia, as if to replace their westward-moving fellow Jews. Speaking to the Diet in 1847, Bismarck predicted a huge invasion of Russian Jews. In the early 1880s, 3,600 Russian Jews had lived in Prussia long enough to be ready for naturalization. After the 1840s, Galician Jews thronged to Leipzig, a city familiar to them because for decades, Galician and other eastern European Jews had come there to buy and sell at the celebrated fair, while German Jews knew well the Hungarian and Polish rabbis and cantors, Hebrew teachers, and other religious personnel who dwelled in their midst.[47]

The influx of eastern European Jews into Germany, by migration or annexation, had a profound impact upon German Jews and the process of Jewish migration to the United States. First, the crude image of the eastern Jew exacerbated problems of emancipation endured by the Jews in Germany. Just as they began to embrace refinement and Germanization, in came their kin, deviating from the bourgeois model. The arrival of eastern European Jews in Germany may have hastened the casting off of Yiddish as the Jewish lingua franca to set off "real" Germans from the uncouth newcomers. Leaders of the Haskalah, such as Mendelssohn, himself a Yiddish speaker, or Naphtali Herz Wessely, the German-born son of Polish Jewish parents, advocated the revival of Hebrew as the Jewish language of discourse because Yiddish bore the stigma of Polish uncouthness. Yiddish, wrote Mendelssohn, "contributed not a little to the immorality of the common man; and I expect a very good effect on my brothers from the increasing use of the pure German idiom."[48]

For German Gentiles, "eastern European" meant something opposed to German refinement and rationality. According to historian Steven Asch-heim, in the eighteenth century, German Jews began to evince an antag-onism to eastern Jews, which grew out of the non-Jewish antipathy for all Jews and from the rhetoric of the advocates of Bildung who claimed that Jews lacked manners, restraint, and reason. German Jewish leaders and opinion-makers subscribed to that argument and sought to remake the eastern Jew and root out the uncivility, emotionality, and noisiness of which Germans accused them. They succeeded impressively in projecting outward the image of the thrifty, industrious, sober German Jew. Part of that success stemmed from the fact that so many from the bottom of the social structure, the Dorfjuden, the peddlers, and their sons and daughters had left Germany for America, making it possible for those who stayed to move up into the middle class. Thus, in the period 1800–1850, Aschheim wrote, "German Jews applied the critique of the ghetto to themselves as well as to other Jews; only when German Jewry was sufficiently confident that its own ghetto inheritance had been overcome did the stereotype of the Ostjude assume its full meaning."[49]

How sharply did the Polish Jews, particularly those of Poznań, differ from their "German" brethren? What made the Polish Jews so terribly distinct? That difference, or the perception of it, may have stemmed, in part, from basic government policy. Prussia acquired Poznań and other Polish areas east of the Elbe in 1793. When, in 1812, Prussia offered eman-cipation to its Jews, it excluded Poznań, thus limiting the offer to those who spoke German and conformed to the image of the refined Jew. The vast majority of the Jews of Posen did not qualify since they clearly spoke Yiddish. For decades, they remained a "tolerated" mass amidst the minority of emancipated Prussian Jews. In 1833, Prussian authorities revised the ordinance dealing with Poznanian Jews, but most of them, about 90 per-cent, still could not become Prussian citizens. The final emancipation of the Jews of Poznań did not occur until 1866. Prussian policy was aimed at the Germanization of the Prussian-Poznanian Jews, offering them monetary rewards in exchange for conversion to Christianity, weakening the power of the *kahal*, trying to wean them away from their usual occupations, and generally making it impossible for them to function without the German language. In 1833, the Prussian government closed the Jewish *Winkelschulen*, replacing them with compulsory Prussian elementary schools. Those Jews who remained went through the process of Germanization, while, importantly, those who left had not.[50]

It was ironic that the Prussian authorities sought to change the economic profile of the Jews of Poznań. Unlike the Jews of Bavaria and Württemberg on the eve of their emancipation, these eastern European Jews engaged in a wider range of occupations and showed up much more often as artisans than did German Jews. Indeed, in 1816, only 7.6 percent of all Jews made a living as artisans within Prussia itself, but 34 percent of those in Posen did. Their involvement with crafts actually made the Jews in Posen more like their coreligionists further to the east—in the rest of Poland, Russia, and Lithuania—and distinguished them from the traders of Germany.[51]

Even when the Jews in Posen worked in trade, they tended to resemble Jews further east. They, for example, ran inns and played a major role in making and selling liquor, a classic eastern European Jewish occupation.[52] Furthermore, as artisans they functioned very much like their fellow Jews in the east, clustering heavily in tailoring. One estimate asserted that 70 percent of all Jewish artisans in Poznań sewed for a living, with furriers, hat and cap makers, lace makers, and weavers constituting the remaining portion. Again, this occupational portrait bore a striking similarity to that of the Jews in the Pale.[53]

The Jews of Poznań remained poor longer and in larger number than those in the rest of Germany. As the economic fortunes of the Jews of other parts of Germany began to rise markedly, the Jews of Poznań began to experience greater pauperization. That, too, distinguished them from their fellow German Jews.[54]

Their living patterns also differentiated them from Jews of Bavaria and Hesse. Poznanian Jews lived in more thickly clustered Jewish enclaves than did Jews in other parts of Germany. They rarely accounted for fewer than one-third of the population of the towns where they resided and constituted 52.4 percent of Kempen, 48.8 percent of Gratz, and 65.4 percent of Fonden. They huddled closer together than did Jews in areas to the west and south, and tended to live in townships and cities rather than rural villages. In the early part of the nineteenth century, up to 60 percent of all Jews in the Rhine province made their homes in the rural areas, whereas less than 5 percent of those in Posen did.[55]

While a full-scale social and cultural history of Poznań's Jewry has yet to be written, traditionalism and piety seemed to hold on longer here than it did in other parts of Germany. Reform did not catch on as broadly among the Jews in Posen, although migrants from Posen to Berlin—let alone to New York, Chicago, and San Francisco—eventually opted for the new variant of Judaism. Traditional Jewish education and rabbinic authority remained in force there longer than in Bavaria or Württemberg, and in many of the newly formed "German" Jewish communities in America, the immigrants from Posen served as lay religious personnel—teachers, cantors, slaughterers, and readers—by virtue of their greater knowledge and piety. As late as 1847, only 25 percent of Jewish children in the city of Poseń and 20 percent in Bromberg, another provincial city, attended state-supported schools, and the traditional heder existed there until the 1870s. Jews in Poznań seem to have clung, by choice, to garb that marked them as different well into the early nineteenth century, and it was not until the late 1850s that "Germanization" made real progress. One Jewish historian, Heinrich Graetz, born in Posen in 1817, noted that "he sprang from that part of Central European Jewry with direct and intimate ties with the Ostjuden."[56]

The social position of Jews in Poznań once again differed markedly from that of Jews elsewhere in Germany. They lived among Gentiles who spoke Polish rather than German, yet had to adjust to German as the official state language. Their Polish townspeople and neighbors with whom they traded yearned to shake off Prussian domination. To Jews, the Prussians represented not only authority but also the promise of modernity and equal rights. This made the process of modernization in Poznań much more complex than in other "German" regions. Here the Jews found themselves caught between two linguistic-nationality groups. They overwhelmingly sided with the state and modernity—Prussia—against the peasantry and the past, the Poles. Their choice had little to do with love of German culture or a desire to integrate into German society but rather with an exercise in reason. While a small group of modern, middle-class Jews identified with German culture and language, most did not. Even in the heady days of the 1848 revolution, when the Poles of Poznań rose up against the Prussian kingdom, chances for the ragtag nationalists to defeat the powerful army from the west must have seemed negligible. For Jews, turning to the victor ought not, at least without more careful research, to be viewed as an embracing of German culture for its own sake. Rather, they shrewdly recognized the odds. Importantly, traditional anti-Semitism flourished among the Polish speakers of the region more than among the Germans, and this also may have influenced the Jewish strategy to ally themselves with Prussia.[57]

Other European Jews of the mid-nineteenth century found themselves in a position similar to that of their sisters and brothers in Poznań: squeezed between linguistic groups and nationalities, none of whom they resembled socially or culturally, undergoing modernization and emancipation, living in relative poverty, and eventually joining up with other immigrants going to the United States.

Jews in western European countries encountered similar situations, raising further doubt as to the sharpness of the contrast between "east" and "west" in Jewish history. Jews in France's Alsace region until the mid-nineteenth century, lived in abject poverty, filling a conspicuous role in society, which earned them the enmity of their Christian neighbors. Here, in the modern, enlightened, democratic France, Jews remained uninte-grated into the larger society for at least half-century after the Revolution of 1789, maintaining traditional Jewish religious and communal patterns. A sizable number of their young people crossed the ocean to America in the middle decades of the century.

These Jews—peddlers, pawnbrokers, horse and cattle dealers, traders in second-hand clothes and petty moneylenders—lived in small towns and villages along the Rhine River. Few worked as artisans, and none of them farmed. Of the 202 Jews who paid taxes in the city of Metz in 1825, only one listed artisan as his occupation, while the majority followed the classic Alsatian Jewish tradition of horse-trading and cattle dealing. Due to the legacy of severe legal restrictions on residence, which had been removed in 1791 and again in 1818, Alsatian Jews resided primarily in small, scattered towns. As of 1808, 74 percent of Alsace's Jews dwelled in villages of fewer than two thousand people, although with changes in government policy and with the decline in peasant agriculture, the number of small-town Alsatian Jews dropped to 19 percent of the total French Jewish population by the end of the 1840s. The change in living patterns came about with the lifting of residential restrictions on Jews, and in the 1840s and beyond, Jews flocked out of these towns to Alsatian cities like Metz, Colmar, and Strasbourg, and to Paris.[58]

Their work distinguished them from the surrounding French farmers. Their commercial concentration and money-lending activities made them bear the brunt of rural unrest; Jews became the target of rioting and physical violence in 1819, 1822, 1830, 1848, and sporadically in the 1850s. An 1822 report in the southern Haut-Rhin district commented that the peasants, angry about their economic distress, blamed the Jews and wanted to launch a "Saint Bartholomew's Day for the Jews."[59]

Linguistically, they stood out as different, too. Native Alsatian Jews spoke a Judeo-German dialect that linguists consider to be similar to Yiddish, a language quite different from that spoken by the Gentiles around them. Moreover, until the 1850s, many German and Polish Jewish immigrants settled there. According to historian Phyllis Albert, they brought their Yiddish with them. Up to the 1820s, instructors at the Talmudic academy in Metz taught in Yiddish and, in that same decade, government regulations stipulated that rabbis had to have at least a rudimentary knowledge of French.[60]

One more group of Jews made up a sizable chunk of the migrant pool to mid-nineteenth-century America. Their experiences—like those of the Jews of Germany, including Poznań, and Alsace—point to the lack of a distinct east-west dichotomy, complex patterns of premigration modernization, and the absence of a simple, single European background. These Jews occupied pockets of a vast, variegated area of the Habsburg monarchy, which in 1867 came to be Austria-Hungary and which included within its borders Bohemia, Moravia, Galicia, Slovakia, and Hungary, among others.

Its Jewry, like the empire itself, defied any categorization, and no single Jewish mode exemplified the experience of all. After all, among those who called the empire home were notable families assimilated in Vienna, Budapest, and Prague. Yet just one generation back, many of these middle-class Jewish city dwellers had lived in the small towns of Galicia, Slovakia, and the rest of the hinterlands, where the masses of Jews still found themselves.

Here, hundreds of thousands could be found living, in extreme poverty in tradition-bound villages that for all intents and purposes resembled the *shtetlekh* under czarist domination to the east. For most, Yiddish served as their mother tongue, and they used German, the language of modernization and of the Austro-Hungarian bureacracy, only when dealing with the larger society. Those two languages could be heard against a chorus of others—Czech, Polish, and Magyar—the languages of the peasants whom they traded with, because these Jews, like their fellows to the west and to the east made a "living" in petty commerce in Bohemia and Moravia, and in the Jewish crafts—tailoring, weaving, and the like—in the areas further to the east, particularly in Galicia, Slovakia, and Hungary.

As in Germany, Jews of the Habsburg Empire were on the move. As they experienced the simultaneous processes of modernization, emancipation, and entry into the middle class, they shifted from the hinterlands and into the cities. The parents of Sigmund Freud, for example, came to Vienna in the 1850s, having left their home in Galicia first for Moravia and only then moving to the empire's capital city. Theirs was a typical mid-century Jewish story of migration across place and class.[61]

A region of contradictions and contrasts, the Hapsburg Empire saw some of the fiercest battles between Reform and Orthodox Judaism. Even the most minor of modifications of ritual created swirls of controversy in the small towns of Galicia and Hungary. In cities like Budapest, Orthodoxy and Reform battled each other, too, the former drawing the support of the newly arrived migrants from the small towns and the latter attracting the already modern and assimilated Jews. Within the borders of the empire, the bastions of Hasidism stood firm in Galicia and Hungary, the enclaves of traditionalism remained solid in Moravia, and the reformers gained some influence in Vienna and Budapest.[62]

Austria was Europe's first nation to link the hegemony of the central state with the condition of the Jews. In 1782, Emperor Joseph II issued the *Toleranzpatent,* which offered economic normalization and Germanization. (As in the various German states, the fortunes of emancipation waxed and waned in the Habsburg monarchy, with rights being given and then taken away according to the vagaries of the political situation. Rights granted in the aftermath of the 1848 revolution were rescinded in the 1850s, and it was not until 1867 that formal equality became the law.) Yet evidence of anti-Semitism cropped up repeatedly in response to economic distress among the peasantry and lower classes, and as a result of the flowering of nationalist and ethnic patriotism among the empire's peoples. As in Poznań, Jews were seen by the surrounding ethnic groups as the agents of not only city and marketplace but, ironically, Germanization.

Modernizing Jews opted to affiliate with German language and culture. German was the language of the state and for Jews it was the logical language to choose. Initially, the state imposed it upon them, but given its similarity to Yiddish, its centrality to business, and its association with *Kultur,* they opted for it. The non-German ethnic groups identified the Jews with Germanness despite the fact that German culture and language were new for the Jews. Jews became pawns in the ethnic politics of the empire, lambasted by one side for not being German enough and by the other for hampering the quest for national self-determination.[63]

The Jewish population of this polyglot area underwent massive changes.

As in Bavaria, they suffered from marriage restrictions and endured other kinds of residential segregation until the 1860s. In addition, Jews—except for a small number of wealthy ones who could purchase the right of domicile—could not settle in Vienna, the Hungarian city of Buda, or, indeed, in most other cities until 1848. But as urban opportunities opened up in the 1850s and 1860s, they migrated en masse from small towns where they lived in thick Jewish clusters to the cities where they formed urban Jewish enclaves.[64]

They learned German, with many of them also opting for Czech and Hungarian, when it became clear that Yiddish would not serve them in the new order, but this transition was slow.[65] Over time, some of the Jews of Austria-Hungary moved up economically, although, like their coreligionists in Germany, they never really abandoned commerce and were able, as the century wore on, to move into its middle brackets. Yet, significant pockets of unreconstructed, untouched Jewish life survived in the eastern back-waters of the empire to the century's end and beyond.

In 1820, a fairly homogeneous Yiddish culture of small-town life based on petty trade, peddling, and a little handicraft characterized the lives of most European Jews. Residents of traditional communities, they differed little from one another. By 1880, new realities had created a variety of Jewish types, and a world of difference separated the Bohemian village shopkeeper, the son of a tailor in a small city of Poznań, the daughter of a Bavarian peddler, and the university student in Berlin drinking up the *Geist* of German *Kultur*.

Despite differences in their economic profile and their stance toward the larger culture, they shared Jewishness. Each one of these archetypical Central European Jews occupied a place shaped by their "otherness" in Christian society. While they would ultimately react differently to the changes around them—one opting for Reform, another staying anchored in tradition, one moving cityward, another to America—their reactions flowed from the fact that being a Jew meant being anomalous.

In the half-century of emancipation, industrialization, and modernization, these Jews—from Alsace in the west to the borders of czarist Russia in the east—sought to take advantage of new economic opportunities and normalize themselves. How they accomplished that varied from person to person and changed over time, although, mostly, Jews positively greeted new options opening up to them and took into consideration their own values as well as outside pressures.

Between 1820 and 1880, some of them, about 150,000 Jewish women and men from across the continent—from Alsace and Lithuania, Slovakia and Suvalk, Moravia and Manchester, Baden, Bavaria, and Bohemia, even from Romania and czarist Russia—decided that despite the promises of emancipation and economic freedom that could be heard in their European homes, America offered better and easier terms by which to work for both.

CHAPTER TWO

"ON TO AMERICA"

A happier generation than ours blesses its palm branches and chews its
unleavened bread by the Mississippi.

You would, most honorable sir, infinitely oblige us, if you would transmit
every particular information relating to the state of the Jews in America. . . .
But you would still more oblige us by . . . establishing a distinct society . . .
about the means of promoting the emigration of European Jews to the
United States, and how such emigration may be connected with the welfare
of those who may be disposed to leave a country where they have nothing to
look for but endless slavery and oppression.

Again I worked in my trade in Edenkoben, Rhenish Palatinate. . . . After
six months I began to think of journeying to blessed America, going home to say
good-bye to my parents and brother and sister.

FOR MILLENNIA, Jews had been "wandering," transplanting themselves to new places. Thus the developments of the mid-nineteenth century
make up one more chapter in an old story. Indeed, in the middle decades of
the nineteenth century, Jewish migrants pouring out of villages and towns
of central and eastern Europe made their way to all sorts of places other
than America. America did not loom as the only, or even the most desirable,
choice from the migrants' perspective at the era's beginning. Over time,
though, migration to the United States became a force in itself, and America
moved from one choice among many to *the* choice above all others. While
small groups of poor young men and women made up the first newcomers,
they swiftly brought over brothers and sisters, parents and friends, recon-
stituting families and communities, and advertising the bounties of life in
America.

In the process, these Jewish migrants created Jewish life in America on
terms quite different than those of Berlin, Warsaw, Hamburg, or Breslau.

As European anti-Semitism worsened, economic opportunities in America blossomed, and Jews formed full-bodied communities, a mythic America became firmly fixed in Jewish imagination. America emerged as more than just another country.

Learning about America

The evolution of the image of America, knowledge of what America "meant," can be traced to the late eighteenth century across much of Jewish Europe in a number of categories: poetry and fiction, journalism and travelers' accounts, hortatory literature to stimulate migration, and—far and away most persuasive—letters of relatives and friends already in America, which in words jingled with coins and resounded with melodies of opportunity.

America became a theme in German Jewish literature in the 1820s and remained a constant for the rest of the century, appearing first in elite literature and then shifting to more mass readership. Heinrich Heine, Ludwig Börne, and Eduard Gans projected an image of America as central Europe's counterpoint: democracy versus authoritarianism, religious freedom versus religious persecution. Influenced in part by the writings of James Fenimore Cooper and Washington Irving, these intellectuals projected a robust America full of novelty and vigor. In their writings they toyed with the idea of America being "the land where many now tired Europeans will find a new birth of freedom and if not they, then their children or grandchildren." While Heine offered a more ambivalent portrait of America than Boerne, stressing its crudeness and vulgarity (attributes he assigned to the masses of European Jews as well), he still underscored that America offered greater hope for Jews than Germany. Reflecting cynically on his own conversion to Christianity, Heine argued that unlike in Europe, "Everyone over there [in America] can find salvation his own way." "Even if all Europe should become a single prison," he wrote, "there is still another loophole of escape, namely America, and, thank God! the loophole is after all larger than the prison itself."

Popular writers also echoed these themes. Poems like "Cristoforo Colombo" (1836) by Ludwig August Frankl, the secretary of the Jewish community of Vienna, or "Deborah" by Salomon Herrmann Mosenthal celebrated the opportunities of American life.[1]

Yiddish and Hebrew writers of the early and mid-nineteenth-century Europe likewise provided information and glowing pictures of American life to Jewish readers. In 1807, Moshe ben Mendel of Hamburg translated into Hebrew a popular German work, *Entdeckung von Amerika* (the discovery of America) by J. H. Campe, intending it for Polish Jewish readers. Ten years later, Khaykel Hurwitz adapted the work into Yiddish. One scholar of Yiddish literature, A. B. Gotlober, asserted that Hurwitz's edition "was so widely disseminated that almost every Jew read it." A Lithuanian *maskil* (an enlightened modern Jewish thinker), Mordecai Aaron Ginsburg, translated it once again into Hebrew as *Galuth Erez Hahadasha* (the Jewish Diaspora in the New World) in 1823 and put out yet another translation, this time in Judeo-German, in Vilna in 1824. Ginsburg's Yiddish translation went through several printings.

Similarly, a Hebrew pamphlet entitled *Hilchot Yemot Hamashiah* (chronicles of the days of the Messiah), published in Germany in 1822, praised America as a land of promise for Jewish people. Furthermore, Isaac Meyer Dick, often cited as the first popular Yiddish writer, introduced America into his novels in the 1850s, and, in 1864, translated some of Benjamin Franklin's aphorisms. In the 1860s, Dick's novels exhorted Yiddish readers to move to America. His characters included Lithuanian and Polish Jews in the United States, a place he called, "God's wonder," who had amassed impressive fortunes, yet remained pious.[2]

Other literary sources provided European Jews with information about America as well and documented the beginnings of the Jewish migration and adjustment. The Jewish press in Europe, in both German and Hebrew, carried frequent articles about the United States in general and its Jewish inhabitants in particular. Publications such as *Der Orient, Allgemeine Zeitung des Judentums, Israelitische Annalen, Israelitische Wochenschrift, Shulamith,* and others presented a steady stream of articles on the "garden of the Lord," "the majestic blessed American coast," or "blessed land of freedom and prosperity." Articles provided concrete information, clearly cast in an upbeat tone. Their writers, based in Europe or American correspondents, portrayed the movement to America as a positive step for the masses of poor Jews from across Central Europe, stressing a mix of economic uplift and religious liberty available to those willing to take a chance. An 1840 article in the influential *Allgemeine Zeitung des Judentums* (founded in 1837) was typical:[3]

> The above mentioned Bavarian Israelite showed us a letter received
> from his brother, who had migrated to New York and had to leave his

wife and child, owing to the restrictions prevailing in fatherland. . . .
He highly extols his present situation and his trade (he is a shoemaker)
guarantees him an ample livelihood even if not wealth. In his letter he
rejoices particularly at the circumstance that his children have an
opportunity to learn a lot and that, along with full civil liberty, an
Israelite also has an opportunity to comply—unhindered—with all
religious prescriptions, as there are three synagogues and all the other
Jewish institutions. He invites his brother also to come over, since he
will surely find a situation there.

This item may have moved some readers to join the Bavarian shoemaker living in New York, just as Dick's novels, Börne's poetry, or Ginsburg's *Galuth Erez Hahadasha* may have inspired others in Posen, Lithuania,
or Galicia to try their luck in America, whatever their occupation.

More likely than not, the letter from America had its fullest impact not
when published in the newspapers but when received directly by the brother
in Altdorf or the sister in Lissa. Letters from America provided the fullest
and most significant source of information about the United States.

The letters served a variety of functions in stimulating and sustaining
the migration process. Obviously, they were the only way kin at home and
those in America communicated with one another, providing information
of safe journeys, economic fortune, marriages, births, deaths, illnesses, and
the like. The letters documented the process of migration and adjustment
itself and offered those at home a glimpse of the opportunities and problems of American life. Letters became the means by which new Americans
called for siblings, parents, spouses, and children to join them. Through
these letters, single men in America announced to the folks back home that
they were ready for marriage and were looking for a young woman who
would journey to America. The transatlantic correspondence attested to
prospects for success in America and to the price to be paid to attain that
goal.

The letters, as the mechanism of family pull, transformed the migration
of individuals into a mass exodus of whole communities. Throughout the
Jewish regions of Bavaria, Württemberg, Baden, Hesse, Posen, Bohemia
and Moravia, Galicia, and Alsace, "emigration fever" raged, and the initial
exodus of a few young people propelled outward many more. A reporter
for the *Israelitische Annalen* reported in 1840 that in the Swabian town of
Ichenhausen, with two hundred Jewish families, sixty Jews were actively
contemplating leaving for America, as were twenty more from the neigh-

boring village of Osterburg, which had a mere twenty-five Jewish households. Events in central Europe and the continued economic and political distress served as forces pushing Jews outward. Novelist Berthold Auerbach summed up the situation in 1851: "I have always resisted the idea of pinning all hope on America, but I'm now constantly forced to that conclusion. If we were incapable of bringing about a condition more worthy of human beings, then I'm afraid that the next generation will be even more so."[4]

Migration, in essence, propelled itself. Its natural dynamic can be seen in part by the failure of the few schemes organized on both sides of the Atlantic to stimulate it. These plans amounted to little because the migration needed no organization, but their very existence served to enlighten Jews of Europe about America as a foil to the poverty and limitations around them. In 1822, for example, a disillusioned and embittered circle of German Jewish intellectuals and activists, including Eduard Gans, who would later become a professor of law, and Leopold Zunz, the founder of modern Jewish scholarship, wrote to probably the best known American Jew of his day, Mordecai Noah, informing him about "the general distress and public calamity under which a great part of the European Jews" found themselves and letting him know that they were "looking with eager anxiety to the United States of North America," and that they would be "happy to exchange the miseries of their native soil for public freedom, which is there granted to every religion." They had heard of Noah's plan to create an asylum for Jews in upstate New York and heartily applauded the idea. Noah's plan amounted to naught, although the idea of organizing a Jewish emigration for a specific American place of refuge was kept alive briefly by Eliezer Simon Kirschbaum, a Galician medical student at the University of Berlin.

Likewise, in the 1830s and 1840s, concrete proposals to acquire land in America for a German and Polish Jewish colony surfaced. Bernhard Behrend of Hesse proposed such a scheme to Baron Rothschild. A pamphlet published in Berlin, *Neu-Judaea,* called for the creation of a Jewish state in America and suggested that Missouri, Michigan, Arkansas, or Oregon might be considered. Needless to say, no such Jewish statehood came to being in the American west.[5]

Similarly, a movement called "On to America" percolated in 1848 in Prague after anti-Jewish rioting that accompanied the revolution. Poet Leopold Kompert became obsessed with the idea of organizing a Jewish immigration to America. "We are not saved," he wrote, and although "the sun of liberty has risen for the fatherland . . . for us it has risen only as a bloody aurora borealis." Kompert and other Jews in Vienna and Budapest, such as Isidor Bush, Sigmund Herzl, and Simon Szanto, despaired of life in Europe for Jews and asserted that by migrating to America, Jews would cease worrying about the "all-but-exhausted problems of Jewish emancipation."[6] As the plans of earlier German groups, such organization was superfluous: the Jews were on to America on their own.

Other schemes arose at various times in the mid-nineteenth century. In the 1850s, a community-financed emigration plan was tried in Alsace, and, in 1853, a committee on the defense of Jewish rights within the Consistory (the French body for Jewish self-governance) discussed facilitating emigration to America. Importantly, some of the poorest Jewish emigrants of this period did migrate with the financial assistance of their communities. At various times, local Jewish communities in Alsace collected money to send the indigent to America. Although the elite wanted to eradicate Jewish poverty by eradicating the Jewish poor, sizable numbers of Alsatian Jews were already leaving for America unassisted, on their own. Additionally, in the late 1860s, the Königsberg Committee of the Alliance Israelite Universelle, founded in 1860 as the first international Jewish defense agency, subsidized the emigration of destitute Russian and Polish Jews to the United States. The Committee ultimately sent fewer than a thousand, but the idea was firmly fixed that America would save Europe's impoverished Jews. As the 1871 report of the Alliance declared: "Emigration! emigration! this is the means of providing for the welfare of the Jews of Russia. And is it then so difficult to promote it? All we have to do is to furnish the cost of travelling from the frontiers of Russia to a German port, and thence to America? That country then undertakes the rest."[7]

Finally, in 1867, an American Jew, Benjamin Franklin Peixotto, advocated the immigration of Romanian Jews to the United States. While the planned resettlement of masses of these Jews was not a goal of most American and European Jewish organizations, Peixotto, a few other notable American Jews, and a Romanian maskil, Aaron Judah Leib Horowitz, author of *Rumaniah Va'Amerika,* ardently hoped to see masses of Jews leave "Rumania, the vale of misery, and come to free America." While Russian and Rumanian Jewish emigration would begin in earnest a decade later, such schemes helped educate the masses in those countries about America as a solution to their problems.[8]

Just as European-originated schemes were superfluous because of the spontaneous ground-swell migration, so, too, American-hatched plans were rarely actualized. Mordecai Noah's bold vision of Ararat, a Jewish colony and refuge in upstate New York, named after the final resting place of Noah's ark, never materialized.⁹ An experiment in Ulster County, New York, did a little bit better. Founded in 1837, the colony "Sholom," under the leadership of Moses Cohen, involved a few Russian Jews. At its peak, thirteen families tried to sustain a Jewish farming enclave that they hoped would attract other Jews from the czar's realm.¹⁰ The 1840s saw a string of other such ideas designed to inspire and facilitate the immigration of European Jews. In 1842, the Jewish Colonization Society of New York toyed with establishing a Jewish colony near Chicago and sent Meyer Klein to buy 160 acres from the government near Shamburg, Illinois. In 1843, the editor of a German-Jewish weekly, Julius Stern, envisioned a Jewish settlement in an area west of the Mississippi River, which he hoped would attract 70,000 Jews so as to ensure statehood.¹¹

The movement of Jews to America assumed the characteristics of the early stage of a mass migration in the 1820s, and it was a self-perpetuating and self-financed exodus. It mainly encompassed young Jewish men and women from the poorer classes of central European Jewry. The migration of these lone individuals, or, more typically, handfuls of young men and young women traveling together as friends, siblings, and kin, propelled outward the migration of others. These young Dorfjuden, peddlers' and cattle dealers' sons and daughters, left Europe with little capital, little formal education, and no knowledge of English. Their leave-taking unleashed a centrifugal force, making life in their home towns less feasible for those who stayed behind. An article in the *Allgemeine Zeitung* of 1839 phrased it aptly for the town of Würzberg: "If the present tendency is to continue, numerous small communities will be compelled to close their synagogues and schools. . . . In many a place, out of a Jewish population of 30–40 families 15–20 people have emigrated, mainly the young and employable."¹²

Who Came and Why

What caused them to make the move? For almost all of the tens of thousands of Jewish migrants, economic motive—broadly defined—was primary. A handful of Jews left Germany, Austria, and Poland for political reasons, particularly in the wake of the failed 1848 revolutions and the concomitant rise in anti-Jewish activity. Anti-Semitism at other points may have also inspired some to leave. It must have been disconcerting for Bavarian Jews to know that shouts of "Banish the Jews to America!" resounded in the chambers of the Bavarian Diet. But political conditions alone did not push the Jews out of central Europe, Bavaria, or anywhere else.[13]

The *vast* majority left their homes for America because in Europe they could neither work nor marry. Of course, the economic lot of the Jews stemmed in great measure from their abnormal political position. Overall, most emigrants found their personal situation altered profoundly by the dissolution of traditional peasant life in which the Jews had played the crucial role of middlemen, and, ultimately, this dislocation propelled their migration.

Emancipation did nothing to stem the tide of emigration. Historian Avraham Barkai has shown that Jewish emigration from Germany flowed, unchecked by emancipation or other political considerations, through the 1880s (the accepted terminal date for the German Jewish exodus) and beyond. Using figures from Württemberg, Barkai asserted that the percentage of Jews among all immigrants from this province increased in the 1860s and 1870s rather than declined with improvements in political conditions.[14]

Similarly, emigration from Poznań, which began in the 1830s and escalated into the 1840s and 1850s, did not abate with complete emancipation in 1866. The year 1871 actually heralded the largest migration from Posen. Neither did emancipation check the flow of Jewish migrants to America anywhere else. For example, one writer from Bohemia wrote that "it was characteristic that despite this emancipation the desire for emigration to North America especially, increases daily. This year hundreds of Bohemians have emigrated. The second-class cabins of the steamer which is to leave Bremen . . . are completely booked by Jews from Prague. The captain was willing to accommodate them with a kosher table."[15] Furthermore, while European anti-Jewish activity subsided in the 1850s and 1860s and emancipation proceeded, Jewish migration out of Germany reached a high point.

Certainly, the increase in Central European Jewish immigration after 1850 derived in part from a technological change. The change from the dangerous crossing as a steerage passenger on a sailing vessel to the safer journey by steam made a difference. Knowing that one had a good chance of surviving the oceanic voyage must have spurred on the somewhat faint-hearted among the Jewish masses. It was in the early 1850s that the steamers captured a majority of the trade at the German ports.[16]

The poorer the Jews, the more likely they were to go to America. In the earlier years of the migration, young men who had apprenticed themselves to artisans found that they could not practice their crafts, either because those crafts were becoming obsolete or because Gentile craftsmen, eager to preserve their monopoly, objected. Young women from impoverished large families who could not find a place for themselves in the rural economy eagerly left for America as well. Other Jewish emigrants came from the ranks of peddlers, petty merchants, or, importantly in the early years, they were their *sons* who could no longer be sustained by the traditional Jewish economy and could not support themselves at home. Artisans represented the most depressed class in German Jewry and, therefore, the largest group of emigrants to America. Indeed, one historian of German Jewry has asserted that emigration to America "probably contributed the single most important factor to the remarkable decline of the Jewish lower classes."

Of course, Jews were migrating within Europe as well in these years. The better off one found oneself, however, the more likely one was to move to a commerical city—Berlin, Hamburg, Vienna, or Budapest—rather than to America. Through the 1840s, Prussian law forbade Jews from Poznań, except for the few emancipated ones, to change residence *within* the Duchy, but they could leave the country. In those years, for example, almost three-quarters of those who left one small city, Ostorowo, came from the very bottom of the economic scale. Later, when they could move to Berlin, some of the more affluent also came to America. One study of emigration from the Bavarian town of Kissingen estimated that the migrants, almost all of whom were bound for America, left with nothing more than their fare in their pockets and that at least 30 percent did not have even that. Their fare came out of the coffers of the kahal. The phrase of the day, *Pattern ist Gelt wert!,* loosely, "it is worth the money to be rid of them" (a good example of the survival of Yiddish; *Pattern* is not German at all), indicated how much the migration, particularly earlier, stemmed from the poor. American Jewish commentators furthermore confirmed the poverty of the migrants to America on the eve of their departure. "Prosperity increases from day to day," asserted the *Wiener Jahrbuch für Israeliten* in 1846, and "those who were beggars when they arrived are rich men after 6 to 10 years and the name *German Jew* has here become a name of honor, a sign of uprightness and honesty."[17]

To be sure, sometimes also the sons and daughters of better-off Jews migrated to America, but their movement came later than that of the masses, and they made up just a trickle in the stream. Only 7.9 percent of those leaving Kissingen in Bavaria between 1830 and 1854 were rabbis and teachers, and a mere 2.2 percent were drawn from the tiny professional class in the town's Jewish community. The Kissingen figures further indicate that "better off" was relative. Since these migrants took entire families with them, their migration expenses amounted to more, and statistics on the amount of capital they had revealed only modest accumulations, not wealth.[18]

A few of Germany's elite Jews, involved in international finance, did send sons to America to set up operations there. With the vast takeoff of American industry in the decades flanking the Civil War, American opportunities beckoned. American business and state-sponsored internal improvements begged for European capital, and a small number of prosperous German Jews came to America.[19] Furthermore, a handful of rabbis and intellectuals also decided to join America's growing Jewish communities, particularly after the 1850s. American congregations, which suffered from an acute lack of religious functionaries, often invited them over. Others responded to numerous advertisements in the Jewish press seeking rabbis, readers, slaughterers, teachers, and circumcisers for the burgeoning American Jewish communities. The rabbis came to the United States well after the mass migration was in full swing. Since the law in much of central Europe required that rabbis speak German and possess a university degree, they brought to America a set of experiences and attitudes that differentiated them dramatically from the masses they were to serve. The rabbis, Reform or traditional, had gone through the process of Bildung, while the masses of immigrants had not. The rabbis had been exposed to German "high" culture during their years in the cities and universities. The vast bulk of the migrants, even those from Bavaria, Württemberg, and the other clearly German regions, left traditional communities that were just beginning to experience Germanization and arrived in America only marginally "German."[20]

Other kinds of variations within the migration point to its economic basis. A hefty—and, unfortunately, inestimable—number of Jewish immigrants, particularly from Posen, Suvalk, and other parts of Poland, migrated to the United States after a stay of some duration in England and sometimes in the Netherlands. Had a search for freedom and equality been their first goal, then England would have been just as fine a place to settle. But the second, and permanent, stage of their migration to the United States reflected a desire for greater economic opportunity, based in part on kin networks already in America and on the powerful draw of the romance of America.[21]

Furthermore, Jewish male migrants from various European countries left for America to escape military service. As Jews had become emancipated, they also became liable for the draft. Some men leaving Württemberg in the 1850s, for example, listed "fear of conscription" as their motive, while a few studies have posited that as early as the 1840s, a small stream of Russian Jews—who were clearly *not* being emancipated—also opted for the United States rather than serve a stint in the czarist army.[22] Additionally, a number of local disasters and crises in the late 1860s, including cholera epidemics and widespread famines in western Russia, particularly Lithuania, Kalvaria, and Suvalk, disrupted Jewish community life and propelled forward a migration to America, whereas idiosyncratic, personal motives also underlay the myriad stories of immigrants wherever they came from.[23]

Age, gender, and family, in addition to poverty, shaped the migration. It clearly began with young, single men, but unmarried women came in relatively large numbers as well. The overwhelming presence of the unmarried in the first cycles of migration out of Jewish Europe attested to the complex connection between economic and political causation. The retention, throughout much of the mid-continent, of restrictions on Jewish marriage through the enforcement of the Matrikel set in motion a process whereby young men, first, left their home towns to go to America to work and marry. The *Allgemeine Zeitung des Judentums,* a constant observer of the migration, reported from the docks in 1839 that among the Jews leaving for America could be seen "many more single people than families . . . who are motivated not by greed but by the conviction that . . . they will not be able to settle and find a family." State law restricted Jewish marriages not just in absolute number but also in relation to class. Jews who could prove that they had a solid chance to earn a decent living could marry. Others were denied the right of matrimony. Thus, for example, between 1830 and 1854, 473 single people left the Kissingen district, although only 31 married couples did so. The singleness of the migration emerged not only by looking at the emigration figures but also from the portraits of the German Jewish countryside, with its glaring absence of young people, and from the situation in early American Jewish communities, where we find a glaring absence of old people and young children.[24]

If men left first, and subsequently either returned—if they had done quite well—or relied upon the mail to find a bride, then small towns of central Europe should have been female-heavy in the marriageable age brackets, while, conversely, Jewish enclaves in America should have had too many men. And that was the profile in the 1820s and 1830s. According to Marion Kaplan, the preeminent scholar of Jewish women in Germany, Jewish women outnumbered men in rural districts. The crisis caused by the male migration revived the role of the *shadkhen* (matchmaker) in Europe, while histories of literally hundreds of Jewish communities in the United States—from Chicago to Mariposa, California, and from Portland, Maine, to Portland, Oregon—pointed to a male-female imbalance in the first decade of Jewish settlement.[25]

Despite the seeming masculinity of the migration, a surprisingly large number of single women joined the first streams of the flood. Women made up 45 percent among those who left Kissingen for America in the 1830s and 1840s, whereas from all of Bavaria from 1830 and 1839, men and women emigrated in roughly equal number, 12,806 and 11,701, respectively. Daughters of the poor, they not only left to follow potential spouses, but they, too, were victims of economic change. Many poor Jewish women in Europe had traditionally worked as domestic servants, while others sewed for a living or played a role in petty family businesses. Just as the economy dried up for men, so it did for women.[26]

Even when the laws limiting marriages—the Matrikel in Germany or the *familienten Gesetz* in Bohemia and Silesia—were rescinded, migration to America continued to attract the single and impoverished. Biographies of young men and women, Jewish immigrants, testify to an almost casual approach toward the decision to move to America and depict an ambiance in which European Jews of this era came to think of migration as an automatic option.[27]

Immigrants left for America in small groups of friends and relatives. Especially brothers and sisters traveled together. Newspapers occasionally reported on organized parties moving en masse, but personal narratives, sketchy for sure, confirmed that the typical migrant group consisted of brothers or sisters or a knot of friends, deciding together to go to America.

Having a relative, a sibling in particular, in America, increased one's own chances of emigrating. Migrations from Bavaria, Bohemia, Silesia, Slovakia, Poznań, and Pomerania all followed family chains. Elaborate networks brought individuals from home villages and cities to relatives in America. Brothers brought each other over to join their peddling operations, while sisters were encouraged to make the voyage to keep house, work, and marry their sisters' and brothers' friends.

Early migration of single people stimulated the larger subsequent flow. The *Israelitische Annalen,* observing the intense out-migration from Württemberg in 1839, correctly judged that "the cause of this strange happening . . . is partly that for the past thirty years, many people had left this place to go to the United States, where they found free work and made a good living; those people invited their relatives . . . provided them with the necessary traveling expenses and prepared everything for their arrival across the ocean." Of the 207 Jews who left for America from the tiny village of Jebenhausen before 1870, 107 involved brother-and-sister family groupings, and no matter the number or sex of the siblings, the process whereby the eldest launched the migration of the rest was nearly universal. Therefore, particular Jewish communities in early stages of formation in the United States tended to be thickly clustered with individuals from the same town. Betwen 1830 and 1865, 28 young men and two young women from the very small village of Demmelsdorf in Bavaria settled in Cincinnati, whereas a few villages in Bohemia sent an inordinate number of Jews to Milwaukee and Cleveland, and Boston saw the transplantation of groups from several towns of Poznań.[28]

In determining which Jews left central Europe, class certainly played an important role. Other factors as well propelled the migration. A number of historians have conjectured that *many* of the migrants came not only from the ranks of the "German" Jewish poor, but that they were also Galicians, Poles, and other eastern European Jews who had been spilling in for decades prior to the migration to America and whose Germanic roots had not sunk down deeply.

Jack Wertheimer, in his study of eastern European Jews in Germany appropriately entitled *Unwelcome Strangers,* asserted that a majority of these transients in fact left for America partly by choice and partly as a result of administrative decrees. Similarly, Moses Shulvass has claimed that of the eastern Jewish newcomers, "many . . . realized, after their arrival in Germany, that for a variety of reasons it could not become their new home. They went on to other western countries." The United States was the most attractive of them.

Parallel patterns may have occurred in Austria-Hungary, where large numbers of Jews from the lands of the Habsburg monarchy also consisted of eastern European Jews, particularly Galicians, whose towns had been incorporated into the empire or who drifted in over the course of decades, eventually opting for America over Bohemia, Moravia, and the like.[29]

From Where They Came

How "German" were the Jewish immigrants of the mid-nineteenth century? While Jews from the Germanic states, particularly Bavarians, constituted the single largest group in the migration, they probably held only a slim lead over Polish, Bohemian, Moravian, Slovakian, French, or even Russian and Lithuanian Jews combined. The exact numbers and breakdowns stubbornly elude historians for a number of reasons. First, the American government—agents at ports of entry, census takers, school authorities, or military officials—never enumerated religion. A Jew from Posen, who may have spoken no German, would have carried some kind of German papers to America. Most of the Jews who migrated to the United States from Prussia actually came from Posen, but historians and others have considered them as German as the Rhinelanders or the Bavarians. Yet the distinction in Posen between "real" Prussians and the *Hinterberliner,* the Jews of the Polish lands, meant a great deal legally, politically, and culturally.

Jewish German speakers could have been very easily confused with "Germans." Since in the mid-nineteenth century Jews from Slovakia or Bohemia would have known some German, they would appear to others as Germans rather than Slovaks or Czechs. That is why many historians, without a second thought, have lumped together Jews from Posen with those from the rest of Germany and thrown Jews from Bohemia, Moravia, and other central European areas into the German cauldron, too.[30] Jews from Galicia were formally subjects of the emperor of Austria. To call them Austrians reveals little about their culture or identity.

Additionally, many American Jews who themselves—or their parents—had hailed from the lands of the east described themselves as "Germans," an identity thought to be prestigious, and ignored their Polish or other roots. The parents of Joseph Proskauer, for example, stemmed from Pressburg in Hungary and Breslau in Silesia, a Polish area annexed by Prussia. But Proskauer always referred to his European background as German. Harriet Levy, who grew up in San Francisco, announced in school that she was German, despite the fact that her parents came from Poland. She later mused: "Why Poles lacked the virtue of Bavarians I did not understand. . . .

I accepted the convention that our excellence was not that of the Baierns [Bavarians] because we were Polish." Indeed, numerous Jews who showed up in immigration records and communal accounts as "English" or "Dutch" actually came from eastern Europe, but they often opted to display the more prestigious western pedigree.[31] Single Jews from various places interacted and intermarried in the United States, blurring national lines. Bernard Drachman, for example, was the son of a Bavarian mother and a Galician father. Since German Jews predominated in New York and Jersey City where the family lived, the mother's Bavarian identity dominated the home. The Galician father, "although born and reared in a Yiddish-speaking environment," followed his wife's linguistic orientation and "did not himself use the Yiddish" in the home.[32]

Congregational formation revealed the ethnic diversity. Since the ritual of Germany and of Poland differed and congregations offered not only places for worship but places for fellowship, German, Polish, Bohemian, Russian, and Lithuanian Jews all formed separate congregations when enough of them clustered. Thus between 1820 and 1830, of the four congregations created, three were German and one Polish; in the 1830s, two German and one Polish; in the 1840s, ten German and five Polish (with an additional seven from other *minhagim*); the 1850s saw sixteen new congregations, three German and six Polish. In the 1850s, the first Russian congregation also came into being.[33]

Yet one more measure of the disparate rather than homogeneous roots of American Jews of the mid-nineteenth century emerges from the various lists of "famous," "first," and "prominent" Jews compiled for a variety of reasons. Of the notable Jews who found their way into Isaac Markens' *The Hebrews In America* (1888), for example, fifteen listed a birthplace somewhere in Germany, seven listed various spots in eastern Europe, and two others cited England, which probably meant that they had been the English-born children of Polish Jewish parents.[34] A somewhat later and less elite list was compiled by Jacob Pfeffer: *Distinguished Jews of America* (1917) extolled self-made Jewish men. Of those who either were born or migrated before 1880 (or whose parents immigrated before 1880), the vast majority came from east of the Elbe. Pfeffer's two volumes may very well have sought to highlight successful Russian and Polish Jews, given that they appeared at the height of the debate over immigration restriction and as such skewed the sample. But Pfeffer nevertheless listed Jews who came to the United States before 1880 from Mariampol in Suwalk, Dembrova in

Galicia, Wolosin in Russia as well as from Bialystok, Kovno, and Lemberg, hardly places associated with the "German" period in American Jewish immigration history.[35] Of the Jewish women included in the multivolume *Notable American Women,* who lived in this era and whose information on European origins was provided either for themselves or their parents, one was Bohemian, three Polish, five German, and one from "Austrian Silesia," a Polish area annexed by the Austrian Empire.[36] Finally, an article on the founders of early Jewish Los Angeles in the 1850s and 1860s highlighted three from Germany, two of whom were listed as Prussians and may therefore actually fit the Polish or Poznanian category, and four who had emigrated from Russian Poland.[37]

Germans did make up the single largest group of the migration. Biographies of individual Jews—those who became well known in commercial, political, and intellectual spheres, and the more numerous ones who never rose above obscurity—pointed to a massive movement of Jews from Germany. That movement proceeded first from Bavaria and then shifted to the other provinces of Germany west of the Elbe River. Histories of most of the Jewish communities in the United States (with the exception of that handful of pre-1820 cities: New York, Philadelphia, Baltimore, Savannah, Charleston, and Newport) began in large measure with the arrival of the first German Jews. Histories of congregations similarly abound with references to German founders.[38]

However, historians who universalize from the German experience, who assume that the years 1820–80 constituted a "German" era in American Jewish history, and who attribute Jewish religious, economic, and social developments in America to Germanness, not only simplify but ignore the sweep of geography and culture from which Jews came to mid-nineteenth-century America. They ignore the fact that in many southern towns, the classic Jewish country store was founded by an Alsatian peddler. As a result of poverty, famines, epidemics, and continuous anti-Semitism, Yiddish-speaking Jews came to the United States from Alsace, often entering through New Orleans. California, and San Francisco in particular, attracted a significant number of them, and one estimate suggested that roughly five to ten percent of nineteenth-century California Jewry hailed from the French provinces along the Rhine. Like their counterparts from Germany, these Jews left France as they began to undergo their first steps into French culture and, thus, were experiencing cultural transitions both in Europe and in America.[39]

Similarly, a sizable, and unfortunately uncountable, segment of the Jewish population streaming into the United States came from various points in the Austrian Empire: Bohemia, Moravia, Slovakia, and Galicia. Significant Czech settlements flourished in Chicago, Cleveland, and Milwaukee. While a smattering of "Austrian" Jewish immigrants were the disappointed participants in the 1848 revolution, the majority made their way to America because of the decline of the Jewish economy, overpopulation, and spiralling anti-Semitism after the 1840s. These Jews, like the "Germans," were generally drawn from the poor and the young, arriving in America from traditional Jewish villages and towns, products of a pious Jewish upbringing. Sons and daughters of artisans and petty merchants, they used family networks to launch and sustain their immigration. Of the Reich family from Kaschau, Hungary, for example, who in America would become the Rich family of Atlanta, the two oldest sons, then early teenagers, were sent to America in 1859 and went to live with friends in Cleveland. In 1861 and 1862, three other brothers joined them on their peddling route up and down the Ohio River valley. In 1849, Abraham Klauber, whose father had succumbed to a cholera epidemic five years earlier, decided that he would be better able to help his widowed mother and younger sister from America than in Chudenitz, Bohemia. He traveled to America with the son of his employer, and the two of them eventually ended up running a small store in the California mining country. Bernard Drachman, later to become an eminent Orthodox rabbi, grew up in the 1870s in a congregation in Jersey City, made up primarily of Jews "from Slavonic lands," some of whom "spoke the pure and undisguised Yiddish of Poland or Russia." In Rokycan, Bohemia, Adolf Kraus's mother took him aside when he turned fifteen and was liable for conscription into the military. She declared: "It is high time for you to go to America. I have secured a passport . . . and a steamship ticket."

Migrants from these various parts of Austria and Hungary defied easy categorization, in part because they hailed from so many different places. In some cases, they came from areas well under the influence of Vienna, while others left places barely touched by that spirit. In America, where their numbers allowed it, they asserted their cultural differences by forming themselves into Hungarian or Bohemian or Galician congregations to sustain fellowship and regional variations in ritual.[40]

Tens of thousands of Jews also migrated from various parts of Poland, including those Polish regions gobbled up by Prussia, those lands that became part of Russia, and those annexed by Austria. Before 1880, immigration even came from such un-German places as Russia and Lithuania. Much of the contemporary journalistic, autobiographical, and biographical material pointed to a steady influx to America from the east. As early as the 1840s, the American Jewish press noted German Jewish antipathy to the eastern Europeans in their American midst. In a Cincinnati Jewish newspaper in 1856, Max Lilienthal, a Reform rabbi, published an attack on the influx of Polish Jews, fearing that their traditionalism would impede Reform Judaism's progress. His colleague, Isaac Mayer Wise, wrote in the *American Israelite* in 1861 grudgingly, that "the best informed Hebraists are Poles and also in this country they can boast upon much more Hebrew and rabbinic learning than any other class of Jews or Gentiles." *The Jewish Messenger* in the late 1860s wrote extensively on the entry of Russian Jews to the United States, and even the German Jewish press recognized the steady flow of eastern European Jews to America.[41]

It is impossible to specify the number of Polish, Polish-Prussian, Polish-Austrian, Polish-Russian, Russian, and other eastern European Jewish immigrants to the United States before the 1880s. Only guesses can be hazarded. One source, for example, estimated that by 1880, and the beginning of the mass immigration from eastern Europe, some 15,000 eastern European Jews lived on New York's Lower East Side alone. Another suggested that between 1820 and 1870, some 7,550 Jews from Russia came to America. In the next decade, a total of 41,000 Russian Jews emigrated to the United States. Historians of Jewish life in the western part of the United States have asserted that Polish Jewry made up a majority of the pre-1880 Jews there. Between 1860 and 1880, more Jews from eastern Europe than from Germany made their way to all of America. Sources from the European side also confirmed a significant Jewish emigration to America from Poland well before the 1880s. The Hebrew magazine *Ha-Melitz* in Odessa wrote in 1869 that "The number of families emigrating from here to America year by year is apparently very large. There is virtually no family in Poland which has no relatives in America."[42]

By the 1840s and 1850s, very few American Jewish communities, the large ones in particular, did *not* see the emergence of both a "German" and a "Polish" congregation. Well before innovations in ritual shook the unity of American Jewish communities along religious lines, ethnic distinctions pitting Germans and Poles against each other rocked the foundations of the emerging Jewish *kehillot*. A Polish congregation in New York, Shaaray

Zedek, came into being in 1840. In 1849, Boston's Polish Jews hired a Polish rabbi from New York to conduct Rosh Hashanah and Yom Kippur services, so that they could pray by themselves. In 1852, Polish Jews formed a congregation in Chicago and in 1858, in Pittsburgh. A Russian congregation was founded in 1852 in New York's Bowery district. On the other coast, Lithuanian and Polish Jews formed their own synagogue in San Francisco in the late 1850s, and scattered throughout California could be heard the sounds of *minhag Polin,* the Polish ritual, interspersed with the German ritual, *minhag Ashkenaz.* Dozens of community histories and voluminous personal narratives of this era testified further to the numerical significance and cultural distinctiveness of the Polish Jews in America during this apogee of "the German era."[43]

Most American Jewish immigrants from England and the Netherlands spoke Yiddish. Polish and Russian in origin, they sojourned in these countries before coming to America. Many of the Polish Jewish tailors who appeared in New York and Boston in the 1870s had lived previously in London, as did a number of the merchants who flocked to California after the Gold Rush, scattering throughout the state, the Southwest, and the Pacific Northwest. The parents of Philip Cowen, editor of *The American Hebrew,* hailed from Prussian Poland but lived for a number of years with a brother in Manchester. David Lubin, a pioneer in agricultural planning, was born in Russian Poland, in a small town near Cracow, and spent part of his childhood in the 1850s in England. And most Russian Jews, petty storekeepers and urban peddlers who in the 1870s founded Chicago's Rodfei Zedek congregation, had lived for a decade or more in parts of the British Isles.[44]

Mass Jewish immigration from Russia did not begin in earnest until the late 1880s, but as early as 1867, a Russian supplement to the Hebrew magazine *Ha'Karmel* asserted that American themes had already crept into Russian Jewish folksongs, particularly into ballads of lament, or *Agune* songs, in which an abandoned wife bemoans her fate. These musical vignettes about heartless husbands who left for America, deserting their wives, bore testimony to a nascent Jewish movement from czarist lands to America. Some young Jewish men left Russia to escape conscription into the military in the 1850s, and by the 1860s, full family groups began to come en masse. The Lipsitz family of Baisogala, Lithuania, for example, left for Detroit in 1868 with children, in-laws, and various other kin active in cigar- and eyeglass-making. The first Lithuanian Jew to come to Chicago, David

Zamenski, arrived in New York in 1860; after he settled there, he arranged for other Lithuanians to follow him. In 1865, enough of his *landsmen* arrived to justify a regular Lithuanian *minyan*. The following year, a second prayer fellowship of Lithuanians was formed. Bernard Hourwich noted in his autobiography that in his Lithuanian village in the 1870s, "there were several courses to be pursued by the young men of Poniemon. One was to leave the country, and seek fame and fortune in other lands, especially America."[45]

No matter where they came from, these young people chose America because of the economic opportunities that awaited them. Contrary to the assertions of many historians, they did not leave as a result of their tangential connections to Jewishness. They had not lost their identification with traditional Jewish life. They were not the least committed, least knowledgeable Jews among their peers. Since the better-off and more modernized Jews of central Europe actually avoided America and moved to cities at home, immigrants to America *may* have been the least modern and the most traditional Jews. They *may* have had worse command of German than their brethren who stayed in Europe and experienced the later, more intense Germanization. Traditionalism can certainly be seen in the publication of special prayer books for travelers, in their references, in the few extant diaries of the voyage, mentioning attempts to observe *kashrut* on board ship, and, ultimately, in the speed with which these men and women reconstituted Jewish communities in America. A newspaper description of a group leaving Oberdorf in Württemberg noted: "The group carries with it a Torah written on parchment, which they solemnly consecrated in the synagogue at Oberdorf before their departure."[46]

Theirs was a *Jewish* migration. Although Gentiles from Central Europe also moved to America in these same years, Jews migrated for distinctly Jewish reasons. The non-Jews were not escaping the civil and religious disabilities that the Jews suffered. Moreover, Jews migrated differently than non-Jews, even if they came from the same country of origin. They came from different regions within those countries, emigrated in different ways, at different times, and at dissimilar rates.

German Gentiles, for example, came from the ranks of the better-off peasantry and small freeholders, migrated as full families, and in these decades hailed primarily from the west of Germany and not from Prussia or the east. The poorer class of non-Jewish Germans went to industrial cities in Germany, and of those who went to America, many returned back to Germany. Not so the Jews. In the non-German regions of Bohemia, Moravia, Galicia, Alsace, Slovakia, western Russia, and Poland—Suvalk as well as Posen—Gentile emigration fell far below the Jewish emigration rate. In most places, a larger proportion of the Jews than non-Jews left for America. Thus, while Jews made up only 1.5 percent of the population of Bavaria, they accounted for almost 5 percent of the state's out-migrants. While Jews represented a relatively small percentage of the population of Posen, 46,640 of them left between 1824 and 1871, as compared with only 18,790 Christians. By 1871, four times as many Jews as non-Jews had left the Polish-German province. In addition, Jewish immigrants settled first and foremost where other Jews made their homes or in places where other Jews could join them rather than among their non-Jewish countrymen.[47]

Where They Went

Wherever in Europe they came from, they met in America. While relatives and friends brought each other over and reestablished in America their Old World networks, clustering in particular American cities and often congregating in the same neighborhoods, the American Jewish communities tended to be polyglot microcosms of the entire European continent. Wherever in Europe they came from, a clear trend of Jewish preference for America over any other possible destination emerged by the mid-nineteenth century. From a Jewish backwater in 1820, America emerged to become one of the most sizable Jewish communities in the world by 1880.

That preference can be seen in part by the escalating numbers of Jews in the United States. No more than 3,000 Jews lived in America in 1825. Dwelling in any significant number in only seven states, American Jews then accounted for only three out of every thousand Jews in the world. The Jewish presence in America doubled between 1820 and 1840, and then quickly doubled again to 15,000. In less than a decade, from 1840 to 1848, that figure once again skyrocketed, going up to 50,000. By 1880, approximately 240,000 Jews made their home in America. Heavily urban, Jewish outposts formed in almost every state and every region.[48]

Settlement patterns within the United States made Jews different from other Americans. In the nineteenth century, the majority of Americans dwelt in small towns and rural areas, and were engaged in agriculture. Jews from the start lived in cities and avoided the land. In general, they opted not just for cities, but for the biggest ones. As early as the mid-1840s, one-fourth of all Jews in America lived in New York City, Philadelphia, and Baltimore. Older cities had Jewish enclaves from before the 1820s and continued to house Jewish communities. Residents of such cities as Cincinnati, Chicago, San Francisco, Cleveland, Rochester, Albany, and Washington, D.C., saw the beginnings of Jewish community life at the same time that these cities themselves took off in the nineteenth century. While in these decades Jews showed up in many agricultural states in the South, Midwest, and West, they planted themselves in the larger towns, opting for Kansas City, Omaha, Mobile, Jackson, and Minneapolis rather than the rural backwaters. Importantly, Jews in nineteenth-century America also found themselves in hundreds of small towns, such as Oswego, New York, Meridian, Mississippi, Shelbyville, Tennessee, and even Cheyenne, Wyoming. These outposts tended to support tiny Jewish communities for just one generation. After a few decades, Jews who lived in small towns usually ended up in larger communities. A string of Jewish "ghost towns" stretched through the Ohio River valley, the Mississippi Delta, and the mining frontier of California and Nevada.

The process of congregation and institutional formation provides the best measure of concentration patterns of Jews in the United States, but other indices also give a clue to the Jewish dispersion in America. Traveler Israel Joseph Benjamin visited America during the years 1859–61 and in his *Three Years in America* wrote of pockets of Jewish life in almost every corner of the country. He commented on the giant Jewish communities in the large cities as well as on the small enclaves tucked away in mining camps and in the Great Lakes region. The account books of several *meshulochim,* messengers collecting money for the needy Jews of Jerusalem, bore witness to the Jewish presence—and largess—in Grass Valley, California, and San Francisco; in Macon, Georgia, as well as Atlanta; Elmira, New York, and Buffalo, too. They collected in Marshall, Texas; Titusville, Pennsylvania; Pittsburgh; Nashville; Boston; Syracuse; New Orleans; and scores of other cities and towns. A *mohel* (ritual circumciser) in upstate New York ushered boys into the covenant of Abraham between 1849 and 1863 in Rochester, Syracuse, Utica, Oswego, Binghamton, and Auburn. Jewish newspapers in the pre–Civil War era found readers in 1,250 places, of all sizes and settings. And finally, an 1872 description of "the American Jew" that appeared in *A History of All Religions,* probably written by the Philadelphia rabbi Sabato Morais, boasted that "the descendants of the patriarchs can be found through the length and breadth of the Union. Whether we travel in the New England

States, or in the distant regions of the West, houses of worship will be met which resound with prayers uttered by the outcasts of Judea."[49]

Jewish dispersion and settlement in the United States moved along certain fairly standard patterns. So standard indeed, that it is possible to delineate a paradigm for Jewish community development. Excluding New York, Baltimore, Philadelphia, Charleston, Savannah, and Newport, which were home to Jews as far back as the seventeenth century, most Jewish communities in nineteenth-century America began in a similar way. A lone Jew or two or three individuals settled first. More likely than not, this represented a second or third stop within the United States for these men, probably bachelors. If life turned out to be good there, particularly if business flourished, they called for brothers to join them in the store. Then they got married, had children, and the outlines of organized Jewish communal life began to appear. In many cases, Jews were among the first white settlers, particularly in dozens of Midwestern, trans-Mississippi, and Far Western places. They arrived early on in the history of St. Louis and Kansas City, San Francisco, Cincinnati, Milwaukee, Minneapolis, and Omaha, responding to the need for small business in these towns in the pioneer stage.

Some communities were formed directly out of the experience of peddling, the premier Jewish occupation of the mid-nineteenth century. Young men newly arrived from Europe donned the peddler's pack and traversed a set region, be it the Mississippi Delta, northern New England, the Ohio River valley, or the Pacific Northwest. If lucky, they graduated to a horse and cart, and finally to a real store. All it took was a few young men who managed to open little shops in a given area to begin the process of organizing Jewish community life. Because of family, business, and religious connections, small Jewish communities maintained close ties with larger ones, which in turn were hooked into even bigger, mammoth communities, such as New York, Chicago, San Francisco, and Cincinnati. Jews in the larger cities provided merchandise and credit, religious services, functionaries, and goods. It was often to these larger communities that young single Jews turned when looking for a spouse, and it was there that the most successful of the small-town merchants moved when looking for wider economic horizons.

This happened in the South. When Jacob Cohen and Jacob Schwartz, peddlers in Mississippi, bought a plot of land in 1849 in Woodville to bury a fellow peddler; when, in 1845, two years before Atlanta's incorporation, a Jewish family from Hesse-Darmstadt, after a sojourn in Philadelphia opened a dry goods store; and when Harris Abrahams and Lewis and Esther Fry, having come from Poland via England, began to trade in Nashville in the 1850s, they not only paved the way for the formation of a Jewish community. They were also replicating the actions of their sisters and brothers in North and South Carolina, Virginia, Louisiana, and Alabama.[50]

This happened in the Pacific Northwest. In 1849, ten years before Oregon achieved statehood, the first Jew made his way to Portland. By 1854 a Jewish woman named Mrs. Weinshank ran a boarding house catering to young Jewish peddlers, and, in 1856, the first Jewish religious service was held. As of 1858, some eight young Jewish men, Bavarians and Bohemians, lived there and did business. Most of them had had several other American homes, and many of them would move on again.[51]

This story, a story of multiple migrations, youthful founders, mixed European origins, small business, and the connectedness between family and community formation, indeed happened *everywhere* that Jews showed up. Wherever they stayed long enough to be visible, wherever even a handful of them plied a trade together, wherever they started families, they banded together to create some kind of semblance of community and started to shape American Jewish life.

CHAPTER THREE

THE TIES OF WORK

Tailors, shoemakers and carpenters earn 20 fl. a week with little effort. . . .
One can live quite decently for half. . . . A girl that is ready to sew earns
7–10 fl. a week . . . no craftsman who is ready to work will have anything to
regret if he comes to America.

Father began life in America, like so many Jewish immigrants did, by walking
the streets of Newark and suburbs, with peddler's pack on his back, filled
with dry-goods and notions.

Where there are no rice-fields, there are no rice-birds; where there is no wild celery,
there are no canvass back ducks; where there is no trade, there are no Jews. . . .
If there is to be a Jerusalem, let Richmond be the place.

THE INABILITY to make a living, get married, and raise a family
pushed tens of thousands of Jewish men and women out of Europe in the
mid-nineteenth century. Their hunch that in America they could do all of
these things pulled them over and led them to New York, Philadelphia,
Chicago, Cincinnati, San Francisco, and indeed to every region of the expanding country. The inextricable connections between work and family as
motives for migration were wound together even more tightly in America,
as patterns of work and patterns of family life bound Jews in America to
each other. How they worked and how they lived, whom they worked with
and whom they lived with merged into a single phenomenon. Jews, immigrants and their children, opted for specific Jewish niches in the economy.
The path from peddler, either rural or urban, to storekeeper, the thick
concentration of Jews in small business, mainly dry goods and clothing,
their reliance on familial and communal credit networks, and the shady
lines between the Jewish entrepreneur and the Jewish worker became elements in an American Jewish economy. This economy could not be sepa-

rated from family life, and the bonds of kinship and matrimony facilitated it. In all of these facets, fluidity and flexibility served as the defining characteristics of the economic adjustment.

The American Jewish economy, epitomized by the small business family dealing in notions or in clothing, offered a curious blend of innovation and conservatism. Innovation made possible the mobility that most—although not all—Jews experienced. They could not remain wedded to a particular craft, mode of operation, partnership, or location and "make it." By improvising and striking out for new methods, products, and places, they took advantage of America's bountiful opportunities. This kind of risk taking, like the attitude that initially brought them to America, demonstrated their future orientation and willingness to defy tradition.

But, at the same time, their tampering with accepted ways of doing business jarred with a trait of fundamental conservatism that they also brought with them. Jewish men, in particular, replicated their European jobs and, by virtue of their work choice, remained connected to a Jewish associational and cultural web. No matter how far afield they went, they never strayed widely from Jewish patterns and Jewish networks: they relied on historic models to guide their economic behavior in America. As merchants, however small, they also depended on order and stability in the world around them. The success of a dry-goods store in Milwaukee or a clothing emporium in Portland presupposed the maintenance of the status quo.

This tension between conservatism and innovation almost universally characterized American Jewish economic behavior. The desire to strike out for the new on one's own and the complex ties that bound them to the old ran through most life histories of individual Jews and Jewish communities. Like the commercial concentration and upward mobility, this tension was a paradigm for Jewish adjustment to nineteenth-century America.

Of course, not all Jewish immigrants in America in the middle decades of the nineteenth century experienced the process in quite the same fashion. Some never succeeded. Stories of failure, poverty, and distress rarely worked their way into family histories, celebratory volumes, or synagogue and communal narratives. But a good number of Jews did not proceed along the proverbial path from "rags to riches." Jews showed up in the New York Poorhouse in the 1820s, 1830s, and 1840s. Luckless peddlers shifted in and out of the Jewish communities, hoping to secure a loan and get back out on the road. Often the appearance of a destitute Jew, either alive or dead, became the impetus for the formation of the earliest community institutions—cemetery, mutual aid society, or congregation. While, initially, the alleviation of economic distress fell in the domain of the individual synagogues and *khevrot* (societies) in larger cities like New York, Philadelphia, New Orleans, or Cincinnati, the problem grew after the mass influx of the poor in the 1820s. Communal leaders sought more efficient, citywide ways to distribute free fuel and clothing, provide loans, give out matzo at Passover, help find jobs, or bury the indigents. From the beginning, Jewish schools subsidized the tuition of poor youngsters, and courts occasionally remanded the "Jewish children of the submerged" to Jewish orphanages. After the founding of Hebrew Union College in 1873, women's groups around the country organized Indigent Students' Aid Societies to raise money to support poor young men who had enrolled. Jewish hospitals had to make special provisions for the care of the Jewish needy, the down-on-their-luck peddlers and domestic servants. According to Isaac Mayer Wise, commenting on the Jewish Hospital in New Orleans, "entire families of poor or homeless Jews would invade it and remain wards of the institution until provided with more suitable quarters." Purim balls and special appeals for contributions to coal, clothing, or matzo funds proved that poverty hovered around the edges of American Jewish life.[1]

Not all Jews did well in America. Orphanages, asylums, and charitable societies proliferated to deal with Jews in need. A continuous stream of new arrivals kept rushing into the Jewish communities, taking the place on the bottom, and replenishing the number of earlier poor immigrants who had begun to inch their way up. Particularly in New York and other large cities, the number of poor Jews throughout this sixty-year span distressed communal leaders. The Jewish poor inspired the many ladies' sewing circles and day nurseries, Purim balls, free schools, and fuel funds.

Settlement patterns of American Jews indicated the existence of poverty. While many Jewish single men and families may have moved from one city to another because they had done well and wanted to do even better, much of the shifting around and nonpersistence that characterized so many communities came from the least successful. Of the fifty children who made up the first "class" of orphans at the Hebrew Orphan Asylum in Baltimore, most came from families on the move. A history of the Jews in Los Angeles noted that in the early years, 1850s and 1860s, "success and a lifetime spent in Los Angeles were the exceptions rather than the rule." Jews came and went from city to city, and usually those who did the least well moved the most.[2]

Various examples of the economically marginal and the unsuccessful surface in the life histories of nineteenth-century American Jews. Jacob Philipson, who with his brother were the first Jews to settle in St. Louis at the beginning of the nineteenth century, were buried at the expense of the Jewish community. David Philipson, a Reform rabbi at century's end, grew up in a "humble home," the child of a mail carrier.[3] Biographies highlight bankruptcies and subsequent impoverishment. Thus the father of Sol Bloom, later a congressman from California, was a victim of the 1873 depression. He lost his small clothing store in Peoria, Illinois. The soap factory owned by the father of Joseph Fels, who himself would later reenter the soap business, failed in 1870. Sam Aaron and his family made some money in California in the 1850s and then lost it. After being wiped out, the family began to move around, first to Salt Lake City, then Galveston, New York City, Butte, and finally Arizona. Community histories, likewise, tell of bankruptcies, bailouts, business failures, and movement out of the community by those looking for better prospects elsewhere.[4]

Jewish women bore a painful brunt of economic distress, partly because they tended to marry men significantly older than themselves, and eventual widowhood meant poverty as well as loneliness. A disproportionate number of Jews in need turned out to be widows. These "indigent sisters from the House of Israel" included both those with and without children to raise. Jewish children turned up in orphanages more often if they had lost fathers than if they had lost mothers, since men could make do, but women had a hard time supporting dependent children on their own. The development of philanthropic organizations for poor Jewish women indicated the extent of this problem, and asylums in a number of cities pointed to both the existence of poverty and its feminine angle. While port cities like New York, Philadelphia, Baltimore, and New Orleans may have had a higher degree of Jewish female poverty than inland and secondary communities, concern for widows and orphans vexed all communities from the earliest years of their formation. Similarly, as early as the 1860s, rabbis began to raise the particular problem of Jewish women deserted by husbands, and, in that same decade, the first evidence in New York of Jewish women engaged in prostitution—usually a by-product of female poverty—was noted by Jewish communal leaders.[5]

Poverty existed among America's Jews, the usual account of historians notwithstanding. Not only did America's mercurial nineteenth-century economy make and break businesses rapidly, but the Jewish sector of that economy constantly endured the influx of new immigrants. The flow remained relatively steady during these sixty years. Newcomers, be they Bavarian Jews or Jews from Posen or from Bohemia, arrived with little or no capital to launch themselves in America. Throughout this period, relatively poor immigrants inundated the American Jewish communities. While those immigrants who migrated from Germany after the 1850s tended to be less impoverished on arrival, they arrived simultaneously with Polish, Galician, and Czech Jews, who landed as poor as had earlier Germans.

Immigrant memoirs abounded with stories like that of Moses Bruml, a young man from Poland, who left Europe in 1849 and remembered that he had only one dollar. Joseph Samuel Mannasse from Filehne, Poland, made it to New York in 1850 with that same paltry amount. A memoir of an immigrant from Hesse-Darmstadt who ended up in Cleveland further indicated the fragile resources upon which the migration hung. He wrote: "About 1850 sister Rosa with several girls went to America, and in due course of time sent me a small sum of money. With this money and what money I had managed to save [I] started for America." The grandfather of Della Adler had tried to plan ahead. He saved his money in Suwalk, Lithuania, and invested in books to sell in America. On the voyage, however, his books and his other possessions were stolen and he joined the masses of others who came with empty pockets. Most Jewish immigrants' money, all they had managed to accumulate in Europe, went into the purchase of passage. Furthermore, for a sizable portion of them—those who could not afford their own fare—extra money to get started in America was out of the question.[6]

Even the "merchant princes," that tiny handful of wealthy Jews who, by the last quarter of the nineteenth century, dominated retailing, particularly department stores, began life in America with little capital. They shared a kind of collective biography. Edward Filene, who came from Poznań, began as a peddler, tailor, and glazier; Lazarus Straus first peddled and then ran a small country store in Talbotton, Georgia; Adam Gimbel left the region of Rheinland-Pfaltz at the age of eighteen with no money and sold from farm to farm around Vincennes, Indiana; Jacob Kaufmann, the son of a horse and cattle trader, also began as a peddler and moved "up" to a store only 17 by 28 feet on the outskirts of Pittsburgh; the owners of Goldsmith's in Memphis, Rich's in Atlanta, and Sanger's in Dallas, and scores of others got started in a similar way.[7]

Members of an even smaller group who entered America's financial elite—the Seligmans, Guggenheims, Lehmans, Goldmans, Wertheims—

also arrived with relatively little. They saved their money and spent little on themselves, set up networks of family distribution, and took advantage of being in the right place at the right time. More solidly German than the masses of Jewish immigrants, almost all of these financiers entered the American economy as peddlers.[8]

Only a few American Jews became department-store magnates, finance capitalists, or anything even close. As a group however, Jews achieved a high degree of economic mobility, and by 1880 represented a fairly solid phalanx of comfortable, middle-class merchants. While some remained poor and some held down jobs as workers, clerks, salesmen, seamstresses, and domestic servants as in Europe, Jews in America mostly worked for themselves.[9]

Jewish economic mobility in the nineteenth century has intrigued historians, just as it has been enshrined in American Jewish mythology. The self-congratulatory "rags to riches" saga has been held up as the paradigmatic Jewish experience. The mobility seems to have been real, although less universal and less rapid than usually thought. That is, nineteenth-century Jewish immigrants to the United States did indeed arrive with relatively little capital, few assets, and no connections other than to their kin and townspeople who had migrated before them, and within the span of several decades moved up markedly to the ranks of the bourgeoisie. Their economic rise contrasted sharply with that of many non-Jewish immigrants of the same decades—for example, the Irish and probably the majority of German immigrants—who contributed a larger number to the ranks of the industrial working class than Jews. How did this happen?

To begin with, some standard explanations can be discounted. Education contributed little; nineteenth-century Jewish immigrants brought little learning with them to America. While no real figures are available to compare American school attendance among ethnic groups in the nineteenth century, biographies of those who succeeded silently attested to the unimportance of education as the avenue to success. Even American-born sons of immigrant Jews entered business more often than the professions, and their "real" education took place behind the counter rather than the scholar's desk.

Secondly, the institutional structure of Jewish communities, embryonic in these years, did not formally provide help to the newcomers to get them started or orient them toward life in America. What formal institutions existed, directed their attention to alleviating the distress of the most needy—

destitute widows and orphans, primarily. Thirdly, Jews did not arrive in America with more capital than did their fellow passengers on the ships from Hamburg, Bremen, and the other European ports, although few landed as destitute as the Irish.

Certain ubiquitous patterns describe, and possibly explain, Jewish economic mobility. Jews began at the bottom, usually as peddlers, sometimes as workers, but always aspired to self-employment. They planned carefully, calculating the right time to move, the right time to invest. Despite the loneliness of bachelorhood, they deferred marriage and family until they could afford such pleasures. They relied heavily on family networks of support, particularly for credit, and small stores that launched some to bigger enterprises drew upon the labor of all relatives. More successful members of the Jewish communities or the ethnic enclaves within them loaned money to poorer, aspiring newcomers. An intricate Jewish web flanked at one end by the peddler and by the manufacturer in the city at the other—with various operatives in between—made Jews responsible to and dependent upon each other. They were all Jews, often compatriots from the same region or town, and this heightened the bonding, meshing economic and communal, religious activities.

Jews in America pursued occupations closely resembling those they had known in Europe. Unlike many other immigrants of the period who went from the peasantry to the industrial proletariat, Jews did not have to reorient themselves from a preindustrial to an industrial economy. The continuity in Jewish occupation from Europe to America served to conserve tradition and maintain links to the past.

On the Road: The Culture of Peddling

Peddling represented the bottom step on the Jewish economic structure and an almost universal male Jewish experience in nineteenth-century America. While other American men—native-born and immigrant—took to the roads to sell, too, only among Jews was it *the* premier occupation. The "Yankee peddler" served New England and the Midwest, while some Irish and German men also took up the peddler's pack. But for Jews, peddling represented a mass experience.

Jewish peddlers shifted in and out of towns and cities, often by the waterways but on foot as well, looking for promising locations to hawk their wares. Peddling linked one Jewish enclave to the next and helped new immigrants scout out possibilities in America and learn where the best opportunities for small business lay. Furthermore, for Jews eager to leave New York, for example, and their jobs of garment workers, clerks, or employees of someone else, peddling offered a way to get up, out, and into self-employment. Requiring little capital, merely a loan for goods, peddling allowed young men a chance to strike out on their own. Biographies of scores of Jewish businessmen out west or in the south began with a stint in New York and a recognition that if they journeyed far afield to peddle, they had a chance to have their own store someday. Peddling could be started up with relative ease. Although states varied as to licensing peddlers, the fluidity of America made strenuous enforcement rare, and most immigrant peddlers plied their trade without official sanction. For many, the possibility of just picking up a bundle and going off into the countryside to sell must have confirmed their ideas that America offered expansive opportunities to those willing to try.[10]

Many opted for peddling as a way to scout out the best location for settlement. Others chose it because their brothers or cousins before them had done so. Yet others fell into it since they could do nothing else, or because circumstances kept them from other occupations. The father of *New York Times* publisher Adolph Ochs wanted to go to college after arriving from Bavaria in the 1840s; but his brother-in-law, with whom he lived, refused and sent him off with a pack. Abraham Kohn, who would later become a figure in Chicago Republican politics, tried unsuccessfully to find a job as a clerk when he arrived in New York from Bavaria. So, he lamented, "as all others: with a bundle on my back I had to go out into the country. . . . This, then, is the vaunted luck of the immigrant from Bavaria!" Bemoaning his fate, he warned other Jewish young men back home—"O misguided fools, led astray by avarice and cupidity!"—to stay at home. In his diary, he indeed mused that he and the thousands like himself might have been better off had they stayed put.

Peddling operated as a bridge occupation. It was something Jewish men or their fathers had done in Europe. Biographies abound of young men who had peddled first in Bavaria and later in Virginia or California. Doing it in America required no great shift in values or life-style.[11] Peddling, furthermore, bridged Jewish life between American Jewish communities. Charles Wessolowsky, a peddler in the South from Gollub, Poznań, served as a circuit rabbi, simultaneously selling his wares and burying, marrying, and consecrating synagogues and cemeteries in the pockets of Jewish settlement in Georgia and elsewhere below the Mason-Dixon Line.[12]

Peddling had yet another meaning within Jewish communities. It provided a common experience for Bavarian, Czech, Polish, Lithuanian, Galician, and Prussian Jewish men. This experience, despite its centrifugality, actually served as a unifying force, representing one step on the road towards creating an American Jewish community. Of the members of the two synagogues in Albany, New York, in the 1850s, for example, approximately one-fourth listed themselves as peddlers at Beth El and one-fourth at Anshe Emeth. Jewish peddlers from Germany, Poland, Russia, and Lithuania all served in the 82nd Regiment of the Illinois Volunteers during the Civil War, presumably relating to each other by virtue of their shared religion and work histories.[13]

Peddling functioned for nineteenth-century American Jewish men as domestic service did for Irish women. Although Jewish communities varied in the percentage of men who made a living in peddling, and although the proportion of itinerant versus sedentary merchants varied over time, in *no* study of a nineteenth-century Jewish community were peddlers ever absent. In Nashville, 23 percent of the enumerated Jewish men peddled in the 1860s. Of Boston's Jews in the years 1845–61, 25 percent did likewise. In Easton, Pennsylvania, the percentage of peddlers among the Jews went from 46 percent in 1840 to 70 percent in 1845 and then 55 percent in 1850. Of the 125 Jewish residents in Iowa in the 1850s, 100 peddled around the state. In Syracuse, two-thirds of all Jews hawked goods along New York's inland waterways, typifying the Jewish pattern nationally, while in nearby Utica, 155 Jews had been listed as peddlers between 1849 and 1871.[14]

Actually, more Jews peddled than these sketchy figures suggest. Transient peddlers often slipped past census takers, compilers of city directories, or leaders of local Jewish communities. Even men who settled down, married, and owned stores spent some of the year out peddling. Enumerated as storekeepers or merchants, they augmented their businesses by selling directly to rural people with limited access to town markets. In addition, owners of stores often employed brothers or other male relatives—the newest immigrants from Europe—to peddle as part of the family business.[15]

Peddlers often accounted for the first Jews in any given town or region. Picking a place as their base of operation, they came in and out with regularity, participating in the developing Jewish religious and communal life; and when conditions allowed it, they ended their wanderings and usually opened a store, often the first in that town. Thus the first Jews of Rochester, New York; Berkshire County, Massachusetts; Sioux City, Iowa; Chico, California; Chicago; Monmouth County, New Jersey; Cincinnati;

Lancaster, Pennsylvania; Atlanta; and hundreds of other Jewish communities had been peddlers, and had experienced their first exposure to America through this age-old European Jewish occupation.[16]

The culture of peddling was sustained by its own lexicon. Peddlers used their own special words and phrases, probably of European derivation, to describe peddling. The "Yankee notions" they hawked were *Kuttle Muttle,* and Jewish peddlers in and out of Chicago would refer to the merchant who outfitted them as "Hershel Ganef," Hershel the thief. They also created small, transient communities. Since peddlers usually did not work on the Sabbath, they congregated in the nearest towns on Fridays and formed a temporary weekly enclave. Simon Wolf's uncle owned a store in Ulrichsville, Ohio; the peddlers who honeycombed the surrounding farm areas repaired there to observe and rest on the Sabbath in the company of other peddlers. The experience of being a peddler did not involve a break with the past, nor did its dispersing pattern destroy community or weaken religious obligation. Indeed, peddlers related to one another as a distinct subculture within the larger Jewish world.[17]

A culture of peddling developed as a result of basic work patterns. Brothers, male relatives, and friends from European hamlets peddled together, spent their Sabbaths together in some small town, and exchanged information about routes and selling strategies. They helped one another and in distress turned to one another for assistance. Hard times they had plenty, with real need for succor. Accidents on the road, nasty customers, stone-throwing rowdies, robberies, exposure to inclement weather, an occasional murder, and, more generally, exhausting days on foot with only paltry sales to show for their efforts, all this happened and made the peddler dependent on others like him for support. The first Jewish institution in Woodville, Mississippi, for example, was a cemetery that came into being in 1849 when two Jewish peddlers had to bury a third.[18]

A Jewish system of credit further solidified links between peddling and traditional Jewish life. Peddlers could not usually get start-up money from standard American lenders, and, indeed, no evidence suggests that they tried. Instead, they turned to fellow Jews to get started. Jewish merchants and manufacturers in cities extended loans, often of fabric, needles, thread, pots and pans, glass and tin, to the newcomers, although cash was also extended sometimes. This helped the lender distribute goods. America was, after all, a country with large numbers of people living in isolated areas, and, in the mid-nineteenth century, railroads had not yet created a national economic system for the distribution of merchandise. For minimum capital investment, Jewish merchants could expect an almost predictable profit, and a string of Jewish wholesale houses could be developed on strategic points along inland waterways to facilitate peddling.

Life stories provide some of the sharpest portraits of this intracommunal credit network. Abraham Abrahamsohn came from Pomerania to the United States in 1849. Destitute and forlorn on the streets of New York, he ran into an old friend who "suggested I go to see a compatriot, Mister Isidor, a very rich Jewish merchant." Mister Isidor learned that Abrahamsohn had been a baker and confectioner, gave him a draft of ten dollars for goods, told him that he ought to make candies and sell them on the street, and advised him that America was "a country where there is no disgrace in any honest work." A Bavarian immigrant, William Frank, got one hundred dollars of credit from Blum and Simpson, Jewish wholesalers in Philadelphia. This supported a year's peddling in Lancaster County. Isaac Bernheim was outfitted by a no-interest loan by the agent of a Jewish manufacturer in 1847. A fellow Jew gave the Guggenheim brothers goods for free to peddle, with one week's grace before they had to start repayment. A Polish Russian immigrant, Zalman Phillips, came to the United States in 1872. Having ensconced his family in Minneapolis, he peddled in North Dakota among the farmers, outfitted by a man named Mr. Sikorsky, one of the "many Jewish jobbers who imported merchandise from the East." According to memoirs by Phillips's daughter, "any Jew who was willing to work could come to these jobbers and get bankrolled to a stock of dress goods and a horse and wagon." Furthermore, Jewish peddlers drifting into Boston sought out the comfortable Jews who sat on the boards of the charitable societies and received interest-free loans—*gemilat hesed*—to buy goods to sell.[19]

These arrangements helped the peddlers make a living and start a family, the twin goals of migration. By and large, the stories of peddlers told of single men, whereas shopkeepers had married. When a peddler could think about opening a small store, he could contemplate getting married as well as bringing over other family members—parents, siblings, and other kin.[20] While some peddlers were married men who had left their wives and children either in Europe or in some settled Jewish community in America, most migrated as bachelors hoping to both marry and achieve economic independence.[21]

Peddlers resorted to several methods for finding a wife. More successful peddlers-turned-merchants went back to Bohemia or Poznań and there married women generally much younger than themselves. The couple then journeyed to America. Others relied on family and friends in larger Jewish cities like Baltimore, Cincinnati, New York, or Chicago to introduce them to suitable partners.

Marriages between former peddlers and the sisters of Jewish merchants solidified existing communal business networks. For example, Abraham Flexner's mother and aunt, immigrants from Rhineland, lived in Louisville with relatives. Flexner's uncle ran a wholesale china business; and "at their uncle's home they met many of the young Jewish merchants or peddlers, who used to spend the Jewish holidays and weekends in the large city." His mother married one of them.

Others met young Jewish women on their trips in and out of the Jewish communities. When circumstances were right, they married. The son of Benjamin Roth of Bavaria had peddled out of Milwaukee, where he boarded with a Jewish family. When he had accumulated enough money to open a store in Monroe, Wisconsin, he married the householder's daughter. Samuel Rosenwald peddled out of Baltimore along Virginia's Winchester Trail. Affiliated with the Hammerslough brothers, a Jewish wholesale operation, Rosenwald married one of his creditors' sisters. As a wedding present, the new couple received the best gift: management of a clothing store in Peoria, Illinois. William Frank, a former peddler from Lancaster County, Pennsylvania, was on his way by train back from Philadelphia to Kilgore, Ohio, where he operated his first store. On the train, as he remembered it,

> sat a young man who, no doubt, observing that I was a follower of Abraham, moved next to me, and during the conversation . . . said he could scarcely await the train's arriving in Lancaster, as he had been married six weeks before and had been away several weeks.
>
> I told him that if I could meet a desirable girl, I would like to marry also.

Frank was in luck. His traveling companion introduced him to his wife's cousin, who boarded with them in Lancaster, and "he knew she would make a good wife." The match worked, and "fourteen days later Uncle Rauh married us . . . at Lancaster, Pa.—Paulina Wormser to William Frank."[22]

Though marriage and the shift from peddling to storekeeping went together, it should not be assumed that peddlers lived at loose ends, bereft of a Jewish community to live in or to provide their basic needs. Cities and towns of every size served as hubs of peddling activity, and peddlers were integrated into Jewish communal life there. Even in the giant of American Jewish communities, New York City, peddlers spent the Sabbath and holidays in worship with fellow Jews, while they also filled their backpacks or wagons, negotiated credit, socialized, and eventually found a spot for a store. Urban Jewish communities housed numerous institutions that catered to peddlers. Jewish wholesale houses relied on peddlers to distribute goods, while boarding houses, often run by women, served the needs of itinerant merchants.[23]

Peddling had its own hierarchy. On the lowest rungs of peddling, occupied by either new immigrants or less successful "old timers," stood the peddler who journeyed by foot, his bundle on his back. Some peddlers, according to Isaac Mayer Wise, carried up to 150 pounds; but the worse off the lot, the less one had to hawk, while the better the credit, the greater one's access to goods. Higher up sat the proud owners of a wagon and a horse or two, who could sell heavier goods, stoves and furniture, rather than just ribbons and thread. Some peddlers specialized and went from home to home and farm to farm with only tin or only crockery. One synagogue in New York was dubbed the "India Rubber shul" because most of its members peddled rubber suspenders.[24] In addition, some peddlers carved out rural areas for their turf, while others worked the cities. Urban peddlers functioned in almost every American city, in close-in residential areas and on the suburban fringe. Before urban mass transit served most city dwellers and when respectable middle class women eschewed the marketplace, peddlers went door to door. The father of Sarah Kussy, an early Jewish resident of Newark, New Jersey, came from Bavaria and began his life in America "by walking the streets of Newark and suburbs with the peddler's pack on his back, filled with dry goods and notions." The Lansburg brothers, Gustav, Max and James, did similarly in Baltimore, Elias Labensky in New London, Connecticut, Fredericka Mandelbaum in New York. Lithuanians, who in the 1870s lived in Boston's North End and founded congregation Beth Abraham, sold to the homes of the Hub City, while Russian Jews, who in that same decade founded Rodfei Zedek, served Chicago's households. Peddling often served as an economic fallback or cushion. Sol Bloom's father went out to peddle on the streets of San Francisco when his stores crumbled, and his young son often helped him; he vividly recalled "trudging up Sacramento Street, or equally steep California Street, half buried under the load." Urban peddling took up the energies of many of Chicago's immigrants in the 1860s from Suwalk and Mariampol. German Jews, likewise, went door to door in many other American cities.[25]

In short, peddling as a Jewish occupation served specific and practical functions for the new immigrants. It helped them accumulate capital and learn about America and Americans. It offered unmarried men a chance to earn money so that they could marry. On the other hand, it grew out of traditional Jewish economic activities and sustained Jewish communal life.

In the lore of American Jewish history, peddling has been seen as *the* route whereby immigrants moved into small or larger businesses. The archetypal peddler has been held up as someone like a Seligman brother, a Lazarus Straus, a Meyer Lehman, or a Meyer Guggenheim: someone who jumped from peddling into the highest rungs of capitalist success. While these immigrants did indeed begin as peddlers and end up as millionaires, most did not; they contented themselves with small stores, selling clothing and dry goods.

In the Workshop: Jewish Artisans and Laborers

Generalizing about nineteenth-century American Jews from the example of the wealthy distorts the actual economic experience of typical business people and also ignores the existence of a Jewish working class. Jews in America in the years 1820–80 sent a smaller percentage of their sons and daughters into factories and workshops than other immigrant groups. But Jewish workers were not unknown and some spent part or all of their lives as employees of someone else, working with their hands, producing clothing, glass, tinware, cigars, and a panoply of other goods. Historians have failed to examine this segment of the Jewish community, important not only in its own right but also in relation to the rest of the Jewish population. Did early eastern European Jews show up here more often than central Europeans? Did the more observant opt for peddling so they could maintain Sabbath restrictions, and did those who flocked to factories not mind working a six-day week? Did men who migrated with wives and children choose laboring for others over peddling to keep the family intact? Or, as historian Stanley Nadel has pointed out in a rare treatment of nineteenth-century Jewish workers, did failed Jewish peddlers swell the ranks of factory workers?

While these questions have been heretofore unanswered, and largely unasked, community histories, biographies, and memoirs list various kinds of mid-nineteenth-century American Jewish manual laborers and artisans. Adolf Kraus from Bohemia did a stint in a paper-box factory; David Amram's father made a living as a ship chandler; and Herman Ickelheimer, a Bavarian-born San Franciscan painted houses all his life. Jacob Lanzit, an immigrant from Posen in the 1850s, worked as a porter, bartender, and peddler. None of these jobs sustained him, so, he said, "I decided to learn a profession, that is to learn either to make cigars or to sew on Singer's machine. I decided for the latter and began to learn in earnest." Ten days later, Lanzit "got into a factory" and joined the laboring class.

In 1852, a letter to the *Asmonean,* a Jewish newspaper in New York, requested that it "enumerate a few trades (exclusive of tailors, glaziers and cigarmakers) in which . . . Jews are engaged . . . bakers, paperhangers, book-binders, pocket-book makers, gold and silver smiths, jewelers, diamond cutters, tin plate workers, gold lace weavers, mechanical dentists, engravers . . . printers and compositors. Shoe and bootmakers, hatters." In the 1870s, efforts were made to assist impoverished Jewish laborers in New York. Organizations, such as the Hebrew Emigrants Workingmen's Institute and the Handworkers' Association, short-lived though they were, called attention to the growing number of Jewish laborers living poorly. The founder of the Institute, J. K. Buchner, a newcomer from either Galicia or Poznań, called upon the leadership of American Jewry to do something for the poor workers who were forced to work on the Sabbath. In the 1870s, Jewish shoemakers in New York formed themselves into the Purim Lodge of the Knights of St. Crispin, a workers' association.[26]

No one in the middle decades of the nineteenth century would have been surprised at the mention of Jewish tailors, glaziers, or cigar makers. While Jews shared workbenches with many non-Jews in these fields, the Jewish glazier, the Jewish cigar maker, and, most importantly, the Jewish tailor were recognizable figures in almost any community.

Glass work, which involved many Jews, actually bridged the peddler's life with that of a worker. The glazier carried a basket and traversed city streets announcing his availability to fix or replace broken windows. The glazier worked for the owner, usually a Jew, of a glass store. According to Judah David Eisenstein, a chronicler of the life of Russian Jews in New York before 1880, "glazing, it appears, was the first occupation of the Russian Jews, who learned the trade while stopping in England on their way to America." As early as the 1850s, Russian Jewish immigrant workers in New

York labored in the trade. The owner of one of Brooklyn's largest glass stores, Jacob Werbelovsky, who migrated from Russia in 1866, began his life in America as an itinerant glazier.[27]

Jewish laborers in cigar making also worked primarily for other Jews. Jewish names, most notably Adolph Strasser's, appeared among the founders of the International Cigar Makers Union of America in the 1860s. Samuel Gompers, who came to the United States in 1863 from London, found his first American job in a factory owned by a Jew from Warsaw. Gompers married a Jewish cigar stripper who also came from England. The future president of the American Federation of Labor then joined a "Hebrew" mutual benefit society, the Hand-in-Hand, founded by other cigar workers. A survey of the occupations of Jews of Utica, New York, in the 1850s and 1860s identified fourteen Jewish cigar makers, outnumbered only by peddlers. In cigar making, particularly before the 1880s, a thin line separated owners from the workers. Many cigar manufacturers began their careers stripping, rolling, and performing other parts of the operation, and, in general, a large number of Jewish factory owners started their ascent from the shop floor.[28]

The fluidity between employee and employer, and between manufacturing and distribution also characterized tailoring and allied needle trades, the giant of nineteenth-century Jewish manual labor. Many Jewish employers began as someone else's employees. Clothing store owners often employed Jewish immigrants to make the garments for sale. Most Jews employed in this field worked for other Jews, although Jewish bosses also hired non-Jews. In New York and other cities, Jews who came from Bavaria and Baden, and later from Poznań, Silesia, Poland, Russia, and Lithuania manufactured clothing. From the 1820s on, Jews worked in all branches of the needle trades as cap makers, hoopskirt makers, furriers, tailors for men and women, and cloak makers. Their concentration in these occupations grew over time. By 1855, 22 percent of New York City's employed Polish immigrants, almost all Jews, wielded a needle; in the 1870s, many Jews labored as cap makers, playing a leading role in an 1872 strike and other sporadic workers' activities.

We do not know who these Jews were, nor can we state with certainty how they differed from their fellows who took to the road to peddle. How many early Jewish garment workers later became owners of garment shops? How many of those who moved from employee to employer hailed from Germany and how many from east of the Elbe? Whatever the answer, it is clear that traditional images of the pre-1880 "German" Jews as entrepreneurs and the post-1880 eastern European Jews as laborers are far too simplistic.[29]

Behind the Counter: Jewish Shopkeepers

Community histories and biographies indicate that many nineteenth-century American Jews who began as laborers in garment, glass, or cigar making ended their careers as self-employed. Often they moved from laborers to capitalists in the same field, but sometimes they shifted into ownership of a small dry-goods store from an unrelated area.

Self-employment was *the* goal, the model, and the defining characteristic of American Jewish economic behavior. By virtue of thick clustering in business, be it a tiny glass shop owned by a Russian newcomer on New York's Lower East Side, a tailoring establishment in Chicago owned and staffed by Poles, or a mighty department store in the hands of a long-time American who began as a peddler from Bavaria, the handling of merchandise consumed the vast majority of American Jews over this sixty-year period. Although statistics are spotty, it seems clear, nonetheless, that throughout this period, Jews concentrated in commerce similarly as in Europe.

Jews brought with them their basic way of working and living. In Europe, they had been admonished to change work habits and wean themselves from trade, but few opportunities existed to do so. In America, opportunities galore opened up to them. They chose, however, to follow familiar lines of work. Just as they eschewed agriculture in Europe, so did they in America, where new western lands opened up for cultivation. Despite prodding from numerous community leaders, they continued to be middlemen, brokers, buyers, and sellers.[30]

In some cases, Jewish men actually brought over to America their European occupation. Isaac Gellis had owned a sausage factory in Berlin and, during the American Civil War, he supplied meat to the Union army. By 1872, Gellis operated a sausage factory and meat-processing plant on New York's Essex Street. The Moses family had been cattle dealers in Germany, and they also dealt in cattle in Easton, Pennsylvania.[31]

Jewish concentration in business, either wholesale or retail, shaped Jewish communal life. Education other than for basic Jewish literacy ranked fairly low in family and communal priorities. The best education that young men obtained occurred alongside their fathers or older brothers in the store.[32] Focus on business also shaped Jewish settlement patterns. Jews moved to follow business opportunities, and they moved to places where they could live among other Jews. Thus, nineteenth-century American Jewish life involved not just migration from Europe, but also secondary and tertiary migrations within the United States, as merchants or potential merchants constantly sought out better sites for commercial ventures.

While the majority of American Jews made their homes in the cities, where, after all, most business was transacted, pockets of Jewish settlement in Alaska, in the Mother Lode, on the southwestern frontier of Arizona and New Mexico, in the Rocky Mountains, on the Great Plains, and on the bayous of Mississippi and Louisiana had all been shaped by Jewish mercantile aspirations and connections. When Jewish young men discovered that a particular town or region lacked a general store, a dry-goods store, or perhaps something more specialized—at later stages of community development—they moved in. In some small towns, Jewish businessmen and their families predominated among the local merchant class.[33]

But whether in a small town or a large city, certain similarities created a homogeneous nineteenth-century Jewish business culture. First, Jews opted overwhelmingly for partnerships with relatives, friends, and coreligionists with similar European origins. Shared business responsibilities solidified close bonds among Jews and made work a Jewish experience. While arguments, breakups, and grudges run like a leitmotiv through Jewish business histories, more often than not, partnerships fostered communal solidarity. Frequently, partnerships created marriages, not only joining women and men in matrimony but strengthening the business venture. Groups of partners joined congregations and benevolent societies, forging connections within the Jewish world.[34]

Just as Jewish merchants provided credit for Jewish peddlers, Jewish shopkeepers obtained capital from one another rather than from mainstream lending institutions. Jews, particularly small merchants, had trouble securing conventional loans, and novice businessmen faltered because of a low level of capital investment for start-up. Dun and Bradstreet, nineteenth-century America's credit reference agency, overlooked small businesses, and its agents made frequent reference in their reports to the untrustworthiness of Jews and to the natural tendency of Jews to default on loans. By and large, they recommended against Jewish merchants as bad risks. Agents tended to lump all Jews together, commenting on them as a group. Thus, for example, an 1849 report on a merchant in Cincinnati noted: "It is very difficult to ascertain what these descendants of 'Abraham' are worth. . . . He is a Jew and with but one exception none of that 'Genus Homo' own any real estate here." Dun and Bradstreet maintained two credit ratings, "Jewish" and "American."[35]

Family, instead, underlay a Jewish communal credit system. Sisters, brothers, cousins, and sometimes even family members still in Europe loaned money. Benevolent societies provided loans to members, while philanthropic bodies extended interest-free credit to the poor to help them launch a store.[36] Successful Jewish businessmen looked out for the interests—both economic and otherwise—of young, rising Jewish men.[37]

Jews generally opted for similar kinds of businesses. Except for cigar making, liquor distilling, and garment manufacturing, they did not choose manufacturing. The Jewish business world centered on general stores in small towns and backwater regions, dry-goods stores in cities, and, eventually, department stores, which naturally grew out of the former.[38]

These kinds of enterprises—stores that sold the basic needs of life—put Jews, whatever the size of town, in highly visible positions. Their stores, which usually clustered in the main business districts, conspicuously displayed on awnings and signs Jewish and foreign names, such as "Levy," "Cohen," "Auerbach," "Friedman," or "Zeckendorf," drawing public attention to the merchants' ethnicity and religion. The closing of businesses for the Sabbath and religious holidays became a constant subject for local newspaper commentary, reminding customers that these merchants differed from the surrounding Christian population.

Jews especially stood out when they engaged in nontraditional merchandising practices. In many towns, Jewish storekeepers pioneered in fixed price, splashy advertising, and "pulling in" customers, standing in front of the store and boldly drawing the attention of the passersby. The parents of Illinois governor Henry Horner claimed to have been the first dry-goods merchants in Chicago to print a price list for customers. In clothing, Jewish merchants pioneered in offering garments "off the rack." The *Cleveland Plain Dealer,* in an 1856 article, lionized a successful Jewish merchant, Isaac A. Isaacs, and noted that "he had many prejudices to contend against, people were adverse to purchasing ready made clothing."[39]

Jewish merchants often diversified, conducting several operations at once. In many southern stores, Jewish merchants sold seeds, nails, paper, and thread, and extended credit to capital-poor farmers, creating a proto-banking system. Many, such as the father of Herbert Lehman in his grocery store in Montgomery, Alabama, brokered cotton on the side. Two Jewish brothers in Statesville, North Carolina, ran a general store that doubled as a bank after the Civil War. They also taught local farmers to identify and bring in medicinal herbs, such as goldenseal root and ginseng, in exchange for goods. They then sold the herbs, tapping into yet another revenue source. The father of San Francisco's Abe "Boss" Ruef and the father of Cyrus Adler both supplemented dry-goods store operation with lucrative real-estate investments.[40]

The Jewish merchant, in small and large towns, came to be identified with civic order and communal stability. Business prospered when order prevailed, and Jewish merchants aligned themselves with the local status quo. While their business techniques may have been unconventional, thus drawing attention to the Jewish shopkeeper as an outsider, their high rates of participation in juries, school boards, city councils, and other agencies of local government countered the image of Jews as strangers. If Gentiles had negative views of Jewish merchants as Shylocks, the Jewish storekeeper who sat on the Mobile school board, the San Bernardino town council, or the Brooklyn Board of Supervisors may have helped dilute hostility.[41]

The Jewish business network extended beyond the urban dry-goods store or the small-town general store. Jews played a role in cigar making and liquor distilling.[42] The number of Jews involved in these industries, however, fell well below that of Jews who manufactured and distributed clothing. The American clothing industry of the mid-nineteenth century functioned on a limited scale, and most American women still sewed for themselves. Yet what garment industry existed in the decades preceding the Civil War, it lay heavily in Jewish hands. In the earlier part of the century, clothing production grew from retail sales. Jews helped create the garment industry through their stores. Jewish merchants with wives, other relatives, and hired hands, if business permitted, sewed in back of the store and sold in front. As a growing American population segment demanded more store-bought garments, many owners of general stores shifted to making and selling clothing.

Regardless of community size or geographic location, Jewish business was inextricably linked to clothing production. In Columbus, Ohio, in 1872, "with only one exception, every Jewish family entered the clothing business, and each located on the main shopping avenue of South. . . . *every* retail clothing establishment listed in the Columbus 'yellow pages' belonged to a German Jew." Of Indianapolis's clothing establishments in the 1860s, 70 percent were under Jewish control. In Milwaukee, Jews owned five of the fourteen largest firms of clothiers and tailors at the end of the Civil War. In the same decade, local press in Johnstown, Pennsylvania, claimed that not a single clothing dealer professed the Christian faith. Although Jews shunned most large industries in Cincinnati, as workers or owners, by 1860, half of the Queen City's Jewish population depended on the production and sales of men's clothing; of the city's seventy clothing firms, Jews owned sixty-five. Poughkeepsie, New York, supported only eight tailoring and clothing establishments in the 1850s and 1860s, but six had a Jew at the helm.[43]

The garment industry, like peddling, made no distinction among Jews. German Jews and eastern Europeans, Jews from Hungary and Bohemians all found a niche in garment making. Jews who marched over to Reform as well as those committed to Orthodoxy engaged in sewing and selling clothing. An overwhelming majority of Jews who belonged to the Baltimore Hebrew Congregation, a decidedly Reform synagogue, and of those who joined the more traditional Chizuk Amuno manufactured men's clothing. Ten of the twenty-four California Jews who in the 1870s contributed money to the Reform movement's Hebrew Union College were involved in clothing. The rabbi of New York's first Russian shul, a clearly traditional institution, Rabbi Ash, left the rabbinate in the 1860s to become a hoopskirt maker. Big-city and small-town Jews equally made a living in this industry.[44]

Jews clustered in all aspects of clothing production. Particularly in New York City, a thriving trade existed in fixing and selling old clothes. Jews, often associated with "slopshops," worked on Chatham Street in Lower Manhattan, carving a particular niche for themselves. Jewish jobbers bought the used clothing, Jewish male and female workers sewed, and Jewish peddlers resold the used garments in New York and through the length and breadth of the South. Many Jewish merchants set up Southern and Western establishments to distribute this particular stock. As early as 1833, a British traveler wrote of the Jewish presence in Chatham Street's second-hand clothing shops, derisively noting: "The inhabitants of this street are mostly of the tribe of Judah: as any body may be satisfied by going into their shops as well on account of their dealings, as their long beards, which reach to the bottoms of their waist."[45]

The Civil War greatly stimulated the garment industry's growth. The tremendous demand for uniforms transformed small stores with only a small sideline business in garment making into workshops and factories to mass produce for the troops. With the war's end, these enterprises shifted to manufacturing civilian clothing, and many of the Jewish owners of used-clothing shops and small retail establishments dipped into available capital to buy sewing machines—invented in 1846—and plunge into the new clothing industry. They made both low- and higher-grade women's and men's clothing, caps, and hats.

In places as far apart as New York and San Francisco, Jews spawned the garment industry. As was the case with old clothing, a Jewish network linked workers to distributors, with family members operating smaller shops. By the 1870s Jews shaped the outlines of what would become the notorious sweatshop system at century's end.[46]

Jewish Women and the World of Work

In the clothing field, as in retail, all family members helped make a living. Like nineteenth-century American children in general, young Jewish people spent relatively little time in school; sons commonly worked with parents in preparation for adulthood.[47]

So did daughters. Indeed, women, especially new immigrants who continued to flood into the United States throughout these sixty years, participated actively in the labor force in peculiarly female and Jewish ways, primarily in family businesses.

Constant references in memoirs and autobiographies to Jewish female work in the nineteenth century contrast sharply with the conventional image of Jewish women of that time as predominantly middle-class—as wives of prosperous businessmen, living a relatively leisured life devoid of involvement in the family's livelihood, whose chief "work" was supervising servants.[48] Certainly, such women existed and their number increased as the century waned. Wealthy Jewish merchants lived in ways commensurate with their status. According to one estimate, one-fourth of all Jews in the antebellum South had enough capital to own slaves. Jews in these years certainly enjoyed a remarkably high level of economic mobility, and the women who in the first decades of their lives in America may have sewed men's pants in the backs of small stores could very well enjoy the luxury of substantial homes and servants in later years. When Esther Levy published the first American Jewish cookbook and guide to household management in 1871, she addressed affluent women.[49]

Non-Jews typically portrayed Jewish women as pampered wives or daughters of capitalists immune from the privations suffered by other women. Echoing centuries' old stereotypes of the rich Jew, a number of American commentators contrasted the privileged affluence of Jewish women with the economic distress of their American—Gentile—counterparts. In 1860, the *Shoe and Leather Reporter,* a workers' publication, declared:[50]

> The Jewess . . . is never known to be engaged in shoebinding or other industrial employment. . . . More than all this, she is never too poor to marry, whilst the beautiful New England factory girl must shrink from a "proposal," if she pauses to consider the life of slavery to which by marriage, [she] subjects herself!

However, Jewish women did work. They brought with them a tradition of female employment within a family economy. While official records may have only portrayed the male "Jewish shopkeeper," gender made little difference behind the counter. Wives of Jewish craftsmen, more likely than not, participated intensively in producing and selling goods. Josephine Goldmark, retelling family stories from nineteenth-century Prague, noted that it was "the custom among middle-class Jewish women a hundred years ago of taking part in their husbands' businesses," and that her grandmother Whele "not only engaged in business, non-domestic, outside the house, but in a concern separate from her husband's, in partnership with one of her brothers-in-law." Similarly, in Poland, Judah Magnes's grandmother managed a store and a farm.[51]

Exact numbers of working nineteenth-century American Jewish women are obscured by their involvement in family stores and shops. Numerous contemporary commentators described women in these roles. The smaller the store, the more likely the wife and daughters worked. Such work often meant the difference between viability and ruin. Opening a store and getting married occurred simultaneously, each making the other possible. Hannah Dernburg Horner's labor in the family grocery store on Chicago's West Side did not only supplement her husband's. "From the beginning," noted her son's biographer, "the guiding force in the business, the pusher," was Hannah. Likewise, the wife of butcher Bernard Nordlinger in Washington, D.C., "could cut up a forequarter of beef just as well as any man." When Julius Mack's grandfather went to San Francisco in 1851 to check out West Coast commercial possibilities, his grandmother operated the Louisville rug and carpet business for two years, providing the family with income while the new venture was getting started.[52]

When husbands died, wives often carried on family businesses on their own. Just one example among many: the widow of Joseph Strauss in Lancaster, Pennsylvania, ran the store from 1866, when her husband died, until 1884, when her sons could support her. This widespread phenomenon was particularly significant, because women married men significantly older than themselves, thus making the probability of widowhood higher.[53]

Married women or widows appeared in many community and family histories as operators of boarding houses. Recognizing the need for feeding and lodging the stream of single men migrating to America, Jewish women turned their homes into businesses. Boarding operations supplemented income from other family business activity, or provided the family's sole support. For the Mayerberg family of Volkovisk, Lithuania, who settled in Buffalo in the late 1860s, the wife's decision to take in boarders meant that they could pay rent. Henry Morgenthau's mother decided to do the same in Brooklyn when her husband's business failed. The first Jewish woman in Portland, Oregon, a Mrs. Weinshank, ran a boarding house for single men, as did Mrs. H. L. Moise in Oakland, California, and Ernestine Greenbaum in Los Angeles.[54]

Jewish women, married and single, sometimes ventured out of the family web to create their own businesses. They started the same kinds of small businesses as Jewish men. Amelia Dannenberg came to San Francisco with her husband in the 1850s from Rhineland and launched her own children's clothing business. By the 1870s, she branched out, manufacturing men's and women's clothing as well. The mother of Judah David Eisenstein, an American Hebraist and maskil, opened a dry-goods store on New York's Lower East Side in 1872 so her son could study full-time. As late as 1879, the Lissner family, German immigrants in Oakland, could not exist on Louis's meager earnings from pawnbroking, so Matilda raised chickens and peddled eggs in the neighborhood. Bella Block had learned millinery work in Bavaria before emigration and owned her own millinery store in Newark, New Jersey, before marriage. Husband and wife combined capital reserves and jointly ran a grocery store. Sarah Goldwater's husband Michael endured so many disastrous business ventures that she decided to put her economic destiny in her own hands and filed a statement in the Tuolumne County, California, courthouse, saying: "from and after this date I intend to carry on and transact in my own name and on my own account, the business of tailoring and merchandising in said city and . . . I will be personally responsible for all debts contracted by me in said business."[55]

Goldwater's public brazenness was unusual, but not her business choice. Daughters, wives, and single immigrant women, many of whom had prepared for emigration by learning dressmaking and tailoring, sewed to earn their bread.[56] Tailors' wives, daughters, and sisters all participated in sewing, making it possible for the "craftsman" to function. In the 1850s, Abraham Flexner's mother lived for a while with an aunt and uncle in Louisville. The uncle sold china, retail and wholesale, while the aunt earned money as a seamstress. Flexner's mother and her sister joined the aunt in sewing, while one Amelia Lezinsky sewed dresses in her husband's fur shop.[57]

Some young Jewish women chose to work as teachers. In New York City as well as in Illinois and California, some had stayed in school long enough to fulfill the requirements for the job. But in these years, Jewish female school teachers were still quite uncommon. Julia Richman, daughter of immigrants from Bohemia, had to defy her father to enter the profession. (In 1884, Richman became the first Jewish woman to be named a principal in the New York City public school system.) It was not common for an unmarried woman to seek her future far from the family economy.[58]

Jewish girls placed in orphanages and schools for the poor learned sewing to become employable, although some institutions also added lessons in umbrella and parasol making and the domestic arts so that the girls could go into service. The first superintendent's report of the Cleveland Jewish Orphan Asylum declared in 1869: "It is our constant aim to raise the girls . . . so that in all the walks of life they are fitted to provide for themselves."[59] This and similar institutions seem to have succeeded in training young women; upon graduation, the Jewish girls usually got sewing and domestic service jobs in Jewish homes. Indeed, Jewish families from around the country wrote to the Cleveland orphanage when looking for servants.[60]

An American Jewish Economy

Jewish immigrants and their families, peddlers, artisans, and small shopkeepers—a growing number of more prosperous proprietors—did relatively well in America. For them, emigration paid off, giving poor European Jews the chance to better themselves. In most communities, they owned more property than others. Few ranked as unskilled laborers. Many paid taxes.

Their success emerged from both new American forces and old Jewish traditions, and it demonstrated the confluence of innovation and traditionalism. The expansiveness of the mid-nineteenth-century American economy, particularly in *their* commercial sector, propelled many upward, allowing them to take advantage of new opportunities. The primitive distribution system and the drift of Americans away from homemade to "store-bought" goods dovetailed nicely with the imported Jewish orientation toward self-employment and business. For "making it" in America, Jews did not have to learn new skills. They did not have to wean themselves from old ways of organizing work and family. Instead, the very economic behavior that had made them pariahs in Alsace, Bavaria, Posen, and Bohemia made them solid, respectable citizens in an America that admired the self-made businessman. America offered Jews not so much a place to pursue new occupations or venture out into previously forbidden enterprises—but circumstances were just right for them to do better in America at the things they had always done. Jews as individuals, family members, heirs to millenia-old tradition, and active participants in the scores of local Jewish communities saw *their* opportunities and took them.

CHAPTER FOUR

THE LINKS OF COMMUNITY

Whereas, The hand of providence is held over our nation as Israelites, we are
prompted by a sense of duty, and to promote our interests and material assistance
for the welfare, happiness and protection to each other . . .

Therefore, we the undersigned, do associate ourselves to provide in time of
health, for each other in time of need, to which the human frame is liable,
and to pay the last duty and homage in that which all living men must fall,
and being creatures while life shall be granted to us, we have formed
ourselves into a body corporate . . .

The organization and development of the Jewish communities all over America . . .
everywhere followed the same pattern.

The young Jewish men felt that organization was necessary for various purposes.
The immediate cause was that we had no suitable way of spending our evenings.
Gambling, resorts and theaters, the only refuge then existing in 'Frisco to spend an
evening, had no attraction for us. We passed the time in the back of our stores and
often times were disgusted and sick from the loneliness of our surroundings.

AMERICAN Jewish immigrants of the mid-nineteenth century avidly
formed Jewish communities. Regardless of where in the United States they
lived, Jewish women and men identified with one another, lived, worked,
and socialized with one another, collectively fulfilled religious obligations,
and created institutions that embodied their sense of belonging while serving practical communal needs. Jewish communities throughout the country
were strikingly similar, in part because Jews moved continuously from place
to place. Therefore, Jews in America lived not just in local Jewish communities but in an *American* Jewish community, not bounded by political lines
of city and state.

Nineteenth-century rabbis and subsequent historians were not pleased with American Jewish communal life. The rabbis complained that lodges, clubs, societies, and other "community" institutions undermined their authority, drained membership from congregations, and encouraged American Jewish indifference to religion. Boston's Rabbi Solomon Schindler, a notable actor in nineteenth-century Reform, lamented not only the lack of Sabbath observance and sparse crowds at his Temple Israel on any Saturday morning but bemoaned that American Jews, ardent joiners of lodges and clubs, "consider their [lodges'] meetings and their prayers to be a perfect divine service." Historians have basically agreed with Schindler.[1]

The history of the B'nai B'rith, founded in 1843, supports this proposition. The organization spread rapidly across America, often taking hold in small towns that had *no* congregation. Its lodges demanded less of the Jews than did congregations. Based on fellowship rather than obligation, they did not monitor behavior or admonish members to close their businesses on the Sabbath and maintain Jewish dietary restrictions. One historian has dubbed the B'nai B'rith "a secular synagogue." It and other lodges seemed to rabbis of the nineteenth and historians of the twentieth century gloomy indices of American Jews' drift away from normative Judaism to the embrace of the bland and pleasant atmosphere of the clubroom, where Jews did not differ from their American neighbors. The rise of these communal institutions, separate from congregations, has been interpreted as evidence of secularization, of "the gradual shift of the center of gravity of Jewish community life from the synagogue and school to the charitable organization."[2]

Historians have located the source of these extrareligious institutions in America's separation of church and state, which spawned voluntarism and pluralism. Since in America, rabbis and other religious functionaries had no state authority and the Jewish community could not levy taxes or enforce its will, Jews freely created, affiliated with, and supported institutions of their choice. They chose those which made the fewest demands upon them. Moreover, historians have argued that in these years, American Jews wanted more than anything else to be like all other Americans and mimicked the national pattern of forming voluntary associations (which French observer Alexis de Tocqueville praised). They chose an American, and rejected a Jewish, model of community organization.

Belonging to a B'nai B'rith lodge or participating in a Hebrew Benevolent Society—in Albany, Georgia, or Albany, New York—often substituted for Sabbath and holiday observance, maintenance of kashrut, and attending to one's prayers. The fact that individual men and women chose to migrate to Nebraska or Oregon or Michigan, far from the safety net of religious services, proved that they had no real concern for Jewish life. Had they been truly committed to living as Jews and observant of tradition, they would never have picked such places, bereft as they were of the synagogue, circumciser, *shokhet* (kosher slaughterer), and *mikvah* (ritual bath).

Some of these assertions are indisputable. The American political structure *did* make the nature of religious behavior a matter of personal choice rather than communal control. That freedom allowed individuals to decide how, if at all, they expressed their Judaism. Nineteenth-century Americans *were* inveterate joiners of clubs and associations, and Jews probably learned from them. Jewish immigrants from nineteenth-century central and eastern Europe were not the most pious or most Judaically learned of their peers. Certainly, the mere act of migration announced their willingness to break with the past. American Jews, like Jews in most places and most times, were also influenced by ideas swirling around them and did not remain impervious to new ways of thinking.

"American" and "Jewish," "modern" and "traditional," "religious" and "secular" did not represent antithetical forces. Men and women who founded new communities and formed new institutions chose to be something of all of these at once. The structure of their communities may have departed from the European model, but they did not reject tradition. These associations may have resembled their American counterparts but were not slavish imitations. American Jews did opt for membership in nonsynagogal Jewish organizations, but did not necessarily cast aside Judaism. In creating a network of organizations, clubs, charities, and lodges, American Jews bridged the Jewish and the American ways of life by establishing mediating structures that organically and creatively, if haphazardly, linked the new with the familiar and the sacred with the profane.

Communities came "from the bottom up." Ordinary Jews—with minimal education, preoccupied with making a living—settled down and fashioned local institutions. These pragmatic people expressed little concern about long-term philosophical problems involved in tampering with tradition or in affiliating with institutions without rabbinic sanction. After all, they came to America because life back home had not worked out for them. Here they rebuilt their lives and created communities that made sense and met their needs as Jews.

American Jewish communal life represented a blending of innovation and commitment. Thousands ventured out to towns and regions with no established Jewish communities. On the eve of this migration, just a handful of them existed. But once Jews settled, they quickly formed Jewish enclaves, clustered in neighborhoods, established families, and created the outlines of Jewish communal life. While many of the institutions existed autonomously—outside and independent of rabbinic authority or religious auspices—and had little or no precedent in Jewish tradition, the men and women who founded and joined them sought to fulfill a variety of Jewish obligations, particularly those of a "corporate" rather than "personal" nature. In communities where kosher meat could not be procured and where religious services were reduced to Rosh Hashanah and Yom Kippur, they felt obliged to bury their dead according to traditional precepts, to sit with their sick, and to provide for their poor. These, they sensed, were nonnegotiable responsibilities of Jews. The ways they fulfilled these commitments blended traditional dictates of Judaism with American needs and opportunities.

To Build a Home

The single men and the handful of women who founded most new Jewish communities felt a keen sense of loneliness in their new "homes." Abraham Kohn of Bavaria lamented that he and "thousands of peddlers wander about America; young, strong men, they waste their strength." Was the money he would make, he asked himself and others like him, "in the wild places of America, in isolated farmhouses and tiny hamlets . . . an equal exchange for the parents and kinsmen you have given up?" Others echoed his sentiments and as quickly as possible sought out other Jews, kin, townspeople from Europe, and friends to compensate for the loss.[3]

To alleviate the sense of isolation, Jews voluntarily chose to live with other Jews. From New York, with its substantial Jewish neighborhoods finely differentiated by ethnicity and class, to small Jewish enclaves in Iowa or Kansas where only a few families made up the community, Jews made their homes with other Jews.

One of the first institutions of community, long before the congregation and even before the cemetery, was the boarding house. Sometimes run by the lone Jewish woman in town or by a Jewish family and often providing kosher food, the boarding houses served as hubs of Jewish activity where single men relaxed and lived among others like themselves.[4] For newcomers with family already in America, kin and community merged, and the first glimpses of American Jewish life as well as the first steps towards making a living were provided by aunts, brothers, cousins, and sisters who had already staked out a spot in America.

Jews clustered in limited occupations and set up stores in concentrated areas. They tended to make their homes in the same business sections where they traded, and the Jewish dry-goods merchant or clothing retailer—more likely than not—lived above, or in back of, the store. Work, family, and neighborhood merged. Adult immigrants from central and eastern Europe tended to be the same age and were involved in the same kinds of marginal businesses, and their American-born children grew up in close proximity to one another.

Family narratives pointed to a high degree of family clustering on particular streets, around courtyards, or in adjoining houses. Hannah G. Solomon remembered vividly her Chicago childhood and her grandparents "when, in later years, they lived on Hubbard Street! Their children had all married and Greenbaums occupied nearly the entire block of green shuttered frame houses." Another memoirist, Mrs. Henry Gerstley, recalled how Plymouth Court, also in Chicago, in the 1860s, abounded with family members. An article on early Los Angeles Jewry, derived from the 1850 census, noted that the eight Jewish men who made up the nucleus of the community lived "with but one interposition" in a row of eight houses, one next to the other. At the end of that decade in Ann Arbor, Michigan, the extended Weil family from Bohemia constituted the entire Jewish community and occupied a string of adjacent homes. In St. Paul, Minnesota, in the 1860s, Yiddish-speaking immigrants from Poland all lived on a single street. According to the 1860 census, Nashville's Jews actually shared a number of buildings in the downtown business district.[5]

Studies of Jewish communities of every size point out that Jews opted for Jewish neighborhoods, making their homes among "their own." They created larger or smaller neighborhoods to which new Jewish immigrants flocked, where they conducted business, and provided communal needs. Isaac Mayer Wise described East Baltimore in the 1850s as a teeming, highly distinct neighborhood. "There seemed to be many Jews there. . . . Women in the small shops carrying children in their arms or else knitting busily. Young men invited passersby to enter this or that store to buy . . . M'zu-zoth, Tzitzith, Talethim, Kosher cheese and Eretz Yisrael earth."[6] Descriptions of Syracuse, Cincinnati, Atlanta, Boston, Chicago, Buffalo, Portland, and Des Moines also portrayed Jewish residential clustering.

In some smaller cities, Jews lived together regardless of national origin. Through the 1860s, German and Polish Jews in Syracuse, for example, lived in the same enclave. In other cities, housing separation occurred. In Des Moines, even the more affluent Russian and Polish Jews of the 1860s flocked to the East Side, while the West Side attracted the Germans. As mid-century immigration intensified, as more Jews not only moved to America but moved within it, and a sizable number entered the ranks of the middle class, cities began to house distinct Jewish neighborhoods, reflecting class and ethnicity. But even if Jews lived in undifferentiated Jewish areas or in Polish or Czech enclaves, they tended to live with other Jews as neighbors and friends.[7]

Jews in Philadelphia and New York, the largest Jewish cities of the pre-1820s era, also congregated residentially, although, before the migrations of the 1820s and 1830s, Jewish housing tended to be less dense than later. In Philadelphia in 1830, Jewish families lived in every ward in the city except for one, while afterwards concentration became pronounced. Of the city's 2,975 Jews, 2,618 lived in the center city, east of the Schuylkill River, as of 1850. New York's Jews also tended to be somewhat dispersed before 1820—Jewish households were enumerated in all but two wards. In 1830, the process of clustering began as 45 percent of New York's Jews lived in the contiguous Fifth and Eighth Wards. After that, residential concentration intensified, and distinct Jewish neighborhoods based on European origin coalesced.[8]

German, Dutch, and Polish Jews spread along Bayard, Mott, Baxter, and Chatham Streets, then crossed the Bowery and moved eastward onto Division, Henry, and Market streets. In the 1840s, German and Czech Jews filtered northward into "Kleindeutschland," the German quarter above Grand Street, and onto Ludlow, Attorney, Clinton, Ridge, Pitt, and Rivington streets. When older New York Jewish residents moved northward in the 1840s and 1850s, Polish and Russian newcomers took over older streets, Chatham, Mott, and Bayard, thus allowing for a continuing Jewish neighborhood presence. In the ethnically based Jewish neighborhoods, language solidified community bonds.[9]

Housing patterns further reinforced the strong bonding that came from shared Jewishness, age, occupation, and experience. Even when Jewish immigrants moved *within* the United States, they tended to follow friends and relatives who had come from the same parts of Europe. Individuals from particular towns in Lithuania or Bohemia flocked to specific American locales, and, for example, most of the Polish Jews who migrated to Des Moines, Iowa, had first lived in Rochester, New York.[10]

It is not surprising that informal communities united these individuals from the beginning. Without any organized institutional structure, they fulfilled obligations to one another. In times of sickness, business failure, or death, Jews turned to neighbors—fellow Jewish immigrants—for aid and support. Newly arrived immigrants made their way from the ship directly to the Jewish neighborhoods and reunited there with friends and family, who invariably provided them with lodging, loans, and advice. Philip Cowen, who migrated with his parents in the 1860s from Poznań via England, remembered that as soon as the family landed, they "sought that section of city that was then the destination of German Jewish immigrants." There they found "countrymen they knew." Later, Cowen's father set himself up as a master tailor on Mott Street, in the heart of the Jewish neighborhood.

Many new immigrants were bachelors, and these young men typically found wives through the community network. Young merchants called for sisters in Europe to marry neighbors in America or served as "matchmakers" in other kinds of ways. A memoir of early Jewish life in Omaha described a "young bachelor by the name of Abram S. Brown, also living in Omaha and working in the Meyer Hellman store in the early '60s. In 1867, when the Aaron Cahns made a trip back to German[y], they brought with them, on their return, a niece, Miss Babette Kohn, who shortly thereafter married Brown." Stories such as this pepper autobiographies and memoirs.[11]

To Bury the Dead

Informal networks of community and neighborhood helped Jews fulfill, without organizational assistance, several commandments: kindness to strangers, provision of free-interest loans, and making a match. Most communities founded after 1820, however, owed their formal existence to that moment when they had to execute yet another *mitzvah*, the burial of the dead. Unlike other forms of assistance, the need to bury forced Jews in a particular town or city to organize themselves into a corporate body to purchase and maintain a piece of consecrated land for a cemetery.

In traditional Judaism, heirs and the community as a whole had the responsibility for burial and maintenance of a cemetery. Communities in

Europe supported one or more fraternal societies, *khevre kaddisha* (holy society), that performed the prescribed rituals surrounding death, from *tahara* (purification and preparation of the body), to *halbasha* (dressing of the body in shrouds), *shmira* (sitting with the corpse until the funeral with recitation of psalms), and the burial itself. In European communities, the *khevre kaddisha* consisted of volunteers, since Jewish law prohibited financial gain from fulfilling commandments of burial. However, membership brought rewards, and these "holy fellowships" wielded power and influence because of their monopoly in performing a sacred function. Obligations of members of the khevre also included *bikur holim*, the visitation of the sick, and comforting the mourners. According to one historian, the khevre kaddisha charged higher dues and initiation fees than other societies supported by the Jewish community, its treasury often exceeding all others, and the honor that went along with performing this commandment caused Jews to covet membership in it.[12]

Jews who migrated to the United States in the nineteenth century believed that this sacred obligation ought not to be abridged. In densely packed Jewish cities on the East Coast or in isolated hamlets on the Nevada mining frontier, they proceeded to make arrangements for Jewish burial, demonstrating the power of tradition even in unlikely settings. Jewish funeral practices in America did change in the nineteenth century, and some aspects were amended with the advance of Americanization and Reform. For example, in traditional European Jewish cemeteries, individuals were interred next to each other in the order of death, men in one section, women in another. In America, in the mid-nineteenth century, Jews established family plots. An 1855 advertisement in the *Asmonean* for a Jewish undertaker in New York suggests that the lay khevre kaddisha was being supplanted by funeral professionals. Isaac Mayer Wise outraged his congregants in Albany in 1849 when he refused to rend his garments at the death of his child.[13]

Despite the drift toward innovation in funeral practices, and despite the general drift toward Reform, attitudes toward burial remained traditional. Jews made elaborate arrangements to transport their dead to cities that had Jewish cemeteries. The early Jews of New London buried in New York; Jews of Norwich, Connecticut, in Hartford; and Jews of Washington, D.C., relied on Baltimore. In Syracuse, in the formative years of the community, Jews contented themselves with a separate section of the city's public burial grounds.[14]

As soon as Jews could—often it was within a few years of the arrival of the first of their number in a given place—they incorporated and purchased a plot of land, thereby creating the first community agency. Burial societies were spontaneous associations that sprang from the grass roots of the community.[15] Sometimes a crisis spurred Jews of an area to form their benevolent society and buy a cemetery. For example, in 1855, a German Jewish newcomer, the owner of a general store in the mining area along California's Kern River, was killed in an altercation with an irate customer. When the handful of Jews in Los Angeles heard about the murder, they banded together to get a deed for a cemetery. Further north, Jews in San Francisco formed the city's first khevre kaddisha during a raging cholera epidemic. In most cities, though, the benevolent association formed under more ordinary circumstances and represented a normal stage of community development.[16]

Often referred to as "benevolent societies"—echoing the Hebrew gemilat hesed—the structure and function of these cemetery associations resembled the traditional khevre kaddisha. They considered burial to be a communal, not a private matter. They subscribed to the traditional view that Jewish burial was an "act of benevolence," an honor for the doer of the deed, and that Jews ought to be buried among other Jews, separate and apart from their non-Jewish neighbors. Several of these societies bore names such as Bikur Holim or Mevaker Holim, indicating that, like their European counterparts, they also visited the sick. One, founded in 1848 in Fort Wayne, Indiana, called itself Chevras Bikur Cholim Uk'vuras Meisim—the society for the visitation of the sick and the burial of the dead. In Philadelphia, as early as 1813, German Jews formed themselves into Hebra Shel Bikur Holim Ugemilut Hasadim—the society for visiting the sick and performing acts of kindness.

Benevolent societies' burials conformed with tradition. In accordance with Jewish law, the simple rites of the Jewish Burial Ground Society in Chicago in the 1840s used rough pine-board coffins draped in black cloth and passed a charity box among the mourners by a collector who intoned the traditional formula, "Charity Saves from Death." Flowers were conspicuously absent. The constitution of Ahafath Achim, a benevolent association in Champaign, Illinois, founded in 1867, required that the *kaddish* prayer be recited at the moment of burial and that all members of the society attend daily services at the home of the mourner.[17]

Like the khevrot kaddisha in Europe, American societies charged dues and initiation fees, which gave members and their families the rights of burial. However, they did not limit the privilege of burial to members and members' families, but almost all declared, as, for example, the Hebrew Society of Hevra Ahavat Ahim (the society of the love of brothers) of South Bend in 1859, that "strangers and indigent Israelites who may decease in our midst" would also be buried, free of charge, "according to the usages of our faith."[18] The societies also used dues to dispense charity and make interest-free loans, again combining the commandment of burial with wide ranging traditional obligations.

Indeed, most burial societies quickly took on other communal responsibilities. The Hebrew Benevolent Society of Atlanta was formed in 1860 expressly to provide burial and relief for the poor. The president of the Charlotte, North Carolina, Benevolent Association was authorized to give out five dollars in charity on his own, although the board acted on requests for larger amounts. Eureka Benevolent Association in San Francisco also maintained a poverty relief fund, as did the 1855 Association for those residents of Houston "professing the faith of Abraham, Isaac, and Jacob." In 1868, the society in Charleston, South Carolina, formed a special Committee on Benevolence, which made a trip north—possibly in conjunction with its members' business—to Baltimore, Philadelphia, and New York to collect money from coreligionists. The trip actually netted $967 for the society. Associations also donated money to suffering Jews in other parts of the United States and in Europe, confirming the Talmudic dictate that "all of Israel are responsible for each other." In as "untraditional" a Jewish locale as Helena, Montana, the Hebrew Benevolent Association, within two years of its 1867 founding, "devoted thousands of dollars in relieving the distressed and afflicted." The president of the association went on to remind Montanans of their obligations and of the reasons for their association:[19]

> You organized the Hebrew Benevolent Association in accordance
> with the strict enjoinment of the Holy Ordinances of Israel; namely,
> to relieve the sick and bury the dead, and you have aided your co-
> religionists beyond the seas—for as sure as you render assistance to
> your fellow men in the hour of distress so shall ye be blessed in this
> world and rewarded in the next to come by Him who is all goodness,
> all charity, and all merciful.

Some burial societies also provided the services of a physician to their members.[20]

The societies easily became social as well as communal and religious organizations. In the larger Jewish communities with numerous burial societies, membership tended to break down along nationality lines. For example, in the wake of the Franco-Prussian War in 1870, Alsatian Jews in Los Angeles split off from the Hebrew Benevolent Society made up primarily of men from Prussian Poland, and formed their own French Benevolent Society. Members of a society shared a great deal, and even in smaller enclaves with more diverse membership, social functions proved vital in the society's life. The Hebrew Benevolent Society of Santa Cruz, California, founded in 1875, included just about every male Jew in the community. A local newspaper described its convivial monthly meeting. Men brought their wives and children, and "some . . . business was transacted, then the meeting adjourned, a hop, playing on the piano, a dinner, toasts, speeches, compliments and good-night all."[21]

In yet another way the American benevolent associations resembled European "holy fellowships" and carried over traditional practices. In Europe, the khevrot kaddisha prepared only male bodies for burial, while women constituted themselves into their own *khevrot nashim* (women's societies) to serve their sisters. In America, women in communities, large and small, also functioned in this capacity and formally constituted themselves into female benevolent associations.[22] Activities in these Ladies' Hebrew Benevolent Associations, as they were usually called, both paralleled and deviated from those of their husbands.

Like men, they performed tahara and tended to the sick, adhering to the tradition that the dead not be left alone before burial. Ahavas Achos (the love of sisters), a women's benevolent association of New Haven in the 1850s, was typical. Its formal constitution mandated a "sick committee" to sit at the bedsides of the dying. Between death and burial, two women remained with the deceased at all times. A specially trained group of ten women washed the body, and all members had to contribute six cents toward the "death cloth" of an impoverished sister. Dues collected also went to charitable purposes. By and large, funds amassed by the women supported the relief of female poverty and distress. And, as with the male societies, women at their meetings also enjoyed themselves and sponsored picnics, "dime parties," and theatricals for pleasure and to fill up the association's treasury.[23]

The similarities between male and female associations should not be surprising. Both served the same religious and communal needs, and most members came from the same families. Husbands belonged to the male association, wives to the female. Indeed, often the leader of the male society was married to the leader of the women's association. Julian Mack's Grandmother Tandler served as an official of the Hebrew Ladies' Benevolent Society, and Grandfather Tandler directed the brother group. Sarah Zlottwitz of Swerenz in Poznań and Jacob Rich from the same town married at San Francisco's Sherith Israel in 1853. At the time of their nuptials, she was the treasurer of the Ladies' United Hebrew Benevolent Society, while he served as secretary of the First Hebrew Benevolent Society, a men's association.[24]

Unlike the male associations, however, women's groups did not hold the cemetery's title. Some women's associations, by charter or tradition, installed men as their chief officers. And unlike the male societies that often divided along a variety of fissures within the community, women's societies encompassed a larger swath of the Jewish enclave. Although evidence is scanty and disparate, it appears that male societies tended to be particularistic and served specific constituencies—members who hailed from the same areas in Europe, clustered in certain trades, lived in a particular neighborhood, or belonged to individual congregations.[25] In New York in 1859, for example, Jewish traveler Israel ben Joseph Benjamin counted some seventeen benevolent associations for men but only seven for women. On the other side of the continent, in San Francisco, Benjamin uncovered one Israelite Ladies' Society to "assist Jewish women in all cases of necessity" and four male khevrot kaddisha.[26]

Obviously, male societies formed first. Jewish communities began with a disproportionate number of men to women; however, within a decade of their founding, the ratio balanced out. The fact that a community supported many fewer women's benevolent societies could perhaps indicate less female poverty or a greater willingness of women to be buried without the rites of the faith, neither of which, though, can be justified by evidence. More likely, female burial and charitable work was performed by and for a more diverse and inclusive group, with Jewish women sustaining pretty much all their sisters and not just some of them.

Whatever their differences, both male and female societies made few distinctions between "secular" and "sacred" functions. Not only did they perform tahara, give charity, and play cards; without rabbinic leadership or sanction, these associations often held worship services and in many cases helped create a congregation as a separate entity. The societies saw themselves as agencies for the preservation of Judaism in its full sense. The Hebrew Benevolent Society of Binghamton, New York, founded in 1862, asked members to pledge to "keep their business establishments closed on the holidays," and both the Woodland Hebrew Association in California and the Hebrew Benevolent Society of Albany, Georgia, supported not only cemeteries but schools for the religious instruction of children. In the 1870s, Dallas's benevolent association had its own Torah scroll, while in the 1850s in Boston, the Chevra Gemilos Chesed found a scribe to write a Torah for them—an arduous and precise task—free of charge. (When the Torah was declared unacceptable by a group of New York rabbis, the khevre paid $110 to buy a proper scroll from a local congregation.)[27]

Benevolent associations often held religious services, particularly in smaller communities, on Rosh Hashanah and Yom Kippur, although members may have met more often in homes to pray. Benevolent associations hired rabbis to lead high holiday services, thus bringing the first religious professional into town. And even in cities with established congregations, numerous khevrot buried their own dead, and members worshipped together without formal synagogue status.[28]

Once they secured a cemetery and established social networks, treasury, and the routine of religious services, members of benevolent associations turned to organizing a congregation. While it is not clear if the motivation for having a formal congregation came from the fact that the benevolent association jarred with the American concept of how a religious community ought to be organized or if the members wanted the professional services of a rabbi or cantor, who might be more willing to serve a congregation rather than a benevolent association, in smaller, newer communities in particular, the people who founded the benevolent association turned out to be charter members of the first congregation. For example, most Jews associated with the founding of the Baltimore Hebrew Congregation had previously belonged—and worshipped—with the United Hebrew Benevolent Society.[29]

Strong bonds linked the benevolent associations and the congregations. Not only did memberships overlap, but new congregations sometimes took over the names of their parent benevolent societies, such as Congregation Bickur Cholim (visitation of the sick) or Congregation Gemuluth Chassodim (acts of loving kindness). A clear case of this—also reflecting problems with Hebrew—happened in Pittsburgh, where what must have been the society of the Bes Olam (the eternal house—the cemetery) became a congregation with a transposed name of Bes Almon (the house of the widower, a meaningless term). Even when such names did not actually connote the benevolent function, the societies often carried them, or their part, to the synagogue. Richmond's Chevra Ahabat Yisrael (the society of the love of Israel), founded in 1839, became Congregation Beth Ahaba (the house of love) in 1841. In most cases, the congregation took over the deed for the cemetery, but not the society's whole range of philanthropic functions. Philanthropic activities flourished outside of the synagogue and functioned in a "secular" framework.[30]

Women's benevolent associations often provided funding for congregations, particularly when members were ready to move out of rented rooms and secure a building of their own. Rabbi Liebman Adler of Detroit's Temple Beth El lavishly praised the women of Ahabas Achjaus on the pages of *Die Deborah*, a German supplement to Isaac Mayer Wise's *Israelite*.[31] In 1859, these Michigan women had donated $250 "with the proviso that steps will be taken speedily towards the earnest realization of the long-discussed building of the synagogue." Adler speculated that the women's largess might "stimulate even more the desire of their husbands to show themselves worthy of possessing such noble and pious wives" and presumably also dip into their pockets to provide for the construction of the synagogue. Interestingly, the women of Baton Rouge's Ladies Hebrew Association manifested the same kind of control over spending *their* money. At their June 28, 1874, meeting they insisted that "the Gentlemen's congregation . . . not use the money collected for rent of lot Cor[ner] North and Church . . . and that the said money only be used for purposes of the Building Fund." That the women in both cases seemed to have the greater sense of urgency about a permanent synagogue structure is particularly noteworthy, for women would not, and could not, be members. In the realm of the synagogue, they had no standing.[32]

The benevolent associations and cemeteries thus served as transitional institutions; they preserved, and brought over largely intact, Jewish traditions of burial, mourning, and gemilat hesed. They joined realms of the sacred and the profane by easily mixing sociability with ritual. They linked individual Jews to an organized community and served as the first step toward the emergence of institution-rich Jewish communities. No wonder then, that Leopold Mayer, an immigrant from Bavaria who came to Chicago in the 1840s, recalled as an old man: "It is remarkable how anxious Jews are to provide a resting place for their dead, when, as yet, they have scarcely a foothold for the living. This is noticeable through all their history. . . . Thus, on my first Friday night in Chicago, I watched, with one of my brothers, at the bedside of a sick child of a friend.[33]

To Aid the Needy

If religious motivation in the sense of spirituality and transcendence explained part of this concern with burial and death rituals, commitment to community and concern for the welfare of fellow Jews probably explained a great deal more. American Jews manifested an abiding concern for the unfortunate among them: the poor, the sick, the newly arrived immigrants, widows, and orphans. In the nineteenth century, philanthropy became the glue that held American Jewry together.

Participation in philanthropic projects and membership in organizations dedicated to the relief of distress involved almost all Jews. While male and female societies functioned separately, and in some cities, different ethnic groups formed their own charities and operated apart from their brethren, philanthropy served, by and large, as a communal umbrella. From advocates of radical Reform to the traditionally observant, all could agree that poor Jewish children should be cared for in Jewish orphanages, that Jewish widows ought to be assisted by their Jewish sisters, and that the Jewish sick would be best served in hospitals under Jewish auspices.

As much of Jewish communal development in America, the philanthropic pattern partially represented an American variant on a traditional theme. Historically, Jewish separatism, shaped by both the ghetto and the strictures of Judaism, meant that Jews "took care of their own." Jewish communal care for the sick, widows, and orphans, distribution of free *matzot,* interest-free loans, grants of clothing, shelter, fuel, and dowries for poor brides all grew directly out of preemancipation experience. Assistance to the needy, according to traditional Judaism, did not derive from a good heart or individual largess but was an obligation for all to fulfill.

Charity, always central to the way Jews defined themselves, easily moved across the Atlantic. In the United States, *tzedakah*—the traditional term that implies the notion of justice, not charity—became increasingly bureaucratic in the nineteenth century. As such, it resembled the emerging American "scientific charity." But its very existence and the degree to which it encompassed most Jews made it more a continuation of tradition than an American adaptation.

Its contours were shaped by American conditions. American evangelical Christians aggressively sought out the poor, offering medical care, food, clothing, and schooling to entice children and adults into the arms of the church. Eager to bring as many souls as possible to Christianity, or, more precisely, to certain Protestant denominations, the evangelicals mounted vigorous, though unsuccessful, campaigns to bring the Gospel to Irish Catholics and Jewish immigrants. They opened schools in neighborhoods with high concentration of poor Jews and offered amusements to youngsters. Missionaries roamed charity wards of hospitals seeking out sick Jews and labored for deathbed conversions.

Jewish community leaders feared the strength of evangelicalism. Philadelphia's Isaac Leeser, for example, advocated the creation of a vast infrastructure of Jewish charitable enterprises to counteract Christian societies. The United Hebrew Benevolent Society in Philadelphia, which Leeser helped create, noted in its annual report of 1825 that "the subscribers . . . appointed a committee on the subject of the children of Moses Isaacs, who have been cruelly deserted by their father and left wholly unprotected, great danger being apprehended that they will be entirely lost as Jews, and brought up as Christians." Indeed, the first Jewish orphanage in New York, founded in 1832, grew out of such motives, as did that city's Hebrew Benevolent Society. In 1859, a group of New York Jews pooled the resources of two smaller Jewish charitable societies and founded a home for orphans, the aged, and indigents after they learned that a Jewish child had been placed in a non-Jewish orphanage and converted to Christianity there.[34]

American Jews also feared that Jewish poverty and social disorganization in America would reflect badly on all. Before the 1820s, individual congregations dispensed aid directly to the needy. But after the massive migrations from central and then eastern Europe, funds of individual congregations, such as New York's Shearith Israel or Philadelphia's Mikveh Israel, no longer sufficed. While these congregations, and the new ones that were founded with dizzying regularity in the years after 1820, continued to succor members, the numbers of Jews outside the synagogue net swelled and required new institutions. Jewish leaders expressed concern over how America perceived them and worried lest Jews be considered burdens on the community at large. The Jewish newspapers and community leaders regularly declared that no Jews lived in the public almshouses, orphanages, and other state-supported institutions. While they did not claim that no Jews needed assistance, they trumpeted the fact that well-off Jews helped those in need. Sabato Morais, writing a thumbnail description of his fellow Jews in America in 1872 for William Burder's encyclopedia of religions, declared:[35]

> They will never suffer the destitute to be an incubus upon society at large. Rarely is any of their faith an inmate of the almshouse, and more rarely is any arrested as a vagrant or an outlaw. Charitable associations supplying food, garments, fuel, and house rent . . . encourage the industrious; hospitals, orphan asylums; foster houses, and homes for the invalid and the decrepit, are supported wherever a Jewish community exists.

The larger the city, the greater the poverty and the more complex the local philanthropic networks. Economically marginal Jews rarely stayed put in the smaller communities, and it seems that Jewish poor from hinterland settlements made their way to New York, Philadelphia, Baltimore, and Cincinnati in search of work and *tzedakah*. Furthermore, port cities, which included New Orleans, had a larger-than-average share of the down-and-out, individuals whose empty pockets kept them from taking advantage of economic opportunities further away. Such cities also maintained relatively elaborate charitable networks. Of course, these same cities also had many wealthy Jews who underwrote orphanages, asylums, hospitals, free loans, and charitable funds.

New York's institutional structure befitted its size, and housing America's largest Jewish community, the city had the greatest panoply of Jewish welfare projects. Indeed, between 1848 and 1860, when Jews made up somewhere between two and five percent of the city's total population, they supported more than ninety-three philanthropic associations. The rest of the city maintained only ninety-six similar institutions. A slew of other Jewish charitable enterprises, such as the Hebrew Mutual Benefit Society and the Hebrah Achim Rachamim, did not get counted because they had not taken out incorporation papers. Yet Jews hardly represented New York's poorest residents; the economically more depressed Irish communities far outnumbered Jews.[36]

Most Jewish historians have asserted that the founders and movers of these philanthropies used the institutions to reshape Jews into Americans. Caring little for Jewishness or Judaism, they aped Protestant American models in the charities they created. This, the historians argue, constituted a radical change in the structure of Jewish life.

Certainly, individual American Jews who organized charitable work sometimes had prior experience in American nonsectarian projects and applied what they learned to Jewish activities. Rebecca Gratz of Philadelphia was an excellent example. Daughter of an old American Jewish family, she had not read the traditional Jewish texts and lacked Jewish literacy. She participated in a general female charitable society in Philadelphia before deciding to found a similar one for poor Jews. Her Female Hebrew Benevolent Society, the first nonsynagogal Jewish charity in the United States, founded in 1819, certainly incorporated some American values into its structure.[37]

Jews active in charitable endeavors learned from Christian and nonsectarian organizations to rationalize philanthropy. In New York, Boston, and Philadelphia, they saw how "friendly visitors" went to the homes of the poor to determine the extent and nature of need. Committees of the benevolent then reviewed applications and decided who got what. Giver and taker were separated by bureaucracy, never establishing a personal bond between them. These institutions defined charity as a privilege, not a right, and their ideology of philanthropy stood in sharp contrast with traditional Jewish precepts of *tzedakah,* which put the burden on the giver and was predicated on close ties between recipient and donor.[38]

American Jews did embrace American ideas about philanthropy. Individuals such as Isaac Leeser and Rabbi Samuel Isaacs of New York applauded the movement of philanthropy out of the congregations, hoping to rationalize it and make it more American. They sought, according to Leeser, to "raise the character of the recipient of charity through a proper discrimination, by aiding those who are most deserving." They also approved of the ongoing movement in America to unite charities and create single, citywide funds, to avoid repeated pleas for money. Many Jewish leaders decried the tendency of Jewish communities to support multiple charitable societies, each representing a different constituency group often based on European origin. They advocated, in Leeser's words, a "united benevolence." Jewish charities, particularly orphanages, sought to mold the Jewish poor into model Americans, emphasizing such values as thrift, sobriety, and hard work. Managers of the Baltimore Hebrew Orphan Asylum very clearly stated that they wanted to produce "good American citizens as well as true Israelites."[39]

In addition, American Jewish charities differed from their traditional European counterparts in the degree to which women led, shaped, and participated in organized good deeds. European communities in Bavaria, Posen, Lithuania, or Bohemia had not supported many charitable organizations founded and directed by women. In America, Jewish women created orphanages, day nurseries, maternity hospitals, soup kitchens, shelters for widows, and the like. Groups such as the Montefiore Lodge Ladies' Hebrew Benevolent Association in Providence, Rhode Island, participated in friendly visiting, gave out coal, clothing, food, eyeglasses, and medicine. The Johanna Lodge in Chicago helped newly arrived single immigrant girls get set up in business. Matrons of the organizations also formally introduced them to eligible Jewish bachelors—often the clerks in their stores—arranged the match, helped finance the wedding, and even loaned money to the young couple to get started. Some of these organizations, such as the Deborah Society in Hartford, Connecticut grew out of female burial societies. Others, such as the Detroit Ladies' Society for the Support of Hebrew Widows and Orphans, started specifically as female philanthropies. Although many of the women's charitable societies had, at some point, a male board of directors or a male president, the mere fact of women's active public involvement represented a departure from the past.[40]

Charities also embraced American methods of fund-raising. In Europe, the Jewish community had the power of self-taxation. As a legal entity, the *kahal* used its treasury to maintain services for the needy. In America, where the state recognized no religious authority and where the Jewish "community" existed only voluntarily, made up of those claiming membership, no overarching body levied taxes to create and maintain institutions. Individuals gave because they wanted to or felt obliged. Thus the traditional tzedakah concept based on justice gave way to the charity concept based on good works.

Most importantly, charitable institutions became membership societies. They assisted the poor primarily by subscribers' dues. The Jewish press drummed up support for various projects and used its columns to tout particular institutions. Various organizations held meetings to acquaint the Jewish public with their worthwhile enterprise, and rabbis preached from the pulpit about the need to give. One American innovation in fund-raising was the charity ball, often coinciding with the merry late-winter holiday of Purim. Purim balls, sometimes costumed or just high-dress events, combined dancing, levity, and the serious business of fund-raising for those in distress. In 1869, for example, Purim balls took place in New Haven, Boston, Albany, Baltimore, Richmond, Philadelphia, Cincinnati, Chicago,

New Orleans, and San Francisco. In 1862, Meyer Isaacs, son of Samuel Myer Isaacs, editor of the *Jewish Messenger*, founded a Purim Association in New York to coordinate the annual dance, and in Philadelphia, a Charity Ball Association came into being in 1869. Annual dinners, picnics, and other social events linked the pursuit of pleasure with the principle of tzedakah.[41]

Some leaders and large givers to Jewish charity maintained only tenuous ties to other aspects of Jewish life. Many of New Orleans's most lavish patrons of organizations such as the Association for the Relief of Jewish Widows and Orphans had no other connections to organized Jewry, and some had married outside the Jewish community. One actually converted to Christianity but continued to donate to Jewish charities.[42]

Yet, it may not be altogether accurate to write off the philanthropists as advocates of assimilation for its own sake. For one, institutions created by philanthropists maintained Sabbath and dietary restrictions. Their schools taught orphans rudiments of Judaic learning along with marketable skills. The Jewish Foster Home of Philadelphia, for example, opened in 1855, would not consider children from families not observing the Sabbath. Asylums typically grew out of fear of the evangelists, underscoring the Jewish motives of asylum founders. The social functions—balls, picnics, and dinners—all solidified bonds of friendship and community among Jewish donors. Advocates of traditional Judaism, including Leeser and Isaacs, played as important a role in these communal organizations as did those who rejected tradition or even personal commitment to Judaism. Finally, the founders of the communal institutions clearly gave their projects Jewish names. They did not seek to submerge the Jewishness of their motives within some generalized American largess. Thus, when the great monument to New York's Jewish philanthropy, the Jews' Hospital, was dedicated in 1855, its English name on the facade was chiseled alongside the Hebrew words *Bet Holim*, the house of the sick. (The name was changed to Mt. Sinai Hospital in 1866 when the hospital opened its doors to non-Jewish patients.)[43]

To Find a Friend

Community, for Jews or non-Jews, involved not just doing things for others but also for oneself. The Jewish communities of the nineteenth century provided places where Jews could socialize with friends, recreate with peers, and foster a sense of belonging. Nineteenth-century Jews made no great distinction between philanthropy and self-help. In the 1870s, the Young Men's Hebrew Association of Boston, founded "for the moral and intellectual advancement of the Jewish population and for the relief of the deserving poor," had an employment bureau, helped peddlers get licenses, distributed food to the poor, visited the Jewish sick in the hospitals, secured the release of Jews incarcerated in local prisons for minor offenses, and provided a place for fellowship and recreation.[44]

In small towns, benevolent Hebrew associations, connected with the grim tasks of mourning and burial, also fostered fellowship and ease. Given the small number of Jews in places such as Helena, Montana, or Albany, Georgia, just about all Jews participated, regardless of where in Europe they had come from. Larger communities offered diverse opportunities, spawning a varied organizational infrastructure. The various associations tended to break down by place of European origin, and as early as the 1860s, *landsmanshaftn,* associations of Jews from particular towns and regions, began to form. These *anshes* (people of) or khevrot (societies), like benevolent associations, offered burial rights along with interest-free loans, medical care through a society doctor, and the chance to be with towns-people in an informal, convivial atmosphere. Actually the oldest New York *landsmanshaft,* the Netherlander Israelitisch Sick Fund Society, was founded in 1859 by Dutch Jews, while in 1864, Jewish immigrants from Russian Bialystok got together to forge a Bailystoker Support Society. Serving newcomers to America, these landsmanshaftn were islands of the familiar in an otherwise new and baffling sea.[45]

For more comfortable American Jews, certainly for children of immigrants, both single-gender and mixed literary societies developed in the 1840s. These organizations offered a varied program of theatricals, musical presentations, debates on political and ethical issues of the day, lectures by well-known individuals, literary discussions, and readings by members of their own literary efforts. Undoubtedly, both before and after the meetings, informal socializing took place, friendships were cemented, business contacts forged, and a good time had by all. Literary societies may have offered a particularly attractive program to individuals with little formal education but nonetheless interested in learning and socializing with other Jews. The Jews of Alexandria, Virginia, actually formed themselves into a literary society first and only later created a khevre kaddisha, attesting to the powerful draw of these organizations.[46]

During the middle decades of the century, such societies combined the intellectual, social, and Jewish aspects. Jews in Davenport, Iowa, founded one, as did their brethren in New York City, Baltimore, New Orleans, Richmond, Virginia, Philadelphia, and elsewhere. These clubs enforced morality and set an elevated tone by banning card playing, smoking, and drinking at meetings. In disallowing such conduct, they may have been reacting to the behavior—perceived or otherwise—of some of the poor immigrants in their midst and may indeed have been advocating *Bildung*. The ban may have had American origins, indicating Jewish assimilation of Victorian standards of respectability and gentility.[47]

Early literary societies paved the way for the 1854 founding in Baltimore of the first Young Men's Hebrew Association. From then on, the YMHA movement spread quickly. Some chapters rented space, while others built their own buildings. All combined literary activities with sports, edifying lectures with exercise and fun. The Newark, New Jersey, YMHA occupied a three story building, completed in 1877, with a gymnasium, two bowling alleys, a chess room, a ladies' parlor, and an auditorium which seated five hundred. In the 1875–1876 season of New York's "Y," members could chose classes in Hebrew language and literature, French, German, and English literature, photography, music, and drama. The association sponsored an orchestra, glee club, employment bureau, and literary society as well as chess and athletic circles. YMHA chapters typically sponsored lecture series on political topics and educational subjects.[48]

YMHAs developed simultaneously with the spread of Young Men's Christian Associations. But the YMHAs were not a reaction against the YMCAs' evangelicalism or exclusionary membership policies, nor should they be viewed as Jewish emulation of Christians. First, young Jewish men did not found their associations because they could not join the YMCA. No evidence suggests, however, that they cared to affiliate with the Christian associations. Most nineteenth-century American Jews chose positively to spend leisure hours with other Jews and had no desire to belong to an organization as overtly religious and missionary as the YMCA. Secondly, Jews gathered together in both informal and formal associations, protean YMHAs, decades before the birth of the first YMCA in 1851.[49]

In both cases, though, young men sought out others like themselves for nonwork companionship. Both Jews and Christians responded to the same nineteenth-century ideas about leisure, which was supposed to build character. Both embodied belief in gender segregation as the most appropriate way to recreate, and both picked up on the mid-century's concern with exercise and physical fitness as tools in molding morally strong men. Both Jewish and Christian associations sought to foster unity among their constituents and envisioned their role as providing a rallying point for all young men of the group, hoping to erase previous divisions and factions.[50]

Although ideas such as these did not grow out of traditional Jewish culture, and, certainly, the format of the associations sprang from the modern American context, the YMHAs maintained strong links to Jewishness. They proclaimed themselves "Hebrew" associations. Their lectures and classes exposed young men to Jewish learning and current events that stressed the bonds of Jewish peoplehood. The New York "Y" even issued pamphlets to the larger public, reprinting outstanding lectures on Jewish topics. Beginning in 1876, it sponsored an annual essay contest on Jewish affairs as a way to actualize its objective of "the protection of Jewish interests." The YMHAs annually celebrated Hanukkah and Purim, often boisterously, while many incorporated the Jewish concern for tzedakah into their program by raising money for Jews in distress. The St. Louis chapter collected two thousand dollars from its members to aid the Jewish victims of a virulent yellow-fever epidemic in 1878, while Boston's association set aside a special time for poor coreligionists in 1875 to come to its boardroom to file relief applications. That year, the Boston YMHA distributed matzo and other Passover supplies to eighteen Jewish families.

YMHAs fostered Jewish religious practice. In 1866, New Orleans members donated one thousand dollars for the construction of a synagogue, and the New York association sponsored an annual examination in Hebrew. At the initiation of the chapter, local rabbis and teachers conducted public testing of the city's Jewish children from the many scattered Jewish schools. One historian of Jewish education, Alexander Dushkin, claimed that this effort by the YMHA represented the first "serious effort to centralize the work of the Jewish religious schools of New York."

Finally, YMHAs grappled with issues of Sabbath observance. Should their facilities be open on Saturday? Should young Jewish men be encouraged to spend their day of rest in the company of other Jews at the YMHA, or should the building close its doors in strict compliance with Jewish law? As of 1875, the New York YMHA decided in favor of a compromise and kept the building open, but only for "light" exercise. Such equipment as the trapeze and the horizontal bars were deemed too strenuous and their use considered a violation of the *halakah* of the Sabbath.[51]

To Covenant as Brothers

The same motives that led Jews to establish landsmanshaftn, literary clubs, and benevolent associations led to the formation of several nationwide fraternal societies with a string of affiliated local lodges. Kesher shel Barzel (chain of iron), founded in 1860, the Order of B'rith Abraham, the Free Sons of Israel, founded in 1859, and the most popular and long lasting, the B'nai B'rith, founded in 1843, all combined ideals of mutual benefit with social and recreational functions. Each offered burial services and widow and orphan annuities, made available interest-free loans to members, and provided cultural and recreational activities. The organizations tended to divide somewhat along the lines of national origin. Kesher shel Barzel primarily appealed to eastern European Jews, Poles in particular, B'rith Abraham enrolled many Hungarians and Germans, and B'nai B'rith, in its earliest years, recruited mostly men of German origin.[52]

Women founded lodges for like purposes. Unabhaengiger Treue Schwestern, the United Order of True Sisters, was founded in 1846 in New York and by 1851 spread to Philadelphia, Albany, and New Haven. Its lodges provided various forms of self-help to members who embellished meetings with secret rituals, garb, and other kinds of paraphernalia. Similar to B'nai B'rith, the True Sisters in some places operated as a kind of female counterpart or, indeed, a ladies' auxiliary to the larger, male B'nai B'rith.[53]

No organization captured the character of nineteenth-century American Jewish communal culture as clearly as B'nai B'rith. Twelve young Jewish men, all from Germany, got together informally on a regular basis on Sundays at Sinsheimer's saloon on New York's Essex Street. These young merchants with a few artisans among them had all been in the United States less than a decade and at Sinsheimer's found a place to relax and interact with their fellows. Four of them belonged either to the Masons or the Odd Fellows. In the 1840s, when those organizations began to systematically reject Jewish applicants for membership, these young Jews decided to create a Jewish equivalent. As they cast about for a name for their new society, they toyed with the idea of *Bundes Brüder,* which in incorrect German was to mean "the league of brothers." They opted instead for the grammatically correct Hebrew, B'nai B'rith, the sons of the covenant.[54] While its name was in Hebrew, its outward form suggested Masonry and it expropriated the secret handshakes, passwords, codes, regalia, and insignia of Masonry. During its early years, the B'nai B'rith articulated a conception of Jewishness that existed outside of the synagogues and rabbinic authority, proclaiming, according to historian Deborah Dash Moore, "a bold new vision of the nature of Jewish identity." As such, the B'nai B'rith represented the "first secular Jewish organization in the United States."55

It certainly did not function any differently than the other, non-Jewish lodges spawned by the economic insecurities of nineteenth-century America, offering their members sickness, funeral, and survivor benefits, and mixing together clubbiness of frequent meetings with insider language and peculiar customs. Like its non-Jewish counterparts, B'nai B'rith fit perfectly the needs of a geographically mobile people. Since the lodges extended over the whole country by the 1860s, a Jew moving from place to place could take his benefits package with him and find a familiar setting among "brothers" in the new town. Indeed, the order issued traveling cards so that members could immediately join a new lodge after relocating. Lodges communicated with one another and reported suspension or expulsion for various infractions or transgressions.56 Like the Masons and other fraternal bodies, the B'nai B'rith frequently housed a library and sponsored lectures and musical programs.

The class of men who joined the B'nai B'rith paralleled those who joined the Odd Fellows and Masons. Drawing primarily from the ranks of small merchants, it probably helped young men make good business contacts and establish their reputation for civic-mindedness. The bylaws of one lodge stated that it only accepted applications from "any Israelite of good moral character." Membership in the lodge could offer a newly minted merchant a chance to announce his worth to the community. Of the thirteen applicants for membership in the Champaign, Illinois, lodge in 1877, all but two listed "merchant" as occupation, while the remaining two wrote down "shoemaker" and "clerk," occupations not terribly far from the majority. More than half of the members were not married, and their age ranged between twenty-one and forty-three.57

Yet, Jewishness never hovered far away from the Independent Order of B'nai B'rith, which should, therefore, not be viewed as a revolutionary innovation in Jewish identity but rather an attempt to find an American idiom in which to express it. Like organizers of other Jewish associations, the founders of the B'nai B'rith and its members in Cincinnati, Philadelphia, Washington, D.C., Louisville, Kentucky, San Francisco, Cleveland, and indeed in almost every cranny of antebellum United States used Hebrew words and Jewish sacred symbols for their order. The secret handshake went along with the traditional *shalom aleichem* greeting; the regalia included the *arba kanfot,* the four-cornered fringed prayer undergarment of traditional Judaism.[58]

In addition, local lodges, chartered by the regional District Grand Lodges—through an 1851 reorganization and constitutional change—were just as likely to choose Hebrew and biblical names as English or geographic designations for their names. So, while the Champaign lodge called itself Grand Prairie Lodge, others went by such names as Asaph, Pisgah, B'er Chayim, Ebn Ezra, Ramah, Ophir, Emes, and Haggai.[59]

More importantly, B'nai B'rith lodges assumed uniquely Jewish functions in local communities. They had a hand in Jewish education, for example. In Albany, New York, the Shiloh Lodge briefly sponsored a full day school, the B'nai B'rith Academy, while the Champaign Grand Prairie Lodge provided instruction for Jewish children on Sundays. In Hartford in the 1850s, the Ararat Lodge provided, as a benefit for members, religious education for their daughters from nine to thirteen years of age and for their sons between eight and thirteen.[60] Elsewhere, B'nai B'rith lodges sponsored lectures by visiting rabbis. The Cumberland, Maryland, lodge organized the celebration of a "Gala Chanuca for the benefit of the congregation," and in 1850 in New York, the order launched probably the first Jewish library in the United States, the Maimonides Library Association. Following suit, lodges in Philadelphia and Cincinnati also decided to start Jewish public libraries.[61]

Descriptions of meetings indicated that Jewishness always found its way onto the B'nai B'rith agenda. At an 1876 meeting of the Paradise Lodge No. 237 in San Bernardino, California, Hyman Goldberg, a visitor from Arizona, launched into a "harangue," in which he "urged his brethren to remember their duties, both as men and Israelites."[62]

Responsibility of "men" alluded to here involved duties to protect their families against economic adversity, and that of "Israelites" included fostering continuity and belonging. On a local level, particularly in smaller communities, B'nai B'rith lodges united Jewish residents. At a time when religious antagonism split Jews along Reform and Orthodox lines and divided them between moderate and extreme innovators, the order offered a neutral place for being just Jewish. According to William Toll's careful study of Portland, Oregon, young men from Bavaria, Prussia, and Poland all joined the B'nai B'rith lodge, thus erasing national fissures that led to the creation of multiple synagogues. Because B'nai B'rith was new and did not sponsor religious services, Jews from Poland and Jews from Bavaria did not have to argue as to which ritual would be used. The American way served as the mechanism for *k'lal Yisrael* (the solidarity of all Israel).[63]

That responsibility went beyond the doors of the meeting house, and the IOBB thus laid the foundations for nationwide American Jewish unity. The B'nai B'rith spoke out on behalf of Jewish political interests and asserted itself as a voice for the Jews. Indeed, the order may be considered the first truly national Jewish institution. The Constitution Grand Lodge, the overarching national body, threw itself into the defense of Jewish rights abroad. In 1851, it wrote letters to Senators Daniel Webster and Henry Clay urging the United States to suspend a commercial treaty with Switzerland, several of whose cantons barred Jewish settlement, and during the Civil War, it stridently protested against General U. S. Grant's order expelling Jews from the "department of the Tennessee." When a virulent cholera epidemic broke out in Palestine, the Board of Deputies of British Jews turned to the B'nai B'rith to coordinate American relief efforts. The order supervised distribution of charity to Jewish survivors of the Chicago fire of 1871. In 1868, the Cleveland lodge brought into being a national orphanage for Jewish children, and members of District 2, covering the Midwest, imposed a surtax of one dollar on themselves to support it.[64]

Thus, if the B'nai B'rith, the YMHAs, and the charitable societies and benevolent associations did not actually reproduce in America Jewish life as it was known in Europe, neither did they reject notions about the solidarity of the Jewish people and Jewish responsibilities for one another. Communal organizations perpetuated aspects of Jewish life by establishing new forms of identity and distinctly Jewish institutions to suit American conditions.

The community structures of American Jews in the nineteenth century can be seen neither as a break with the past, nor as the tradition's unbroken "chain of iron." American Jews believed they were both responsible to the past and unfettered by it. They viewed themselves as fully capable of changing forms when it suited their needs. They created a set of institutions that adopted some functions of the European *kahal* with its formal, legalized powers of taxation and enforcement, but did so in an American way, based on voluntarism, pluralism, and freedom. They established institutions and practices that may not have had precedent but which owed their existence to Jewish exposure to American life.

Those structures could be American and Jewish at once, because the women and men who founded them did not worry about the ideological implications of freedom of choice. When Jews formed a landsmanshaft, planned a Purim ball, or gathered together to found a lodge of the United Order of True Sisters, they rarely stopped to think about historical and cultural implications of their actions. Rather, much of American Jewish communal life grew out of an unself-conscious recognition of need: need for economic security, need for support in time of crisis, need for friendship, and need for community. American Jews engaged in these activities because they wanted to and because they had to.

Communal institutions of American Jews sprang, leaderless, from the grass-roots level. Little conflict accompanied their founding or their functioning, since no group had a stake in the maintenance of one kind of structure over another. Community organizations did not pit an ideologically oriented elite, worried about the underlying dilemmas of the conflict between modernization and tradition, against a pragmatic laity that *only* wanted to see results.

Not so religion. Here, conflicts became all too real when rabbis, fully aware of the ramifications of these issues, confronted congregations of ordinary Jews with their own agenda.

CHAPTER FIVE

STRIVING FOR THE SACRED

The [Jewish] inhabitants of San Francisco are not wicked and sinful, any more than
are the [Jewish] people of European cities. True, there are some who desecrate the
Sabbath, but then there are many who keep it sacred. There are those who partake
of the forbidden food, still there are many who are very strict in the observance.

I dwell in complete darkness. . . . religious life in this land is at the lowest
level. . . . Under this circumstance my mind is perplexed and I wonder whether
it is even possible for a Jew to live in this land.

Our reception of the Torah was, for us, like the moment that our people received
the holy covenant on Mount Sinai. It was a sacred moment for our congregation
and one full of awe. Our eyes were raised up to heaven and we called out,
"As our hearts were filled with the fear of God on this day, so may it be
all the days of our lives on the earth."

Our strength is frittered away by every community's acting independently
of all others; since scarcely two congregations in any one city even, have a
mutual good understanding between them.

THE PRACTICE of Judaism, with its cultic rituals and its complex
obligations for personal and collective behavior, had for millennia distinguished Jews from those around them. In Europe, to be a Jew and not a
Christian meant that one adhered to an intricate code of distinctive behavior that governed what one ate, how one marked the days of the week, the
cycles of the month, and the seasons of the year, the fabrics one wore,
relations between husbands and wives, how one prayed, and indeed almost
all aspects of life. To be a Jew, however, went far beyond what one did or ate
or intoned. Jews considered themselves a people. In the classic formulation
of Judaism, God (the transcendent), Torah (the law), and Israel (the people)
could not be separated. Jews distinguished themselves from those of other
faiths by their belief system, their public religious behavior, and their personal behavior.

The transplantation of Judaism to America seemed unpropitious and inorganic. Judaism drew no boundaries between the personal and the communal, yet an industrializing nineteenth-century America increasingly marked a sharp line between home and work, self and society, private and public. Traditional Jewish life centered on a highly structured, empowered community that enforced proper behavior and insisted that in matters of piety individuals had little choice. America, on the other hand, had evolved into a society that assumed that matters of faith ultimately rested with the individual and concerned no one else.

Rabbinic law did not allow for spontaneous innovation in ritual practice and carefully delineated the power of religious authorities to determine questions of personal status, liturgy, and rite. Yet in America, numerous new religions and sects cropped up—Millerites, Shakers, Mormons, Disciples of Christ, Unitarians, and Christian Scientists, to mention but a few—attesting to the indifference of the state toward religious behavior and the mood of experimentation within established denominations. Even the most hierarchical nineteenth-century American religious groups saw lay members challenge established authority, question beliefs, and demand changes in ritual. Dissident sects became new denominations, replete with clergy, institutions, and often their own insurgents challenging one aspect or another of the new "orthodoxy." The early nineteenth century also saw the final disestablishment of religion in the various American states, signifying the erosion of the status and power of the clergy—and religion—in all America.[1]

Still other elements shaped religious behavior and challenged traditional Jewish practice in this country. Westward movement and constant mobility tended to break religious control. Americans changed denominations with the same ease they changed residences, and churches competed with one another for members. Indeed, Protestant churches differed primarily in the social and economic class of their members and not in belief systems. During the middle decades of the nineteenth century, denominations diluted theological differences. Those of Calvinist origins, for example, blunted their harsh preachings of eternal damnation to compete for crowds on Sunday. Ultimately, a generalized American Protestantism developed, with few differences separating one Protestant denomination from the other.[2]

The massive influx of immigrants from Europe introduced new religions and challenged traditional religious communities. Lutherans, for example, could have been just as likely Germans, Swedes, Norwegians, or

Danes as old-stock Americans. Fissures within the Lutheran church over language developed along national lines, producing rival, ethnic-based Lutheran churches in America. Similarly Catholicism, the domain of Americans of English origin in 1820, rocked under floods of Irish, German, and French-Canadian immigrants, with each group bringing their own saints, festivals, clergy, and language, and thus threatening the church's claim to universality. [3]

Finally, women participated actively in nineteenth-century American church politics, in striking contrast to European Jewish practice. The "cult of true womanhood," which assigned to women the domain of morality and goodness, defined religion as falling within the proper female sphere. As religion faded in significance in Victorian America, women, powerless in the political arena, and the clergy, stripped of state support, found natural allies in each other. The world of the churches by and large became theirs. [4]

Traditional Judaism, like immigrant Catholicism or Lutheranism, faced the challenge of a pluralistic and privatized American religious culture. It was not surprising then that some aspects of Jewish religious practice underwent radical change and emerged barely recognizable at the century's end. Other elements remained constant, testifying to the power of tradition. But most aspects of Jewish religious behavior fell between these two poles and appeared as a mix of *both* innovation and constancy, transition and tradition, Reform and Orthodoxy. What changed and what stayed the same? How did American Jews, the masses and their rabbis, blend tradition and innovation? Answers to these questions provide the key to understanding the nature of adaptation to America.

The Rise of Reform

The emergence and spread of Reform Judaism in nineteenth-century America demonstrated how Judaism was changing and that American Jews considered themselves agents of innovation. The first such effort occurred in 1824 in Charleston, South Carolina, at Beth Elohim Congregation. A dissident group, "the Reformed Society of Israelites for promoting true principles of Judaism according to its purity and spirit," asked for a shorter service, an accompanying English translation of some prayers, and a few other, minor modifications. These lay people from some of Charleston's most elite Jewish families believed that they should be able, "from time to time," to change "such parts of our prevailing system of Worship, as are inconsistent with the present enlightened state of society, and not in accordance with the Five Books of Moses and the Prophets." The rejection of their request by the *parnassim* (trustees) of Beth Elohim led to a short-lived withdrawal, although the secessionists eventually returned to the congregation. [5]

The impetus for Reform came mostly from the laity and its focus on practical ritual problems. Congregations in one city after another pushed for changes. Many tampered with elements of the service before they hired a rabbi or during the frequent hiatuses between rabbinic professionals, justifying reforms on practical grounds rather than biblical justifications or elaborate intellectual rationale. For example, most confronted the problem of where to seat women when the congregation bought its first building, usually a former Protestant church, which did not have a set-off women's section. Other matters of design also forced innovation. The former churches did not have a central reader's desk but did have an organ. Lay leaders had to decide what to do about these structural problems and usually left the building intact and altered the service.

The laity had no particular vision of what ought to be—they just knew what they did not like and had some inkling of what would improve it. They preferred some English in their service, a rabbi to deliver a sermon, and perhaps an organ to accompany prayers. They generally liked the idea that their houses of worship resemble those of their Christian neighbors. Over time, some often pushed for choirs and demanded that men not be required to don the traditional *tallit* (prayer shawl) and *yarmulke* (head covering). They considered it appropriate that Jews behave with decorum in their synagogues, and synagogue boards banned spitting, walking around during services, voluble talking, loud praying at one's own pace, and other "uncivil" acts. They wanted to give the synagogue all the dignity of an American religious institution. [6]

The gradual trickle of European-trained rabbis to the United States, particularly after 1850, changed somewhat the process of Reform. These rabbis who pressed for ideologically based innovations came from traditional homes in Europe and began their careers as strictly observant young men. However, as central European governments mandated university training for all clergy, they came into contact with secular learning, cosmopolitan culture, and strands of thinking that jarred with the Judaic system. For some, the percolating movement for Reform in Germany offered a way to reconcile Jewish and modern modes. [7]

When they arrived in America, often invited by congregations searching for religious leaders, they introduced a theoretical rationale to justify
and spur on the process of reform. Rabbis such as Isaac Mayer Wise and
David Einhorn, who led the moderate and the radical factions within American Reform, as well as Max Lilienthal, Samuel Adler, and Kaufmann Kohler
strove to impose a philosophic order onto the hodgepodge innovations
cropping up in America.[8]

At their various conferences, such as those in Cleveland in 1855 and
Philadelphia in 1869, in the prayer books and other texts they edited,
such as Wise's *Minhag America* and Einhorn's *Olath Tamid*, and, ultimately, during the deliberations of the crowning institutions of the Reform
tendency, the Union of American Hebrew Congregations (1873) and the
Hebrew Union College (1875), the rabbis asserted that they, men of the
nineteenth century, had the right to excise, add to, and alter the corpus of
Jewish law. Assertion of the right to change Judaism to fit the time and place
characterized both the radical faction associated with Einhorn and the
Reformers of the East Coast, and the more moderate wing linked to Wise
and the Midwest.[9]

The rabbis claimed that some practices jarred with American conditions and that they could nullify them. They could also tamper with the
service and eliminate some basic elements in the Jewish credo. They rejected
such core ideas as the impending arrival of a Messiah, in whose wake the
dead would rise, the reestablishment of a Jewish kingdom in Zion, and the
notion of *galut*, the Jewish exile.

Reform-oriented rabbis sought to purge American Judaism of elements
that conflicted with modernism and the *Zeitgeist* of rationalism. Thus, a
tradition begun during the Babylonian exile in 586 B.C.E., whereby Jews
outside of Palestine celebrated a second day of all holidays in order to
ensure observance of the festivals at the same time with their brethren in
Jerusalem, no longer made sense. Calendars and clocks—accurate ways of
measuring time—obviated the need for this *sheni l'yom tov*. In addition, the
rabbis rejected the obligation of an additional day of holiday for Diaspora
Jews because they rejected the notion that they lived in exile. Why, asked
Reform rabbis, should American Jews mourn for Zion and recite lamenta-
tions over the destruction of the Temple in Jerusalem on Tisha b'Av, the
ninth day of the month of Av? In America, Jews no longer lived in exile—
this was their land of freedom. Einhorn, Wise, and the others eliminated
this summer fast day for its inconsistency.

They also purged those aspects of Judaism that governed personal behavior. They rejected regulations of diet, Sabbath, and family relations as being outside the realm of religion, asserting instead that only the ethical elements of Judaism were of divine origin and obligatory. They denied the binding nature of *halakah* (Jewish law) as embodied in the Talmud and turned to the Bible as the fundamental source of Judaism. Judaism, they asserted, constituted a religion, not a legal system.[10]

Historians of American Judaism, regardless of their personal religious orientation, have focused on the nineteenth century as the age of Reform, as a time when Jews in their new American home eagerly shed the restraints of the past and rushed into innovation of both public rites and private codes of behavior. While some historians have applauded this liberation from the shackles of the past, others have lamented the abandonment of tradition and Reform's sundering of Jewish unity. In either case, they have worked on the assumption that *reform* (lower case) meant the same as *Reform* (upper case) and that change involved an all-or-nothing formula. Tradition, historical scholarship has declared, died fast, and had it not been for the eastern European influx after 1880, normative Judaism would have disappeared from America. Historians have also asserted that much of Reform stemmed from the desire to present Jews and Judaism as being the same as Christians and Christianity, and that Reform mimicked Protestantism. More than anything else, nineteenth-century American Jews wanted to fit into America and opted for a protestantized ritual, stripping Judaism of all that made it alien, including the concept of peoplehood, and dismissing the belief that "Israel and its Torah are one."

The Drift toward Change

American conditions made the practice of traditional Judaism if not impossible, then certainly difficult. In the relatively homogeneous communities of Europe, a single rite prevailed, but in the "melting pot" of the nineteenth century, American Jews divided along national or ethnic lines, which in turn led to the splintering of communities, and making the term "Jewish unity" an oxymoron. While the most common split occurred along the lines of *minhag Ashkenaz* (the German rite) and *minhag Polin* (the Polish rite), Jews from Bohemia, Lithuania, Russia, and various other geographic subdivisions felt most comfortable praying with their own. As soon as enough of their landsmen settled in a particular city, they coalesced into a khevre that eventually transformed itself into full congregational form.[11]

Rabbinic authority, so central to traditional Judaism, could not be maintained in America either. Institutional conflicts between rabbis and their congregations ran rife through the communities. Squabbles over ritual and fights over petty insults and questionable behavior in almost every congregation pitted the previously privileged rabbis against the now empowered American laymen. Since in America the congregations came first, created from the grass roots, dues-paying members treated congregations as their domain. To the congregation, the rabbi was an employee with a contract, serving at the pleasure of the board (parnasim). The rabbis, trained to believe in the principle of *mare d'atra*, that authority rested with the rabbi of the place, engaged in endless arguments, disputes, and even occasionally physical confrontations. Rabbis, many of whom actually did not have formal ordination, went from congregation to congregation, city to city, and disputes between them and the laity erupted everywhere.[12]

In addition, the balance of religious power between Jewish men and women shifted a bit under the pressure of new conditions in America. While membership in the synagogues was limited to men, who alone could be rabbis and participants in congregational ritual, women earned new roles in public Judaism in a particularly American way. Although they did not have voting rights in the synagogue and had to be expressly invited to attend congregational events, they involved themselves in the congregation's life.[13] Women seem to have attended the synagogue more often than they did in Europe, and their physical presence, usually in a special women's section, invited comment by rabbis. Mothers commonly brought their children to Sabbath services. David Philipson, writing about his childhood in Sandusky, Ohio, in the 1860s, recalled that "on the Sabbath morning the boy [himself] attended divine service with the mother, as he had done for years."[14] Women in America also played a major role in congregational finances. In numerous cities, the funding for the synagogue building came from women's pockets directly or from women's fund-raising efforts. For example, the women who belonged to Baton Rouge's Ladies' Hebrew Association recognized that although they did not belong to the "Gent's Congregation," they had raised the money and could dictate the terms on which it would be spent. Within the synagogues, the *k'lay kodesh,* the holy objects—Torah covers, binders, curtains—were either made by the wives of members or purchased with money the women raised.[15]

Jewish women in America asserted themselves within their communities and congregations in ways that departed from traditional practices, although they did not necessarily do so in order to further reform. In many congregations, women wrestled control of the female auxiliary, the ladies' benevolent associations, from the male leadership by the 1860s and 1870s. These associations had begun with men as the leaders and women as the members, but in synagogues across the country, women came to be comfortable with power and asserted their right to direct their own organizations without male assistance.[16] As founders of schools, particularly in the early stages of community formation, and as teachers, women helped shape an American Jewish culture that balanced change with tradition. Innovations in education, such as the creation of the Jewish Sunday school, came from women who sought to preserve, through new kinds of schools, traditional piety. Women wrote much of the popular, religiously oriented fiction of the nineteenth century geared toward the preservation of Judaism and set in sentimental devotional terms. Appearing in such Orthodox-oriented newspapers as the *Occident* and *Jewish Messenger,* women's fiction stressed their role as the anchors of traditionalism.[17]

One benchmark on the journey to the creation of a modernized American Judaism can certainly be seen in the issue of mixed seating. Importantly, women participated little in the debate over where they should sit in the synagogue, and the arguments either for or against came from men. While the issue of who sat where in the synagogue raised a mighty polemical storm in rabbinic circles, caused congregational secessions, and provided the basis for a number of court battles as well, women themselves contributed little to the debate. Isaac Wise actually remarked that the girls at Beth El in Albany balked when he suggested mixed seating and "objected strenuously to sitting among the men."[18]

The drift toward Reform seemed inexorable. From the vantage point of the traditionalists, American Jews were rushing mindlessly into the arms of Reform, which, to them, deviated from Judaism, constituting a new religion that threatened the unity of the Jewish people. As of 1880, only a handful of congregations, Baltimore's Har Sinai, New York's Emanu-El, and Chicago's Sinai Congregation, had been founded as expressly Reform temples. The scores of congregations that evolved into Reform had been founded as traditional institutions. According to the more pious, their members had abandoned the faith of their fathers out of convenience and lusting after American ways. The rhetoric of Orthodox rabbis, such as

Baltimore's Abraham Rice, gloomily predicted the demise of Judaism in the United States and stressed the absolute incompatibility of the faith of Israel with the spirit of America. Writing back to Europe, Rabbi Bernard Illowy described America as[19]

> an unclean land, a land that devoureth its inhabitants, whose people, being blind, are to be considered dead, as . . . the sun of wisdom shines not upon them, many are ignorant, yet all are wise and intelligent in their own eyes, though they know not the law.

Ironically, many traditionalists among the American Jewish clergy themselves picked up on innovation and tinkered a bit with the service and tacitly admitted that in America, Judaism could not remain unchanged. Isaac Leeser, the *hazan* (cantor) of Philadelphia's Mikveh Israel, was a staunch defender of tradition but recognized the need to respond to American conditions. While he emerged as the major opponent to Reform on a national level, using his newspaper, the *Occident,* to attack tampering with tradition, at Mikveh Israel, he, too, innovated. For example, instead of facing the ark of the Torah, Leeser turned around and, like a Protestant clergyman, prayed facing the congregation. He advocated catechism for children, weekly sermons, and translations of the prayer book, the Bible, and other texts into English. He encouraged the efforts of women in Philadelphia and elsewhere to set up Jewish Sunday schools, again breaking with the past. Like the Reformers he decried, Leeser looked more often to the Bible than the Talmud to justify his actions, and he enthusiastically embraced American culture, hoping to link it to traditional Judaism.[20] Similarly "orthodox" rabbis, such as Bernard Illowy, who at various times served New York's Shaarey Zedek, Philadelphia's Rodeph Shalom, as well as congregations in St. Louis, Cincinnati, Baltimore, and New Orleans, ranked themselves among America's most traditional but sanctioned the confirmation ceremony.[21] In the 1870s, congregations that had described themselves as traditional also began to alter the traditional format. A group of prosperous Orthodox Jews founded Congregation Hand-in-Hand in New York's Harlem in 1873, and had no problem reconciling their statements of traditionalism with mixed seating.[22]

Over the course of the 1860s and 1870s, one congregation after another either adopted Wise's *Minhag America* as its text or joined the Union of American Hebrew Congregations after its founding in 1873. By 1880, the majority of American Jews who belonged to synagogues allied themselves with Reform. In small towns that could support only one synagogue, *Minhag America* seems to have been the most popular prayer book; its title, which juxtaposed the Hebrew word for custom with a bold proclamation of its placement in America, may help explain its appeal.[23]

Historians have agreed with the traditionalists' lament that normative Judaism was on the way out in nineteenth-century America. The thrust of the scholarship has documented the lives of Reform rabbis, the rise of Reform congregations, and Reform's institutional triumphs. In part, the scholarship has reflected the novelty of insurgent Reform and the absence of traditionalist institution building before the 1880s. But in most large American cities, individual synagogues were created as traditional secessions from reforming parent bodies. Adas Israel, for example, split from the Washington Hebrew Congregation in 1876, and traditionalists in Baltimore founded Chizuk Amuno in 1870 as a rejection of innovations at the Baltimore Hebrew Congregation. Actions of traditionalists were dwarfed, according to historians, by the organizing zeal of the Reformers on both the congregational and national level.[24]

Balancing Acts

Nineteenth-century traditionalists understood that Reform appealed to American Jews because they wanted to blend in and shed the appearance of foreignness and distinctiveness. They believed, however, that neither ordinary Jews nor modern rabbis had the right to reshape normative Judaism in a new mold. They viewed all alterations, additions, and excisions as throwing out the inheritance of the past for convenience's sake. They interpreted Reform as a rejection of tradition and predicted a quick demise of Judaism in America.

They failed to see that American Jews were looking for ways to be both Jewish *and* American. American Jews sought to create new traditions that would harmonize Judaism and modern American life. Reform Jews built lofty temples that invested Judaism with all the trappings befitting a dignified American religion. Yet, at the same time, they drew attention to their distinctiveness. They etched visible Jewish symbols on walls and windows—stars of David, the Ten Commandments, Hebrew letters—announcing to anyone who passed by that this was not a church but the house of worship of a distinct people with its own language and iconography.[25] Even when the chiselled letters on the synagogue were in English, they connected the building not just to the Jewish religion but to the Jewish people. Thus Cincinnati's Congregation B'nei Israel, dedicated in 1852, stated on its front in both English and Hebrew that "Ye shall make Me a sanctuary that I may dwell in the midst of Bnei Israel, nor will I ever forsake My people Israel, said the Lord."[26] The Reform congregations were particularly enamored with oriental architectural motifs, symbolized by the Moorish style (sometimes called Byzantine or Saracen). Few other American buildings of the middle and late nineteenth century were built this way, and certainly no churches were bedecked with the minarets, lacework, and other design elements redolent of the East. If Reform Jews wanted to emulate Protestantism, they could have found a more appropriate design for their synagogues than this one, which linked the Jewish people to their Levantine roots (and which was all the rage among the Jews of European cities) rather than to their American neighbors.[27]

Reform advocates felt a sense of urgency that, without change, Judaism would die in America. Reformers, like the traditionalists, feared that America's openness would erode Jewish culture. They, too, lamented the decline in personal observance of tradition and took this to be a sign of the crumbling of the centuries-old distinctiveness of the Jews. Wise, for example, noted that before the advent of Reform, "many Portuguese [Jewish] families died out, others amalgamated with their Christian neighbors, and again others forgot entirely all about Judaism. Hence it appears that their . . . orthodoxy was inefficient to preserve Judaism with . . . vitality."[28] The two camps differed, however, on the question of how to inspire greater observance of tradition and on the degree of flexibility allowed the Jews in religious practice. They clashed over who had the right to determine the contours of compliance, with the Orthodox side asserting that rabbinic law, the Talmud and its commentaries, had been fixed and could not be tampered with, while the Reformers considered the process to be evolutionary, in which rabbis of the nineteenth century had as much right to determine its nature as rabbis of centuries past.

To Live as a Jew

American conditions made the observance of traditional practice difficult although not impossible. Provisions for kosher slaughtering, the maintenance of a *mikvah,* the ritual bath in which married women had to immerse themselves after their menstrual period, the annual need for Passover matzo, which had to be baked under highly supervised conditions, all posed problems for the new communities both in their formative years and in subsequent decades. Although rabbis and others lamented the falling away from the strict practice of kashrut, *niddah* (laws governing sexual relations within marriage), and other elements of halakah, in fact, American Jews went to considerable lengths to make observance possible.

That Jews created and sustained benevolent associations, cemeteries, schools, and congregations, attested to the desire of average women and men to live as Jews. In most places, the idea to form a Jewish "association" came from the bottom up; and long before any rabbis arrived on the scene, lay people tried to provide for their own needs. Jewish religious life began with the first burial and with improvised services in the back of a store, in someone's home, and sometimes even above a saloon, as in Appleton, Wisconsin, in the 1860s.[29]

The constant arrival of Jewish newcomers kept religious institution-building alive. From the 1850s on, a steady stream of newcomers from the various regions of Poland, Lithuania, and western Russia formed traditional khevrot and small *anshes* (people of) in New York, Chicago, Detroit, Syracuse, Omaha, Providence, and elsewhere. They banded together into minyanim (prayer quorums), study groups, benevolent associations, and landsmanshaftn to pray with their fellows in a traditional manner, recreate, and receive mutual aid. These newcomers entered into established Jewish communities but created their own, familiar houses of worship and stimulated the observance of traditional practices.[30]

Jews without any formal training in ritual matters attempted to fulfill as many communal requirements as they could. Often, for example, in accordance with Jewish tradition, marriages were solemnized by laymen, who also officiated at funerals. Individuals with just a little bit more learning than the mass stepped in to serve as preachers of sermons, readers of the Torah scroll, or leaders of worship services. In the 1860s, one Hyman Goldberg, an immigrant from Russian Poland, served as *m'sader kiddushin* (the arranger of nuptials) throughout California, as did Simon Jackson, Jacob Rich, Mark Israel Jacobs, and Joseph Newman. These businessmen had just enough Jewish knowledge from Europe to conduct such rites.[31] Throughout the United States, lay people initiated Jewish worship and filled the roles that in Europe and later in America professionals would handle. Adolph Ochs's father, Julius, served as a surrogate rabbi in Knoxville, Tennessee, after the Civil War; Bernard Nordlinger, a peddler from

Alsace, impressed the Jews in Macon, Georgia, with his Jewish knowledge. They asked him to stay on as a "rabbi." Neither man had any kind of ordination or extensive education.[32]

Even some of those who eventually became full-time rabbis, indeed even some major players in the religious debates of the period, had no formal rabbinic training. Bernhard Felsenthal, for example, had been a teacher in Bavaria. When he came to America in 1854, he settled in Indiana and again taught in a Jewish school, did some private tutoring, and contributed to various Jewish periodicals. According to his daughter, he got involved in the local congregation, and "towards the end of that time [began] performing some of the functions of rabbi, though it is clear that he did not then nor for some years after think of himself as a rabbi or even as one looking forward to a rabbinical career." Felsenthal moved to Chicago, where he worked as a bank clerk. But when he and other members of Congregation K.A.M. seceded to form a Reform *verein,* which became Sinai Congregation, he was asked to become rabbi in 1861. Indeed, some of Wise's rabbinic rivals expressed doubts concerning his claim to the rabbinate. But his congregants, readers of the *Israelite* and *Die Deborah,* seemed not to care. In America, the laity made the clergy, and not ordination conferred by other rabbis.[33]

Whatever the title or learning of their leaders, Jews in America sought to build communities and have in their midst individuals who could help them fulfill requirements of Jewish life. That communities in their early stages considered it enough to have a factotum, a Jew who could teach, circumcise, chant, and slaughter, attested not only to the primitive level of communal life but also to the fact that nonrabbis among the immigrants brought with them Judaic knowledge and ritual skills. Individuals such as Joseph Raphael Spiro in Providence, Rhode Island, in the 1850s—one of hundreds of his kind—did not hold themselves up as more pious, learned, or invested with more authority than any other Jew. This combined *shokhet-mohel-hazan-ba'al koreh* commonly held down some other kind of job and lived in the community among his peers. Ritual matters were decided, it seems, informally by all members of the Jewish association or congregation, and a kind of democracy by default characterized this leaderless stage in American Jewish community development.[34]

These efforts, chronicled in hundreds of community histories and synagogue annals, indicate that by moving to America, Jews had not removed themselves from the corpus of Jewish law or the context of Jewish life. They hoped to live as Jews, and the evidence on burial practices indicates that they intended to die as Jews. They also hoped to bring up their children as Jews.

No element demonstrated Jewish commitment to tradition more boldly than their retention of *milah,* the circumcision of infant sons. Itinerant *mohelim,* or circumcisers, ushered baby boys into the covenant of Abraham all over America, just as they would have, had they lived in Europe.[35] In upstate New York, in the Rocky Mountain West, or in the deep South, these functionaries linked dispersed Jewish communities and attested to this tradition's persistence. Circumcisers traveled hundreds of miles to attend to the ritual. Parents considered the ceremony a crucial, unalterable part of their lives.

Vast distances, primitive communication networks, and poor transportation made it difficult for circumcisions to take place always on the eighth day after birth as mandated by tradition. Therefore, communities with a number of Jewish families advertised in the Jewish press for mohelim, hoping to find someone who could also slaughter meat, read Torah, teach children, and sound the *shofar* (ram's horn) on the high holy days.

Certainly, changes took place in the setting for the *b'rit*. One observer, an anonymous traveler from Germany in the 1850s, noted that "under the impact of English-American prudery," circumcisions in America were done at home rather than in the synagogue, as had been common in Europe. But no matter *where* it took place, the widespread practice of this rite, with no American or Christian equivalent, indicated that Jews who moved to America did not reject the "covenant."[36]

The practice of kashrut, while not as universal as circumcision, continued as well. Fewer American Jews steadfastly clung to elaborate dietary prohibitions than did their kin in Europe; a vast range of contemporary documents bear witness to kashrut's erosion in America.[37] Clearly, keeping kosher in America posed problems. Few individuals trained in *shekhita* (ritual slaughtering) migrated to America, and the Jews scattered to hundreds of towns across tremendous distances lived where no provisions for kashrut existed. Furthermore, the absence of legally sanctioned authority to supervise and enforce the elaborate process of preparing kosher meat left American Jews concerned about kashrut vulnerable to butchers of dubious honesty who claimed that the meat they sold was ritually acceptable. In Jewish communities without rabbis, the shokhet had to be responsible to the lay people not knowledgeable of rabbinic law. Frequent charges, countercharges, and suits over the provisioning of "kosher" meat may have discouraged some American Jews from observing the dietary restrictions. American Jewish memoirs and autobiographies made ample reference to eating all kinds of food, regardless of its kashrut.[38]

The poor were particularly hampered, since the cost of kosher meat put a burden on their meager budgets, while the affluent and those with extensive ties to American society may have found the inability to sit down and eat a meal with non-Jews a social and business liability. The appearance in 1871 of a kosher cookbook, Esther Levy's *Jewish Cookery Book,* was intended to prove to the "Jewish public," to "our sisters in faith," that "without violating the precepts of our religion, a table can be spread, which will satisfy the appetites of the most fastidious." The book targeted a comfortable audience, for example, households that employed domestic servants. Levy pitched her argument to her readers in culinary rather than halakic terms. Jewish women, she argued, should consider keeping kosher. "Some have," Levy said, "from ignorance, been led to believe that a repast, to be temptuous, must unavoidably admit of forbidden food." She presented recipes that would "show how various and how grateful to the taste are the viands of which we may legally partake."[39]

Some Jews, who could not easily get kosher meat or who did not observe all the multifarious restrictions, still refrained from eating pork. Marcus Spiegel, an immigrant from Bavaria, active in the early Jewish community of Chicago, wrote in his letters home from Civil War military service that he would eat just about anything except pork. Aaron Haas of Atlanta remembered that in the 1850s, "it was impossible to keep a kosher table, [but] there was never a piece of hog in my father's house, nor was milk or butter on the table with meat." On the other hand, a Mrs. Ullman in St. Paul, Minnesota, tried to observe the dietary restrictions all year long, but during the harsh Minnesota winters she consumed bacon.[40] Scattered evidence from studies of very small Jewish communities suggests that Jews who did not observe kashrut all year made strenuous efforts to do so during Passover, along with the eating of matzo. Thus, the miniscule Jewish enclave in Nevada City, Nevada, in the 1850s, brought in a shokhet from San Francisco before the spring holiday.[41]

American kashrut existed along a continuum, and individual women, as managers of their kitchens, picked and chose from the complex set of requirements and restrictions. Bernard Drachman, remembering his youth in Jersey City in the 1870s, claimed that his Bavarian-born mother kept a kosher home, but did not "conform in every way to the precepts of Orthodox Judaism" at her table.[42] How widespread were such attempts at quasi kashrut? Although a definitive answer is impossible, the few references to everyday practice indicate that the move from strictly traditional eating to all-American dietary habits probably did not proceed in a unilinear way.

Yet, one community after another supported a *shokhet* (a ritual slaughterer), and Jews in small towns commonly sought one. Early in the history of many Jewish communities, benevolent associations placed advertisements in Jewish newspapers offering employment to a Jewish "jack-of-all-trades," a combination shokhet, mohel, cantor, and teacher. When hired, this individual often represented the first Jewish functionary in the town.[43] In the absence of a central community board, individual congregations throughout this half-century hired their own slaughterers of meat. In Buffalo, Baltimore, Columbus, New York, Philadelphia, Chicago, Milwaukee, Washington, D.C., Omaha, and, indeed, just about everywhere, some Jews deemed the observance of the commandments of kashrut worth the expenditure of communal funds. On just one day, September 15, 1865, seven congregations in such disparate places as California, Kentucky, Alabama, Illinois, Ohio, and Louisiana placed notices in the *American Israelite* for shokhetim. Indeed, between 1823 and 1880, almost one hundred cities and towns either supported a shokhet or advertised to find one. Congregation B'nai B'rith in Los Angeles, for example, employed a slaughterer as early as 1861, while such small towns as Elmira, New York, Akron, Ohio, Fort Wayne, Indiana, or Portland, Maine, supported a resident shokhet, although not always continuously. An itinerant rabbi in the late 1870s claimed that a hotel in Selma, Alabama, maintained a kosher dining room;[44] and Jewish orphanages and hospitals provided kosher meat to inmates. [45]

Rabbis, congregational officers, and slaughterers frequently bickered with one another. The slaughterers and butchers were frequently accused of selling unkosher meat. Charges and countercharges were aired volubly in public and sometimes ended up in American courts. These controversies indicate that at all times some Jews in Portland, Oregon, Omaha, San Francisco, Savannah, Buffalo, Baltimore, and New York cared deeply about the traditional dictates as to what a Jew could and could not eat.[46]

A number of congregations employing a slaughterer argued with him over the carefulness of his work even after they had clearly moved to Reform. Well after the leaders of the Akron Hebrew Association made the wearing of head coverings for men optional during services, after they instituted confirmations, and, indeed, after they adopted the Reform prayer book *Minhag America,* they still argued with their shokhet over his meticulousness. B'nai Israel in Columbus, Ohio, belonged to the Reform alliance, the Union of American Hebrew Congregations (UAHC), but continued to employ a ritual slaughterer, and Adath Joseph in St. Joseph, Missouri, also kept a shokhet on its payroll until 1885, long after it had joined the UAHC. At Lancaster's Shaarey Shomayim, men prayed without prayer shawls in 1867, and the sounds of an organ resounded in the synagogue the following year. But as late as 1877, the congregation still paid a shokhet.[47]

There is also evidence that individual Jews persisted in their efforts to maintain dietary tradition despite many obstacles. Remembering his youth in Illinois and San Francisco in the 1860s and 1870s, Sol Bloom insisted: "I am sure that until I was at least twelve or thirteen I never knowingly ate a mouthful of food that was not kosher." Even on a long train trip from the Midwest to California, he and his family eschewed any unsanctioned food.[48] In incipient Jewish settlements, before a "community" took shape, families observed kashrut. Jacob Klein, for example, came to Omaha in 1873 and, together with three other Hungarian families, hired his own slaughterer; before 1820, Isaac Polok, the first Jew to live in the nation's capital, employed Raphael Jones to provide his household with kosher meat. Samuel Adler married Sarah Sulzberger in the 1850s and moved to Van Buren, Arkansas. Before they left, Sarah's father, Leopold, taught his new son-in-law the craft of *shekhita,* so that they could make a kosher home where no Jewish community existed. An extended family of Weils from Bohumelitz in Bohemia moved to Ann Arbor, Michigan, over the course of the 1840s and 1850s. As the only Jews there, they slaughtered meat for themselves and for the Jewish peddlers who hawked goods through the state. According to the *Helena Daily Independent,* a Mrs. Sabolsky, who with her husband opened a store in the Montana town in the 1870s, was "probably the most orthodox Jew in the state. . . . So rigid was her observance that she might be said to have been a vegetarian. . . . At times there would be killed for her a chicken according to the rules of her religion, and that was the extent of her meat eating."[49]

What about Sabbath observance? If the rabbis of the time are to be believed, most American Jews viewed Saturday as a day to make money rather than refrain from workaday pursuits. Both Reform and traditional rabbis railed at their congregants for neglecting their religious obligations in favor of keeping open their stores.[50] David Einhorn of Baltimore's extreme Reform Har Sinai tried to induce his members to close their businesses on

Saturdays, as did traditionalist Bernard Illowy. The son of Rabbi Gustave Gottheil of New York's Emanu-El noted that on the Sabbath, "we walked there [to synagogue] and we walked back, as riding on Saturday was not considered good form even for the Minister of a Reform congregation."

In the 1820s and 1830s, congregations attempted to fine Sabbath violaters but over time dropped such punishments. Instead, their bylaws stipulated that ritual honors during the service and positions on congregational boards would be limited to those who closed their shops on the Sabbath. As of 1847, Louisville's Adath Israel adopted rules that withheld the honor of reading the Torah or sounding the shofar from those who violated either the Sabbath or the code of dietary restrictions. The effect of such measures is not clear.

Such innovations as upgrading the Friday night service and the more revolutionary Reform experiments making the Sunday morning service the showcase of the Jewish ritual week involved as much a frustration with congregants' disregard for the Sabbath as a desire to mesh with American Christian rhythms.[51]

Rabbis had a particular stake in increasing Sabbath observance. If their members worked on the seventh day, who then would sit in expensive, newly constructed synagogues, participate in dignified services, and hear lofty sermons? One of the justifications for Reform was that American Jews, young ones in particular, found the traditional service alien and odious, and that unless worship became an aesthetically and spiritually meaningful experience, they would drift away from Judaism in disgust.

Therefore, the paltry crowds that came to Reform temples on Saturdays must have been particularly disheartening. Additionally, the few faces that the rabbis saw from the pulpit were increasingly female. In 1877, for example, Wise reported on his journey to the West Coast. In Sacramento, he noted, "the service is orthodox. *Minhag Polen.* I went to the synagogue Sabbath morning, and found besides the Vice-President . . . who took the place of the absent Hazan, nine more men, five boys (three of them mourners) and one lady. I was told here that all over California this is the case." Wise also noted that "as a general thing the ladies [in California] must maintain Judaism. They are three-fourths of the congregations in the temple every Sabbath and send their children to the Sabbath schools. With a very few exceptions, the men keep no Sabbath." Solomon Schindler of Boston sneered that Jewish men went off to the lodges and left wives to go to the synagogue. Sarah Kussy, writing of her girlhood in Newark in the 1860s, remembered that "Father, while not as deeply pious as mother, was nonetheless ardently Jewish. During his early married life he had kept his shop closed on the Sabbath. As the growing neighborhood brought with it increasing business competition, he yielded to the pressure of circumstances and kept it open."[52]

Still, Sabbath observance was not an all-or-nothing proposition, and American Jews observed it in varying degrees. While it is hardly noteworthy that rigid traditionalists, such as Abraham Rice in Baltimore or Judah David Eisenstein in New York, marked off the Sabbath in a punctilious and uncompromising way, others did so, too. Adolphus Solomons, a printer and stationer in Washington, D.C., in the 1860s and 1870s, a figure of note in District of Columbia politics, refused President Ulysses Grant's offer of appointment to a local post because he could not work on Saturday. The Greenbaum family, leaders in Chicago's Reform community, employed a "*Shabbos goya*," a Christian woman, to light the fire and perform other domestic tasks forbidden to Jews on Saturdays. Financier Jacob Schiff, who belonged to New York's Emanu-El, the apogee of Reform, described himself as "inclined by principle to devout observance" and refrained from working on the Sabbath. The Gerstley family spent every Saturday morning at Chicago's K.A.M. congregation despite—as the daughter recollected— long and incomprehensible German sermons. Victoria Jacobs and her household in San Diego in the 1850s were ever mindful of the "day of rest." The young girl's diary alluded weekly to Shabbat, both in terms of Fridays, when she, her mother, and the other women were always "busy cleaning for Sabbath," and Saturdays, when family and friends got together in pleasure, eschewing work, refusing to ride in carriages, and, in general, taking into account the various restrictions of the day.[53]

Jewish newspapers reported some darkened and shuttered Jewish businesses on random Saturdays. The *Jewish Messenger,* a traditionalist newspaper published in New York, glowed with pride as it reported that as far away as Stillwater, Minnesota, the shopkeepers, Levy and Daniels, hung in their store window a prominent sign, reading: "No business transacted from Friday Evening at Sunset till Saturday at dusk." Similarly, a Jewish merchant in New Brunswick, New Jersey, stated boldly in the city directory that "this store is closed from Friday evening to Saturday evening, at half past seven."[54]

And as with kashrut, keeping the Sabbath may have occurred along a continuum of behavior. Although traditionalists saw Sabbath observance as an all-or-nothing proposition, ordinary American Jews probably picked and chose from among the restrictions and rituals. Merchants, for example, occasionally opened their stores Saturday afternoon so that they could first attend Sabbath services in the morning. B'nai B'rith lodges scheduled balls for Friday nights, thus violating halakah, but bringing members to a social event with other Jews on the Sabbath. While Sarah Kussy's father did sell goods and handle money on Saturday, he "never failed on Friday night and Saturday noon to bless his children, chant the *kiddush* [benediction over the wine], *bentsh mezumen* [say Grace after meals in unison], sing psalm 144 Saturday at dusk, and make *havdole* [a ceremony to mark the end of the Sabbath and the beginning of the new week]."55

If the Fourth Commandment dictated that Jews "remember the Sabbath day and keep it holy" and tradition spelled out what Jews could and could not eat, it also enjoined them to "teach diligently" their children the basics of Judaism. Again, American conditions made full compliance difficult, and although the European patterns could not persist, many Jews found ways to fulfill this obligation.

Both Reformers and traditionalists agreed that American Jewish children lacked solid Jewish education, and that the obligation to provide it fell on parents and, ultimately, on the community. They disagreed, however, as to what constituted an adequate education. David Einhorn, a firm believer in the uplifting power of German, thought that through that language, Bildung would take place. Wise, a firm advocate of Hebrew, insisted on Hebraic instruction. In addition, Leeser and others on the Orthodox end tended to favor all-day schools as the best way to educate Jewish children, while Wise endorsed American public schooling for secular studies and advocated supplemental, afternoon Jewish institutions.56

Whatever their ideal of education, rabbis of these years painted a bleak picture. Parents, they said, were neglecting the Jewish education of their children, a harbinger of bad times ahead for Judaism in America. American Jews, wrote Wise, "have no solid basis, no particular stimulus to urge on the youth to a religious life." Wise predicted imminent doom for that life and urged that "if we do not stimulate all the congregations to establish good schools . . . the house of the Lord will be desolate or nearly so in less than ten years." Leeser, Wise's traditionalist rival, worried that without religious education, children would lose a sense of Jewish peoplehood. He argued for Jewish day schools because "a community of education will excite a community of feeling."57 In America, the rabbis asserted, Jewish children needed to be fortified with Jewish knowledge to ward off the Christian evangelicals. Throughout the country, they decried the sorry state of Jewish learning for the young and believed this caused adult indifference.

Historians have accepted this diagnosis of the low state of Jewish education in the nineteenth century. They have taken it as a symptom of the general lack of regard for traditional practice and of the meager Jewish learning that the immigrants had brought with them from "Germany."[58]

Once again, rabbis, and subsequent historians who have relied upon them as sources, failed to see important American developments. First, a great deal of borrowing from American education took place, indicating that Jews cared enough about the issues to survey the American scene for appropriate models for educating their children. In Europe, children did not learn from specially written texts but began their studies in the original sources and at a very young age plunged into Torah, Talmud, and Hebrew commentary.[59] In America, special educational materials were published for Jewish children. Isaac Leeser's *Catechism,* Simha Peixotto's *Elementary Introduction to the Scriptures for the Use of Hebrew Children,* and other books, pamphlets, and magazines, such as Max Lilienthal's *Sabbath Visitor,* aimed at Jewish youth, conformed to modern pedagogic ideas that children needed a differentiated approach. Unlike traditional Jewish education, this approach was based on the notion that children were not adults and had to be taught through specially crafted media.[60]

European Jewish communities provided much more in the way of formal education but only for boys. Mid-nineteenth-century America offered equal levels of public education for girls, and the various Jewish schools in America, whether communal, congregational, or private, soon followed. Although girls in some cases sat in separate classes in America, they learned the basics of Judaism the same way their brothers did.[61]

In America, parents and lay people played a major role in establishing and maintaining Jewish schools. Special parent committees hired teachers, determined curricula, and observed classrooms. Indeed, the very idea to open a school, whatever its format or structure, originated more often with parents than rabbis. At Cincinnati's Talmud Yelodim Institute, for example, lay people controlled the school, and the congregational board could hire and fire teachers.[62] Even community-based schools, such as New York's Hebrew Free School, which opened its doors in 1864 in response to the prowling missionaries on the East Side, owed its founding to laity.[63]

The Jewish press published a multitude of advertisements placed by small Jewish communities seeking teachers who could also perform other functions.[64] Indeed, in hinterland Jewish communities, some mechanism for educating children preceded, or occurred simultaneously with, the formation of a congregation and happened well before the first rabbi appeared. Community histories and histories of Jewish education of this period make frequent reference to the widespread use of private Judaic tutors.

Two Jewish women in Atlanta began teaching children in their home more than a decade before men banded together into a formal congregation. In Petersburg, Virginia, the school followed the congregation by just one year. Jews in Ft. Wayne, Indiana, founded their Congregation Achdut Vesholom in 1848 and in the same year added a school. Some twelve years later, thirty-four students, both boys and girls, attended the school fifteen hours a week. Even in remote Woodland, California, Jews maintained a school that in 1879 enrolled thirty children. Wise, a constant critic of American Jewish education, wrote in amazement at the Hebrew proficiency and knowledge of "biblical history and catechism" of the boys and girls in Calvert, Texas, in 1880, and marveled at the skill with which "they translated so readily" from the Hebrew.[65]

In Philadelphia, Richmond, Charleston, New York, Atlanta, and elsewhere, Jewish women organized schools in a grass-roots, improvised manner. Rebecca Gratz had no Jewish precedent for the opening of her Jewish Sunday school in Philadelphia in 1838. In Europe, teaching was the domain of men. But Gratz, Rachel Cohen-Peixotto, and the other "ladies" who helped found the school, open to "all who are hungry for the bread of life" and "not limited to any member [of Congregation Mikve Israel] or class of children," believed that they had both a right and a responsibility to pass on Jewish learning. Gratz was not influenced or supported by the developing Reform tendency; she and the like-minded women of Charleston's Beth Elohim Congregation who began a Sunday school in 1844 represented traditional forces within the community. Despite the Sunday School's unconventionality in *form* and its obvious adaptation of the Christian Sunday school model, it grew out of a traditionalist impulse.[66]

However effective or ineffective the schools may have been, however much or little substantive Jewish learning was transmitted, Jewish women and men who migrated to America and then moved around within the vast country did not link their migrations with the abandonment of the obligation of "teaching diligently." Lay efforts in Jewish education combined the desire to maintain Judaism with innovations stimulated by the American environment. Both motivations underlay the efforts of Jewish women and men as they created new kinds of schools in order to preserve Jewish identity and literacy.

Some elements of the 613 mitzvot, the corpus of commandments, were much more private in nature than Sabbath observance, retention of kashrut, or Jewish education, and their historical patterns are more difficult to measure and analyze. Probably no aspect of personal religious practice was as intimate as the commandments of family purity—those regulations regarding marital relations and the obligation of married women to immerse themselves in the mikvah after the completion of their menstrual period. Frank discussions of sexuality and female body functions of traditional Judaism jarred with nineteenth-century American standards of appropriate topics for refined public discourse. This dissonance between the Jewish and the American tradition may explain, for example, why women's writings of this period, including letters, memoirs, and novels, mutely refused to comment on this practice. Minutes of the congregations' meetings in one community after another only sporadically refers to the construction and maintenance or to a controversy over the supervision of the ritual bath. While traditionalists denounced American Jewish women for their failure to fulfill the mitzvah of niddah (ritual impurity), noting that "the daughters of Israel were estranged and their children born of the ritually unclean," the frequency with which congregations built and maintained such facilities indicates something else. Well into the 1870s, congregations, including many reformed ones, constructed mikvaot for the wives of their members, and possibly for other, more traditional Jewish women in the community. The benevolent society, the khevre, often provided for this need.[67] In 1857, San Francisco's *Weekly Gleaner* announced that "the managers of the Hebra Shomre Shabbat hereby give notice to the scrupulous Israelites that a proper Mikweh is now constructed at the Bath Establishment of Dr. Brun, North Beach. Those whom such an arrangement interests may avail themselves of it. 'Mikwe is die erste von de drei mitzwoth vat belongt zu die Weiber. [Mikvah is the first of the three commandments for women—expressed here in combined Yiddish, German, and English]'."[68] From the 1830s through the 1870s, some Jews in New York, Philadelphia, Hartford, Baltimore, Buffalo, Providence, Easton, Pennsylvania, Louisville, Chicago, Cleveland, and, most likely, elsewhere as well seemed to have followed this ritual practice.[69]

The nearly universal public celebration of certain Jewish holidays also suggests that Jews preserved tradition in an American format and willingly stood out as different from their American neighbors. During the fall holidays of Rosh Hashanah and Yom Kippur, the New Year and Day of Atonement, almost all Jews closed their stores. Men and women who otherwise observed few or no elements of the tradition came to the synagogue. American newspapers commented annually on the visible store closings and, in smaller communities, remarked how the Jewish holidays had brought about a virtual standstill in certain trades. Jews who spent the whole calendar year seemingly living like all other Americans, on these days, at least, demonstrated their distinctiveness. After all, Rosh Hashanah and Yom Kippur had no American or Christian equivalents, and these "days of awe" were precisely when Jews revealed their otherness.

In communities with no congregation, individual Jews banded together for the holidays into makeshift minyanim, prayer groups, in the back of stores, in lofts, or in their homes and either conducted services themselves or hired an itinerant prayer leader to lead services, read the Torah, and sound the ram's horn. A Jewish resident of Placerville, California, for example, described to the readers of the *American Israelite* how families in this mining town marked off the beginning of a new Jewish year in 1873. He wrote that "on Rosh Hashanah and Yom Kippur we manage to have services . . . conducted by some volunteer chasan [cantor] and reader from our midst. We have no preaching, yet have these exercises generally the effect of healing all dissensions that may have arisen through politics, for, in the matter of politics, our Jews are not so united."[70]

These festive days, replete with themes of reckoning and repentance, may have inspired recollections of the traditions of childhood or of pious European parents. The holidays may have provoked a desire, as the correspondent from Placerville noted, to assert the solidarity of all Jews in a context separate and distinct from Christians. In 1858, a layman delivered the Yom Kippur sermon in San Francisco and asserted that "it is a day on which even those of the faith who, throughout the year, are lax in their religious observances, feel it incumbent to join again with their brethren, and humble themselves with a contrite heart before the Almighty." Congregation Achdut Vesholom of Ft. Wayne, Indiana, moved to mixed male-female seating in 1862 and had adopted the radical *Olath Tamid* prayer book. But when Rosh Hashanah and Yom Kippur came around, men and women sat separately and traditional *mahzorim* (prayer books) came out of storage.[71]

Similarly on Passover, non-observant or minimally observant Jews again showed at least temporary concern for the details of halakah. Jews living in embryonic communities worried about how to secure enough matzo, and Jewish bakers in large cities, New York, Baltimore, San Francisco, and Cincinnati, distributed unleavened bread throughout their regional hinterlands. In the first year of Jewish life in Nashville, Cincinnati bakers began to ship matzo to the tiny enclave. Southern Jewish merchants on working trips to New York brought back matzo. A notice in 1869 in a San Francisco Jewish newspaper noted that one M. L. Caplan from Sitka, Alaska, had arranged for matzo to be sent to that remotest and perhaps coldest of Jewish settlements. Isaac and David Wallace of Statesville, North Carolina, removed all the breadstuff from their home for Passover. When, during the Civil War, a group of Union soldiers foraged on their property, they could find only the crisp, unleavened bread. "More hard tack," the disgusted Yankee soldiers were reported to have said.[72]

Communal celebration of the mid-winter festival of Purim, which also could not be linked to any American or Protestant holiday, was widespread. Typically, communities sponsored masked balls to support Jewish charities. In Baltimore in the 1860s, Jews invited non-Jews to the festivities, and a Purim Association coordinated the fun with the serious business of disbursing the money. Although it is hard to know how many of the revelers at the balls *also* fulfilled the obligation of listening to the reading of the scroll of Esther, the Purim ball phenomenon illustrates the ways in which Jews in America sought to keep some elements of tradition—in this case, Purim's public merriment and concern for the poor—in an American format.[73]

The continuity of Judaism in America, as elsewhere, required more than anything that Jews marry other Jews. How often did nineteenth-century American Jews marry outside the group? How did their patterns differ from those of their sisters and brothers who remained in Europe but migrated to Vienna, Berlin, Budapest, or Paris? In American intermarriages of the nineteenth century, did the non-Jewish partner become a Jew, or did the Jewish partner sever bonds with the Jewish community? Again, how did American trends differ from those in contemporary Europe? While the history of Jewish intermarriage and the communal fate of the intermarried in nineteenth-century Europe and America still awaits its scholar, scanty evidence seems to indicate that in Europe, intermarriage tended to accompany conversion to Christianity. Deborah Hertz and other historians asserted that Jewish women in cities such as Berlin were more likely than their brethren to choose a non-Jewish spouse. Those who married Christians gave up membership in the Jewish community as part of their marriage choice. Their decision to convert to Christianity seems not to have been based on changes in religious sensibilities; it often stood as a legal, if not practical, prerequisite for the marriage. Thus, to marry a non-Jew also meant becoming one.[74]

America saw a different pattern. Although the descendants of the earlier, Sephardic Jews did intermarry frequently, the post-1820 Jewish immigrants did not. Before the large-scale migrations, the paucity of potential Jewish mates tended to impel Jews into marriages with non-Jews. After the massive immigrations from Germany, Poland, Alsace, and elsewhere, Jewish men and women had ample opportunity to choose from among their people. Jews went to tremendous lengths to find Jewish spouses, including writing back to their European hometown, tapping friends and family for introductions to suitable partners, and even journeying across the ocean, which attests to the widespread desire of Jews to marry "according to the laws of Moses and the children of Israel."[75]

To be sure, in the years 1820–80, individual Jews, primarily men, married across religious lines, although no real numbers are available. One estimate for Los Angeles County for the years 1850–76, a place and time in which Jewish women were a scarce commodity, claimed that fewer than 25 percent of all Jews married non-Jews. A study of Portland, Oregon, during that same quarter century uncovered no such unions.[76] However, stories from the Southwest told of Jewish merchants married to Indian or Mexican women, while in New Orleans, Jewish men took French Catholic women into matrimony. Even Jewish women sometimes married out of the group, and of the five boys circumcised in Augusta, Georgia, in 1846, three had Jewish mothers and non-Jewish fathers.[77] Individual biographies contain scattered references to intermarriage, as, for example, Abraham Flexner's *I Remember;* he indicated that his deeply Orthodox mother did not mind that "two of her sons married Christian girls, who became not daughters-in-law, but daughters."[78]

Both traditional and Reform rabbis condemned intermarriage. Einhorn warned that "each intermarriage drives a nail in the coffin of Judaism," while Wise denounced any rabbi who would officiate at a mixed marriage. When Philadelphia's Samuel Hirsch decided to sanctify a marriage between a Jew and a non-Jew, his congregation balked and criticized the decision. Congregational bylaws usually denied rights of membership to those who married outside the community, and the khevre kaddisha refused burial rights to them. B'nai B'rith lodges debated over, and usually blackballed, applicants whose spouse was not Jewish by birth.

American Jewish novelists further presented sentimental literary portraits of the stresses and strains of immigrant life and often included a heartless son or daughter who broke their parents' heart by opting for love across religious lines.[79] Still, the number of personal narratives, family histories, and community studies containing details of intermarriage is vastly overshadowed by the number of reminiscences and recollections pointing to a fairly self-contained Jewish social life, which would have precluded the opportunity to meet and marry someone from another religious tradition.

In America, the non-Jewish spouse was usually a woman, since Jewish men did most, although not all, of the out-marrying. These women converted to Judaism with some frequency, and this was also a departure from the European pattern.[80] Whereas in Europe the marriage of a Jew to a Christian usually drew the Jew out of the kahal, the opposite seems to have happened in America. Conversions to Judaism must have been common enough for Einhorn to include in his prayer book, *Olath Tamid,* a ceremony on the acceptance of a convert into the congregation. In 1869, a Philadelphia conference of rabbis considered various issues involved in the process, such as whether a male convert had to undergo circumcision.[81]

Personal narratives confirm the impression that non-Jews who married Jews in America sometimes chose to become Jewish. Marcus Spiegel, for example, a Bavarian immigrant who peddled goods through the Ohio territory, met and fell in love with Caroline Hamlin. After the couple's August 1853 civil ceremony, they moved to Chicago where Spiegel's extended Jewish family made its home. Caroline undertook a study of Judaism, converted, and lived the rest of her life as a Jew. When Marcus went off to military service during the Civil War, he wrote back and reminded Caroline to keep the children home from school on Jewish holidays and get the house ready for Passover. Jacob Lemann, a Jewish merchant in Donaldsonville, Louisiana, brought his Catholic-born wife, Marie, to New York to be formally converted under the supervision of Rabbi Max Lilienthal. After she accepted the name "Miriam" and the burdens of the commandments, the couple went through a traditional Jewish wedding ceremony. In Santa Cruz, California, in 1877, Emma Schlutius submitted to an examination by an improvised *bet din* (rabbinical court), in this case a panel of three laymen, in order to be converted to Judaism. She chose the Jewish name of Esther and proceeded then to be joined in marriage to Abe Rotschild.[82]

Isaac Wolfe Bernheim who came to the United States from Baden in 1867 at the age of 19, went the typical route of Jewish male immigrants of these years and took up the peddler's pack.

The peddler depicted with hooked nose and stooped shoulders in the short story, "My Speculation in China Ware" fits the physical stereotype of the Jew prevalent in nineteenth-century caricature.

The challah cover (1852) of green brocade with red velvet uses the American eagle with thirteen stars as its central motif. The Hebrew above bears the name, probably of its owner, "Gedalia, the son of Shimon Halevi called Ullman." "Behold that the Lord has given you the Sabbath," is stitched underneath.

Talmud Yelodim, supported by wealthy members of the community, served the poor children of Cincinnati's Jewish community c. 1870.

ORIGIN OF THE RITES AND WORSHIP OF THE HEBREWS.

A richly detailed 112-page book by a cantor who served in Boston and San Francisco explains Judaism's symbols and rituals.

Title page of America's first book of Hebrew poetry, its first Yiddish book, *Shir Zahav L'chavod Yisrael Hazakane* (a song in honor of ancient Israel) by *maskil* Jacob Zevi Sobol (New York, 1877).

Masthead of *The Asmonean*, founded by English-born New York merchant Robert Lyon in 1849, showing an American flag and eagle along with a star of David. The Hebrew reads across the top and bottom, "Two are better than one" and "The triple thread will not be broken quickly."

Philadelphia artist, Joseph Abrahams, wove together Jewish, Masonic, and American themes in this *mizrach*, used to orient worshippers to the eastern wall of a home. The prominent Jewish images, the Torah scroll, the two tablets, the lions of Judah, and the Hebrew words are joined by the two Liberty figures, popular in 1876, the year of the nation's centennial. The tiled floor appeared often as a symbol of Masonry.

Important repositories of Jewish folk art, Torah binders were common in Central Europe. Mothers usually embroidered them for their sons' circumcisions. The binders were then wrapped around the Torah for the bar mitzvah at age 13. This one was made for "Gabriel, son of our honorable teacher Rabbi Eliyakim ha-Levi, born under a good sign of Monday, the 26th of Tammuz [5]629. May he be raised by God to Torah, and to the canopy of marriage, and to good deeds. Amen. Selah." An American flag sprouts from the words "may he be raised."

A *shivti,* or paper cut, a traditional Jewish art form brought to America from Germany, Holland, and eastern Europe, like a *mizrach,* was used to mark an eastern wall for home prayer. Here Jewish and American motifs appear. The twin American flags in the upper corners set off the Hebrew words "This is God's gate" and "I am ever mindful of God—forever."

In 1877 the Grand Union Hotel, Saratoga, N.Y., refused accommodations to Joseph Seligman, a prominent Jewish banker. *Puck* depicts Jews with large hooked noses and mocks their social climbing.

Nineteenth-century American popular culture, under Protestant influence, often depicted Jews as victims of the evils of Catholicism, as shown in this engraving from *The Jewess*, performed at the Boston Museum.

Although few Jews advocated separate Jewish schools, noted cartoonist and
virulent anti-Catholic Thomas Nast made the hooked-nosed Jew a major player
in the common school debate, equal to the simian-like Irish Catholic.

The Peddler's Wagon. Artist C. G. Bush. Courtesy of the Library of Congress

The peddler's hooked nose indicates that a Jew is showing clothing to these farm folk.

"The Hebrew Purim Ball at the Academy of Music, March 14," *Frank Leslie's Illustrated Newspaper* (1 April 1865). Courtesy of the Library of Congress

Nineteenth-century American Jews widely celebrated Purim, both by the giving of charity and the merriment of parties and costumes. Costumes worn here were both specifically Jewish, like the dreidel (the top with Hebrew letters), and typical of American balls. The artist indulges in stereotypical images, giving several partygoers exaggerated hooked noses.

"The Jewish Passover of 1868." *Frank Leslie's Illustrated Newspaper*. (10 April 1868.) Courtesy of the Library of Congress

A matzo factory on New York's Chatham Street. In the accompanying newspaper article describing Passover, the baking process is detailed and Jews are described as people with "inky hair, hooked noses, stooped shoulders." The writer considered them a "distinct race" who never part with an atom of their national identity."

"The Chanuka Celebration." *Frank Leslie's Illustrated Newspaper* (3 January 1880). Courtesy of the Library of Congress

A Young Men's Hebrew Association Hanukkah pageant

The B'nai B'rith contributed *Religious Liberty* to the 1876 Centennial Exposition in Philadelphia's Fairmount Park. Devoid of Jewish images, the statue's base reads "Dedicated to the United States by the Order of B'nai B'rith and Israelites of America."

Completed in 1866, San Francisco's Temple Emanu-El with its onion-shaped domes and façade festooned with stars of David, dominated the city's skyline.

IN MEMORY OF THE CONFIRMATION

OF

ON THE

CONGREGATION.

MINISTER

Confirmation certificate designed by "Rev. Dr. Sonneschein" stresses that confirmation for boys and girls serves the interests of the Jewish religion, community, and family (1872).

Kehilat Kodesh B'nai Yeshurun (Plum Street Synagogue), Cincinnati. Dedicated in 1865, this Moorish-style synagogue embodied its rabbi Isaac Mayer Wise's aspirations for American Jews and Judaism.

This B'nai Brith membership certificate (1856) with American and Judaic images attests to the benefits of joining the Order. The husband as protector of his family is juxtaposed with the sick man and his family in their hour of need. Moses, Abraham, and Isaac on the sides are topped by the American shield and eagle.

Strouse Brothers. Nineteenth-century American Jewish businesses usually involved partnerships of brothers.

Like many nineteenth-century American Jewish merchants, Hutzler Brothers in Baltimore sold dry goods and produced and marketed ready-made clothing. They pioneered in the "single price" (1873).

Levi Benjamin, a founder of the Baltimore Hebrew Congregation, gave this silver charity box in 1851 to his daughter Henrietta. Children often had their own boxes and put a few coins in before the lighting of Sabbath candles (1851).

Shaaray Hashomayim Synagogue around 1864, with a membership of fewer than twenty families, was depicted in the lithograph *A View from Madison* (Wisc.) showing that city's important buildings.

These three anecdotes, among many others, suggest that being Jewish in America was not a tremendous burden or liability from which acculturating Jews sought escape. Nor did Gentiles necessarily see it as something repugnant. Indeed, many Jews clung to their Jewishness even when married to non-Jews.

Jewishness as a set of religious obligations did not stay the same in America because local conditions differed radically from what the immigrants had left. The disinterest of the state in religious matters gave the masses of Jews the chance, and challenge, to craft for themselves the kind of Judaism they wanted, choose leaders they preferred, and shape institutions and practices that made sense to them. The absence in America of a kahal that could enforce behavior, determine patterns of leadership, and set terms for membership empowered Jews to do those things for themselves. In America, lay people decided the terms of religious life. They created congregations from the ground up and shaped ritual practices. They defined who was a rabbi and, indeed, who was a Jew.

American Jews demonstrated a deep wish to live as Jews despite their decision to venture out into places where few accoutrements of Jewish life awaited them. They maintained those elements of the tradition that they could. The movement toward Reform did not signify a desire to discard completely the distinctiveness of Jewish culture or to become *k'chol hagoyim* (the same as all other peoples).

In an unself-conscious and haphazard way, these nineteenth-century American Jews put together religious structures with elements that did not necessarily appear consistent or make sense if measured in terms of halakah, but that, nonetheless, satisfied their needs. They wanted to succeed economically, participate in Jewish life, be accepted by their neighbors as equals, and, ultimately, balance the dictates of their Judaism with the dictates of their Americanism.

America allowed for religious pluralism, and Jews suffered little for their distinctiveness. They could celebrate holidays when no one else did, they could emblazon their buildings with Hebrew letters and Jewish symbols, and they could boldly state that the Christianity of the majority of Americans was not theirs. They could press for full inclusion in the political and cultural life of the nation and yet proclaim that they also had their own, unique agenda.

CHAPTER SIX

LOOKING OUTWARD

Politically, the Jew has the same rights as the Christian. He may rise to every
office and every dignity. . . . In politics every difference between
Jew and non-Jew is gone.

I am a Jew, when Saturday, the seventh day, comes; I am one on my holidays;
in the selection and treatment of my food; it was always written on my doorposts.
. . . But when I . . . take a ballot in order to exercise my rights as a citizen.
Then I am not a Jew, but I feel and vote as a citizen of the republic,
I do not ask what pleases the Israelites.

We are always reluctant to obtrude our opinions upon the public attention,
and generally seek to keep our own counsel.

THE JEWS who came to America in the nineteenth century brought
political traditions and patterns of interaction with non-Jews different than
those they would find in the New World. In contrast to Central Europe,
which predicated the Jews' acceptance in public life on their transformation, to become an American did not require toning down one's Jewishness.
American Jews who held public office, sidled up to those with power,
belonged to non-Jewish fraternal lodges, and served in the military did not
hide their Jewish identities or transform themselves into "model" Americans as defined by Gentile sentiment. Instead, many used their participation
in American institutions to be Jews and help their coreligionists at home
and abroad.

With the exception of the intellectual elite and the rabbis, few European Jews had forayed far from the all-Jewish, small-town world of family
and community. They conducted business with non-Jews, but as immigrants, they had no real experience in sharing institutions in a pluralistic
environment. The franchise in much of Central Europe extended only to a

few Jews, and the vast majority came with no exposure to secular politics. Of course, Europe was changing rapidly throughout the nineteenth century, and Jews who migrated later in the century often had experienced secular schools, the army, lodges, and other "nonsectarian" institutions. This brief exposure, however, was relatively limited.

America offered naturalization and citizenship to all white males, and immigrants attained them easily, regardless of religion or class. All immigrant men had an equal chance to participate in the political affairs of their communities, and Americans boasted of their openness to all European immigrants.

Despite sporadic, often violent outbreaks of anti-Catholicism and antipathy toward Irish immigrants, as exemplified by the Know-Nothing party of the 1850s, over the nineteenth century, American politics moved toward greater inclusion of men from diverse backgrounds. Starting in the 1820s, states dropped religious and property qualifications for voting and office holding. American politics became a checkerboard of ethnic alliances bolstering the local and national party structure. Ethnic and religious interest groups along with regional alliances helped hold the amorphous, nonideological parties together. Diversity served society as a whole, connecting voters to parties through particularistic group agendas and loyalties.

Politicians and writers celebrated America as a land where men of diverse backgrounds created something new. A campaign song in the 1810 gubernatorial race in New York purposefully jingled:

> Come Dutch and Yankee, Irish, Scot
> With intermixed relation;
> From whence we came, it matters not;
> We all make, now, one nation.

In the same vein, Ralph Waldo Emerson prophesied that "in this continent—asylum of all nations—the energy of Irish, Germans, Swedes, Poles, and Cossacks, and all the European tribes . . . will construct a new race, a new religion, a new state, a new literature."[1] Reformers such as Horace Mann promoted common schools as "the great equalizer of the conditions of men . . . the balance wheel of the social machinery," erasing the distinctions of Europe and creating citizens with a common culture and outlook.[2]

This rhetoric presented opportunities as well as dangers to Jews. On the one hand, they welcomed participation in public life after being rigidly excluded from it in Europe on the basis of their Jewishness. Conversely, the ultimate American vision pictured a future where distinctive cultures and backgrounds faded under the beneficent sun of American liberty, forging a homogenized American nation.

Nineteenth-century American Jews voted, ran for office, and joined militias and Masonic lodges. However, they did not do so to the detriment of group solidarity and allegiance. They did not hide who they were and participated in mainstream institutions to advance the interests of their people.

In the Realm of Politics

In partisan politics, Jews deftly balanced their effort to blend in with their Christian neighbors and the pursuit of their own needs. While political issues kept changing during these years and American Jews increased in number and diversified, Jewish male participation in American politics remained constant.

First Jews entered politics as businessmen. Local politics in America rested heavily with the mercantile class, and Jews as merchants had a particular stake in the stability of their communities. Customers recognized their faces from behind clothing and dry-goods stores' counters, and the names on the ballots matched up with those emblazoned on store awnings. Reputation earned in business lent them the aura of upstanding men of substance. When, for example, Samuel Hirschl ran for town council on the Republican ticket in Davenport, Iowa, in 1851, the local newspaper commentated that "Mr. H. is a well known citizen and property holder and no doubt will make an excellent officer." Through their entrepreneurship, Jewish businessmen served on county boards, city councils, school boards, in state legislatures, and as mayors in every region and community. In smaller communities and in the newly settled West, Jewish merchants were mainstays of town government. The first Jews did not show up in Portland, Oregon, until the 1850s, but by 1880, two had served as mayors, and the city council regularly held meetings in the store of Rosenblatt and Blaumer. Jewish office holders rarely pursued politics as a career or won elections to further a particular ideology. Rather, they saw public service as befitting a merchant—custodian of public order.[3]

Secondly, Jews participated most often and most intensely in local politics, because local governments dealt with issues that mattered most to Jews and non-Jews alike. The vast majority of Jewish office holders tended to be relative newcomers to the jurisdictions where they ran for and held office. Not only had many come from Europe, but most had lived elsewhere in the United States. Participating in local politics may have offered a way to solidify business contacts. Generally, larger American cities saw fewer Jewish office holders.[4]

After the 1850s, like the American polity itself, Jews divided themselves evenly between Republicans and Democrats, with the Republican party holding a slight edge among Jewish voters. Local conditions rather than national ideologies determined party affiliation. In the larger cities in particular, class or place of origin in Europe influenced Jewish party preference. Thus, in Chicago, Jews of German origin supported the Republican tickets, but the Yiddish-speaking Jews from Bohemia on the West Side voted Democratic.[5] Jews in Los Angeles tended to be Democrats, while those in Milwaukee typically cast their ballots in the Republican columns.[6] Although the Jews of New York City allied with Tammany Hall until the 1870s, Jews played key roles in local Republican ranks in Philadelphia, Rochester, and Louisville.[7]

The parties courted Jews and other ethnic groups. Boss Tweed, for example, helped subsidize the *Hebrew Leader* and *Die Yiddishe Zeitung* to advance Tammany's interests among Jewish voters in New York, while Chicago's Democratic party in 1879 purposely nominated Adolph Moses for superior court to break German Jews' Republican proclivities. The Moses nomination and the Democratic courting of the "solid Jewish vote" caused a storm of controversy. Under the headline "The Mistakes of Moses," the Republican *Chicago Tribune* editorialized that Democrats erred in believing that "the rite of circumcision of itself qualifies a man to be a judge of the Superior Court of Cook County."[8]

American Jewish newspaper editors and rabbis proclaimed volubly that no Jewish vote existed, nor should it. In the polling booth, they insisted, Jews behaved like Americans. "With politics," wrote Isaac Leeser in 1855, "Jews have little concern, except to vote for those whom they individually may deem most fitting to administer the offices created for the public good." Newspapers such as the *Occident,* the *Jewish Messenger,* and the *American Israelite* speculated on the negative effects of Jewish participation in visible partisan politics, concluding that such behavior could ignite the sparks of anti-Semitism. Thus, after Adolph Moses lost the judgeship in 1879, the *Occident* claimed that "for the next four score years, no Israelite can ever attain a judicial position in Illinois, as the deep prejudices and religious intolerance of our citizens will not permit of such an event." The Jewish press regretted that Chicago's Jews had been used by the Democratic party for its own purposes and said that, in the end, the Jews would suffer.[9]

Non-Jewish politicians and party operatives assumed that Jews, like all other Americans, voted out of group interest, supporting their friends and opposing their enemies. Occasionally, disappointed candidates vented their anger on "the Jews" whose "political cabal" helped tighten the "Jewish economic stranglehold" on the nation.

For example, William J. Dyer, an unsuccessful candidate for a seat in the Oregon territorial legislature in 1859, blamed his defeat on the Jews. Being the editor of the *Oregonian*, Dyer used the Portland newspaper to pronounce that "The Jews of Oregon . . . have assumed an importance that no other sect has ever dared to assume. . . . They have leagued together . . . to control the ballot box. . . . They have assumed to control the commercial interests of the whole country by a secret combination." In response, Oregon Jews did not deny the fact of group voting. Instead, Jewish merchants in Portland canceled all their advertisements in the newspaper.[10]

The skittish Jewish elite, nervously listening to such rhetoric, conspicuously asserted that Jews voted purely on the basis of their American concerns, pursuing no specifically Jewish agenda. This assertion, though, reflected wishful thinking. Jews did participate actively in partisan politics around the country. They held offices and made unpopular decisions that, potentially, could inspire anti-Semitism. Morris Goodman sat on the first city council of Los Angeles, Maier Zunder on New Haven's School Board, Abraham Kohn served as Chicago's city clerk, and Marcus Katz as the treasurer of the San Bernardino, California, Board of Supervisors. Gerson Herman ran for New York's Board of Supervisors with Tammany's backing. Bernard Goldsmith and Philip Wasserman were elected mayors of Portland, Oregon. Twenty Jews served in the United States Congress between 1820 and 1880, and hundreds of other Jews defied the dictum that Jews should steer clear of politics and not hold any office.[11]

To what extent did Gentile voters identify candidates and officeholders as Jews? While it is hardly possible to reconstruct what went on in voters' minds, newspapers in smaller communities noted frequently, and often positively, the Jewishness of individuals running for office.

Jewish politicians themselves rarely changed their names, and most of the Jews who held local public office affiliated with and often assumed leadership roles in synagogues and benevolent associations. Clearly, Jewish candidates and officeholders did not try to conceal their religious affiliations.

Despite the generally positive reception Jews received in America, Jewish communal leaders on the national level feared that Jewish political participation would stimulate anti-Semitism. Sporadic anti-Jewish statements, which sometimes accompanied Jewish participation in politics, fueled these fears. In 1860, for example, Polish-born Bernhard Marks ran for a seat on the school board in the California mining country and won. A slew of letters in the local newspapers angrily denounced the election of a man who does not "attend Church." In an 1850s campaign in Detroit, German Republicans attacked, in the press and on the campaign circuit, a Jewish Democratic candidate as a Jew. In 1863, the Detroit *Commercial Advertiser* condemned several Jews running for office and advised voters not to support the "hooked nose wretches [who] speculate on disasters and a battle lost to our army is chuckled over by them, as it puts money in their purses." A study of Philadelphia found that "politics seemed to bring forth isolated, and apparently a-typical, bursts of anti-Semitism."[12]

Calls for Jewish aloofness from active political involvement came more often from traditionalists such as Isaac Leeser than from reformers such as Isaac Wise. Indeed, nineteen of the thirty-one Jews who joined the Reformed Society of Israelites in Charleston, South Carolina, in 1824, that first venture into the reform of Judaism in America, actively participated in Charleston's public life—in contrast to the more aloof traditionalists on the Adjunta (board of trustees) of Beth Elohim.[13] They undoubtedly feared that politics bred easy social relations with non-Jews and recognized that in postemancipation Europe, Jews devoted to politics tended to be the least involved in the *kahal*.

Synagogue board members did not accept admonitions against Jewish involvement in politics in general, but they strongly opposed any rabbinical political action. The world of politics, they believed, should be off limits for rabbis, and congregational boards repeatedly attempted to muzzle their clergy. Rabbi Morris Raphall, for example, enjoyed a relatively amicable relationship with the lay leaders of New York's Congregation B'nai Jeshurun until he signed a letter in the *Jewish Messenger* favoring the election of a particular candidate for judgeship. The board censured him. At Cincinnati's B'nai Yeshurun, the board told its rabbi, none other than Isaac M. Wise, that it "disapproves of all political allusion" in sermons and ordered him to "discontinue same." Wise, a staunch Democrat with pro-Southern leanings, incurred the wrath of his heavily Republican congregants—as well as readers of the *Israelite*—for his political, proslavery statements in the 1850s and early 1860s. Two dozen subscribers to the *Israelite* sent a letter to the *Cincinnati Daily Times* to register publicly their displeasure with Wise's foray into politics. "We had supposed," they wrote, "when we subscribed for his paper, that it was his purpose to make it a religious paper, totally eschewing all political subjects." Imagine their anger when Wise urged the readers of his newspaper to vote Democratic and support the Dred Scott decision. In 1861, Philadelphia's Rabbi Henry Vidaver resigned his pulpit at Rodef Sholem and returned to Germany, most probably because members resented his proslavery, anti-Union stance.

On the other end of the spectrum, members of Har Sinai Congregation in Baltimore ordered the abolitionist-minded David Einhorn to cease offering antislavery sermons, and Baltimore Jews held a protest meeting, asserting that Einhorn did not speak for them. After antiabolitionist mobs destroyed the printing presses of his publications, *Sinai* and *Der Wecker,* Einhorn fled Baltimore for the more hospitable climate of Philadelphia. Samuel Adler, who also professed strong antislavery views, angered members of New York's Emanu-El, many of whom had Southern business ties, with his politically charged rhetoric. Although the political positions of Wise, Einhorn, and others irritated their congregations, the real issue came down to a deep conviction among the American Jewish laity that rabbis and politics did not mix. Politics, they believed, was too important to be put in the hands of mere religious functionaries.[14]

Nineteenth-century American Jews did have a specifically Jewish political agenda, although never so labeled. A broad range of personal, local, national, and international issues concerned American Jews, making political insulation impossible.

In establishing and maintaining Jewish institutions, Jews dealt with those in power and maintained contacts with the political system. Most Jewish orphanages, hospitals, and other asylums held state charters and often owed their founding to the financial contribution of state governments. The New Orleans Home for Widows and Orphans began with a six-thousand-dollar gift from the Louisiana legislature, while New York's Hebrew Benevolent Society financed its building with contributions from city and state. Jewish orphanages, in particular, depended on close cooperation with juvenile authorities, making sure that Jewish children in distress not be sent to evangelical or other "nonsectarian" institutions.[15]

Jewish cemeteries and synagogues also needed charters from local and state governments. In Washington, D.C., the tiny Jewish community of the 1850s sought to amend an 1844 law providing for the conveyance of real

estate to the trustees of institutions for religious worship, so that the synagogue, Washington Hebrew Congregation, could enjoy the same rights as
churches. Members of the Washington Jewish community turned to Captain Jonas P. Levy, a naval officer and Mexican War hero living in Washington and known in powerful political circles, to make the right contacts
for them. Since Congress held legislative authority over the District of
Columbia, Levy used his political networks to secure passage, in May 1856,
of "An Act for the benefit of the Hebrew Congregation of the City of
Washington," which gave the synagogue the same rights and privileges that
protected Christian churches.[16] Western towns often gave nascent Jewish
communities outright gifts of land to build their institutions.[17]

Jews in nineteenth-century America appealed frequently to American
courts to settle internal community disputes. Courts heard complaints
arising out of the slaughter and the kashrut of meat being sold by butchers.
Jewish groups often asked city councils to regulate the provisioning of
kosher meat. In the first half of the nineteenth century in particular, Jews
tried to involve secular government in the maelstrom of the kosher meat
business. New York's Common Council granted Congregation Shearith
Israel's 1813 request to have the exclusive right of slaughtering and selling
kosher meat. A faction in the synagogue, then New York's only one, petitioned the Council to repeal the monopoly, which, the petition said, was "an
encroachment on our religious rites and a restriction of those general
principles to which we are entitled." In response, the aldermen did an
about-face and removed Shearith Israel's license.[18]

Furthermore, congregational schisms over Reform led to court battles
over which group owned the building and cemetery, who could vote in
congregational elections, and, in essence, which group—the traditionalists
or the reformers—was right. When the Baltimore Hebrew Congregation
made changes in ritual in 1857, Jonas Friedenwald, an advocate of tradition,
obtained a court order forbidding the board from renewing the rabbi's
contract. In 1870, Friedenwald again secured a court injunction, this time
to prevent a mixed choir in the congregation. Even when personality, and
not ideology, was the issue, Jewish congregational politics not infrequently
ended up in court. In the late 1850s, members of New York's Kalvarier
Congregation squabbled over representation on the board of trustees, and
one disgruntled faction sued another. Repeatedly, intramural Jewish conflicts became extramural as one group or another used American political
institutions for the furtherance of Judaism as they saw it.[19]

Jews participated in the political system in order to ensure equal treatment in American society. Well into the second half of the nineteenth century, some states maintained restrictions on office-holding, limiting it to professed Christians. Jews did not sit by idly; they did not want to put up with being treated as second-class citizens or to eschew those states to avoid controversy. Instead, they used their contacts in the non-Jewish world to press for equality. Beginning in the 1790s and continuing into the 1820s, Jewish merchants in Maryland, Solomon Etting, Bernard Gratz, Jacob Cohen, and others, worked through sympathetic Christian legislators to repeal the restriction on Jewish office-holding. Represented in the legislature indirectly by Thomas Kennedy of Hagerstown and Colonel W. G. D. Worthington, Jews proclaimed that, as permanent residents of Maryland, they demanded political rights due to all men. They persisted in pressing for their rights, despite the strident anti-Jewish rhetoric of their opponents, who called Thomas Kennedy a "Judas Iscariot" and accused him of being "one-half Jew and the other half not a Christian." Within one year of the 1825 passage of the "Jew bill," which allowed for Jewish office-holding, Solomon Etting and Jacob Cohen successfully ran for the Baltimore City Council.[20] Jews and their allies challenged restrictions on office-holding in Rhode Island, North Carolina, and New Hampshire in 1842, 1868, and 1877, respectively, although these states harbored smaller Jewish communities than Maryland—the issue served a more symbolic function, as Jews demanded the rights claimed by all men.[21]

Jews also used the political process to ensure that they were not penalized for practicing their religion. In the 1870s, for example, "a young lady of a prominent Jewish family . . . was anxious to be appointed in one of the departments [of the federal government]." However, as a Sabbath observer, she "conditioned that she need not work on Saturday." Simon Wolf, a figure in both local, Washington, D.C., and national politics, intervened on her behalf directly with President Rutherford B. Hayes, securing her appointment in the Interior Department, which stipulated that she be excused from the office on her Sabbath.[22] In 1850, the United States government entered into a commercial treaty with Switzerland. Several Swiss cantons forbade Jews from conducting business within their borders. American Jews argued that this disadvantaged them as American citizens and that the United States government must not condone discrimination. Jews wrote articles, circulated petitions, and held public meetings. They paid personal visits and sent strident letters to powerful congressmen, such as Henry Clay, Daniel Webster, and Lewis Cass, demanding abrogation of the treaty. Joseph Abraham of Cincinnati noted in a letter to Daniel Webster: "As a member of the Jewish Church, and one of the proscribed . . . jealous of our rights . . . having for centuries been under the ban of persecution, [I] watch with a vigilant eye, encroachments on our rights."[23]

Closer to home, American Jews also kept a "vigilant eye" on the passage of state and city laws that made it illegal to operate businesses on Sunday, the Christian day of rest. These laws posed a harsh burden on observant Jews, because they could not work on Saturday either. Even the less observant Jews who did not mind buying and selling on Saturday found it irksome that the Christian weekly calendar would apply to all. From 1816 on, Jews challenged in court legal restrictions on merchandising on Sunday in Virginia, South Carolina, Maryland, Ohio, Iowa, Pennsylvania, Louisiana, and elsewhere. They argued that Jews, while different than other Americans who worshipped on Sunday, still deserved an equal chance to make a living. When, in 1867, one Mr. Frolickstein in Mobile, Alabama, was fined twenty-five dollars for violating a city ordinance by selling a pair of shoes on Sunday, his lawyer stated in court that Frolickstein considered himself "a strict member of the Jewish Church, and believing in the religion and faith of the Jewish church; that according to the religious faith of the Jews, Saturday is the Sabbath and that day the defendant *does no work,* because he is so commanded by the law of Moses." Jews challenged such ordinances in a way that drew public attention to their differences with the majority Christian American polity.[24]

Even when the debate about Sunday closings sparked anti-Semitic political rhetoric, American Jews did not retreat from protest. In 1855, for example, the Speaker of the California House of Representatives, William Stowe, attacked Jews as unworthy and undesirable residents, "who only came here to make money, and leave as soon as they effected their object." He then proposed a special head tax on Jews to deter their settlement in California. What had provoked Stowe's ire was the refusal of a Jewish firm in Santa Cruz, his home district, to sign a petition in favor of a state Sunday closing law he had introduced. Instead of being frightened into passivity, Jews of California fought back aggressively in local newspapers. H. J. Labatt, a San Francisco Jewish businessman, penned a passionate response for the San Francisco press, challenging the powerful Speaker of the House. Labatt asked:

Are you ignorant of the number of families arriving [on] every steamer, and of the Jewish faith, to make California their home? Are you ignorant of the brick synagogues [Jews are] erecting in our large cities for family worship? Are you ignorant of the permanent benevolent societies, which extend the hand of charity to their bereaved brethren, and relieve the state, county, and city of taxes for almshouses, hospitals, asylums, etc.? If you are ignorant of these facts, then you are basely ignorant.

Jews in Los Angeles persuaded the editors of the *Star* to reprint Labatt's letter, and the editor of the *Star* not only agreed but added his own note, accusing the Speaker of "bigoted prejudice and falsehood." Noisy protest meetings took place in San Francisco and Sacramento, boldly warning that "the Jews are alive and watching over their rights; it takes a shrewder and more influential man than Mr. Stowe to frighten them. . . . The Jews have too many sincere friends in this country."[25]

American Jews also battled the overtly evangelical public school education. As the public school movement advanced in the mid-nineteenth century, more and more Jewish children attended state-run schools. In the earlier part of the century, Jewish children attended Jewish day schools. But as cities and towns began to provide systems of mass education, Jews abandoned particularistic schools, which taught English, often German, and other secular subjects as well as Hebrew and Judaica, in favor of public education, providing supplementary Jewish learning for their children themselves. Increasingly, though, Jews came into conflict with the thinly veiled Protestant ideology of public education.[26]

In the latter part of the century, Jewish women began to opt for careers as public school teachers. In smaller communities, with few educated people to draw upon, local rabbis taught public school.[27] Some Jews also served on school boards in various communities. Isaac M. Wise, for example, an advocate of public education for Jewish children and passionate enemy of the evangelicals, sat on the Cincinnati public schools' Board of Examiners. Thus the issue of the Christian orientation of the curriculum became increasingly pressing.[28]

As early as 1843, Jews in New York spoke out against New Testament readings and the use of other clearly Christian classroom materials. In what historian Diane Ravitch has called "the Great School Wars" in 1840s New York, Jews and Catholics opposed the Protestant curriculum. The *New York Herald* remarked sarcastically in 1840 that the battles over textbooks had made Jews and Catholics allies for the first time in 1,840 years.[29] In

Cincinnati, the Board of Education voted at the end of the 1860s to end Bible reading and mandatory prayers. The Protestant clergy of the city objected, mounting a campaign to reinvigorate the schools' Christian content. The threatened re-Christianization of schools brought together some Jews, Catholics, and freethinkers of the Queen City into an alliance to maintain the religiously neutral status quo. In 1872 in Columbus, Ohio, the board of Congregation B'nai Israel went on record against Christian songs in public schools, demanding that officials "put a stop to this." Isaac Mayer Wise may have stated the widely accepted Jewish position on the need for religious neutrality in state institutions most succinctly in 1869: "All sects are entitled to equal rights hence all versions of the Bible must be read in the public schools or none."[30]

American Jews also worked aggressively on behalf of their coreligionists around the world. From the second decade of the century through the 1880s, the defense of Jewish rights abroad stood high on the American Jewish agenda. American Jews considered themselves responsible for Jews in distant lands and used political contacts to that end. As early as the 1810s and 1820s, Mordecai Noah, a journalist, dramatist, and founder of Tammany Hall, sought to stimulate a large-scale Jewish immigration into the United States from central Europe. He hoped to establish a Jewish agricultural colony in upstate New York to be peopled by European newcomers. Although Noah's plans never materialized, his ability to tap members in the New York legislature for support and his manipulation of the press to dramatize the plan demonstrated the usefulness of a political career for a Jew who was bent on doing something for his brethren, "the race of Jacob. . . . from the four quarters of the globe."[31]

In 1840, a Catholic priest and his servant in Damascus, Syria, disappeared. A rumor spread that they had been victims of Jews, kidnapped and killed so that their blood could be baked into Passover matzo. The Ottoman authorities, eager to placate the Christian minority in the empire, arrested several Jews, tortured them, and elicited "confessions." The government then rounded up numerous Jews, sentenced seventy-two to death, and indicated that up to thirty thousand others were suspected of complicity. The United States government actually registered its first horrified reaction at this blood libel before Jewish protests sparked, and American Jews did not organize until a month after their English and European coreligionists had done so. But when they did, American Jews in city after city put together protest meetings, enlisted notable Gentile politicians and clergymen, and demanded that the government use its diplomatic influence to relieve the Jews of Syria. "Resolved," read the Philadelphia meeting's official document, "that, in conjunction with our brethren in other cities, a letter be addressed to the President of the United States, respectfully requesting him to instruct the representative of the United States at Constantinople . . . to procure for our accused brethren at Damascus an impartial trial."[32]

Less than two decades later, in 1858, American Jews once again turned to the U.S. government to press for Jews abroad. In this case, a young Jewish boy in Bologna, Edgar Mortara, had been abducted from his home by Vatican police after a Christian servant of the family told Catholic church authorities that she had had him baptized. Officials decreed that the six-year-old was a valid Christian and, therefore, should not live in a Jewish family. Jews around the world protested, and American Jews joined in the chorus of outrage. They organized meetings, urging the government to use diplomacy to secure the return of the boy to his family. Two thousand Jews attended a rally in New York City alone, demanding President Buchanan's intervention. The United States government, the meeting resolved, should commit a "simple act of humanity" and assert "its moral influence in favor of oppressed humanity, everywhere, and at all times." A delegation of Jews from Philadelphia went to Washington to press the reluctant president, who disagreed with the Jewish position. "The Israelites were in many countries cruelly treated," begged members of the delegation, accompanied by two congressmen as a visible symbol of political ties. And even now, the delegation said, "we are cramped in body and mind, since oppressors keep down our natural energies." Their choice of pronouns is particularly revealing: in the matter of Jewish rights, even when it involved Jews a continent away, "we" rather than "they" was the word of choice.[33]

American Jews used their political clout, however measured, on behalf of Jews in Palestine, Romania, Russia, and elsewhere throughout the middle decades of the century. As early as 1867, American Jews asked Secretary of State William Seward to investigate, through the ambassador to Turkey, the deteriorating status of the Jews of Romania and, a year later, pressed for a congressional resolution protesting their mistreatment. In 1870, President Grant, sensitive to Jewish pressures, appointed Benjamin F. Peixotto, a leader of the B'nai B'rith, as U.S. Consul in Bucharest, where he served the United States and kept tabs on escalating persecutions.[34] American Jews also pressed the government to monitor persecutions and intercede on behalf of Russian Jews, victims of pogroms and banishments heaped on top of their usual disabilities. In 1869, the B'nai B'rith lodge in Washington, D.C., sparked local and national concern about the Jews in the Russian province of Bessarabia, where officials ordered Jews to leave the city of Kishinev. In part because of the lodge's location in the nation's capital, the protests of the lodge reached the Department of State, which added them to the petitions from other American Jews.[35] Further, Rabbi Hayyim Zvi Sneersohn, in the United States to collect money for poor Jews in Jerusalem, persuaded American Jews to set up a meeting with Secretary of State Hamilton Fish and President U. S. Grant. Sneersohn asked the American leaders to remove the American consul in Jerusalem because he had been deeply involved with missionaries there, bent on converting the Jews.[36]

American Jewish leaders cared so deeply about the defense of Jewish rights abroad that, in the aftermath of the Mortara case, they created the first truly national Jewish organization, the Board of Delegates of American Israelites. While nominally apolitical, it coordinated Jewish responses to overseas crises over the course of the next decades. (In 1878, it merged with the Union of American Hebrew Congregations.) The Board of Delegates, made up of representatives from the congregations, also attempted to tackle such thorny issues as Jewish education, the clergy, the provision of charity, aid for immigrants, and the collection of Jewish statistics, and in general hoped to foster a degree of Jewish unity in America. But its energies went primarily toward the coordination of Jewish efforts on behalf of their coreligionists abroad. The Board raised money, activated political networks, lobbied government officials, and stimulated the consciousness of non-Jewish Americans to the dangers faced by Jews in other lands.[37]

Indeed, these activities created a new class of American Jewish leaders who did not emerge from the synagogues and the religious establishment like Leeser or Wise. Such political men as Simon Wolf and Adolphus Solomons surfaced as secular leaders and Jewish power brokers. They somewhat resembled *shtadlanim* of premodern Europe, the well-connected Jews who shuttled back and forth from palace to ghetto, pleading the case of the Jews to princes and representing the state to the Jews. Both Solomons and Wolf were deeply involved in party politics. Both lived in the District of Columbia and developed ties and friendships with powerful national leaders. To be sure, they used contacts to advance their own careers. But they also coordinated Jewish politics and pressed for Jewish rights abroad. Solomons, a traditional Jew, a printer and stationer, who had been elected to the House of Delegates of the short-lived territorial government in the District of Columbia during the early 1870s, mediated between the Board of Delegates, its secretary Myer S. Isaacs, and the State Department in the 1870s, during the Romanian crisis. Solomons described to Isaacs his discussion with Secretary of State Fish: "I asked him if he had heard of any outrages having been perpetrated upon our people in Smyrna and he said they knew of none." Solomons then described to the secretary the plight of the Levantine Jews.[38]

Wolf had a longer and more thoroughly political career and was closely associated with Ulysses S. Grant. He worked with the Board of Delegates, and it was he who induced Grant to appoint Peixotto to the Romanian post.[39] Wolf and Solomons very self-consciously displayed their Jewishness and protested against anti-Semitism not just in other countries but in America as well.

Clearly, American Jews had a political wish list that distinguished them from other citizens, and they did not hesitate to publicize their particularistic stake in American politics and diplomacy. Because they felt responsibility to other Jews, they willingly stood out as different in America and pursued a course of action that labeled them as being somehow out of the mainstream. While historians may in retrospect judge their efforts as "timid" or paltry from the vantage point of the late twentieth century, nineteenth-century American Jews rejected advice to eschew politics.

The Civil War and Jewish Unity

The Civil War put unique strains on American Jews. Jews lived on both sides of the Mason-Dixon Line and ideologically fell on both sides of the slavery question.[40] They voted for all parties and most of the factions within them. They donned uniforms of blue and of gray[41] and, as civilians, rallied to the Union and the Confederate causes.[42]

Jews felt regional loyalties, and thousands served and died as volunteers in both armies. A few special Jewish companies were formed, such as the 82nd Regiment of the Illinois Volunteers, made up of many recent arrivals from Lithuania, Russia, and Poland.[43] Synagogues on both sides announced special days of prayer, invoking God to grant victory, while rabbis enthusiastically cooperated with their respective governments and Jewish women sewed for their troops and tended to their sick.

Although the Baptists, Methodists, Presbyterians, and other denominations split into separate churches along regional lines over slavery, Jewish "unity" prevailed.[44] The B'nai B'rith continued to function as though no "fire bell in the night" had been sounded, as though no storm of secession brewed and no war had torn the country in two.[45] After the war, it took decades before the wounds of war would be healed on a national level. But Southern Jews moved north, Northern Jews moved south, families that had had young men fighting for both armies got back together, and the new Jewish communities, made up of Union and Confederate veterans alike, took shape as though nothing had happened. For example, in the tiny Jewish enclave of Marshall, Texas, Emanuel Kahn went off to fight for the Confederacy, but his brother Lionel joined a Union brigade. After the war, both men returned to Marshall, picking up where they had left off. Rabbis who had ardently supported North or South found themselves, after the war, behind pulpits in the other region, with no lingering antipathy about wartime politics marring their relationships with new congregations.[46]

But even amidst the pressures of war, Jews pursued a group agenda. They made it clear that they expected to be treated like all other participants. Jews in both the North and the South pressed their respective governments to extend to rabbis the same benefits enjoyed by Christian clergy. The standing law clearly stated that a chaplain must be "a regularly ordained minister of some Christian denomination." The Confederate command quickly dropped the word "Christian," although the number of Jewish soldiers in any one regiment was so small that none elected a rabbi as chaplain. The absence of Jewish chaplains never became a controversy.[47]

A different story unfolded behind Union lines. Jews tended to cluster in certain regiments, and Jewish soldiers clearly wanted to have a rabbi, if only for symbolic value, as chaplain. Indeed, the 65th Regiment of the Fifth Pennsylvania Cavalry, under the command of a Colonel Max Friedman, voted Sergeant Michael Allen, a Hebrew teacher who had studied for the rabbinate, as chaplain. When a YMCA field worker discovered this violation—Allen was neither ordained nor baptized—a controversy ensued, and under the threat of dishonorable discharge, Allen resigned his commission. The regiment, however, went on and voted in another Jewish chaplain, this time Arnold Fischel of New York's Shearith Israel, an ordained rabbi. When Fischel applied to the the War Department for his commission, he was turned down, and a flurry of Jewish protests, petitions, sermons, meetings, and enflamed editorials in the Jewish press followed. Rabbi Isidor Kalisch noted in a letter to Congress that the Jewish soldiers "have the same right, according to the constitution of the U.S. which they endeavor to preserve and defend with all their might," and that he hoped Congress would "make provisions that Jewish Divines shall also be allowed to serve as chaplains in the army and hospitals of the U.S." The Board of Delegates held protest meetings and petitioned Congress. It is not clear whether the masses of Jews felt the outrage as strongly. Partly out of a sense of professional pride, rabbis may have reacted particularly sharply, but some highly visible members of the Jewish community also publicly asserted demands for equality. Despite the exigencies of war that made any protest and dissension dangerous, Jews willingly spoke out against government discrimination.[48]

In the Union and the Confederacy alike, anti-Semites charged Jews with disloyalty, claiming that Jews used the war for economic advantage. In fact, the Civil War did bring some benefits for the Jewish economy, activating the small clothing industry in which Jews were already engaged. Their relative prosperity probably stimulated jealousy and resentment. The Mack brothers of Cincinnati, for example, small-scale tailors before the war, received a contract for uniforms from the government. Henry Mack, who served as chair of the Hamilton County Military Committee, benefited from an upsurge in business and, despite his service, was accused of dealing in contraband cotton.[49] Also, in small towns, particularly in the South, Jewish merchants had access to capital and goods not available to many non-Jewish families.

On the national and local levels, both North and South, Jews were accused of profiteering and treachery—and they protested assiduously. In April 1862, citizens of Thomasville, Georgia, held a public meeting about the unpatriotic behavior of Jewish storekeepers, resolving to ban any new Jews from entering the town and to banish those already there. Jews reacted swiftly. Thirty Jews serving in the Tattnall Guards, Company C, First Georgia Volunteer Regiment, wrote an angry letter of protest to the *Savannah Republican,* proclaiming their patriotism and insisting that Jews behaved no better and no worse than anyone else. Jews in Savannah met at a public meeting, decrying the "wholesale slander, persecution and denunciation of a people" and claiming that the Thomasville incident had "no parallel except in the barbarities of the inquisition and the persecutions of the dark ages."[50]

Northern Jews, not immune from the anti-Jewish hysteria impelled by war, also reacted sharply to anti-Semitic accusations, diatribes, and perceived injustices. In 1862, General Grant issued Order #11, which called for the expulsion of Jews from the military district under his command, including Mississippi, Kentucky, and Tennessee. Grant accused "Jews, as a class [of] violating every regulation of trade established by the Treasury Department." Jews throughout the United States assembled protest meetings and activated political networks to get the order repealed. Under its terms, the Jewish community of Paducah, Kentucky, then some thirty families, actually had to leave the town within twenty-four hours. Only two ill women were left behind. The Jews of Paducah reacted aggressively. They dispatched Cesar Kaskel to Washington to plead with Congress and President Lincoln, who also received angry delegations of Jews from Louisville and Cincinnati. Indeed, Lincoln found himself swamped with documents of outrage from Jews across America, such as the one written in St. Louis on January 5, 1863: "In the name of that Class of *loyal* citizens. . . . In the name of the thousand of our Brethren and our children who have died and are now willingly sacrificing their lives . . . for the union . . . we Enter our Solemn Protest against this Order, and ask of you—the Defender and Protector of the Constitution—to annull that Order."[51]

When General Grant ran for president on the Republican ticket in 1868, the Democratic party reminded Jewish voters of the infamy of Order #11. Some Jewish community leaders joined them in a crusade against Grant, and Isaac M. Wise, a long-time Democrat anyhow, urged Jews to defeat the general, since "none in this nineteenth century in civilized countries has abused and outraged the Jew" worse than Grant. "If there are," he chided the fainthearted of his fellow Jews, "any among us who lick the feet that kick them about and like dogs, run after him who has whipped them, if there are persons small enough to receive indecencies and outrages without resentment . . . we hope their number is small." Charles Moses Strauss, who later became mayor of Tucson, Arizona, lived in Memphis at the time of the 1868 election campaign and organized a meeting of Tennessee Jews to urge the defeat of Grant. Herman Hellman of Los Angeles similarly asserted that he could not vote for someone with Grant's history.

Not all Jews shared Wise's sentiments, however. Some New York Jews organized a "Grant and Colfax" club, and Simon Wolf ardently supported Grant. After Grant was elected, Wolf acted as a broker between the president and the Jews, and pointed out to Grant numerous ways in which he could demonstrate that he harbored no ill feelings towards Jews. He induced Grant to appoint Jews to public offices, to attend synagogue dedications, and the like. Others, such as Samuel M. Isaacs of the *Jewish Mes-*

senger, feared repercussions of overt warnings of Jewish retribution at the ballot box and raised the alarm that Jews should not assert the existence of a Jewish vote or a Jewish interest in the election outcome.

Although the Jewish vote was relatively minor and Jews did not speak with a single voice about General Grant, the Civil War experience nonetheless illustrated the emergence of self-conscious Jewish politics in mid-nineteenth-century America. Despite wartime tensions, Jews asserted their rights as Americans and their self-worth as Jews. Union propaganda, laden as it was with evangelical rhetoric, certainly stimulated negative feelings against Jews as merchants, foreigners, and non-Christians.[52] The government barely tolerated dissent of any kind.[53] But Jews did not passively accept injustices; they protested, petitioned, and issued strident declarations that they deserved the same rights as all other Americans.

In the columns of the Jewish press, a lively debate raged over the nature of Jewish participation in politics. Although some insisted that Jews not draw attention to themselves in the political realm, many behaved contrary to this advice. The political parties recognized the potential of ethnic appeals to Jewish voters, suggesting that non-Jewish politicians did not think their Jewish neighbors an apolitical people with no group agenda. Indeed, they often feared irrationally the level of Jewish political cohesion. Despite the numerical insignificance of Jews in the American electorate, even Grant felt obliged to make overtures to Jews to prove that he had never been an anti-Semite.[54]

With Other Americans

Jews also participated in American life outside the realm of partisan politics. Here, too, rabbis and communal leaders insisted that Jews behaved, or ought to behave, just like other Americans. In fact, Jews engaged in public life in distinctly Jewish ways. In America, as in Europe in this era, sizable numbers of Jews became Masons. Closely connected to mercantile life, Masonry provided a natural meeting ground for Jewish merchants and their non-Jewish peers. In smaller communities, the Masonic lodge often housed the town's only library. Masonry espoused universalism, brotherhood, tolerance, and morality, ideals that any fair-minded nineteenth-century man could subscribe to regardless of creed. Many Jews therefore perceived no barrier to membership.[55] Indeed, much of the Masonic ritual, iconography, insignia, and lore picked up on Jewish themes. After all, Masons traced their lineage back to the workmen who built Solomon's Temple in Jerusalem, and claimed that the Jewish books of the Bible, the Talmud, and the Kabbala (tracts of Jewish mysticism) contained hidden references to Masonry. The Masons used numerous Hebrew words, including *El Shaddai* (almighty God), *kedem* (east), as well as the "Ineffable Name" of God. This fact must have made a Masonic meeting in New York, California, Portland, Chicago, Atlanta, or Boston an experience not jarring with Jewish identity.[56]

Although freemasonry came to articulate a more strident Christian tone, and anti-Semitism began to crop up in lodges in America as well as in Europe later in the century, Jews felt very much at home among their Masonic brothers in the earlier years. Congregations and benevolent societies often used Masonic halls as their first places of worship, indicating the lodges' Jewish membership and a spirit of cooperation between Masons and Jews of the town. In St. Louis, after a group of rowdies threw stones through the window of a home where a minyan prayed, the Masonic lodge offered its rooms for safer worship.[57] At many synagogue dedications, Masons marched solemnly in their regalia, participating in, and sometimes leading, the *hanukkat ha'bayit* (dedication) by inspecting the cornerstone. At the dedication of Rodof Sholem in Petersburg, Virginia, in 1876, the Masons laid the cornerstone at the request of the congregation, and woven into the Jewish ceremony were the plumb, square, level, candles, the symbolic cups of corn, oil, and wine of the ancient Order.[58] Masonic symbols were carved on the tombstones of Jewish members interred in Jewish cemeteries, set against the Hebrew words, and Jewish artists used Masonic motifs in their work, particularly in fashioning *mizrakhim* (plaques to mark off the eastern side of a house) and on Hanukkah lamps.[59] Since Masons participated in members' funerals with their own rite, not infrequently a Jewish burial service was accompanied by the appropriate Masonic rituals. Indeed, when Rabbi Abraham Rice objected to the involvement of the Masons at a Jewish funeral, a handful of irate members quit the Baltimore Hebrew Congregation and founded Har Sinai Verein, America's first explicitly Reform congregation.[60]

Jewish membership in the Masons, the Odd Fellows, the Knights of Pythias, and the other fraternal orders demonstrated how Jews sought equality and integration into America, and at the same time continued to behave as Jews. These lodges offered a chance to socialize with other Jews away from the tumult of synagogue politics and congregational bickering. In small towns, membership in these lodges was close to universal. A correspondent for the *American Israelite* wrote in 1875 about Eureka, Nevada: "There is scarcely a Jew in the place but what is a member of either the Masonic or Odd Fellows societies. Many hold membership in both orders."[61] Jewish leaders, including rabbis, belonged to the lodges as well, and Isaac Wise rationalized: "Masonry is a Jewish institution whose history, degrees, charges, passwords and explanations are Jewish from the beginning to the end."[62] Rabbis, such as Polish-born Wolf Edelman of Los Angeles, took part in the dedication of the Masonic Hall, describing Masonry as "an ancient and honorable institution."[63] While some Jews belonged to all-Jewish lodges, most clustered where their brethren predominated. Of the sixteen lodges in late-nineteenth-century San Francisco, Jews joined only lodges that had other Jewish members and shied away from special German-language ones.[64] In Johnstown, Pennsylvania, as of the 1850s, a visible number of the Jewish men participated, but because of increased anti-Semitism, not a single Jew remained affiliated by century's end.[65]

Similarly, lodges of other national fraternal orders, such as the Odd Fellows, attracted many Jewish men from the merchant class, made their halls available to congregations without buildings, and participated in synagogue dedications. Reform and traditional Jews alike found reason to participate in these lodges, especially if they wanted to enhance business and even political contacts.[66]

Jewish men joined other kinds of secular associations in nineteenth-century America—fire companies, militias, athletic clubs, relief associations, civic organizations planning Fourth of July and Washington's birthday parades, and others that stressed civility and civic-mindedness in the context of leisure-time pursuits.[67]

Jewish women, on the other hand, participated less frequently in public activities and joined non-Jewish associations less often than their brothers. Except for spotty references to Jewish women in Washington, D.C., and Santa Cruz, California, few memoirs mention Jewish women joining the Order of the Eastern Star, the women's Masons auxiliary.[68] Jewish women did join some secular, service-oriented associations. In smaller towns, where the Jewish community sponsored few charitable projects, Jewish women played a role in supporting local orphanages and shelters. But in larger Jewish enclaves, New York, Chicago, and Philadelphia, Jewish women spent their time working for Jewish philanthropic institutions.[69] This pattern of female seclusion reflected the greater religious tradition of women.

Married Jewish women both worked in small family businesses and ran their homes, and therefore had significantly less leisure time than their husbands. In any event, women did not need to develop political or mercantile relationships in the larger society, and socializing through Jewish organizations served their needs. For Jews, the public, even the nonpolitical, realm remained primarily a man's world.

Historians have asserted that nineteenth-century Jewish immigrants readily joined German American associations and identified themselves strongly as Germans. One scholar posited that Jewish immigrants from Germany "brought with them a highly developed double culture," German and Jewish.[70] While some educated German Jews who came to America later were steeped in German culture and had mixed with non-Jews in Germany, most immigrants were Dorfjuden. These peddlers from Bavaria and tailors from Posen, who acquired minimal education in Europe and spoke little or no German, hardly identified with German culture. These Jews did not participate in German-American communal and cultural life.

Some American Jews did mingle in several of the elaborate German cultural institutions of the nineteenth century. They mostly participated in those that had no Jewish equivalents. A young Jewish man interested in athletics had no Jewish place to turn to to fulfill that interest. The YMHAs only slowly developed sports facilities and programs. The New York chapter, which was the most elaborate YMHA in the United States, installed its gymnasium only in 1875 and hired a sports instructor in 1880.[71] A Jew avid for sports probably turned to the German athletic clubs, the *Turnvereine,* which usually offered membership regardless of national origin.[72] Similarly, there were no Jewish singing societies, and a Jew with a good voice and love of music could join the *Sängerbünde* or *Gesangvereine* in the German communities.[73] Certainly no American Jewish community sponsored a *Schützenfest,* a rifle meet, while the German community offered opportunities to develop shooting skills.[74] Jews also participated in various aspects of American German *Kultur,* including theater, some journalistic ventures, a few German academies, and, in rare instances, German lodges, such as the Teutonia Verein or the Sons of Hermann.[75]

While it is impossible to arrive at a count of Jewish participants in German communal life, their presence was visible, although it may have been overstated. As patrons of German theaters and opera halls or as purchasers of German books, they were said to show up far out of proportion to their miniscule numbers when compared to Christian Germans in

New York, Chicago, Cincinnati, and Milwaukee. After an 1875 performance of the German Opera Troupe in Cincinnati, the *American Israelite* boasted that "the majority of the audience [was made up of] Israelites," thereby proving that, unflattering stereotypes notwithstanding, American Jews supported genteel culture. On the other hand, anti-Semites also claimed that Jews dominated German institutions, pushing out the Christians who rightly belonged there. One commentator, no friend of the Jews, noted in 1858 that eighty percent of those who attended German plays were Jews: "If you, reader, go to the New York theater you may see for yourself, but if you can't see, your nose will tell you among what Germans you find yourself." A German journalist visiting America claimed with a degree of envy that "German Jews in America gain in influence daily. . . . They read better books than the rest of the Germans, the booksellers tell me."[76]

Some Jews participated with zest in Germanic institutions and in the picnics, balls, and parties that went along with membership. Rabbis and other Jewish community leaders routinely showed up at German festivals and civic ceremonies. Isaac Wise claimed to have founded Albany's first German singing society.[77] Simon Wolf and Oscar Straus had close political ties with Germans, particularly those from the liberal wing of the Republican Party, such as Carl Schurz. Locally, Jews and Germans often acted together politically.[78] The first Jews to participate in organized labor traveled in German socialist circles. Conrad Kuhn, a Jewish cigar maker, served as president of New York's German Central Union, while the New York Sozialistische Turnverein elected Sigismund Kaufman the speaker of the party.[79]

A few Jews expressed almost mystical connectedness to German culture. David Einhorn, for example, spoke eloquently about Germanness as the soul of Reform Judaism. "Is not the German spirit," asked Einhorn, "the bearer of Reform Judaism? Where the German language is banned, there Reform Judaism is nothing more than a glittering veneer." Simon Wolf joined all kinds of German organizations in Washington, D.C., and proudly announced, "I am a German by birth," although he quickly added, "an Israelite by faith, and I trust a thorough American by adoption."[80]

Some American Jews, such as Wolf, considered themselves Germans as well as Jews, but the extent of Jewish identification and involvement with the German American communities has been overstated. While for some, participation in German events involved a strong assertion of Germanness, for many others it offered a way to see a play, hear an opera, or read a book in a language more familiar than English.

Participation in German activities also seems to have provided an early transition for many Jewish immigrants. In Portland, Oregon, in the 1850s, when newcomers made up the bulk of the city's Jews, Jews belonged to the local Turnverein and some even held offices. Yet by the 1870s, the club had no Jewish members. Perhaps by then Jews felt at ease enough with English and with America, and also, the Jewish community maintained an elaborate set of institutions of its own, so they could look for pleasures outside of the German world.[81] In the larger cities, Jews clustered in particular German clubs, such as New York's Orpheus Gesang Verein, which had a predominantly Jewish membership.[82]

There is no way to determine how many of the Jewish consumers of German culture actually hailed from Germany. Undoubtedly, some were athletically minded young men from Posen or Slovakia. As a native of Bohemia, Wise had no German roots, but he participated. Bernard Drachman's father, an immigrant from Galicia and a traditional Jew, eagerly accepted an invitation to become a member of a Jersey City German-American political group but predicated joining on a change in the organization's constitution that would state that membership was open to all regardless of place of birth.[83]

If Jews joined German cultural institutions, they never fully integrated into the German American communities. In Philadelphia, Syracuse, Cincinnati, St. Paul, and other places, Jews did not inhabit the same neighborhoods as Germans.[84] In addition, while finding common cause with German Americans in politics or athletics, Jews did not forget that back in Germany, anti-Jewish feeling ran rife and that immigrants from Germany had not necessarily shed the sentiments of the homeland. Thus, for example, Sarah Kussy's Bavarian father participated in German politics, lived among Germans in Newark, and spoke German at home, "interspersed with Yiddish words and sayings." But, says Kussy, "father would from time to time voice his apprehension: 'Where there is *Ashkenaz* [a German], there is *rishes* [Jew hatred].'"[85]

Beyond the circles of Ashkenazim, American Jews took tentative steps toward participating in their new country's cultural life. A few Jewish playwrights, journalists, and artists showed up in the 1820s and then in increasing number over the course of subsequent decades. By and large, they did not draw attention to their Jewishness in their cultural endeavors, nor did they disassociate from Judaism in order to win acceptance. Mordecai Noah, Isaac Harby, Solomon Nunes Carvalho, Adolph Ochs, and Henry Heyman all played key roles in their Jewish communities. But their drama, art, music and journalism resembled that of other Americans of the time, giving no hint of Jewishness.[86] The scarcity of Jews in these fields may have made them aware of their outsiderness and deterred them from linking art and ethnicity.[87]

A small number of Jewish young men attended America's colleges, in this period still primarily classical in their orientation and Christian in grounding. An even smaller number taught in American colleges. According to Wise, as of 1867, only six young Jewish men from Cincinnati had ever attended college. The first Jewish student graduated from Harvard in 1870, although Yale and the University of Pennsylvania had enrolled a few Jewish students earlier.[88] Oscar Straus recalled from his undergraduate years at Columbia University in the late 1860s: "I came . . . almost a stranger to a strange land . . . not as well dressed as most of my class-mates, with no social standing and a Jew."[89] Jewish students found themselves adrift among the Christian majority, but the experience of marginality did not scar them or cause them to resent their Jewishness, nor did they try to "pass" as something other than Jews. Louis Ehrich, a student at Yale in the 1860s, participated in the activities of New Haven's Jewish community, contributed articles to Jewish newspapers, and observed, somewhat spottily, Jewish festivals and holidays. When Louis Brandeis came to Harvard, he turned to the Jewish community of Boston for support.[90] Jewish communal leaders and rabbis of the latter part of the century, such as Cyrus Adler, Bernard Drachman, Simon Tuska, and Henry Schneeberger, all attended college in the mid-century, a time when a Jew on campus was a rara avis, yet they went on to carve out careers in Jewish life.[91]

If Jews taught at colleges, it was almost exclusively in the realm of Judaically oriented subjects of the classical curriculum. One exception, James Jacob Sylvester, briefly taught mathematics at the University of Virginia in 1841, but the appointment of a Jew and an antislavery advocate raised enough ire among powerful Virginians to have him ousted. "The University of Virginia belongs to the people of this Commonwealth. . . . The great body of the people in this Commonwealth are by profession Christians," they declared.[92] Those Jews who taught at colleges taught Hebrew, Bible, rabbinics, and sometimes German. Sigmund Waterman, for example, was an active member of New Haven's Jewish community and taught German at Yale. In 1845, he arranged for the first rabbi to speak on campus, bringing Samuel M. Isaacs from New York to address the overwhelmingly Christian student body "on the Present Condition and the

Future Spiritual and Temporal Hopes of the Jews."[93] In 1846, Isidor Lowenthal, an immigrant from Posen, served as a tutor and professor of Hebrew and German at Lafayette College in Pennsylvania. In 1866, courses in rabbinic literature taught by Jews were added to the curriculum of Columbia College and the University of Pennsylvania. In 1872, the Jewish communities of Los Angeles and San Francisco jointly petitioned officials of the University of California to "provide, even though in a moderate way, for instruction in Hebrew." The memorialists added that "Israelites on this coast," have "a strong predilection for this ancient tongue, whenever any of us seek to acquire a liberal education." A recent arrival in San Francisco, a Russian Jew named James M. Phillips, was offered the post approved by the university president, Daniel Coit Gilman.[94]

In sum, American Jews participated in American public life in the mid-nineteenth century demonstratively as Jews. They announced assertively that they would stand up for themselves, pursue a Jewish position on important policy issues, organize communities in distinctly Jewish ways, and pray according to their rites. Jews openly welcomed non-Jews to watch them in prayer and ritual. Public officials marched in processions to dedicate new synagogues and Jewish community institutions. Christians attended circumcisions and Jewish weddings. Indeed, so many non-Jews attended Jewish services that Rabbi Simon Tuska, the first American college graduate to become a rabbi, wrote a book in 1854, *Stranger in the Synagogue,* providing guidance in Jewish worship for the non-Jew. Conversely, rabbis spoke from the pulpits of Protestant churches, educating the Christian public about the Jews in their midst. Indeed, when Isaac Wise preached in Omaha on "The Wandering Jew" to a Methodist Congregation, he noted that "fifty years ago it would have looked miraculous for a rabbi to preach to a Methodist congregation; but now and here it is nothing strange."[95] Jews built large and imposing synagogues often in a Moorish style that diverged from the American preference, not tucked away in the interstices of the city but boldly announcing the Jewish presence. As one visitor to San Francisco noted, "The most sumptuous ecclesiastical edifice . . . is undoubtedly the synagogue. I put it first because for its position of one of the highest points in the city it attracts the eye before all the Christian churches. It testifies likewise to the local importance of the Jewish element."[96]

In participating in American life, American Jews walked a tightrope, claiming that in public matters they did not differ at all from their fellow citizens and yet, at almost every turn, drawing attention to their distinctiveness. When proclaiming patriotism, they spoke about a special Jewish stake in American society. At a centennial tree-planting ceremony at Mount Vernon in 1876, a representative of the Union of American Hebrew Congregations exclaimed: "Here, near his final earthly resting place, then is it fitting that the nation celebrating its first century should be greeted by the descendants of a people of FIFTY centuries' history. . . . here, in a land where the great code of Sinai binds a people in bonds of love and justice, we join our fellow-citizens of all denominations in rejoicing in the jubilee of the Republic."[97] Likewise, when American Jews invoked the memory of Abraham Lincoln, they presented not just a generalized portrait of the sixteenth president, martyr for the Union, fallen leader, and great emancipator—the usual statement of eulogy. Jews depicted him in their own, Jewish way. They cited his friendships with individual Jews and his special fondness for the Jewish people. They claimed for Lincoln personal qualities that made him almost a Jew. Isaac Wise had not been such a great partisan of Lincoln's in the war's early years but claimed that Lincoln, *"in my presence,"* professed Jewish ancestry. A rabbi in California eulogized Lincoln by telling his congregants that both "Moses and Lincoln loved people. . . . Moses and Lincoln were people who did things at the risk of their lives. . . . Moses affected Lincoln's philosophy as the philosophy of the Pentateuch dominates much of the American way of life."[98]

By proclaiming loyalty to America and describing the depth of Jewish participation in its life, Jews asserted their sameness with Americans, yet linked that sameness to Jewish difference. On the eve of the Fourth of July, 1857, the *Jewish Messenger* wrote: "Tonight, before we retire to rest, and after saying our usual prayers, let us exclaim [the words of "The Star Spangled Banner"] with every other American heart, that is, if the noise of the street does not drown out our voice."[99] The implication was clear. Out on the streets, making all that noise, thronged everyone else. Jews had to explain that, although they stood aloof from the crowd, they felt no less loyalty to the land, no shallower commitment to "the country that opened its arms to receive . . . our ancestors" than did those whose claims to Americanness rested on firmer grounds.[100]

Jews participated in American life as Americans. They participated in American life as Jews. And they participated while being ever mindful of the eyes of Christian America measuring, assessing, and judging them.

CHAPTER SEVEN

IN THE EYES OF OTHERS

We congratulate ourselves because nothing is so indicative of a city's progress as to see an influx of Jews who come with the intention of living with you and especially as they buy property and build among you because they are a thrifty and progressive people.

It is very difficult to ascertain what these descendants of "Abraham" are worth. . . . He is a Jew and with one exception none of that "Genus Homo" own any real estate here.

Why are greenbacks like the Jews?
Because they issue from Abraham and know not their redeemer.

NINETEENTH-CENTURY American Jews experienced contradictory relationships with their Gentile neighbors. On the one hand, Christian Americans welcomed them; in word and deed, America truly differed from any other Diaspora home. On this side of the Atlantic, no legacy of state-supported exclusion and violence, encrusted aristocracy, no embittered peasantry, or legally established church hierarchy manipulated centuries-old Judeophobia. Many Americans prided themselves on their openness to Jews, often because of sentimental attachments to the people of the Bible. Many took it as one of the hallmarks of America in general and their town or region in particular that individuals of different religious traditions could live side by side. As early as 1819, clergyman William D. Robinson, in a pamphlet entitled "Memoir, addressed to Persons of the Jewish Religion in Europe on the subject of Emigration and Settlement in the United States of North America," penned an invitation to the Jews of Europe to come and settle in America. Robinson hoped that Jews would leave Europe and envisioned settlements of "Jewish agriculture spreading throughout the American forests, Jewish towns and villages adorning the banks of the Mississippi and the Missouri."[1] More than a half-century later, Daniel Coit Gilman, in his inaugural address as president of the University of California, extended a welcome to all, including the "many among us . . . who look for a Messiah yet to come."[2] Senator Zebulon Vance of North Carolina traversed the South, giving his "Scattered Nation" speech to Jewish and non-Jewish audiences alike, and praised the Jews of America and their ancestors of ages past.[3]

On the other hand, despite tolerance and pluralism, Christians still articulated negative stereotypes about Jews. They wrote and spoke about the Jews' treachery and dishonesty in business at the expense of honest, hardworking Christians, about the Jews' eternal curse for the killing of Jesus and the damnation that awaited the unbaptized, their uncouth behavior and social abnormality, and their retrograde religion. Christians saw the Jews and their religion as fundamentally different and flawed. Nineteenth-century American Christianity was basically evangelical and the mere existence of Jews and Judaism threatened its vision of America as a Christian nation. Tolerated or not, Jews were outsiders.

If American Jews heard contradictory voices around them and could not decide whether America really differed from other countries or if it represented a kind of promised land, historians have not been able to decide which strain predominated either. Scholars have been split between those who emphasize the existence of a vibrant anti-Semitic culture in America and those who argued that anti-Semitism hovered only on the margins of society, limited to the lunatic fringe and to mere footnotes in text.[4]

The debate over anti-Semitism in America has hinged on questions of emphasis and, in most cases, looked at symbolic evidence rather than substance.[5] Some historians noted that in America, Jews encountered little overt hostility and they listed the leveling impact of the frontier, the constitutionally guaranteed religious equality, shortages of labor, and an obsession with skin color, which empowered whites regardless of ethnicity and creed, as the reasons. Others have pointed to scurrilous rhetoric in fiction and journalism, on the stage and in songs, rhetoric that could be heard from the pulpit and, occasionally, from the politician's stump that attacked Jews and Judaism. These historians insisted that this constituted a substantial anti-Semitic tradition. In the main, historians have opted for either one or the other position, *or* they have contended that neither predominated and that American views of the Jews fell into an ambivalent zone, bouncing back and forth between deep affection and scurrilous hatred.

The scholarly debate skirts the question of whether stereotyping constituted anti-Semitism. No one would deny that American popular and elite literature, theater, cartoons, advertisements, and jokes portrayed the Jews in a set of flat images that, whether positive or negative, had little to do with Jews as real people. This way, American Gentiles manifested ethnocentrism. They saw in their midst a people whom they perceived to live and look different, and they used and explored that difference for their own purposes.

But, by the standards of the nineteenth century, did the popular projection of such images mean that anti-Semitism flourished in America? How often and under what circumstances did words become deeds? Did the structure of American public institutions exclude Jews, relegate them to second-class citizenship, or deny them the rights available to other—Christian—Americans? How did America compare to Europe?

Certainly, America's diversity was one important difference from countries of both eastern and western Europe, where anti-Semitism had been and remained a potent political force. Although the vast majority of Americans belonged to some Christian denomination, religious, ethnic, and racial heterogeneity minimized Jews' otherness. Moreover, American culture diffused authority. No single institution, region, or class spoke for all of America; anti-Jewish sentiments articulated in one place or by one individual, however prominent, did not necessarily reflect majority or official opinion.

Indeed, America's contradictory images of and attitudes toward Jews mirrored contradictions in the Americans' self-image and national identity. White American Christians used Jews, Native Americans, Irish immigrants, and blacks as mirrors by which they defined themselves.[6] Nineteenth-century observers of the American people and later historians, such as Frederick Jackson Turner, Daniel Boorstin, and David Potter, as well as anthropologists, such as Margaret Mead, emphasized the jumble of seemingly oppositional beliefs and values held by the Americans. Michael Kammen has called Americans a "people of paradox."[7] Americans have at once exhibited or espoused individualism and cooperation, idealism and practicality, freedom and order, generosity and greed, tradition and innovation. Alexis de Tocqueville noted in his classic, *Democracy in America,* in 1835, that Americans cared little for ideas, rarely attended church but considered themselves a deeply religious people.[8] Americans prided themselves on their openness and tolerance toward people of different origins and at the same time articulated profoundly xenophobic and racist ideas that held up the white Protestant of English origin as representatively American, the ideal type.[9]

These contradictory messages grew out of the strains of a society faced with vast opportunities for growth and yet fearful of what growth would bring, a society that celebrated the ideal of the independent, yeoman farmer but moved inexorably into industrialization.[10] This society, which venerated the bonds of family and close-knit community, saw men and women moving about at a frantic pace over vast geographic areas in search of economic opportunities, straining the bonds of kinship and breaking up communal solidarity.[11] This society, which believed itself, unlike all other countries, to be based on ideals of democracy, equality, and liberty, denied basic benefits of citizenship to blacks, Indians, and others.[12] Committed to the separation of church and state and to religious diversity from almost the beginning of national existence, Americans celebrated the wall erected between the affairs of the soul and those of citizenship. Yet, American Protestants, strongly rooted in the evangelical tradition, believed that their democratic system grew out of Christianity and that the two were inextricably bound to each other.[13]

Thus, it should hardly be surprising that Americans espoused jarringly contradictory attitudes about Jews. Anti-Semitism surely existed in nineteenth-century America, and nineteenth-century Americans surely welcomed Jews into the ranks of equal citizenship. Probably no issue loomed larger than the inherent incompatibility between the notion of America as a religiously tolerant and diverse society, and a deep American commitment to evangelical Protestantism. Americans prided themselves on their hospitality to foreigners and believed that all differences would be eroded under the powerful influence of the American environment. Yet they lived in a race-conscious society that doled out rights along racial lines. Americans celebrated success in the marketplace but sneered suspiciously at those who did not till the land. They professed a belief in social egalitarianism, no doubt a legacy of the frontier, precisely at the time when their economic elite became increasingly concerned about symbols of status. Finally, Americans were entangled in a tug-of-war between ideals of community and mobility, tradition and modernity. In each one of these paradoxes of self-definition, Protestant Americans used Jews to work out solutions.

Jews, different, exotic, and identifiable, provided a perfect medium by which Gentiles could test their values. The Jewish tradition was external to America. To depict a Jew in a play or to preach against Judaism in a sermon was to hold up something alien to America. Yet, unlike blacks, Indians, or Chinese immigrants, the Jews functioned inside the American framework. As "white" people, they voted, held office, served on juries, bore arms during wars, and lived as close by as the local dry-goods store. However strange Judaism may have seemed, American Protestants steeped in the Hebrew Bible had a reference point when discussing Judaism, as opposed to, for example, Asian religions. Being outsiders and insiders at once, Jews stood out as emblematic of all that one either liked or disliked about modern America. The enemies of the Jews as well as their defenders, average Americans as well as systematic thinkers used these people, different in religion, occupational structure, and cultural background, as symbols to explore the meaning of their own society and values.

Jews and Judaism, Christians and Christianity

The existence of Judaism in America challenged the way Americans defined religion. Many Americans committed to the separation of church and state also feared for the health of Christianity, by which they meant Protestantism, in America. Many incidents cited by contemporary Jews and subsequent historians as evidence of anti-Semitism were not in fact specifically targeted against Jews and Judaism. Jurisdictions enacted Sunday-closing laws and added Christian content to public school materials not so much because they disdained Jews but because they feared widespread irreligion among Christians. Moreover, many Protestants worried about the immense influx of Catholics, whom they saw as a potent threat to their civilization.[14] When the Supreme Court of Georgia declared in 1871 that "the Christian Sabbath is a civil institution, older than government," its primary concern was that Christians were defying the dictate that "law fixes . . . the Sabbath day all over Christendom, and that day, by Divine injunction, is to be kept holy."

Jews certainly suffered from ordinances that forbade mercantile activity on the Lord's Day and believed that such regulations had been aimed at them. But states and towns in which few or no Jews lived passed such laws more often than did jurisdictions where Jews swelled the shopkeepers' ranks. Jews suffered from what in the late twentieth century might be called "institutional anti-Semitism," a public policy intended for other purposes but hurting Jews disproportionately.[15]

During the Civil War era and through the 1870s, American evangelicals pressed for a constitutional amendment that would acknowledge Christianity as America's religion and recognize the authority of God and Jesus as fundamentals of the polity. Many influential Americans supported the proposed amendment, including a Supreme Court justice, several governors, and college professors. Despite wide endorsement, the amendment died in the House Judiciary Committee in 1874 and never made it to the floor of Congress.

Isaac Leeser, members of the Board of Delegates, and other Jewish leaders saw this proposed amendment as an attack on Jews. Yet the amendment reflected the evangelicals' anxiety over secularization of American life, the rise of scientific challenges to orthodox Christianity, and the increasing number of Catholics who constituted a majority in many American cities. Although the amendment's advocates occasionally cited "infidels, Jews, Jesuits" in one breath, for them, Jews were an afterthought rather than the lightning rod whose presence sparked the movement.[16]

A few states required that officeholders be practicing Protestants well into the late nineteenth century. New Hampshire did not repeal its religious test until 1877, the last state in the country to do so. Jewish leaders asserted that these laws were motivated explicitly by antipathy to Jews, but as in the Sunday-closing issue, the framers and supporters of the laws usually had Catholics and nonbelievers in mind when deciding to limit public offices to professing Protestants.[17] Nonbelievers, that is, atheists, still could not hold office in Maryland after passage of Thomas Kennedy's "Jew Bill" in 1824.[18]

Of course, Judaism was a minority religion, stigmatized for centuries in Christian Europe, and it stood outside the American mainstream. That European heritage produced sporadic acts of exclusion, harassment, or plain intolerance in America. Jews who grew up in the mid-nineteenth century recalled that as schoolchildren their Christian classmates taunted them as "Christ killers." When Cornell University offered Felix Adler a position to teach Hebrew language and literature in 1874, the *Christian Statesman* asserted that "Christianity is imperiled in consequence."[19]

Some Americans saw Judaism as a threat to the fundamentally Christian nature of the nation already under attack from many quarters. Judaism and Jews, they believed, had an almost mystical power to survive against all odds. In this view, Judaism—unlike Presbyterianism or Methodism—constituted an ossified form, impervious to the pressures of modernity and jarring to American values or common sense. When Warder Cresson, member of a notable Quaker family in Philadelphia, converted to Judaism in the

1840s, his family sought to have him legally declared insane.[20] A Christian clergyman who participated in informal religious discussions with Chicago's Bernhard Felsenthal asked the rabbi to describe the "manner in which the Jews of today prepared their temple sacrifices." Some believed that Judaism was a bigoted, intolerant religion, which taught care for one's own, but inculcated an aloofness towards others, causing them to exclude outsiders. Had Judaism kept up with the times and responded to its environment, Christian critics implied, it would have become more liberal, more loving, more democratic, and essentially more American.[21]

Judaism appeared to be inconsistent with America because it bred intolerance and group chauvinism, as opposed to the American self-perception valuing openness and liberality. A reporter for the *Chicago Daily Democrat* noted in his coverage of the 1851 dedication of Congregation Kehillath Anshe Maariv: "No person that has made up his mind to be prejudiced against the Jews ought to hear such a sermon preached. It was very captivating and contained as much real religion as any sermon we ever heard. . . . We never could have believed that one of those old Jews we heard denounced so much could have taught so much liberality towards other denominations and so earnestly recommend a thorough study of the Old Testament."[22]

Because of the perceived incompatibility of Judaism and America, public officials were not always keen to see Jewish religious institutions arise in their "Christian" communities. The Maryland legislature, for example, refused to incorporate The Scattered Israelites congregation in 1829, just a few years after the "Jew bill" controversy. By its refusal it sent a hostile message to the state's Jewish population. (Governor Thomas King Carroll intervened, and the next year Congregation Nidche Yisrael—also known as the Baltimore Hebrew Congregation—received a charter from the state legislature.) In 1844, the municipality of Boston likewise turned down the request of Ohabei Shalom to buy and enclose a portion of the municipal cemetery for Jewish burials. (The congregation found a suitable burial ground in East Boston instead.)[23]

American commentators depicted Judaism as sui generis, and its transplantation to America became a subject of immense interest. American writers, clergyman, and commentators of all kinds differed widely in their assessment of the religion of the Jews. Was it a degenerate religion, responsible for the evils of civilization and the degraded state of the Jews, from which its misguided followers ought to be weaned? Did it nobly link present with past? Should Christian Americans show Jews—a very special group of nonbelievers—the truth of the gospel, or should Judaism be left undisturbed as a testimony to American liberality?

Traditional Christian ideas about Judaism found a home in America, and despite the ethos of religious tolerance in American rhetoric, popular, folk, and "high" culture persisted in the notion that all Jews, for all times, carried a curse for the killing of Jesus. When Judah P. Benjamin of Louisiana walked out of the Senate chambers during a heated debate over slavery and secession in 1861, his colleague from Massachussetts, abolitionist Henry Wilson, condemned him as a descendant of "that race that stoned Prophets and crucified the Redeemer of the World," while the tremendously popular novel of 1880, *Ben-Hur,* clearly placed the Jews at the scene of the crime, leading the frenzied mob. In Wallace's panoramic book about the conversion of an aristocratic Jew to Christianity, Jews bore responsibility for the crucifixion on Calvary: "Jews from all East countries and all West countries, and all islands within commercial connection . . . went by in haste—eager, anxious, crowding—all to behold one poor Nazarene die, a felon between felons."[24] In 1872, a Jewish benevolent association applied for a Texas state charter, and one legislator objected to sanctioning a "Christ killing association."[25] A popular nineteenth-century joke, with variations to suit local conditions, involved a simple mountaineer or cowboy who had just left a camp meeting. Upon seeing a Jew, he struck him down with force. The bewildered peddler, or shopkeeper, asked what he had done to incur such an attack, and the Christian replied, "You crucified our Lord." When the Jew explained that the event had taken place some eighteen hundred years earlier, the ignoramus replied that he thought that it had happened only recently and begged the Jew's pardon.[26] Hymns and sermons, religious pamphlets and Sunday-school lesson books emphasized the damnation of the Jews as killers of Jesus. A popular black ballad sung throughout the free and the slave communities intoned unmistakably:[27]

> Cruel Jews, jes look at Jesus . . .
> Dey nail him to de Cross . . .
> Dey rivet His feet . . .
> Dey hang him high . . .
> An' dey stretch Him wide . . .
> O de cruel Jews dun took ma Jesus

Organized American Christianity devoted tremendous energy and resources to converting Jews. Evangelicals controlled almost all of the nineteenth-century Protestant denominations. They viewed the transplantation and flourishing of Judaism in America as an affront to American society's fundamental nature, which had been and ought to remain Protestant. The formation of Jewish communities and the founding of synagogues for Jewish worship contradicted the basic truth of America as a Christian society, which predicted the universal acceptance of the Christian gospel. When, in 1843, New Haven's Jews formed Congregation Mishkan Israel, the *New Haven Register* expressed a mix of dismay and disappointment. "Whilst we have been busy converting the Jews in other lands," speculated the paper, "they have outflanked us here, and effected a footing in the very centre of our fortress. Strange as it may sound it is nevertheless true that a Jewish synagogue has been established in this city and their place of worship . . . was dedicated on Friday afternoon. Yale College divinity [school] deserves a Court-martial for bad generalship."[28]

Not all American Christians supported the drive to convert Jews, however. Some opposed it for theological reasons, while others distrusted the evangelicals and their quest for an American religious orthodoxy. Yet others decided that these missions were squandering vast amounts of money and energy, since Jews would never see the truth. Some Americans just thought that the whole idea smacked of illiberalism and intolerance. In 1816, *Niles' Weekly Register* sneered at the fact that missionary groups had spent $500,000 over five years "for the conversion, real or supposed, of *five Jews*." The *Philadelphia Sunday Dispatch* cynically noted in 1871 that the Society for the Promotion of Christianity among the Jews could boast that it had, after considerable effort, converted, "a sixth of a Jew per annum."[29]

Nevertheless, conversionists far outnumbered their opponents. Such organizations as the American Society for Meliorating the Condition of the Jews, founded in 1820 in the afterglow of the Second Great Awakening, struggled throughout the half-century to bring about a Jewish acceptance of Jesus. All over the country, in large cities and small towns, bands of Christian men and women set up programs to attract Jews, particularly women and children. Evangelicals, despite their continuing failure, established themselves in storefronts in Jewish neighborhoods, roamed the streets looking for Jewish orphans and poor children, tried to get courts to remand destitute Jewish youngsters to their care, stalked the charity wards of hospitals looking for expiring Jews to make last-minute deathbed conversions, and employed a handful of Jewish converts to Christianity, such as Ephraim Epstein, Louis Meyer, Isidor Lowenthal, and others, to spread the word among their coreligionists still in darkness.[30]

Christian advocates of conversion tirelessly prodded their Jewish friends to accept the truth. Rebecca Gratz, for one, maintained amicable relations with a number of Christian women. Yet her friendships were always strained by these women's incessant efforts to ply her with pamphlets about Christianity. When her brother married a non-Jewish woman, Gratz worried that her new sister-in-law would carry on a conversion campaign within the family circle.[31]

The writers of religious fiction exploited the theme of the conversion of Jews. Poignant stories and novels portrayed the good Jews, usually the ones least attached to money and with attractive physical features, as converts. Jewish women, whom Gentile American writers portrayed in more positive terms than their brothers, generally showed up in sentimental stories about Jews who saw through the sham of Judaism and its worship of money, and opted for the true faith. A short sentimental piece in an 1821 issue of the *Ladies Literary Cabinet* saw a beautiful, dying Jewish girl, who had secretly found her way to Christianity, extracting a last request from her beloved father. "My dear father, I beg you," she intoned, "never again to speak against Jesus of Nazareth! . . . I know that he is a Saviour, for he has manifested himself to me since I have been sick, even for the salvation of my soul." The father, deeply moved "after committing to the earth his last earthly joy," went and found a Christian Bible. "This he read; and taught by the Spirit from above, is now numbered among the meek and humble followers of the Lamb!"[32]

While conversionists may have been noticeably unsuccessful in winning over many Jews, they enlisted a number of notable Americans. John Quincy Adams, James Monroe, college presidents, ministers, lawyers, captains of industry, and legions of street evangelists who sang hymns and distributed Bibles, assumed that to convert a Jew constituted a great act of loving-kindness. How better, after all, to show one's appreciation of the Jews as a people than to offer them the gift of Christianity?[33] How better to prove the tolerance of American culture than to allow Jews to share its greatest gift?

Interest in the restoration of a Jewish homeland illustrated the paradox of American Christians' attitudes toward Jews among them. Almost all restorationists participated in conversionist work as well, although some pious Christians opposed missions to the American Jews because they believed that the restoration of the Jews to Palestine would precede the Second Coming and they wanted to see Jews reach Zion in their unconverted state. As an 1849 writer for the *Puritan Recorder* noted, the presence of the Jews "is a standing proof of the verity of our holy oracles; and many of the glorious prophecies of the Bible are yet to be fulfilled by their restoration to national greatness, and God's favor."[34]

Judging from the tone of restorationist rhetoric in published writings and sermons, these visionaries of a Jewish commonwealth in the Holy Land clearly saw themselves as the friends of the Jews and as agents in the fulfillment of centuries-old Jewish dreams for a return to Zion. In 1841, the leader of the Mormon church, Joseph Smith, sent an elder, Orson Hyde, to the Holy Land to prepare for the imminent return of the Jewish people. As Hyde wrote back, "It was by political power that the Jewish Nation was broken down, and her subjects dispersed abroad: and I will hazard . . . that by political power . . . they will be gathered and built up." A speaker at the 1878 First International Prophetic Conference in New York City extolled the Jews for their power of survival. "Can the world," he asked, "show anything like it? Twice 1,800 years old, they saw the proud Egyptian perish in the water of the Red Sea; they heard the fall of great Babylon's power; they witnessed the ruins of the Syro-Macedonian conquests. And now they have outlived the Caesars, and outlived the dark ages." What the restorationists said and did connoted something else. They sought this return to Zion not to help the Jewish downtrodden but to hasten the Second Coming, which many believed would happen only after the ingathering of the Jews to their land. By implication, they were not too eager to see the Jews move en masse to America.[35] Indeed, if the restorationists wanted to see a Jewish return to Zion, they were probably willing to bid farewell to the Jews of America. When, for example, John Adams wrote to Mordecai Noah in 1819, "I really wish the Jews again in Judea as an independent nation," he, by implication if not by design, was also hoping not to see them in Boston.[36]

American Protestants shared no single view of the prospects for Judaism in America and of the possibility that it could survive in a land of freedom and tolerance. Some asserted that such an illiberal religion as Judaism could never really thrive in America, while others feared the mythical power of Judaism to outlive other civilizations. Both extremes stressed the unbroken chains that bound the Jews of the nineteenth century with ancient ideas and forms. In the press and in sermons, Americans marveled at the ways in which Jews banded together to keep their archaic faith alive and how, despite migrations, persecutions, and new environments, they had not swerved from or altered religious practice. On the day after Yom Kippur in 1859, a reporter for the *Gazette* of Alexandria, Virginia, voiced his personal feelings as a "reflecting Gentile," on the rite he had just witnessed: "Here we have the remnant of a once renowned nation firmly adhering to the custom of their fathers, which they have preserved amidst the greatest afflictions and calamities which ever befel [*sic*] a people."[37] Lydia Maria Child, who visited New York's Shearith Israel in 1841 at Rosh Hashannah, experienced this same awe at the antiquity of ritual and the historic connections between the Jews of her own day and those of the past. While she decided that the Jewish ritual lacked the solemn dignity and deep faith of a Catholic service, "there is something deeply impressive in this remnant of scattered people, coming down to us in continuous links through the long vista of recorded time . . . keeping up the ceremonial forms of Abraham, Isaac, and Jacob."[38] Indeed, even when criticizing the ambience of the synagogue, American writers invoked the past, placing American Jews in the pages of history. In 1844, the Reverend Mr. Wells in Boston found the synagogue Ohabei Shalom "not a comfortable or decent place for the performance of the service which thousands of years ago swelled through the arches of Solomon's Temple."[39]

At a time when Protestant orthodoxy had lost its grip on the churchgoing public, when the clergy and church establishment experienced a decline in power and status, and when the sharp theological distinctions between denominations faded, the descriptions of traditionalism in Jewish ritual could be seen as the counterpoint to the American experience.[40] While American Christians relegated religion to the sphere of the female, the sentimental, and the inconsequential, Jews seemed to preserve their ancient faith intact. This sounded potentially positive. After all, America was the land of progress. Modern people did not remain mired in the dogma and formulations of the murky past. But Jews did. Jews prayed, maintained religious practices, and organized religion the same way their ancestors had in the biblical past, while Christians opted for progress.

Some Christians believed that this preservation of Judaism as a relic of the past would be short-lived, that it would have little prospect for survival in America. A religious tradition born in the Levant and sustained by European persecutions, could hardly thrive in America's free air. Some were even somewhat saddened by this realization. Longfellow's poignant "Jewish Cemetery at Newport," written in 1852, elegaically reflected:[41]

> Pride and humiliation hand and hand
>> Walked with them through the world where'er they went
> Trampled and beaten were they as the sand
>> And yet unshaken as the continent

But in America, where they suffered no "humiliation," and were not "trampled" down, they could not survive:

> But ah! what once has been shall be no more!
>> The groaning earth in travail and in pain,
> Brings forth its races, but does not restore.
> And the dead nations never rise again.

The theme of the disappearance of "backward" peoples and races ran through much of nineteenth-century anthropological and ethnological literature. Scientists argued that if lesser races and inferior cultures could not adapt to the demands of the modern world, they would vanish. Jews, like American Indians, had to adjust to new realities or find themselves pushed out of history. Longfellow's "Jewish Cemetery at Newport" could be juxtaposed with his "Hiawatha" (1855), in which the poet described the beauty, the oneness with nature, and the inevitable disappearance of the American Indian.[42]

Americans pointed to some specific aspects of Judaism as the evidence of its backwardness. The practice of gender segregation in the synagogue came under particular attack as an "oriental" atavism, a "mistreatment" of women, and a "great error of the Jews," in which "she [the Jewish woman] is separated and huddled into a gallery like beautiful crockery ware, while the men perform the ceremonies below." Christian leaders, rather than womens' rights advocates, insisted that the position of women in Jewish ritual did not fit into the American framework. It was out of step with modernity, an era not surprisingly ushered in by the advent of Christianity. "It was the author of Christianity that brought her [the woman] out of this Egyptian bondage," wrote one commentator, "and put her on an equality with the other sex in civil and religious rites."[43]

Because of this fixation on Judaism as an inanimate reminder of antiquity, writers and journalists paid scant attention to the rise of Reform. Perhaps the exotic and unintelligible features of a traditional service made for better copy than, for example, one in which men and women sat together, prayers were offered in English, and the rabbi faced the congregation. It may have also been that by updating Judaism to fit the conditions of American life, Reformers denied evangelicals one of their well-worn images of Judaism as an unbroken connection to the past, which could not grow of its own accord. A writer for the *Cleveland Leader* in 1869 expressed shock when he saw that "Hebrew prayers are abolished as unintelligible, the law of Moses is declared to have had only a temporary authority, and the doctrines of the Messiah and of the restoration of Israel are spiritualized. . . . The 'peculiar people' are giving up their greatest peculiarity."44 Similarly, the Omaha *Evening Bee* in 1879 poked fun at the reformed Rosh Hashanah service, held in a Unitarian Church, in which "service was rendered in the old Hebraic language; and a somewhat talented young man . . . presided at the organ. This time, when this essentially Christian instrument was prohibited in the Jewish church, but progressive ideas have wrought innovations. . . . [a] congregation whose ancestors have for nearly 2,000 years denied that Christ was God, worshipping the Unitarian God of the Jew in the Unitarian church of the Christian, presents to America in the 19th century, an illustration of the adage 'Extremes meet.'"45

The scant attention to the reform of Judaism stood in sharp contrast to the extensive coverage given to traditional Jewish practices, holidays, and rituals. American newspapers, particularly in smaller cities and towns, devoted numerous articles to Judaism as a faith and to its oddities and peculiarities. The articles were often of a strictly informational nature, educating readers about the high points of the Jewish calendar, elucidating some Jewish customs, and offering straightforward, if not always accurate, details about the faith of their Jewish neighbors. The *Argus,* of Albany, New York, told its readership, for example, that "yesterday the orthodox Hebrews celebrated the feast of 'Ab' or the 'black feast.' It began on Sunday morning and lasted until last evening. The feast commemorates the destruction of the two temples in Judea." A writer for the *Santa Cruz Sentinel* covered the local Purim ball in 1878 and reported that "the schoolhouse was well filled. . . . Prof. J. M. Lesser delivered a lecture on the occasion which was often interrupted by applause. He spoke of the historical event to which the feast relates, with sufficient humor to make it enjoyable, mingled with historical fact to make it interesting, and enough pathos in order not to take from the solemnity of the occasion." The article went on to describe how the "Hebrew children promenaded through the hall, masked in costume."46

Reporters of local newspapers wrote about various Jewish gatherings, including weddings, dedications of synagogues, and circumcisions, and reported on these grand and glorious, albeit strange, events. Writing for a

Nevada City newspaper in 1857, a reporter put under "Local Affairs" the fact that "we were induced to witness the rite of circumcision at the house of a Jewish friend on Wednesday." After detailing the rites, including the "nipping in the bud," the reporter suggested that "those curious in such matters are advised to obtain further information by seeing for themselves, or consulting a rare old book a part of which is said to have been written by Moses."[47]

Local newspapers also reported on Jewish weddings, described as lavish galas demonstrating intense Jewish commitment to family and the Jews' tendency to flaunt wealth. Jewels, silk, flowers, rich food—all swirled around these events that brought together relatives and Jewish friends from far and wide. When Bertha Weiner and William Baer got married in Cleveland at the Eagle Street Synagogue in 1867, the local press noted the immense crowd, full of relatives and friends who had spared no expense to come "from nearly every town on Lake Superior, and also from New York, Pennsylvania, Virginia, Michigan, Illinois and other states." The *Standard* of New Bedford, Massachusetts, claimed that at the wedding of Julius Goldbeck and Riecke Cohen, an eighty-six-year-old uncle of the bride had traveled all the way from Posen, some three-thousand miles, just to be present.[48] A reporter for the *Express* in Lancaster, Pennsylvania, covered the wedding of Fannie Loeb in 1873 and chronicled the lavish festivities, rich clothing, and sumptuous feast. So many uninvited people crowded in to see the interesting ritual under the canopy, that the floor of the synagogue collapsed. The reporter ultimately decided that even his presence had been in poor taste and concluded: "By invitation the reporter of the *Express* was present, and although we do not approve, as a general thing, of laying matters so sacred before a curious public, yet the occasion was so interesting, so novel, so grand, so impressive that we cannot refrain from a description of it."[49]

Articles describing dedications of synagogues emphasized the grandeur of the new structure and the triumphalism of the participants. When in 1869 a reporter for the Los Angeles *Star* covered the dedication of Congregation B'nai B'rith, "one of the grandest spectacles that was ever witnessed in Southern California," he informed his readers, the vast majority of whom were not Jewish, that the members of the "Hebrew Synagogue . . . may well feel proud of their house of worship. It is the most superior church edifice in Southern California."[50] Similarly, an article in the *Mobile Register* in 1853 waxed eloquent about the synagogue, the Jews, and the beneficence of America in general and the Alabama city in particular, asserting that "the synagogue is worthy in all respects the high character of our Jewish brethren for wealth, intelligence, and character. How proud must the enfranchised descendants of the patriarchs have felt yesterday who were some times since the slaves and serfs of Russia, Austria and Prussia. Poor Poland."[51]

How might non-Jewish readers have felt when somehow their weddings, their churches, and their ceremonies were measured up against those of the Jews? While these articles had been written just to report to the public about the interesting and notable activities of local Jews, the tone conveyed a sense not only of Jewish singularity but superiority, at least when it came to spending money. After all, if the Jewish congregation was the "most superior," then all Christian edifices had been found wanting. If the Jewish wedding was "so novel, so grand, so impressive," then comparable ceremonies among American Christians paled.

Articles detailing the various aspects of Judaism constantly gauged the worth of Jews and their religion. A notice in the San Francisco *Herald* on the local celebration of Purim in 1851 connected this "celebration of Israelites," with the fact that they constituted "a numerous and intelligent class, conducting themselves with great propriety and decorum, industrious and enterprising, and worthy members of the community."[52] Likewise, articles consistently linked the religious life of the Jews with money. In 1872, the *Spectator* in Hanover, Pennsylvania, kept tabs on Jewish holidays, offering readers a steady stream of information on Passover, Sukkot, Purim, and the like. On Rosh Hashanah, it noted that "the worship commenced in the morning as soon as the day dawns. . . . each of the men did wear a white linen garment, without pockets, which is preserved until their death and then becomes their shroud. It is said that no pockets in this garment signifies the fact that you can not take any money with you when you die."[53]

Almost yearly, newspapers across the country commented on how the Jews' fall holidays brought about a cessation of business for everyone. Readers in Davenport, Iowa, learned on October 1, 1867, from the local *Gazette* that the Jewish year of 5628 had begun, services had been held with many attending from Rock Island, Moline, Le Claire, and Geneseo, and "most of the Jewish places of business were closed." The *News* of Denver wrote in 1865 that "today is some sort of holiday for the Jewish persuasion, unknown to us Gentiles." Some Jews, obviously not included amongst "us," must have protested; the next day, the newspaper expanded its holiday coverage: "Yesterday was the opening of the Jewish year 5626, and consequently was a gala day with our Jewish residents. . . . This will account for the closing of the business houses of this class yesterday." Likewise in 1880, the reporter for the *Sentinel* in Eureka, Nevada, surveyed the town and wrote: "Some idea of the number of merchants in Eureka who belong to the Jewish faith could have been formed between dark on Friday and the appearance of the stars last night, that period embracing their Day of Atonement. Main Street, usually dull at this season of the year, presented an almost deserted appearance, and one calculated to give even a callous reporter the blue devils."[54]

Mixing together welcome and praise with traditional Christian antipathy for Judaism, Gentiles surveyed curiously the new faith that was being transplanted on to their shores. Christian opinion divided along a variety of lines as to the worth of Judaism and its viability in American society. Judaism was not just another denomination in a religiously pluralistic society—it offered Americans a chance to assess *themselves*.

Jews with Money

No set of images demonstrated contradictory American views of Jews more graphically than those juxtaposing Jews and money. Discussions of Jews and business also demonstrated American confusion about money-making, profit, and class relations. Americans considered themselves idealistic, willing to sacrifice comforts for the pursuit of the lofty ideals of democracy and freedom. Their public discourse sneered at the evils of commercialization, lauding the simple yeoman farmer, content with and ennobled by his meager plot. They projected America as a nearly classless society, devoid of Europe's extremes of abject poverty and fabulous wealth. At the same time, though, Americans aspired to material success and set about creating social institutions and public policies aimed at economic expansion. Their rhetoric about national creed asserted that the widespread prosperity itself proved America's uniqueness; yet, however they lionized the small-time farmer, businessmen wielded power and made America a business civilization.

Jews provided a medium by which these conflicting values about the commercial life were played out. Jews—associated with business and almost totally absent from agriculture—became symbols of material acquisition. In the press, theater, literature, and politics, they were linked with money.

At times, this linkage earned Jews the praise of their neighbors. Their critics, however, also built arguments about the incompatability of Jews with American, Christian culture around the issue of money.

Connecting Jews to money-making grew out of a millenium-old experience. European Christians depicted Jewish commercialism negatively, despite the fact that the European economy depended thoroughly on Jews. In America, on the other hand, Jews found themselves equally praised and condemned for their supposed money-making prowess. Either way it served as the central and most often invoked image of the Jews, used to delineate the positive qualities of real—that is native and Christian—Americans.

Some non-Jewish commentators noted that Jews actually enriched the communities in which they lived because they made so much money that their tax payments were far out of proportion to their numbers. The *Richmond Whig* stated in 1866: "We hail their [the Jews'] presence in the Southern States as an auspicious sign. . . . a more industrious . . . class of the population does not exist. They interfere with no one, mind their own business, observe their religious ceremonies, and pursue their peculiar enjoyments and indulgences. We hope they may never leave us. When they do, we shall begin to fear that we are giving over to ruin."[55] Other commentators complained that Jews made that money by cheating, exploiting, underselling, and tricking honest Christian townspeople who worked hard and struggled to make a living in nobler ways. A writer for *Alta California* wrote in 1852 that the Jews' "religion is but in name, a cloak for avarice. . . . Gold seems to be their only God, and the shrine of Mammon the only one to which they kneel." *Niles' Weekly Register* held up the fact that "they will not sit down and labor like other people—they create nothing and are mere consumers."[56]

Civil War tensions heightened this perceived connection between Jews and money. Across the country, anti-Jewish sentiment flared. Jews were accused of disloyalty and cowardice, of being unpatriotic, and contributing little to the war effort. Jews, it was said, made a profit off the suffering of real Americans.

Wartime anti-Semitism illustrated most dramatically how Christian Americans used Jews as the foil against which they defined national values. The massive internal crisis of the war challenged the basic meaning of American society. It demanded tremendous sacrifice from ordinary citizens for ambiguous goals. While the war was "sold" to the public—on both sides of the Mason-Dixon Line—in terms of lofty and noble sentiments, in actuality, economic interests of powerful Northern industrialists and wealthy Southern planters set the agenda.[57] Politicians tried to ease the dissonance between the aims of the masses, upon whose cooperation the war effort depended, and those of the economic and political elite by draping the war in highly-charged evangelical Christian symbols. This made the Jews—the outsiders—convenient targets. The public identified them with that part of the business sector that they recognized most immediately.

A string of incidents across the country indicated how deeply Gentiles saw the Jews as the profit hungry "others." General Grant's Order #11 had forced the Jews of Paducah out of their homes, and the citizens of Thomasville and Talbotton in Georgia demanded the expulsion of their Jews. They all used economic arguments against the Jews. Confederate Congressman Henry S. Foote from Tennessee, along with several of his fellows, proclaimed that Jews controlled nine-tenths of the Confederacy's commerce, and that powerful Jews, such as Judah P. Benjamin, the "brains of the Confederacy" were allowing Northern Jews to infiltrate the South and gobble up property.[58] In cities and towns throughout the North and South during the Civil War, individual Christians accused "the Jews" of profiteering from the suffering of others. Indeed, the Civil War represented a high point in American anti-Semitism and came closest to replicating the European experience. As Detroit's *Commercial Advertiser* saw it, Jews were the only group to profit from the war; while others bled, "the people who look up to Abraham as their father . . . [the] hooked nose wretches speculate on disasters and a battle lost to our army is chuckled over by them, as it puts money in their purse."[59]

With money came power. After the heat of the Civil War, anti-Semitism toned down. But some Americans emphasized that the Jews' economic prowess enabled them to gain great influence. Politicians, they maintained, courted the Jews. Newspapers noted routinely when distinguished non-Jews participated in Jewish community celebrations. The presence of governors, mayors, and Christian clergymen at dedications of synagogues figured boldly in the descriptions of these events. Who could but fail to be impressed at reading in the Washington *Star* in 1876 that President Grant, his son, the vice president, and other "prominent personages" all showed up at the dedication of the orthodox Adas Israel? Outside of the nation's capital, other distinguished Christians, powerful and important officials, attended similar Jewish assemblies, and their presence, as a testimony to the power of the Jews, was duly noted in the press.[60]

At times, Americans protested the influence and power amassed by Jews by virtue of wealth. The *Oregonian,* during a local political controversy in 1858, decried that Jewish power clearly derived from money. In a broad stroke it stated that "the history of the Jews is but a history of a great variety of ways and means adopted by them to obtain money and power." The editorial ended with the familiar refrain: "Do you know of a Jew who ever drove an ox team across the plains, or engaged in an Indian war to defend the homes and firesides of our citizens on this coast, or on any other frontier?"[61]

Because of their mercantile inclinations, Jews served to contrast with the positive attributes of the Americans as strong, virile, adventurous, and productive farmers and mechanics who worked with their hands. While few works of popular fiction and theater made Jews the central protagonists or even chief antagonists, Jews served as the foils against which the Americans' sterling traits could be measured. If Jews sold goods, Gentiles produced them. If Jews stayed inside behind their counters or in their "slop shops" in dank basements picking rags and sewing old clothes, Christians worked outside in the fresh air of their fields. If Jews slipped in and out of town with their peddlers' packs on their backs, the authentic Americans sank their roots in the soil and created communities.

The mid-century credit reports issued by agents for R. G. Dunn in response to loan applications depicted Jewish apartness in a unique, self-contained business culture. Communications from every region and every-size town commented on the Jews' extraordinary ability to make money through "mysterious" business practices that these agents claimed they could not understand, differentiating Jews from true Americans.[62] "No one knows," wrote one of these investigators, "as the pecuniary affairs of Jews are usually in the dark." Jews, said the reports, had extraordinary business skills and created a closed world that non-Jews could never penetrate or fathom; Jews never told the truth about their business affairs, and only the unusual "white Jews" could be counted on to be honest.[63] Credit reporters also believed that Jews first and foremost took care of one another, cared little about their creditors, lied, and never invested in real estate because they would not commit themselves to American communities. One reporter wrote back from Middleton, Missouri, in 1849: "A German Jew . . . does a small business. No one has any idea how long he will continue to do business here or where he will be a year hence. Tricky . . ." An agent from Cincinnati noted that a Jewish firm was "doing an excellent business . . . character and habits good. Considered good by all the dealers, but they are

Jews, and their ancestors took Jewels of the Egyptians when they left Egypt and never returned them."[64]

In literature, drama, journalism, and within the world of business itself, the imagery about Jews and money asserted either admiration for the frugal, hard-working men and women who added to the community's tax rolls, or loathing for the avaricious shopkeepers, peddlers, and creditors who sapped the resources of other Americans. Whichever direction it took, it offered Gentiles a picture of a group of people who all behaved the same—but differently than other Americans. The contrast between Jews and Gentiles ran throughout nineteenth-century literature and popular culture, highlighting the difference between city and country, money and goodness, vice and virtue, displacement and rootedness.

Whether praised or condemned for their commercial prowess, Jews deviated from other Americans, and money-making defined the Jew just as charity defined the Christian. Because the wealthy philanthropist Judah Touro of New Orleans was known for his largess to Jews and non-Jews alike, the *New Bedford Mercury* reported that "he gathered money with honest Judaical eagerness, but gave it away with true Christian liberality."[65] A memoir writer, reminiscing about the early gold-rush days in California, remarked that one "could easily gauge the prosperity of a mining town by the number of Jewish shopkeepers it maintained and the size of its Chinatown."[66] Encoded here was not only the positive view of Jews as agents of prosperity, but Jewish distinctiveness. Indeed, thousands of comments in American newspapers, plays, poems, novels, stories, and essays developed the theme of Jewish "otherness."[67] Real Americans, in the excitement of California of the 1840s, dug for gold, sweated, exerted energy, lived a rough out-of-doors kind of life, and produced something. Jews—and the other "others," the Chinese—lived apart, differently, no matter what they added to the commonwealth.

In a guidebook to New York City, Corneluis Matthews offered this description of the Jews' Chatham Street in 1845:

The Jews were as thick with their gloomy whiskers, as blackberries; the air smelt of old coats and hats, and the sideways were glutted with dresses and over-coats and little, fat greasy children. There were country men moving up and down the street, horribly harassed and perplexed, and every now and then falling into the hands of one of these fierce-whiskered Jews, carried into a gloomy cavern, and presently sent forth again, in a garment coat or hat or breeches, in which he might dance, and turn his partner to boot.

The metaphoric Jews here could be identified by physical appearance, smell, "fat greasy children," aggressive business techniques, and their intrusion into public space. To them the "country men," newcomers to the city, were easy marks to buy their goods. Jews corrupted these innocents, selling them clothes to be donned for such commercialized vices as dancing. They destroyed good, decent Americans—and, by implication—the basic values of the culture.[68]

In some literary pieces, the Jewish merchant, often a pawnbroker, has a heart and in the end helps the American hero. In such popular novels as Albert Aiken's *California Detective* (1878) or *Morgan Or the Knight of the Black Flag* (1860) by Edward Judson (who later wrote under the name Ned Buntline), Jews made money as pawnbrokers, peddlers, or shopkeepers, while other Americans did not. The Jewish merchant usually stole, cheated, or tricked the hapless American hero. George Lippard created Gabriel Van Gelt, a villainous character whose Jewish identity "was written on his face as clearly and distinctly as though he had fallen asleep at the building of the Temple at Jerusalem." Lippard's 1844 novel, *The Quaker City,* with a Jewish character who lives off the misfortunes of an unlucky American, sold some forty thousand copies within a year of publication. The Jewish pawnbroker in *Phantom Hand* (1877) offers assistance to a Christian in need but still earns a profit off the economic woes of Gentile Christians. In contrast, Christians emerge as noble farmers embodying American values of family, community, honesty, and hard work, although they are often in distress.[69]

Throughout the nineteenth century, Jews were used to condemn materialism and acquisitiveness, as though Americans had no interest in such goals. There is no reason to presume that Jews had any greater interest in upward economic mobility than did all other Americans. But Gentile writers, ministers, and lecturers played upon the image of the Jew as money-maker to exculpate the masses of Americans who themselves seemed to be putting economic advancement over community, God, and family by abandoning farms and small towns for the big cities where money could be made. By portraying the Jewish peddler as luring farm women into buying unneeded cheap trinkets, writers and orators posited the Jew as the agent of rural discontent, an alien disrupting the heretofore idyllic tranquility of

American life. The Chatham Street Jew who sold flashy, poorly made clothes to urban newcomers embodied the American fear of the corruption of city life.

The rhetoric had clear implications. Without the Jews, Americans would have been content with what they had. But the Jews, outsiders with no stake in rural American, Protestant culture, came with their wares and their profit motive, bred unhappiness, and undermined the values of traditional American life. The blame for the breakdown of these values, accordingly, lay with the Jews and their alien, commercial ways. Throughout this, Jews served as symbols of other Americans' confusion about their own value system. Except for the Civil War incidents, however, the use of Jews in solving the American dilemma did not move beyond words to deeds.

Caste and Class

Another pervasive American idea maintained that Jews used their money crudely and flaunted their riches. It posited nouveaux riches Jews whose money was tainted by social impropriety. This stereotype spilled beyond rhetoric. Jews found themselves frozen out of some American social institutions. By the 1860s and 1870s, resorts, hotels, clubs, and other kinds of elite recreational institutions that had previously welcomed Jews began to snub them. An 1868 guidebook to New York pointed out that a new hotel specifically excluded Jewish guests. Despite the fact that "the people of Israel" had tried every possible means to gain entry, the management triumphed in keeping them out. A similar volume for Atlantic City warned Christians away from the kosher Atlantic Hotel in 1867 by letting them know in advance that "it is . . . chiefly, if not entirely, held for the use of the persons of the Hebrew faith and mostly those of greatest wealth."[70]

Saratoga Springs, New York, had for years been a popular summer vacation spot for affluent Jews and non-Jews alike. But, as upper-class Protestant vacationers became conscious of a Jewish presence there, they feared an invasion of their turf. As early as 1868, a Gentile man wrote to his sister from Saratoga, complaining that "the Jews flock to Union [Hotel] this season. Have literally run away all the old habitués."[71] In 1877, Joseph Seligman, a prominent banker and crony of U. S. Grant, was refused admission to Saratoga's Grand Hotel. As the management explained it, Christians would stay away if the hotel attracted "colonies of Jewish people," considered "obnoxious to the majority of guests." Further, wealthy

Jews brought along their less well-off coreligionists who expropriated the good seats at the theatrical performances, and "old customers stood while a shoemaker or tailor from Chatham Street occupied prime seats."[72] Two years later, the owner of Coney Island's Manhattan Beach Hotel also decided that the kind of guests he wanted for his swank establishment avoided places where Jews, "contemptible as a class . . . [and] a detestable and vulgar people," congregated en masse, bringing their own picnic food, and the hotel excluded them.[73]

Even in the West, which lacked most Eastern social hierarchies, elite institutions began to exclude Jews in the late 1860s. Portland's prestigious Arlington Club, founded in 1867 as a spot for the upper business class to meet, barred Jews from membership soon thereafter. This was particularly striking because Portland not only housed a large, comfortable Jewish mercantile class, but Portlanders had elected two Jews to the mayoralty in the 1860s and 1870s.[74]

The social snubs and the imagery of uncouth wealthy Jews functioned on a variety of cultural levels. Undoubtedly, many upper-class Americans, the kind of people who frequented Saratoga or Coney Island, probably did not like Jews and therefore preferred not to vacation with them. But more was at work than overt anti-Semitism. Coney Island, Saratoga, and other vacation areas "democratized" by the 1870s as increasing numbers of non-affluent urbanites, often from the working classes, took advantage of organized trips to these popular spots. Commercialized amusements for the masses, considered tawdry and cheap by the elite, developed alongside the older, genteel haunts of the wealthy.[75] Indeed, in the Coney Island affair, Austin Corbin, the president of the Manhattan Beach Company, noted that the Jewish invasion set in motion a process whereby "the Jews drive off the people whose places are filled by a less particular class. The latter are not rich enough to have any preference in the matter." Corbin asserted that the lower strata did not like Jews any better than did the higher-class vacationers, but their limited means constricted their options. What seemed to be going on here then was not just a rejection of Jews, but a rejection of the new Coney Island, the Coney Island that saw boatloads of proletarians, single men and women, families with children, transforming the once exclusive zone for the wealthy into a class-contested space.

In the post–Civil War world, one's leisure-time activities—clubs and resorts—made statements about one's social standing. They were not just places to recreate. Where one vacationed, and with whom, indicated status, giving Americans a way to prove that they stood above someone else.[76]

With the hardening of class divisions after industrialization, Americans tried to sort out the paradox of extremes of wealth existing in a society claiming near classlessness. Egalitarianism came into direct conflict with the clear reality that American society sharply divided into haves and have-nots. Focusing their rhetoric on gentility and style allowed privileged Americans to enjoy their wealth without making it seem that wealth was an intrinsic end in and of itself. Elite Protestants could contrast the honorable and refined nature of their wealth with the ill-begotten, ill-used wealth of the Jews.

The frequency with which the advocates of exclusion used words like "vulgar" and "crude" indicated that within the reaches of affluence, elite Protestants felt the need to create distinctions between themselves and Jews who might have just as much, or more, money. Those who in the 1870s sought to differentiate between their affluence and that of Jews did so at a time when a public debate raged over class, wealth, corporations, and the seeming incompatability between American ideals and the growing social discrepancies among Americans. This affluent Christian stratum sought to prove that its wealth functioned more nobly than Jewish money since it was born of gentility and refinement. The Jews, on the other hand, constituted "a pretentious class, who expect three times as much for their money as other people." The "other people" could enjoy their money without guilt because they had not been corrupted by it and spent it with grace.[77]

Resort owners, who may or may not have reflected the opinion of their guests, made no distinctions among Jews. For them, Jews served as a collective symbol of alienness, of being different from everyone else and at odds with ideals of Christian America.

The Leopard's Spots

How did Gentiles explain the Jews' unique economic proclivities? What factors explained the inextricable ties between Jews and money? What did Gentiles see as the source of the Jews' crude and boisterous public behavior? Did Jewish business practices and cultural styles grow out of historic experiences, or were they innate Jewish characteristics over which the individual Jew had no control? In the middle decades of the nineteenth century, American scientists and scholars were tremendously interested in race theory as it applied to American Indians, blacks, and the Chinese. At times, they used race—a set of inherent, natural characteristics—to make sense of Jewish behavior as well.

Before the 1880s, when social Darwinism and other theories of biological determinism dramatically shifted the debate on race, only a handful of articles posited the Jews as a singular race whose culture reflected innate, inborn traits. Popular writers, on the other hand, had throughout the mid-nineteenth-century decades focused on the physical appearance of Jews as the key to understanding their moral character.[78]

Scientists paid much greater attention to the physical characteristics of blacks, American Indians, and other distinct groups in the American population than to those of Jews. Much of the early nineteenth-century ethnological writing about Jews reflected the predominant belief that environment shaped physical appearance and that climate rather than biology was the key factor. Lydia Maria Child, a New England abolitionist and reformer, commenting on her first visit to a synagogue, which was her first exposure to a group of Jews, was "disappointed to see so large a proportion of this peculiar people fair-skinned and blue-eyed." Having expected to see the "dark eyes, jetty locks, and olive complexions of Palestine," she concurred with the scientists who argued that "colour is the effect of climate."[79]

Some ethnologists, however, speculated about the possibly fixed and biologically determined nature of Jewish traits. Reflecting this view, a few scholars in the 1850s and 1860s studied Jewish jaws, foreheads, and other body parts as they searched for the pure Jewish type. This "type," they believed, held the key to explaining the origins of Jewish behavior. John Beddoe, a British ethnologist whose work circulated widely in scientific circles in the United States, noted that Jews always had "full and prominent" eyes, "though the brow is well marked." Jews were further characterized by a "somewhat heavy though rounded" lower jaw "with a receding chin and full lips." An American scientist, Josiah Nott, in *The Physical History of the Jewish Race* (1850), went even further, and using the popular science of craniometry, which linked intelligence to head size and shape, concluded that the Jews' "Caucasian heads have never failed to show their full measure of intellect, a sufficient proof that, a truly great race, when unadulterated, can never sink to the level of an inferior one." He asserted that the Jews constituted a pure race that "has preserved its blood more . . . than any other of antiquity" and despite persecution "in *no instance* has it lost its own type, or approximated to that of other races."[80]

Other Americans also believed that Judaism had survived because the Jews had remained a racially pure group. They connected Jewish religious behavior with the Jewish racial type. In 1870, a woman writing for the *San*

Francisco Bulletin said: "I have always coveted the purity of lineage, and the steady persistency . . . of the Hebrew race."[81]

Throughout these decades, popular writers fixated on the physical appearance of Jews to explain character and intellect. Their belief that "biology was destiny" actually preceded scientific theories in explaining Jewish behavior by racial categories. Popular fiction, cartoons, and theatrical renditions of the Jew constantly referenced the Jewish body type and facial characteristics. Noses, in particular, served as indices to the Jews' moral and mental capabilities.[82] Novelists, for example, readily depicted the archetypal Jew's probing eyes, hooked nose, and stooped physique as evidence of depravity and avarice. The inherent evil of Moses Tubal, a character created by John Beauchamp Jones in his 1849 *Western Merchant,* manifested itself in his "prominent nose, high cheek bones, and sparkling eyes . . . [of] a cunning Jew, in quest of a location to cheat his neighbors and spoil the regular trader's business." The very popular book *New York by Gas-light* (1850) by George G. Foster stated clearly that "the roundness and suppleness of limb, the elasticity of flesh, the glittering eye-sparkle—are as inevitable in the Jew or Jewess, in whatever rank of existence, as the hook of the nose which betrays the Israelite as a human kite, formed to be feared, hated, and despised, yet to prey upon mankind."[83] Henry Wadsworth Longfellow, in a travel sketch sent back from Europe in 1835, surmised that his fellow passenger on a train had to be a Jew by virtue of "the customary hooked nose and half-moon of his tribe." But, beyond physiognomy, the man's Jewishness was confirmed by the fact that "though he could hardly be less than sixty years old he travelled day and night, so as to avoid paying for lodging." Anyone but a Jew would have parted with a few cents and had a good night's sleep.[84]

The Jews as Others

Whether seen as adherents of a faith out of step with American Protestantism, financial wizards, social climbers, or members of a distinct race, Jews were different. In the press, on the lecture circuit, and from the pulpit, Gentiles either praised or condemned the Jews just because they seemed to stand apart from other Americans.

Gentile attitudes revealed more about Gentiles than about real Jewish behavior patterns. In Western communities, for example, where the shaky state of law and order vexed community leaders, the "American Jew" stood as an exemplar of someone who showed "respect for *our* laws . . . [and] never violates them" (emphasis added). In a society concerned about the excesses of drinking, the Jews were "men . . . marked for their sobriety." In an era when the women's rights movement sparked public discussions about the breakdown of acceptable gender relations, Jewish women retained a "chaste and decorous demeanor and their freedom from the fearful scandal to which their Anglo-American sisters are so fiercely addicted." As American cities became the home to increasing numbers of the poor, Jews were touted as having no beggars among them, and their well-endowed communities took care of their own, making sure than none became public charges. The *Los Angeles Daily Star* perhaps captured the tone of Jewish otherness best in 1869, when it generalized: "It is not in a spirit of praise or exaggeration that we commend our citizens of Israelitish extraction. We commend them for their commercial integrity and their studied insulation from the prevalent vices of gambling, lechery, and inebriation, for their individual and class benevolence, and for their courteous demeanor."[85]

Statements of admiration for Jews always contained within them not so subtle hints that, somehow, Jews were not quite like everyone else. Their business acumen provided a case in point. Jews could turn a profit where Americans could barely eke out a living. An 1878 *Los Angeles Herald* piece praised merchant Bernard Cohn, who served on the city council, as "one of our leading Hebrew citizens," and imbued him with abilities beyond the average. Cohn served as a "vigilant and unceasing enemy to anything like jobbery in our municipal affairs. No African in the woodpile could conceal himself so thoroughly as to escape his lynx-eyed watchfulness." A compliment, certainly, but the praise implied that non-Jews ought to be on guard against his uncanny ability.[86]

Importantly, these blanket hyperboles assumed, as did the vicious stereotypes of exclusionists, that Jews somehow fit into fixed categories and behaved in uniform ways, with no gradations or shadings. Unlike other Americans, some of whom drank and some of whom did not, some of whom worked hard, saving their money, and some of whom loafed around, frittering away their earnings, Jews as a class, a race, a nation behaved the same. Jews were held up as standards of incomparable moral behavior against which Americans measured themselves and found themselves wanting. The mythically admirable Jew could be as dangerous to the Jewish people as the mythically evil one.

White Christian Americans were not alone in holding up this singular image of Jews—as somehow beyond ordinary people's abilities or as a nation whose history had somehow marked it as different—worthy of emulation. Black preachers, educators, newspaper writers, and politicians created a mythic Jew who persevered despite adversity and offered him as a yardstick against which their people should measure themselves. Pinkney B. S. Pinchback, briefly a Reconstruction governor of Louisiana, exhorted an audience in Louisiana in 1876 to think about the Jews whenever they felt dejected. "Like you," he consoled them, "they were once slaves and after they were emancipated they met with persecutions." But now, despite all that adversity, Jews have emerged as "leaders of education and princes of the commercial world. . . . What an example for you, my people."[87]

Images of Jews articulated by blacks served their particular interests just like those articulated by all other Gentile Americans regardless of race, class, region, or ethnicity. Such images created a singular "Jew" who, for better or worse, represented certain values and behavior patterns. Was this, then, anti-Semitism? How widespread was anti-Semitism in nineteenth-century America? How thoroughly was American society defined as inherently Christian, how deeply Jewish participation in it resented? Certainly, throughout these decades, Jews suffered in the public realm because they were Jews. When President Grant proposed that Simon Wolf become Recorder of Deeds of the District of Columbia, "a protest had been filed with the Senate Committe on the score," wrote Wolf in his memoirs, "that I was a Jew," and should not hold such an august office. (But Wolf got it.)[88]

Political campaigns sporadically brought out the latent anti-Jewish sentiment. In 1875, in a countywide election for school superintendent in Oroville, California, one candidate's supporter attacked the other one as the Jews' candidate and concluded a letter to the local newspaper with a vicious diatribe: "Jew Dave Hecht, the greatest living untruthful gorilla of the age, whose impudence got him the nomination for coroner on the Republican ticket, may be seen free of cost at his place of exxhibition [*sic*] (a Jew rag store) scratching his hand."[89] Indeed, hostility towards Jews could arise in almost any political or legal controversy that happened to involve a Jew and a non-Jew. An 1859 trial in Milwaukee pitted a Jewish client with a Jewish lawyer against a Christian client represented by a Christian attorney. In his summation to the jury, the Christian attorney exclaimed that "all Israelites, since 1800 years, made their living by stealing, lying, etc., and that what a Jew should state under oath, the jury should not believe." To discredit the "Jewish" side, he maintained that all Jews "have been branded thieves, liars, and swindlers, by all civilized nations."[90]

Anecdotes scattered through the autobiographies of nineteenth-century American Jews indicate that Jews could be the victims of harassment and sporadic violence. Bernard Drachman recalled his childhood in Jersey City in the 1870s being punctuated by schoolmates' taunts calling him "Jew," "sheeny," and "Christ killer," while Henry Morgenthau, growing up in the 1860s in Brooklyn, remembered: "I had my little difficulties in school: I well remember how one of the boys told me that he deeply sympathized with me, because I would have to overcome the double handicap of being both a Jew and a German." Leo N. Levi, a B'nai B'rith leader, had been a law student in the 1870s at the University of Virginia. Here, according to his biographer, the young man's "courage and manliness . . . were put on trial. As so often happened to our coreligionists, he was taunted with being a Jew, and he resented it verbally and physically. He won the admiration of his quondam antagonists."[91] School children throughout America were reported to have sung this jingle:[92]

> I had a piece of pork, I put it on a fork
> And gave it to the curly-headed Jew
> Pork, Pork, Pork, Jew, Jew, Jew.

Sometimes, Jews even endured physical harassment and violence. Bands of vandals once threw stones through the windows at Jews at prayer in St. Louis; in Weatherford, Texas, in the late 1850s, someone posted a note replete with skull and crossbones on Alex Sanger's door, warning him to get out of town or face dire consequences. (He remained.)[93]

But did these incidents constitute anti-Semitism? By European standards, they hardly seemed substantial; American anti-Semitism appeared tame. However starkly Christian Americans stereotyped the Jews, these words rarely led to action. Efforts to limit public life participation to Christians failed. As of 1880, no state restricted office-holding to Christians. Although Jewish immigration into America continued unabated, efforts to make public institutions emblems of Christianity made little headway. Jews increasingly participated in political and cultural activities without suffering or being stigmatized. In this respect, traditions of tolerance beat out the evangelical impulse.

Even during the Civil War, the highest point of anti-Jewish sentiment and activity, scattered incidents rarely went beyond rhetoric. Most Jews lived through this anti-Semitic nadir unscathed, possibly unaware of the events, apart from the flurry of editorials in the Jewish press.[94] Acts of public tolerance offset almost every act of anti-Semitism. General Grant's commanding officer, General Henry W. Halleck, and Lincoln himself rescinded Grant's infamous order and made efforts to quiet down the smoldering Jewish protest. Public opinion, at least as expressed in the Northern press, did not support the measure. Similarly, when in 1864 General Benjamin Butler accused Jewish soldiers of displaying cowardice in battle, General George B. McClellan, his superior, wrote to the *Jewish Record*: "My attention [was] never called to the peculiarities of Jewish soldiers, when I was in command. . . . I have never had any reason to suppose them inferior to their comrades of other races and religions, or to their decidedly belligerent ancestors."[95] Indeed, every anti-Jewish statement in the press or in literature can be matched by utterances praising the Jews, commending them for contributions to civilization, and welcoming them into America.[96]

Because of the Christian religious inheritance and the American ambivalence about diversity, Jews functioned as a medium by which Americans resolved their own culture conflict. Should America be Christian or not? The only way for them to know was to look at the one clearly non-Christian religious community in their midst. Was there a single American culture to which all should conform? One way to explore this was to focus in on a group who seemed to be both American and something else at the same time.

Needless to say, some disliked Jews because they were not Christians, and others felt that rich Jews strangled the economy. But an equal, maybe bigger, number of people held that American society ought to be open to all religious and national groups and that a person's religion should be no one else's concern.

Liking them or not, native-born Christians noticed that Jews were different. Foreigners in the main, they lived apart. Urban dwellers in a society that celebrated the rural life, they stood out. Merchants and peddlers, they pursued occupations different from those of most other Americans. They banded together in distinctive institutions and set about the task of creating vibrant communities that could sustain a sense of peoplehood.

These attitudes and images never fell into neat categories and, indeed, went beyond ambivalence, since that term implied two stark opposites. Rather, Jews and their religious tradition showed up in an ever-changing kaleidoscope of contradictory, intersecting, and inconsistent pictures. The splintered images that Americans held about the Jewish newcomers reflected a variety of attitudes, fears, and concerns about the culture itself.

Critics of the Jews generally evinced a lack of faith in the integrative power of American culture. As they witnessed immigrants with alien traditions and cultures streaming into America, the defenders of the old order feared that inherited values and forms of the past could not survive the onslaught. They lamented the passing of the virtues of the simple past. They perceived around them the crumbling of a Christian-based, small-town, rurally oriented commonwealth. Jews served as one, though not the only, possible cause of the decline in American life. Critics used the Jews as a symbol of the decay of traditional values as nineteenth-century Americans embraced new ideas, new forms of expression, and new ways of living. For many of the critics, the problem of the Jews was a problem of an alien people threatening the already shaky social order. The fact that the Jews seemed to preserve their ancient faith, while Americans were rushing towards irreligion and innovation, only compounded the "Jewish problem."

Supporters of the Jews, their defenders and advocates, also worked out their stance toward American culture as they made sense of the Jewish presence in their midst. By and large, the defenders of the Jews stood on the side of "progress" and modernity, and to them, Jews as a people represented a welcome challenge to the old order and the bounty of commerce. By the hearty welcome extended to the Jews and by their expansive statements that Jews surpassed average Americans in lawfulness, sobriety, good citizenship, and morality, these liberal-minded Gentiles testified to the tolerance of their commonwealth. They eagerly welcomed the prosperity that they believed Jews would bring.

But whatever Gentiles said, Jews were becoming part of the social and political fabric of America, creating communities all over. The labors of the restorationists and the efforts of the conversionists amounted to little, and Jewish institutions and Jewish life took hold in America. Those Americans who envisioned the demise of this once proud but now decadent religion miscalculated, and the very ongoing process of Jewish immigration, which swelled unabated and unchecked by the rhetoric of anti-Semitism, bore witness to the Jewish attraction to America and to the other, louder voices of welcome and inclusion.

Jewish women and men set about the task of creating communities and forging an American Jewish culture that recognized the simultaneous reality of American anti-Semitism and American tolerance. They molded a culture that incorporated the American cacophony and yet, at the same time, looked inward to reflect their own internal, group values.

CHAPTER EIGHT

INSIDE/OUTSIDE

In this country, wrested from tyranny and devoted to liberty, the Jew can,
like his ancestors in the days of Solomon, "sit under his vine and his fig tree,
with none to make him afraid."

"All Israel are brethren," and although we differ in several insignificant matters and
quarrel upon some important ones; yet we are brethren, we are Jews, and the Jews,
like the God they worship, are immortal. . . . we are less faithful than our
forefathers . . . we may even be somewhat lethargic, but let circumstances abide
requiring us to manifest the integrity and solidarity of our faith, and we are
as ready to manifest it, as our forefathers were.

IN 1876, the B'nai B'rith, American Jews' largest mass-membership organization, unveiled a statue in Philadelphia's Fairmount Park as the Jewish
contribution to the nation's centennial festivities.[1] Sculpted on the order's
commission by Moses Ezekiel, a B'nai B'rith brother and an artist of some
renown, the monumental marble group, *Religious Liberty,* made no mention in its iconography of Jews, Jewishness, or Judaism. While its images
were stock symbols of American patriotism, the words chiseled on its base
proclaimed that this gift to the American people came from the "Order of
B'nai B'rith and Israelites of America." The artist, B'nai B'rith, and, by
extension, American Jews celebrated America by invoking both the American and the Jewish idiom. The central female figure of the work, "Liberty,"
wearing the Phrygian cap with a thirteen-star border, clasped a scroll of the
Constitution in her left hand, while her right hand shielded a young, naked
boy, the "Genius of Devotion," who held aloft a lamp. In the foreground, to
the right of the woman and the boy, an eagle, "Freedom," engaged in
triumphant battle against a snake, "Intolerance."

Jews and Gentiles alike understood that the eagle and the Constitution scroll were the symbols of religious freedom and separation of church and state. Moses Ezekiel occasionally employed biblical themes in his work, and, of course, American Jews continually articulated devotion to America's tolerance of religious difference.[2] B'nai B'rith members, Philadelphians, and out-of-town Jewish visitors to the World's Fair recognized the statue's Jewish origins because the order's national governing board, the Constitutional Grand Lodge, repeatedly implored them to contribute funds to this Jewish expression of belonging in the national holiday. Readers of the *American Israelite* knew the statue as well, because Isaac Mayer Wise wrote editorials endorsing *Religious Liberty* as a Jewish statement of participation in America's festivities.[3]

But did Jews view the statue differently from Christians? Did it stir in them specifically Jewish emotions? To those who did not know the statue's Jewish background, it could be an artistic representation of one element of the American political creed, consistent with the nation's celebration. But to Jews, the statue announced that no matter how small their numbers or how recent their arrival, they were as much part of that birthday celebration as anyone else. They wanted to honor that element of American culture that made America so singular to them as Jews.

A covert political message was encoded in the statue as well. In the 1870s, Jews worried that the evangelicals bent on the Christianization of America would create a social order from which Jews would be excluded. As Adam Kramer, chairman of the Union of American Hebrew Congregations' committee on the "Israelites Centennial Monument," wrote in 1873, "we are aware of the attempts being made to insert religious doctrines in the fundamental law of the land. These designs . . . must be frustrated by the wisdom and patriotism of the people." He hoped that this statue, designed and dedicated by American Jews, would "forever admonish" the American people to remember that "in freedom and harmony there is safety, whilst by a system of intolerance and discord there is danger."[4]

In 1867, a Jewish woman in San Francisco gave birth to triplets, all boys. A first for the West Coast, the human-interest story made the local press. The father, Henry Danziger, a pawnbroker from Poland naturalized in California in 1855, served as an officer in the benevolent society Chebra Achim Rachmonim and as a junior warden in the nearly all-Jewish Progress Masonic Lodge No. 125. He decided to invite local military and civic leaders to the triplets' circumcision, at which the Masonic lodge was to present the father with appropriate medals. According to the *San Francisco*

Evening Star, Danzinger had been "advised" to name the three babies "after some men now holding high official positions in the Union," but the father abjured. "My children shall be named after my fathers—Abraham, Isaac and Jacob," he forthrightly announced. At the brit, he pronounced their names: Abraham Lincoln Danziger, Isaac Andrew Jackson Danziger, and Jacob John Conness (John Conness was the senator from California) Danziger. Without much difficulty, he thus combined his bonds to his "fathers" of tradition and his loyalty to those of his newly adopted home.[5]

Both anecdotes illustrate the complex process of building a *Jewish American* culture that deftly counterposed its two adjectives, its two identities. Jews drew attention to themselves as a distinct group in American society who still resembled all other citizens. Through newspapers, novels, the visual arts and architecture, schools and clubs, American Jews created forms of expression that blended dictates of peoplehood with demands of citizenship. They took into account what other Americans thought of them but simultaneously remained true to their own sense of self. American Jewish self-expression of the nineteenth century reflected the multiple identities and loyalties of these new Americans.

Critics have typically depicted American Jewish culture of the nineteenth century as shallow, materialistic, and derivative, a product of nervous newcomers fearful of drawing attention to themselves and eager for "currying favor with the native Protestants." One scholar has characterized the pre–Civil War American Jewish landscape as a "cultural wasteland," while another, studying the 1870s, asserted that the "spiritual and intellectual life" of American Jews had sunk to "a low ebb. . . . American Judaism, particularly Reform Judaism, was evolving as a haphazard, reflexive Jewish reaction to the exigencies of socio-economic considerations." American Jews labeled themselves "Israelites" or "Hebrews" rather than "Jews," according to historians, proving that they projected themselves as a religion, pure and simple, denying peoplehood, distinctive values, history, and identity.[6]

Historians have compared the culture of the Jews who migrated to America between 1820 and 1880 unfavorably with that created by the more numerous Jewish immigrants who arrived after 1880, who sustained mass-circulation Yiddish newspapers, vibrant Yiddish theaters, Yiddish music halls, hundreds of schools, political clubs, cafés, and bookstores.

But if historians understand past cultures in their own terms, as patterns of response and meaning that anthropologist Clifford Geertz has called "webs of significance," they would not judge a culture as rich or

poor.[7] In this context, American Jews in the middle decades of the nine-
teeth century expressed themselves in ways that made sense to them as
immigrants to a new social and cultural reality where the past could be only
a rough guide. They sought new ways to express old values.

What "significance" did nineteenth-century American Jews attribute to
Jewishness and Americanness? How did these new Americans see themselves as Americans and as Jews? What forces shaped their visions? How
did those visions resonate in the institutions they built and in the ways they
looked outward toward America and its people?

The Jewish immigrants who arrived at the start of the mass migrations
of the mid-nineteenth century found few vehicles for group self-expression
to articulate a sense of self. No newspapers, magazines, or publishing
houses gave voice to Jewish values. No schools existed to formally transmit
identity, and no Jews wrote novels, plays, or poems for a Jewish public.
Jews in the small pre-1820s communities relied on imported European
products, and in their few synagogues, Jews spoke to themselves rather than
to other Americans about Jewishness. Where Jews participated in the cultural life of their communities, as dramatists and journalists, for example,
they *never* drew attention to themselves as Jews and eschewed Jewish
topics, themes, or motifs.[8]

Over the course of the sixty years after 1820, there came into being
dozens of newspapers and magazines in English, German, Hebrew, and
Yiddish, as well as Jewish poetry, novels, short stories, and editions of
sacred texts. Literary societies and institutions of learning were founded at
every level and artists began to craft in an American Jewish style. Some of
these vehicles for Jewish self-expression attracted little financial or popular
support and lasted only briefly, while other means spanned decades and
demonstrated the appetite of American Jews for Jewish news, ideas, and
materials. These activities indicated their willingness to stand out as distinct
from their American fellow citizens while they claimed for themselves a
place in their new homes.

American Jewish Arts

Jewish art and architecture provided a case in point. After the 1840s,
American Jews built their synagogues with bold Jewish motifs emblazoned
on the outside, self-consciously opting for styles virtually unknown in
American churches. Jews built synagogues largely in the Moorish or Byzan-

tine (sometimes even called Egyptian) style at a time when urban European Jews were also choosing eastern-style structures. Indeed, when San Francisco's Emanu-El Congregation on Sutter Street was dedicated in 1866, the local press described it as "foreign" in appearance. The label did not deter other congregations across America from linking themselves with this exotic appearance. For small-town Jews from Posen and Bavaria, the Moorish mode did not resemble any of the old world structures they had known, but it did not look like other American religious structures either.[9] Stars of David, decalogues, and Hebrew letters all announced that these buildings—bearing such clearly non-English names as Beth Israel, Adas Yisroule, Ahavas Achim, Mishkan Israel, Knesseth Israel, Shaaray Tefiloh, Shaarai Shomayim, Shaare Zedek, Berith Kodesh, Achim Sholom, Nifutzoth Yehudah, Rodef Shalom, Magen David, Shaaray Hesed, and Anshe Hesed—belonged to people who did not shy away from acknowledging their distinctiveness. The Washington Hebrew Congregation, one example of the many congregations with English names, also had a Hebrew name, Shaare Zedek, which at some point, probably in the 1870s, was lost, perhaps when the perceived demands of America came to outweigh those of tradition.[10]

The handful of Jewish graphic artists, such as Moses Ezekiel, Solomon Nunes Carvalho, Theodore Sydney Moise, Max Rosenthal, Toby Rosenthal, and Gustave Henry Mosler, relied heavily on biblical motifs that were understandable and presumably inoffensive to American Christians, yet clearly part of Jewish tradition. Biblical themes allowed them to be both Jewish and "everyman's" with the same strokes of their brush or chisel.[11] Painter and daguerreotypist Carvalho, for example, an observant Jew and activist in various Jewish communities, earned an 1852 Diploma and Silver Medal for Ideal Painting from the South Carolina Institute for his work called *The Intercession of Moses.* Other of his history paintings included *Moses at the Battle of the Amalakites, Moses Receiving the Law on Mount Sinai,* and *Cain Receiving the Curse of the Almighty,* and he also sculpted a bas-relief entitled *Israel.*[12] Although Moses Ezekiel eschewed the notion of "Jewish art," he asserted that "everybody who knows me knows that I am a Jew—I never wanted it otherwise." To Ezekiel's chagrin, the label stuck, and both Jews and non-Jews identified him as a "Jewish sculptor."[13]

American Jewish folk art also linked the two traditions. For example, papercuts, mizrakhim (markers for eastern walls), and Hanukkah lamps twinned Masonry and Judaism, while Torah binders, challah (Sabbath bread) covers, and other religious artifacts combined Jewish and American motifs.

Jewish women in Germany traditionally decorated swaddling clothes for baby boys as Torah binders, which were tied around the Torah at the time of the young men's bar mitzvah, and the custom continued in the United States. One made in New York in 1869 was adorned with the word "Yigdal"—the opening line of a prayer and also perhaps a mother's wish, since it meant "he will grow"—with an American flag sprouting from the final letter. Similarly, central European Jewish immigrants transplanted to America micrography, a specifically Jewish art form of reproducing biblical passages in tiny letters. Artist David Davidson, for example, used this traditional medium to do portraiture, a common American form but alien to traditional Judaism.[14] The producers of these and numerous other material artifacts, from lofty synagogues to homey wall hangings, developed styles that tied together Jewish and American ideas.

The Written Word

Like the popular arts, the American Jewish language reflected a blending of traditional Jewish and contemporary American identities. Jews wasted little time trying to decide what to call themselves, both among themselves and when they faced the outside world. While some Reform leaders preferred the names "Hebrew" or "Israelites" for their biblical connotations, shying away from the word "Jew" because it implied nationality and anti-Semites used it, most mixed terms with no regard for ideological or political impact. If "Hebrew" sounded more refined than "Jew," or if "Israelite" indicated a religion rather than a distinct people, the masses were oblivious. Writing to the *American Israelite* from a gold-rush town in California in 1873, a member of the small community referred to "our Jewish children" and "a Jewish maiden," while a decade earlier a letter writer from Nevada said in the *American Hebrew* that the "principles of the Jewish faith" were being advanced in that outpost by the formation of a benevolent society.[15] In 1864, the United *Hebrew* Benevolent Society of Boston dedicated itself to "secure . . . the cooperation of the Jews of every nationality . . . to dispense the charities of the Israelitish persuasion."[16] The *Hebrew* Ladies Benevolent Society of Albany, Georgia, indicated in its minutes that on February 20, 1878, "the jewish [*sic*] ladies of Albany" met and that the society would invite to membership "every israelitish [*sic*] lady above the age of 13."[17] By and large, formal institutions—synagogues and benevolent associations—used the term "Hebrew" more often than the other two, but ordinary men and women had no problem calling themselves "Jewish." Nor did they believe that "Israelite" referred to their religion alone.

Newspapers written by and for Jews also blended Jewish and American modes of expression. The press probably served a broader base of Jewish America than any other institution, bridging regional, ideological, and linguistic divisions. The first American Jewish publication, the *Jew*, edited by New York printer Solomon Jackson, offered "a defence of Judaism against all adversaries," especially the evangelicals.[18] On the eve of the Civil War, seven English and two German publications served Jewish America.[19] By 1880, seventeen Jewish newspapers and magazines flourished in New York, Philadelphia, New Orleans, Cincinnati, St. Louis, San Francisco, and Chicago.[20]

Journalism enabled Jews in different communities to communicate with one another. Newspapers such as Isaac Leeser's *Occident*, which began in 1843 out of Philadelphia,[21] Isaac M. Wise's *American Israelite* (1854) and *Die Deborah* (1855) from Cincinnati,[22] and the *Jewish Messenger*, edited by Rabbi Samuel Myer Isaacs in New York from 1858,[23] covered events of international and national importance and published fiction. They detailed the happenings of Jewish life in every corner of the United States, emphasizing the unity of the Jewish people. Communities throughout the country sent notices to these newspapers, chronicling the rise and fall of congregations, schools, and khevrot, describing outstanding achievements of members, alerting readers to incidents of anti-Semitism, or pointing with pride to examples of goodwill on the part of Christian neighbors. Communities struggling to build a synagogue or purchase a Torah appealed directly to better situated Jews for funds, and editors often accompanied requests for assistance with their own statements of support. So, when in 1871, Anshe Emeth in New Brunswick, New Jersey, wanted to outfit its new structure, it naturally turned to the readers of the *Israelite* for help.[24]

Editors, rabbis, and correspondents traveled regularly to the various outposts of Jewish life and wrote back about the towns they visited, the people they met, and the stresses and strains of American life. By publishing travel accounts and letters from the hinterlands, newspapers functioned as conduits for Jewish information. In February 1857, for example, a San Francisco Jew could learn about the Jewish community of Davenport, Iowa, in the *Occident:* "We are progressing slowly but surely. . . . There are enough Israelites . . . for three times a minyan. . . . There are at present, as far as my knowledge reaches, a congregation each in Dubuque, in Burlington and Keokuk, all in Iowa."[25] Likewise, Jews in those Iowa towns could find out from the *Jewish Messenger* in 1859 that, according to a correspondent, Rabbi Henry Abraham Henry, "in the far distant land of California, the Jew, notwithstanding his desire for wealth, does not forget the God that made him, nor the religion which has at all times been the rock of his support."[26] Regional papers, such as California's *Voice of Israel* (1856) and *Weekly Gleaner* (1857), served the same function for West Coast Jewry,[27] and, in 1877, Rabbi Edward Morris Benjamin Browne—nicknamed "Alphabet"—tried to bring together Jewish communities below the Mason-Dixon Line through the *Jewish South* published in Atlanta.[28] This linkage of Jewish communities through newspapers fit the high rates of Jewish mobility. Jews contemplating relocation to another region had a handy reference guide in these newspapers, while those back home got news of friends and family who had moved away to new places.

The Jewish press aggressively detailed the persecution of Jews in Europe and the Near East as well as incidents of anti-Semitism at home. It also heroically portrayed famous Jews, such as Moses Montefiore in England and Judah Touro in the United States. This fostered a palpable sense of belonging to a worldwide community and substantiated vague feelings of Jewish identity. Ironically, while the American Jewish communities often found themselves beset by internal disputes and national organizations had difficulty sustaining harmony or breaching the gap between traditionalists and reformers, the press created a sense of a worldwide Jewish community. The idea that Jews in one community had a responsibility to those in another, to be expressed in financial aid, political pressure, or welcoming of new immigrants, ran through the American Jewish press, indicating a strong sense of peoplehood.[29]

Although the newspapers varied in outlook and ideology, they all espoused Jewish unity, identity, and survival in America. The *Israelite* and its companion paper, *Die Deborah,* clearly reflected their editor's Reform outlook, while the *Occident* and the *Jewish Messenger* squarely fell into the traditionalist camp. *Israels Herold,* edited by forty-eighter Isidor Bush, styled itself into a literary publication to uplift the Jewish masses and lasted a mere three months.[30] English-born Robert Lyons began publication in 1849 of the *Asmonean,* dedicated to fostering a "Congregational Union of Israelites in the United States, and the general dissemination of information relating to the people."[31]

These newspapers relied upon both paid agents and volunteers to drum up subscribers, penetrating Jewish communities across the country.[32] The publications survived in part on advertisements from Jewish businesses, those which carried specifically Jewish goods and those owned by coreligionists. They published the writings of both rabbis and lay people, and of a strikingly large number of women, to whom traditional Jewish forms of publication were closed. Indeed, in the first year of the *Jewish Messenger,* a "New York Jewess," writing under the nom de plume Miriam, first begged her readers' pardon, for "it may appear presumptuous in a female to enter into comments upon scriptural themes, but the daughters of Israel have always felt that allegiance to Zion was paramount to every other sentiment." Editor Isaacs quickly appended a note, applauding "Miriam" and encouraging other women: "We hope to see many Miriams in the field."[33]

The Yiddish press began to form by the early 1870s. J. K. Buchner published his lithographed *Die Yiddishe Zeitung,* Tzvi Hirsh Bernstein launched *Die Post* in 1870, and Henry Gersoni began *Die Idishe Post* in 1874, the same year that Kasriel Sarsohn offered the public *Die Yiddishe Gazeten.* In 1872, Sarasohn had also tried his hand at *Die New Yorker Yiddishe Tsaytung.* All of these papers were published in New York, hoping to make a profit and provide news and other reading matter to the growing Yiddish speaking public in America. While the Yiddish press would not achieve stability or attract a massive audience until the first decades of the twentieth century, the early Yiddish newspapers in America, which appeared less than twenty years after the first Yiddish publication in Russia (1863), anticipated later developments. Some of the newspapers, such as Buchner's, appealed to a specifically working-class audience to forge trade unionism among Jewish laborers. Most stood on the traditional side of American Jewish life, engaging in anti-Reform polemics. As full-service papers, they mixed politics, original literature, and editorials; however, they found themselves severely handicapped, at least initially, by the lack of Yiddish printing presses in America. Tzvi Hirsh Bernstein, for example, at first tried to use the Hebrew presses at Frank's Printers but found the type inappropriate and, instead, imported letters and type from Vilna and Vienna. These pioneer Yiddish journalists primarily wrote in *Dietshmerish,* a Germanized Yiddish. The established English-language American Jewish newspapers, particularly Wise's *Israelite,* mocked the very idea of journalism in "jargon."[34]

Moreover, a small community of Hebraists, *maskilim,* in New York and Chicago tried to launch a Hebrew press. Some of these advocates of the Hebrew language arrived in the United States as early as the 1850s, making a living as teachers, religious functionaries, and printers. In the 1870s, such journals as *Hatzofe B'Eretz Ha-Hadash* (the scout in the new land) reprinted articles from European Hebrew journals and reported on local developments. The weeklies, *Hadashot Yisraeliyot* (1871) and *Hechal Ha'Ivriyah* (1877), attacked Reform Judaism and tried to promote Hebrew language, literature, and traditional Talmud scholarship. According to one study of the early American Hebrew press, "the literary quality did not fall generally below that of the European Hebrew newspapers of that period."[35]

Jewish journalism in America hoped to create a national Jewish culture, foster unity, and awaken the Jewish masses to their stake in contemporary issues. Jewish literature, in these four languages, did the same. Close links bound together journalism and literature, since newspapers published poetry and short stories, and serialized novels, introducing the reading public to a stable of authors. The Jewish press devoted a great deal of space to literature. Leeser, in the *Occident,* promised novelists and poets that by writing in a Jewish idiom, they would help all Jews "by aiding them to rise in public estimation, and to become known for something nobler than the mere acquisition of wealth, which the world believes is the only pursuit in which Jews can excel."[36]

Before the mass migrations from central Europe and the formation of the Jewish press, American Jews who happened to write fiction, poetry, and drama built a fairly thick wall between their art and Jewishness. Jewish themes and subjects never figured in the literary output of Isaac Harby, Mordecai Noah, Jonas B. Phillips, and Samuel H. B. Judah.[37] After the 1840s, however, poets and novelists explored explicitly Jewish issues, including family loyalty, communal solidarity, history, anti-Semitism, and the Bible. Jewish women, in particular, swelled the ranks of novelists and poets whose work usually appeared first in the press. They wrote in sentimental terms, encouraging pride in Jewishness, loyalty to people and family, and devotion to God. Not unlike other female writers of the mid-nineteenth century, Jewish women, such as Penina Moise, Rebekah Gumpert Hyneman, Marion Hartog, Celia Moss, Octavia Harby Moses, Rose Emma Salaman, Martha Allen, Adah Isaac Menken, and—best known by the end of the 1870s—Emma Lazarus, turned to the columns of the Jewish press to express their Jewish peoplehood and American patriotism, and to celebrate women as mothers and defenders of Israel.[38]

When they wrote for non-Jewish publications, they also identified themselves with Judaism and Jews. Penina Moise, a native of South Carolina, who had been asked in 1856 by the rabbi of K. K. Beth Elohim to compose a series of hymns to be accompanied on the newly installed organ, published in *Fancy's Sketch, Godey's Ladies' Book,* and elsewhere. In 1820, she obviously referred to Jews when she addressed her poem in the *Southern Patriot* "To Persecuted Foreigners":

> If thou out of that oppressed race
> Whose name's a proverb and whose lot's disgrace
> Brave the Atlantic—
> Hope's broad anchor weigh;
> A Western Sun will
> Gild your future day.

Similarly, in the late 1870s, Emma Lazarus wrote (although not published until 1882) *Songs of a Semite: "The Dance to Death" and Other Poems* in which she placed herself under "The Banner of the Jew":[39]

> Oh deem not dead that martial fire,
> Say not the mystic flame is spent!
> With Moses' law and David's lyre,
> Your ancient strength remains unbent.
> Let but an Ezra rise anew,
> To lift the BANNER OF THE JEW!

Connections between mid-nineteenth-century American Jewish literature and a public assertion of Jewishness can also be seen in the fiction produced by none other than Isaac M. Wise. The galvanizer of the Reform movement was discouraged, as he later recalled, that "there simply was no Jewish literature in the English language . . . [He] became furious, rushing impetuously through the materials on hand, but in vain. There was nothing." He took it upon himself to remedy the situation and published in the *Israelite* and *Die Deborah* eleven English and sixteen German novels plus hundreds of poems.[40] Gothic in style and historic in setting, Wise's novels celebrated the bold courage of Jews in past eras, glorious moments in their battles for freedom, and assertions of their national independence. *The Combat of the People* (1859) pitted Hillel against Rome's Herod, while *The First of the Maccabees* (1860) retold the story of the Jewish revolt against the Syrians. Wise situated some of his other works in Germany, depicting Jewish resistance against and triumph over Christian oppression. *The Convert* took place in nineteenth-century Bohemia—Wise's birthplace—from which the tale's hero, intensely loyal to Judaism, fled to America, the best place to return to the Jewish faith.[41]

Under Wise's influence a number of others also dabbled in Jewish novel-writing. Their novels were first serialized in the *Israelite,* and many of them were subsequently published by Cincinnati's Bloch and Company, owned by Wise's brother-in-law. One of them, *The Count and the Jewess,* set in sixteenth-century Prague, dealt with anti-Semitism, love across religious lines, and Jewish solidarity. Written by a physician, Nathan Mayer, this novel began a long literary career that saw four other novels and scores of poems published in the *Israelite.* Mayer's 1867 novel, *Differences,* probed Jewish life in America during the Civil War and was perhaps the first novel to examine American Jewry.[42] The *Israelite*'s literary editor, H. M. Moos, came out with a play in 1860, *Mortara; or, The Pope and His Inquisitor,* in verse form, retelling the story of Catholic iniquity and Jewish courage, while his *Hannah; or, A Glimpse of Paradise* (1865) depicted the life of a German Jewish peddler in America. Moritz Loth, another protégé of Wise, published *Our Prospects* in 1870, a fictionalized Jewish defense against Christian charges.[43]

Jewish writers wrote not just in English. Wise wrote several of his novels and much of his poetry in not quite grammatical German, while *Die Deborah,* his German-language newspaper, published literature similar to the English material of the *Israelite.* A small number of Hebrew and Yiddish literati also published in America, although Hebraists and Yiddishists formed a separate literary community. The nascent Yiddish and Hebrew press devoted space to literature, and poets, in particular, explored what it meant to be American and Jewish. The earlier and more thoroughly developed Yiddish press also opened its columns to Hebrew writers. *Die Yiddishe Gazeten* made room for Hebrew poems during its brief existence, publishing, of particular note, the work of Jacob Zvi Sobel.[44]

Sobel, a native of Kovno, Russia, was typical of the small band of maskilim in late-nineteenth-century America. He made his way to New York by the early 1870s, teaching Hebrew there and in upstate Elmira. He sent back several articles to the Russian Hebraic press, including an upbeat piece on the state of the Jews in America, entitled *"B'sorot Tovot"* (good tidings). In the mid-1870s, he published a book of poetry, *Shir Zahav l'Yisrael Ha'Zakane* (a golden song for old Israel), which he then translated into Yiddish. Likewise, he became involved with the New York organization Hovevei S'fat Ever (lovers of the Hebrew language).[45]

The Hebrew and Yiddish literature, like the press, tended to deride Reform Judaism. The Yiddish and Hebrew papers published anti-Reform diatribes, and Sobel, in *Shir Zahav,* depicted the bewilderment of a young Polish Talmud student confronting Reform Judaism in America. The pious fellow entered what he thought was a factory, where he was required to remove his head covering, and to his dismay realized it was a Reform temple.

Hebraists aligned themselves with traditional Judaism, and traditionalists supported the development of a Hebrew-based culture. As early as the 1860s, the *Jewish Messenger* published occasional Hebrew poems, such as Isaac Goldstein's Hebrew dirge on Lincoln's death, which appeared in the New York Orthodox paper in May 1865. Joshua Falk Ha-Cohen, who arrived in the United States in 1858, also used the columns of the *Messenger* to publish Hebrew materials. Yet, despite this alliance, at least one Reform rabbi participated in the movement for Hebrew literature. Henry Gersoni, who served in Reform-style pulpits in Macon and Atlanta, Georgia, as well as in Chicago's B'nai Shalom, sent regular items to the Hebrew press in Europe, translated Longfellow's poetry into Hebrew, and in 1870 helped to found a Yiddish newspaper, *Die Post,* which also published Hebrew materials.[46]

In the mid-nineteenth-century decades, Jews in America also wrote, published, and presumably purchased sacred texts. In the 1810s American Jews relied on Europe for prayer books, Bibles, *haggadot* (texts for the Passover seder), Hebrew grammars, and, indeed, any kind of printed Judaic material. By the end of the century, American Jews still imported books from abroad but had begun to craft American texts and contribute to the world of Jewish writing. Partly intended as an antidote to the tracts of missionaries, and partly because the number of Jews had grown, the publication of Judaic materials for American Jewry began as early as the 1820s and 1830s.

In 1826, Solomon Henry Jackson, a New York printer who edited the anti-evangelical newspaper, the *Jew,* published his own English translation of the Sephardic rite daily prayer book, with accompanying Hebrew text. Then, in 1837, Jackson published the first American haggadah.[47] From the 1830s through the 1850s, Isaac Leeser scored several firsts in American Jewish publishing: among others, the first volume of published sermons by an American rabbi, the first primer for Jewish children, and the first Hebrew-English Bible translated in America.[48]

A variety of problems in American Jewish life encouraged, by default, the publication of multiple prayer books: the growing tension over Reform and the assertion of the reform-minded that modern Jews could make liturgical innovations, the splintering of American congregations along nationality-rite lines, and the lack of any kind of central, unifying governing body. Rabbis, such as Leo Merzbacher, Isaac M. Wise, David Einhorn, Benjamin Szold, and Marcus Jastrow, among the better known, all edited and published their own prayer books. Over the course of the next half century, American Jewish intellectuals and writers produced numerous prayer books, sermon collections, educational materials for children, a few learned essays, editions of nonliturgical traditional texts, and some speculative works on Judaism.[49]

Exact figures on the sales of these works do not exist, but the public must have been willing to spend some money on them, because so many were published. The space devoted to literature in the press, the growth of the press itself, and the steadily increasing number of books published indicated that Jews of nineteenth-century America had some appetite for Jewish reading. Judah David Eisenstein, writing back to Russia in 1873, lectured his supercilious readers that Jewish learning existed and flourished in America, and that at least New York's Bet ha-Midrash ha-Gadol on Ludlow Street had "Jews engaged in study. . . . It has many books, as in the great houses of Study in Poland."[50]

Ancillary institutions made it possible for Judaic writing to take shape. Publishing houses equipped with Hebrew type put out Jewish materials, bookstores distributed books, and literary societies fostered a readership. In 1854, Isaac M. Wise's brother-in-law, Edward Bloch, a fellow immigrant from Bohemia transplanted to Cincinnati, entered into a partnership with the enigmatic rabbi and launched his publishing company that started *Die Deborah,* and the *Israelite,* and printed numerous novels by Jewish authors on Jewish themes. Bloch also made available such scholarly material as *A Guide for Rational Inquiries into the Biblical Writings* by Isidor Kalisch. Recognizing that there was a small but palpable Yiddish and Hebrew reading public in America, Bloch imported books and reprinted European works, sometimes transliterating Yiddish words in Latin characters.[51] Over time, non-Jewish publishers also made available the work of Jewish writers, both European and American, while newspapers, such as the *Occident,* the *Jewish Messenger,* and the *American Hebrew,* used their presses to print book-length materials. By the early 1870s, a New York printer, M. Toplowsky, used his facilities to publish Yiddish materials as well.[52]

Bookstores in New York, Chicago, San Francisco, and elsewhere carried lines of Jewish reading material. As early as 1849, the newly arrived immigrant from Bohemia, Isidor Bush, tried his hand at a Jewish book mart on New York's Grand Street. Although its name, "Bookstore, neue Buch-, Kunst- und Schreibmaterialienhandlung" (new books, art and writing materials), indicated a general store, it offered Hebrew and English-language Jewish books, Jewish ritual objects, and Jewish periodicals in multiple languages. Bush's bookstore, designed to provide financial backing for its owner's *Israels Herold,* failed.[53] In the mid-1850s, Rabbi Samuel Myer Isaacs operated a Jewish bookstore out of his home and served as American agent for several books published in England as well as for newspapers published abroad and in other American Jewish communities. He carried almanacs, prayer books, ritual objects, and Jewish art (including pictures of the British philanthropist Moses Montefiore, suitable for framing).[54] Isidor Choyinski ran a successful bookstore in San Francisco, which offered Jewish books and printed materials to West Coast Jews. As of 1880, New York Jews could avail themselves of five such enterprises, two of which, Kantrowitz's and Sakolski's, were "longstanding and have made their owners rich."[55]

In 1845, Isaac Leeser founded a Jewish Publication Society to stimulate the publication of Jewish materials in the United States, deemed paltry and inconsequential by many at the time. He hoped the Society would produce anti-evangelical literature while elevating the intellectual level of the Jewish communities. The society issued a dozen booklets in its "Jewish Miscellany" series, a few written by Leeser himself but most published earlier in Europe. The society and the knot of Philadelphians behind it envisioned primarily a membership organization that eschewed any profit motive, hoping instead to entice modest Jews to pay one dollar a year for a projected series of eight booklets. The plan far exceeded the society's means. It failed to issue the anticipated number of books, and a fire on December 27, 1851, marred its hopes for two decades.[56]

Yet the idea did not expire with the flames of 1851, and, in 1867, the Board of Delegates of American Israelites chose a committee of three—Isaac Leeser, Marcus Jastrow, and Samuel Isaacs—to plan for another Jewish publication society. The Board of Delegates knew that just the previous decade, Jews in Germany had organized the *Institut zur Förderung der israelitischen Literatur,* and the American group wanted something similar. The following year, Mayer Sulzberger, a Philadelphia lawyer, issued a call in the *Occident* to the Jews in America, particularly those with means, to promote a publication society "whose activity shall foster native talent, and whose munificence shall enable all to drink draughts of wisdom at its fountain so that in all the land it shall be said of us: "Behold, Israel is a wise and an understanding people."57

By 1871, the American Jewish Publication Society, headquartered in New York and supported by Reform congregation Temple Emanu-El, came into being. (Similar societies were developing in western European countries at the same time. In 1868, French Jews founded the Société Scientifique Littéraire Israelite, and, soon thereafter, the Society of Hebrew Literature was established in England.) Like its earlier incarnation, the American Jewish Publication Society looked outward at the missionaries and published such materials as Rabbi Frederic da Sola Mendes's *Jewish Family Papers; or Letters of a Missionary,* a defense of Judaism. It also looked inward and offered American Jews a one-volume translation of Heinrich Graetz's *History of the Jews.* Indeed, the publication society sought to create a Jewish public literate in its own history, knowledgeable about itself.58

Poor funding, its almost exclusive New York base, and the absence of real leadership at its helm explained its short life. But its formation and Leeser's earlier effort indicated that at least some American Jews felt the need for the self-conscious production of a Jewish culture that experimented in nontraditional forms, disseminated Judaic material to a non-scholarly public, and functioned in tandem with the synagogues and schools as an agency of Jewish education and defense.

Individuals as different in ideology as Wise and Leeser agreed on the need for an American Jewish literature and its commitment to Jewish learning. Despite an opinion expressed at the time that America was a Jewish cultural backwater, the American effort did not take shape much later than that in older and more highly developed communities in western Europe. The heavy reliance on British and German materials demonstrated that American Jews functioned in a worldwide Jewish network, speaking an idiom not all that different from their coreligionists in Europe. Texts that crossed national lines replicated the movement of people and the feelings of unity among the Jewish people.

American Jews had more success in establishing Jewish schools than in spawning literature. While such issues as the educational level, reading habits, and breadth of consciousness of the immigrants before migration to America defy easy categorization, their class backgrounds made it improbable that they had much access or exposure to Jewish learning or books in Europe or much knowledge of Jewish events beyond their immediate locale. Yet, once in the United States, they expressed a strong interest in the preservation of Judaism and in inculcating, through education, Jewish literacy in their children. Both rabbis and lay people defined early on Jewish education for their children as a crucial element on the communal agenda. In Akron, Ohio, for example, the handful of Jews who first settled there tried to provide Jewish education before they consecrated a cemetery or formed a congregation.[59]

American Jews taught Judaism to their children in various ways. Some used congregationally sponsored day schools, others sent their children to private Jewish academies, Sunday schools, or relied on private tutors.[60] English, German, and Jewish subjects were taught in private academies in New York, San Francisco, Atlanta, Savannah, and San Bernardino, California,[61] while elsewhere congregations operated such schools.[62] In Philadelphia, the public school system sanctioned and provided some funding for Jewish day schools. The Hebrew Education Society, founded by Isaac Leeser, carried the official sanction of the city's board of education.[63]

Some of these schools thrived; others did not. Success depended on a variety of factors: size and wealth of the community, availability of trained personnel, and the provision of public education. Depending on their means, Jewish parents in New York could choose from a number of different academies, from teachers who advertised their services in newspapers, from congregationally sponsored schools, from traditional Talmud Torahs, Sunday schools, and the like.[64] Parents in smaller towns had fewer choices. Jewish parents in Sandusky, Ohio, for example, may have felt quite frustrated in the 1870s at the paucity of Jewish learning. No local children could attain a high level of proficiency in Hebrew. They must have been duly impressed when in 1873 the young David Philipson got up on the *bima* on his bar mitzvah and "read the opening portion of the Torah . . . from the scroll, a feat never before achieved by any lad in the community."[65]

Rabbis and other communal leaders vigorously argued over what kind of Jewish education best suited American children. Some, such as Leeser, believed deeply that only a Jewish investment in parochial schools would serve American Jews. Jewish children, he believed, had to be fortified to deal with the American, Christian world; since the public schools were hardly religiously neutral institutions and tried to convert Jewish children, they should not attend. Leeser considered the low level of Jewish learning a particular problem in a democratic society and asserted that only a rigorous Jewish education would adequately prepare the child to participate in Judaism as an adult. To fulfill these twin goals, Leeser saw to the publication of pedagogic materials for Jewish children and the creation of America's first institution of Jewish higher learning, Maimonides College, which opened in Philadelphia in 1867.[66]

Although concerned about the same issues, Wise saw the public schools as important crucibles in molding American Jewish citizens and, therefore, advocated an extensive system of afternoon schools for Jewish public school students. "Should our children," Wise asked readers of the *Israelite,* "be educated as Jews only or even as foreigners in language and spirit, or should they be educated as Americans, as citizens of the same free country, to be with them one harmonious people; or should we foster that unfortunate prejudice that pressed so many bitter, burning tears from most of us, and from our fathers in the old country? Answer yourselves which system will do the one, and which must result in the other."[67]

Wise wanted America's Jewish children to assert their Jewishness proudly and not cower in separate institutions. He hated the evangelicals with no less fervor than Leeser but believed that Jewish participation in American schools would defuse the Christian missionaries' efforts. He refused to give these tax-supported institutions over to them, asserting that Jews had the right to demand that schools indeed be neutral. Like Leeser, Wise wanted to foster Jewish survival through education but assumed that synagogue schools, employing scientific pedagogic methods, directed by American-trained rabbis (naturally, products of his Hebrew Union College, founded in 1873), and buttressed by special child-oriented publications, such as the *Sabbath Visitor,* edited by his friend and Reform associate Max Lilienthal, could provide a solid foundation for young Jews.[68]

If Wise and Leeser argued for quite different types of institutions, they showed remarkable agreement about the content and purpose of Jewish education. They sought to teach Hebrew language, Bible, customs, and prayers to sustain Judaism as a religion. They wanted to secure the survival of the Jewish people as a distinct entity within the American polity by fostering group feeling and identity. No voices in the community denied that Jews needed special knowledge to be Jews, and none envisioned a future in which Jews would cease to be a distinct group with feelings of belonging to an entity with roots in the past and affiliation to "Israel" around the world.

The Languages of American Jews

Probably no element in their culture revealed as much about the ways in which nineteenth-century Jews in America saw themselves as their language. What language, or more appropriately, languages, did they speak? What values did they attribute to their various languages, and how did they project themselves linguistically to the American people among whom they had chosen to live? American Jews debated over what should be the language of the worship, of instruction, and of the home. Each of their languages presented a different problem or issue. For example, *if* any vernacular language was to be added to the service (traditionalists refused to tamper with the Hebrew liturgy), which should it be? Should Jewish schools emphasize teaching ritual and Bible in English, comprehensible to American-bred youngsters, or should they teach Hebrew? The proponents of English clashed with those who advocated the use of Hebrew as the only mode of religious expression, who in turn pitted themselves against the lovers of German. Despite the fact that all three groups denigrated the use of "jargon," that is, Yiddish, that language functioned as a medium of communication, too.

From Europe's linguistic crossroads, where multiple languages existed side by side, Jewish immigrants came to a nation committed to a single language. In their everyday lives, Jews picked up English, broken though it may have been, out of necessity. The peddler on the road or the shopkeeper behind the counter had immediate reason to learn the language of customers. One ordinary immigrant, writing to his newly arrived brother in Baltimore in 1854, made clear the linkage between language and work. "An ordinary laborer," Jacob Felsenthal glowed about California, "gets four to five dollars per day, so you can imagine what wages are paid. I am sure you already speak good English. I do too as my wife is an American born in Boston, and does not speak a word of German."[69] Newly arrived Jewish immigrants learned English from one another, from the more acculturated families in the boarding houses where they lived, on the street, and possibly from customers rather than in any formal classes or institutions provided by the American or Jewish communities.[70]

Rabbis and other communal leaders born and educated in Europe also had to learn English—as their second or even third language—in order to communicate effectively. Isaac Wise, a native Yiddish speaker who first had to learn German to qualify for the rabbinate, claimed that he had long yearned to leave Bohemia for America and acquired some English from a set of English books he came upon in a Prague bookstore. Indeed, he boasted that those books made him "a naturalized American in the interior of Bohemia."[71] Rebekah Kohut remembered that when her father, a Hungarian-born rabbi, came to America in 1867 unable to handle English, "his first purchase . . . was a copy of a daily newspaper. His second was a German-English dictionary. He read the first, word for word, with the aid of the second. Soon he was more American than the Americans," issuing a rigid decree that from then on, only English could be spoken in the household.[72]

Unlike some other immigrants of the mid-nineteenth century, few Jewish community leaders doubted the need for Jewish children to grow up fluent in the tongue of their new home. Groups of German immigrants who settled in Texas and the Midwest sought to preserve intact the German language and culture. They saw the vastness of America as an opportunity for transplanting their native culture unchanged and created enclaves where they fostered the exclusive use of German.[73]

Not so Jews. Jewish schools and orphanages used English as the language of instruction. Many communal leaders, eager for the English-speaking children to see their Jewish and American lives connected to each other, pressed for the inclusion of English into the synagogue service. When, in the 1840s, New York's Congregation B'nai Jeshurun invited Samuel Isaacs to its pulpit from London as the first rabbi to preach in English in America, it launched a tremendous drive for rabbinic personnel who could speak the language. English-speaking rabbis were in big demand thereafter.[74] Leeser, Wise, and even the highly traditional Abraham Rice urged Jewish schools, particularly all-day institutions, to place English high on the curriculum, produce reading material for children in English, and ensure that the words of the service be comprehensible to those who knew only English. Solomon Carvalho, whose wife, Sarah, joined other women to found the Hebrew-English Sunday School in Baltimore in 1857, urged the parents: "educate your children in the English language . . . and have the divine principles of their religion taught and explained to them in the vernacular of the country."[75]

Carvalho directed her admonition at those Jews who held up German as a sacred tongue, as a language par excellence for Jewish discourse. In central Europe, German had been considered the language of refinement and cultural sophistication. A good secular education required mastery of German, which in turn was essential for entry into the higher echelons of business and the professions. Even in the towns and cities of eastern Europe, where German was not the native language, German spoken without a Jewish accent marked a woman or man as someone who traveled with ease in the two worlds.

American rabbis such as David Einhorn wanted to give primacy to German in the service and in the rabbi's sermon. The majority of nine-teenth-century congregations at one time or another employed a German-educated rabbi who indeed delivered his sermons in German, and many memoirs of American Jews of those years recalled, not often fondly, that, "we had to go to service every Saturday morning, and as it was in German, it was inexpressibly tedious and I invented a headache whenever I could."[76] Most Jewish all-day schools included German in the curriculum, B'nai B'rith lodges sponsored German lectures, and synagogues and benevolent societies routinely wrote their constitutions and kept their earliest records in German.[77]

This celebration and use of German did not mean that a sizable number of Jewish immigrants to America actually felt comfortable in German, using it with accuracy and ease, or that they attributed to it the mystical force that Einhorn did. The children of German-speaking immigrants quickly became English speakers, and expansive statements of Einhorn or Chicago's Bernhard Felsenthal about the Jewish affinity for German may indeed have been a last-gasp effort to revive it. Memoirs described the boredom of the children who had little knowledge of and probably even less love for the language. Rabbis steeped in German *Kultur* wanted American Jews to dignify themselves by sharing in their love of that language. But these rabbis rarely had the laity on their side on the language issue. For example, when Bernhard Felsenthal became a trustee of the Jewish Orphan Asylum in Cleveland in 1875, he pressed for German to be equal in the curriculum to English. He found himself heavily outnumbered by his fellows on the board. The superintendent of the orphanage clearly stated that "the education of our orphans . . . is American and Jewish at the same time." He saw no reason to educate them in the idiom of Goethe and Schiller.[78] Einhorn and the other Germanophiles saw German erode before their very eyes as organizations such as the B'nai B'rith formally adopted English in 1855 and congregation after congregation dropped German to keep minutes in English and voted to adopt Wise's English language prayer book, *Minhag America*. By doing so, they also endorsed the concept of *minhag America,* an American rite in the English language.[79]

Some rabbis may have addressed their congregations with German sermons and intoned prayers translated from Hebrew into German not because they venerated German, but because so many knew no English, or at least not enough to orate in it. They or their congregants may have felt uncomfortable with English overlayed with a thick central European accent. Until the end of the 1870s, when the first American-born, American-trained rabbis were ordained, rabbis by and large spoke German. Before the graduation of the first classes from Hebrew Union College, all rabbis were imported to the United States from Europe. Until then, regardless of the laity's preference in the matter of language, congregations had little choice. In 1866, for example, Chicago's Bene Shalom Congregation advertised in the *Israelite* for a preacher fluent in both English and German. After two years, the board hired Aaron Messing, who never felt comfortable in Engish, spoke it haltingly, and always opted to preach in German, not out of love of the language but out of discomfort with English.[80]

For many immigrants, even those from "Germany," German had not been their mother tongue; they learned it for either business or bureaucratic reasons. At the point of their departure, only the very tiny stratum of rabbis, intellectuals, and political activists in Germany had a firm grasp of German. Ordinary Jews migrating from Poland, Galicia, Lithuania, and even Bohemia, Moravia, and Hungary had not. But as secularization progressed, they came to see it as a language more prestigious than the familiar Yiddish, which had been lambasted by Christian advocates of *Bildung* as well as by Jewish intellectuals and maskilim as a mongrel dialect.

Thus, although synagogue and benevolent society constitutions and minutes appeared first in German, they abounded with errors in spelling and grammar. The women and men who held the pens may have never formally learned German or may have had just a few years of elementary education. They might very well have been Yiddish speakers who believed that documents of such importance ought to be written in a "real" language.[81]

Even many immigrants from Germany found German difficult to handle. Isaac Bernheim, an immigrant from Baden who came to Kentucky in the late-1860s, described one of the German Jewish bachelors who frequented his store as someone handicapped by the fact that he "wrote German badly and had not learned enough of the English language to read or even to write or speak it with any fluency."[82]

Among intellectuals as well, attachment to German was not terribly strong. American Jews produced much more in the way of English and even Yiddish literature than they did German. Wise's German paper, *Die Deborah,* with its chatty tone, informality, and avoidance of political issues, took second place in communal importance after the *American Israelite.* Few Jewish institutions, certainly not synagogues, bore German names. Occasionally, a local group formed a *Frauen Verein,* but much more commonly, these associations were called by Hebrew names, such as Chebra Gemilath Chassodim U'bikkur Cholim, B'nai B'rith, Kesher shel Barzel, and the like. In fact, the few synagogues that used the term *Verein* to describe themselves announced their Reform orientation. While Jews of German background could also be found in the ranks of the traditionalists, the celebration of German and the audible declarations of Germanness tended to be synonymous with Reform.

It is hard to gauge how much Hebrew the immigrants knew before coming to America or how much their children learned afterwards. Certainly, only a few of the European Hebraists and traditional scholars journeyed to America. Yet in letters of ordinary Jews and in their communications with Jewish newspapers, Hebrew words cropped up, pointing to some familiarity, if not competence, with the "holy tongue." After the death of a Jewish child, A. Sand from Leavenworth City, Kansas Territory, told readers of the *Jewish Messenger* in 1858 that "much trouble was experienced by its parents to bring the child to *kever Yisroel* (a grave in Israel)," while Victoria Jacobs of San Diego, in her diary of the 1850s, peppered her English with *"yomtov"* (holiday) and *"mazeltov."*[83] Furthermore, ordinary Jews in cities and towns across America gave their institutions Hebrew names, demonstrating again that they knew something of that language and sensed that sacred matters would be best articulated in the original language of Jewish piety. A group of lay people who seceded from Rochester's Berith Kodesh in 1870 first dubbed their new congregation Elon Yerek and then changed it to Aitz Rah-Non, two different Hebrew phrases for a green or new tree. Hebrew remained very much the tongue of the holy to these nineteenth-century American Jews.[84]

With the exception of Einhorn and the small circle around him, most rabbis, school directors, editors, and communal figures, regardless of religious orientation, believed firmly that Jewish children needed to know Hebrew, whether it be just enough to read prayers or to read with comprehension. The Jewish orphanages, usually very practical in their missions, taught the Hebrew language along with carpentry for boys and needlecraft for girls, while the New York Young Men's Hebrew Association offered prizes to local boys and girls in the 1870s for showing off their Hebraic proficiency.[85] Wise proudly reported in the *Israelite* how school children in remote communities recited Hebrew lessons for him, while Leeser in the *Occident* similarly touted evidence of interest in the language. In 1859, for example, he greeted warmly the arrival of Rabbi Henry Vidaver, a Warsaw-born Jew who came to Rodeph Shalom in Philadelphia. Vidaver had translated some German poetry into Hebrew, and Leeser waxed eloquently that "the lovers of the sacred tongue will be pleased to notice that we have in this country another who knows how to employ the language of Israel to express the tender emotions of the soul."[86]

Traditionalists and most Reformers wanted to strike a balance between English and Hebrew in synagogue and school. They differed over the weight given to each. Leeser, the traditionalist, would not tamper with the actual content of the service but considered the English sermon a reasonable addition. Wise, who ardently advocated Hebrew instruction in American Jewish schools, put English into his *Minhag America* but also retained much of the Hebrew in the text, except for selections that he excised for ideological rather than linguistic reasons. Reform-oriented rabbis who attended the 1869 Cleveland Conference adopted a plank stating that "urgently as the cultivation of the Hebrew language, in which the treasures of divine revelation are given and the immortal remains of the literature," should be felt, "it has become unintelligible to the vast majority of our coreligionists; therefore it must make way, as is advisable . . . to intelligible language in prayer, which, if not understood, is a soulless form." Reform advocates still saw the connection between Hebrew and the preservation of Judaism. Even Chicago's ultra-Reform Temple Sinai included Hebrew among subjects in its school until 1879.[87]

Why this attachment to Hebrew? It had, after all, been the language of prayer for centuries and American Jews, conscious of this legacy, balked at replacing it fully with an alien tongue, be it English or German. Perhaps, it was because Hebrew remained ensconced in the Jews' inner realm, the synagogue, and did not complicate their relationship with non-Jewish neighbors. Using it ritually carried few negative implications. Indeed, it bore a degree of prestige in America. After all, it was the language of the Bible. Protestant clergymen revered it, and American colleges and theological seminaries taught it. By retaining Hebrew for ceremonial purposes, Jews situated themselves in America as the heirs of the biblical tradition. When Abraham Kohn, the city clerk of Chicago and an observant Jew and ardent Republican, wanted to give the newly elected president Abraham Lincoln a token of his appreciation, he personally decorated a silk flag with a Hebrew text from the Book of Joshua: "Every place that the sole of your foot shall tread upon, that have I given unto you, as I said unto Moses."[88] Far from stigmatizing Jews, the use of Hebrew in religious worship could be acceptable even to those acculturating. It did not embarrass them, no negative attitudes surrounded its use, and it even had a degree of prestige in Christian America.

On the other hand, Yiddish or variants of Judeo-German, which were also spoken and read throughout this era, lacked such prestige. When in the 1840s, a group of Jews founded a congregation in Easton, Pennsylvania, they wrote their constitution by transliterating German words in Hebrew characters, full of "Yiddish that took account of every peculiarity of German script . . . with occasional characteristically south German phonetic spellings."[89] Yiddish served as the medium of communication in the congregations, khevrot, anshes, and landsmanshaftn founded by various groups of eastern European Jews from the 1860s on. The amount of editorial space Isaac Wise gave to the lambasting of "jargon" in the *Israelite* suggests that the language was used prominently and publicly. Moses Mielziner, a Posen-born, Berlin-educated rabbi who was an ardent lover of German and hater of Yiddish, came to New York's Anshe Chesed Congregation in 1865, and as his wife remembered, "Moses . . . was imbued with a love for purity in language, and always expressed an abhorrence of a mixed tongue. He watched with distaste the development of Yiddish."[90]

American Jews wrote numerous letters in Yiddish to families back in Germany and to other parts of Europe, testifying to the persistence of the language, while the interspersing of Yiddish words into German or English materials further indicated that nineteenth-century American Jews existed in a multilingual world. Jacob Lemann, an immigrant from Hesse and a Jewish merchant living in Donaldsonville, Louisiana, in the 1850s, kept his business records in Yiddish. The fathers of Judah Magnes and Bernard Drachman were Yiddish-speakers who in America married "up" into German families and then felt compelled to give up their Yiddish. David Magnes, an immigrant from Russian Poland who came to San Francisco in the 1860s, married a woman from East Prussia, a "lover of German culture [who] did her utmost to see that German was spoken and written by the family."

Certainly, the tens of thousands of Jewish immigrants from Posen, Galicia, and Bohemia, particularly in the earlier decades of the century, had to have been Yiddish speakers. German had barely seeped into these regions' Jewish communities, and those few elite Jews who knew German there tended to be the wealthier and more educated, precisely those who eschewed America but moved to Berlin, Budapest, Vienna, and Prague instead. Immigrants from these regions who came to America after the 1850s would have had some exposure to German prior to migration, but by then, others were coming to America from places further east, from Suwalk, Lithuania, and other areas that were still largely untouched by German culture and speech. For these immigrants, Yiddish was the everyday language used with family and friends. American Jews in the mid-nineteenth century certainly spoke, wrote, and read Yiddish. Yet it may have functioned as a kind of underground language, deprecated by many, spoken only in privacy or in snatches interspersed with German and English. Lambasted from every side, Yiddish speakers submerged their linguistic identity into an undifferentiated mass of "German" Jews moving along the road toward learning English. As Jews sought to take on the trappings of respectability, they became less willing to speak or admit to speaking Yiddish.[91]

The short-lived *Hebrew News,* an English-German-Hebrew-Yiddish New York newspaper of the early 1870s, typified the linguistic complexity of American Jewry. An editorial of 1871 justified the use of Yiddish in the name of the "hundreds of thousands of our brothers [who] live here. Those arriving every day speak and understand no other language but the one spoken among our brothers in Russia and Poland."[92] The function of English was obvious. It spoke the words of the future, of work and livelihood. Hebrew and German stood in the middle. Both languages represented different aspects of refinement and higher values, the former looking inward to the culture of the Jewish people, the latter facing outward, representing the central European lingua franca of civility.

Being Jewish / Being American

What, then, did being Jewish mean to these men and women as they became American? What did they actually say in their various languages, in their newspapers, poems, schools, synagogues, and in their homes? What did being American constitute, and how did they balance out these two identities? Obviously, no single paradigm represented Jewish acculturation, and no single model encompassed the experiences of tens of thousands. Indeed, the same individual could both praise America as the closest approximation to the Jews' promised land and lambaste it in no uncertain terms for its Christian evangelical aims. A single person might claim for the Jews a special identity, different from that of all other Americans, venerate the Jewish past, and yet decry traditional practices as anachronistic and out of place in modern America.

When it came to defining America, the immigrant Jews and their children knew that they had arrived in a place that offered them liberties and opportunities unknown in Europe. They described America in their letters, memoirs, sermons, and newspapers as Europe's polar opposite. All of the liabilities of their home countries—the restrictions and the virulent anti-Semitism—faded in America.

Given that the Jews' economic misfortunes had launched the migration, America's material expansiveness made them eloquent about the "land glorious and free."[93] To Isaac M. Wise, the openness of America made it more than just another spot in the Jewish Diaspora but a place replete with transcendent meaning. "Moses," he wrote effusively, "formed one pole, and the American Revolution the other, of an axis around which revolved the political history of 33 centuries" of Jewry.[94] Isaac Bernheim, who would eventually rise to fame and fortune in the liquor-distilling industry in Kentucky, arrived relatively poor in New York in 1867 and expressed the optimism characteristic of American Jews on a more prosaic level. Despite the emptiness of his pockets, he *knew* that America was the right place for him. "I saw New York in all its splendor and glory. . . . the signs . . . bearing German-Jewish names all along the street instilled me with courage."[95] American Jews welcomed the chance for political participation, competition in the marketplace, and structuring their Jewish institutions as they wanted them.

But naive they were not. They recognized the fact that the germs of anti-Semitism infected America as well, that pockets of hatred existed. America, while more tolerant and open than Europe, still lagged behind their image of a paradise for the Jews. Samuel Rosenwald, a Jewish merchant in Springfield, Illinois, wrote back to family in Germany in 1881: "I quite forgot that you wanted to be exactly informed about the Jewish question, although there is not much *Rischus* [anti-Semitism] here, yet we are not on the same level with the Christians. . . . In business one hardly ever hears anything like that, but the children often hear about it, and that is unpleasant enough."[96] Not surprisingly, a degree of timidity ran through their self-expression. They did not know exactly with whom they were dealing and how far they could push group interests.

But American Jews spoke out when they felt slighted. They sent stinging letters to newspaper editors to protest outrages and used their numerical power, however meager, to register their ire at the ballot box. For example, an irate Jew wrote to the Milwaukee *Sentinel* in 1858 after a particularly vicious piece of reportage: "Do we live in the fifteenth century to throw a stigma of hatred on the Jews?" He obviously worried little about "rocking the boat."[97] On a private level, Jews reacted when they believed that their people or their religion had been attacked. During the Civil War, Lazarus Straus, a successful businessman in Talbotton, Georgia, decided that he and his family would not continue to live in a town where a grand jury referred to the "evil practices" of the Jews. According to one of his sons, Lazarus, he "immediately let it be known that he would move away from a community which had cast such a reflection on him as the only Jew living in their midst." Despite the pleas of local Christian clergymen and town officials that he stay, he left in anger.[98]

Jewish leaders feared, perhaps out of proportion to reality, the power of the evangelicals who envisioned a Christian America in which the unconverted would see the light and in which Jews and Judaism would cease to exist. Part of nineteenth-century American Jewish culture, including philanthropy, education, journalism, and Reform Judaism, developed in reaction to missionary pressures. Only by providing Jewish services to the poor, fortifying children with Jewish education, countering evangelical arguments point by point, and modernizing Judaism to make it meaningful to modern women and men could the evangelicals be undermined. Jewish writers and orators did not hesitate to take on the evangelicals and boldly excoriated them. Rabbi Pinchas Wintner of Mt. Zion Congregation in St. Paul, Minnesota, in the 1870s, attacked them in a Purim address, which the next day appeared boldly in print in the *St. Paul Pioneer*. He called the evangelicals the "Hamans of America," alluding to the villain of the Purim story, the Persian who wanted to kill the Jews. "They emerge," stormed Wintner, "from their hiding places from time to time in different shapes and colors as politicians, pietists, heads of churches, narrow minded ministers, missionaries."[99]

But the evangelicals did not represent all of America. On balance, the tone of nineteenth-century Jewish culture expressed a basic trust in the American system and its people, and took statements about goodwill and tolerance at face value. Because Jews believed in the American creed, they did not hesitate to draw attention to themselves as somehow different, yet at the same time entitled to equal access to the bounties of America. They unabashedly celebrated holidays with no American equivalents—Rosh Hashanah, Yom Kippur, Purim, and Hanukkah—and opened the doors of their synagogues, benevolent societies, and homes to non-Jews to observe them at these rites. They invited their Christian neighbors, including clergymen and public officials, to their weddings, circumcisions, and dedications of their synagogues.[100]

Probably all American Jews in the middle decades of the nineteenth century agreed that America offered them greater opportunity to make a living, build homes without restriction, shape communities as they chose, and jump into the political fray without stimulating anti-Semitism than any other spot on the globe. They differed among themselves, however, as to what such an open society would mean to Jews and Judaism in the long run. Rabbis and newspaper editors arrayed themselves along a spectrum of opinion, from that of Baltimore's Rabbi Abraham Rice, who feared that that openness would lead to the destruction of all that distinguished the Jew, to that of radical Reformers, who envisioned a kind of universalistic Judaism that would usher in an American messianic age of progress. The former adamantly maintained that it did not matter where the Jews lived— they had a fixed body of law, a fixed liturgy, and a fixed identity, and from those there could be no digression. The latter just as ardently argued for the elasticity of Judaism, epitomized in Rabbi Emil Hirsch's inaugural sermon at Chicago's Temple Sinai in 1880: "A world of thought and sentiment in which our fathers moved and lived is taking leave of us—the children."[101]

But in their private writings, in the ungrammatical, poorly spelled constitutions of their *khevras,* and in their actions in benevolent societies, synagogues, Masonic and B'nai B'rith lodges, neighborhoods and family circles, the majority of American Jews showed themselves to fall sloppily, and unself-consciously, in the middle. The great disputes of the rabbis and the points of ideological departure meant little to them. Instead, ordinary women and men, small businesspeople concerned with everyday matters, Jews *and* Americans, pragmatically saw themselves to be both bound by the past and freed by the present. They did not feel compelled to define why they behaved the way they did either as Americans or as Jews. They picked and chose those aspects of Judaism that made sense to them and adopted those aspects of American culture that fit with their definitions of themselves as Jews. Like most newcomers to America, they believed, if their actions tell us what they thought, that to add on a new layer of identity did not require a total stripping away of the old one and that past and present, tradition and modernity, could coexist in harmony.

POSTSCRIPT: BEYOND 1880

IN THE mythology of American Jewish history, 1880 begins the decade of the great watershed. With the beginnings of the Jewish exodus from eastern Europe to America the following year, a new kind of Jewish life burst upon the scene. A complex Jewish world, rich in institutions, pulsating with diverse political, religious, literary, and social ferment, came into being. America became one of history's largest and most influential Jewish centers. The story after 1880 has been the story of the new arrivals who in America opted overwhelmingly for urban life, New York in particular. Here, these women and men of the working class founded theaters, newspapers, labor unions, schools, and cafés in densely packed neighborhoods that echoed with the sounds of Yiddish. The new immigrants demonstratively asserted their Jewishness and did not hesitate to subscribe to socialism, Zionism, Orthodoxy, and other ideologies out of step with American culture.

The usual telling of the story of the American Jewish experience beyond 1880 has indeed pitted the new Jewish immigrants against the Jews of America, the "German" Jews, by then comfortable, Reform, and put out by two million immigrants, many poor, all alien. Out of a mixture of paternalism, sincere concern for the poverty, disease, and shabby housing of their fellow Jews, and fear that the outlandish behavior of the "Russians" would jeopardize their own secure place in America, the American German Jews created a string of institutions, ranging from settlement houses to health stations, schools, and hospitals, to transform them into acceptable, proper Americans. The "uptown Jews," because in New York many had moved north of Lower Manhattan, tried to remake their eastern European coreligionists in every possible way. They tried to wean them away from socialism, traditional Judaism, loud and boisterous behavior, and the Yiddish language—in essence from everything that made them uncivil.

Indeed, the stock narrative has posed the years from 1880 through the 1920s as the period of conflict between the German and eastern European Jews in America, in which the former group, uncomfortable with Jewishness but at ease in America, sought to hold onto communal power and minimize the alienness of the newcomers, and the latter group, comfortable with Jewishness but ill at ease in America, resented the efforts at transformation and persisted in behaving as they wanted. Ultimately, by sheer power of numbers, the eastern Europeans triumphed, gained control of the machinery of American Jewish life, and created a very different kind of Jewish America.

While this standard version has a dramatic ring to it, it is based on a misunderstanding of the era before. It ignores the striking similarity in the motives for migration, aspirations for success in America, and the cultural identification of Jews both before and after 1880. Indeed it is much more accurate to talk about a century of migration and consider the immigration from the 1820s through the 1920s as a single movement that began in western Europe and moved gradually and unevenly to the east. Since the migration set in motion in the 1820s had continued largely unabated, with obvious peaks and valleys in the process, the "American" Jews who awaited the new arrivals may have been in America one year or five or ten years rather than a full half-century. All of them had hardly completed acculturation. The Jews who lived in America on the eve of the great exodus from eastern Europe represented people in different stages of that process, from the grandchildren of Bavarian immigrants of 1820 to Suwalkers, themselves just "off the boat." For this reason, 1880 represented less of a watershed in American Jewish history than an intensification of a force set loose well before. A newcomer in 1881, for example, could dock in New York, buy a Yiddish newspaper, see a sign for a landsmanshaft of an eastern European town, hear the voice of a Russian Jew peddling in the streets, and drop into a traditional house of worship to recite prayers just as at home.

Moreover, the Jews who came to America in the six decades before the end of the nineteenth century represented a geographically broader swath of Europe than the term "German" could convey. Jews from Poland and Galicia, Lithuania and Hungary, Moravia and Bohemia arrived alongside the "Germans," who themselves ought not to be viewed as the bearers of the culture of Goethe and Schiller or as the starry-eyed revolutionists of 1848. Peddlers and horse traders, impoverished sons and daughters of petty merchants and artisans with skills unusable in the industrializing Europe, the immigrants from Bavaria, Hesse, Baden, and Württemberg differed little from those from Suwalk, Posen, and Slovakia. With the exception of a thin layer of intellectual and rabbinic leadership, they did not come to America modernized and Germanized, and, indeed, they had been no more affluent or equipped to enter into the American economy than those who arrived after 1880.

Their migration, settlement, work, communal life, religious patterns, and forms of participation in American life presented much greater diversity than has heretofore been assumed. They did not, for example, all become wealthy and Reform-oriented, nor did they desire to Americanize at the expense of their loyalty to Jewish identity. And furthermore, membership in a Reform congregation, the B'nai B'rith, or a Masonic lodge did not mean that one had opted for Judaism as just a religion, casting off notions of Jewishness as group identity. Indeed, the behavior of the mid-nineteenth-century Jews, their philanthropic endeavors, and their efforts to succor Jews in distress around the world indicated that they viewed themselves as bound up with a group of people with whom they shared a common history and fate.

But the era after 1880 did usher in a new period in American Jewish history. It was not that those who arrived in the four decades after 1880 subscribed to a fundamentally different view of their Judaism or came out of a profoundly different Jewish culture. Rather, they showed up in America in numbers so much larger than the immigrants of the previous era that they had a greater impact on the institutions and communities in which they lived. After all, in the sixty years between 1820 and 1880, 150,000 Jews, at the most, arrived in the United States, whereas between 1880 and 1925 (despite the dislocations of World War I), over two and a half million arrived.

In addition, after the 1880s, immigrant Jews in a few cities, primarily in New York but also in Chicago, Philadelphia, Boston, and Baltimore, found themselves in large enough concentration to shape public institutions and make a full-scale Jewish culture possible. Whole neighborhoods spoke the language of Jewishness, and a Jewish street culture emerged, spawning a natural constituency for newspapers, theaters, unions, cafés, and bookshops, and facilitating an almost wholly Jewish life. By dint of numbers, public schools in Jewish neighborhoods, as one example, became Jewish schools, not in curriculum but in clientele. In this kind of soil, Jewishness as ethnicity flourished and made it possible to just "be" Jewish, without much concern about what the "Americans" would think.

To be sure, the solidly all-Jewish neighborhoods and their distinctive ethnic culture grew in part out of the eastern European experience, where Jews lived in greater density than their brethren further to the west. Additionally, many post-1880 newcomers had been urban dwellers in Europe, as compared to the villagers and small-towners who made up the bulk of their predecessors. But, beyond this, America had changed by the 1880s, and its transformation shaped the new-style Jewish life. If, in the 1820s and 1830s, the route for an unskilled, unlettered Jewish immigrant to achieve economic mobility lay literally on the road, in the 1880s and 1890s it offered itself in the cities. The burgeoning of the garment industry and the process of urbanization put an end to the possibility, or need, of advancement by peddling or small-town merchandising. Thus, the city streets, where the new culture of *yiddishkayt* throbbed, offered the same economic opportunities that fifty years earlier had pushed young immigrants to disperse across the nation and content themselves with a few Jewish families for a community.

The end of the nineteenth century also saw a reorientation of American culture itself, which made possible an intensely Jewish self-expression. The cultural hegemony of a Protestant, New England elite and a Victorian ethos that stressed propriety broke down. Commercialization helped stimulate a variety of particularistic cultures—working-class, popular, and ethnic. Spectator sports, the "yellow press," vaudeville, and mass-market dime novels defied the notion of uplifting culture and created an environment in which a Jewish popular culture of theater, humor, and newspapers could develop.

All institutions of Jewish culture conveyed a sense of Jewish distinctiveness. They benefited from the fact that America had ceased to be a country dominated by native-born Protestant men and women of English origin. Jewish ethnicity and group identity partly owed its existence to the fact that millions of other immigrants—Italians, Poles, Greeks, Hungarians—had also created their own enclaves replete with institutions and modes of cultural expression, thus defying the old-style idea of America. The Jewish Lower East Side in New York or the Maxwell Street area in Chicago existed as the Jewish counterparts to Little Italy or the Slavic Back-of-the-Yards. Jews did not stand out as unusual when asserting their distinctiveness from the "real" Americans. Additionally, the rise of the Irish to political power in city halls across America in the 1880s opened the door for Jews and others to assert unabashedly their group interests and clamor for representation.

If, then, the new age of American Jewry owed its existence in part to a new age in American history, so, too, a new chapter in the history of the

Jewish people was being written in Europe, leaving its mark on the Jews of America. In the final decades of the nineteenth century, as political emancipation in western and central Europe became complete and universal, political anti-Semitism, particularly in Germany, Austria, and France, became a fact of life. Pan-Slavic and Pan-German movements raised questions about the nature of Jewishness and the rightful place of the Jews in European society. Racist scientific theories held up the biological superiority of certain "types" to prove the inherent, fixed inferiority of the Jews. These were the decades of the Dreyfus case and of the anti-Semitic street politics of Karl Lueger's Vienna. These were also the decades that witnessed the publication of Theodore Herzl's *Der Judenstaat* (the Jewish state) and Leon Pinsker's *Auto-Emancipation,* and the decades of Bilu and the founding of the first Jewish agricultural settlements in Palestine. At the end of the nineteenth century, the notion that Jews represented a people apart, a belief shared by Jews themselves as well as their enemies, came to be translated into the first outlines of a movement to reestablish a Jewish homeland. The Jews of America, the newcomers in particular, knew about these developments and, like their European brethren, asserted a new Jewish nationalism that played itself out in America.

These worldwide changes in Jewish culture as well as the transformations of the American economy and society altered the nature of American Jewish communal life. However, in their reasons for coming to America, in their Jewish identity, and in their embrace of America, the post-1880 immigrants differed less from those of the half-century earlier than the mythology has assumed. They did not feel their Jewishness more deeply or experience American life less timidly than those who came before them. They, too, would enjoy economic mobility, find some of the innovations in religion appealing and acceptable, pick and choose from traditional practices as fit their circumstances and predilections, express deep affection for their adopted land, speak eloquently about its opportunities and freedoms, and, over time, become American. Both groups, like the bulk of the other immigrants who made their way to America from Europe, would find ways to be both American and something else at one and the same time. Ultimately, the nature of American society made it possible for them to climb some of the rungs of the ladder toward the middle class, create the kinds of religious and communal institutions they preferred without state interference, and function within the majority culture, yet at the same time retaining loyalty in words and deeds to a people, a heritage, and a past.

NOTES

Chapter One. In Europe's Heartland

First epigraph quoted in H. I. Bach, *The German Jew: A Synthesis of Judaism and Western Civilization* (New York: Oxford University Press, 1984), 93; second epigraph quoted in Jacob Katz, *Jewish Emancipation and Self-Emancipation* (Philadelphia: Jewish Publication Society, 1986), 67.

1. Naomi Cohen, *Encounter with Emancipation: The German Jews in the United States, 1830–1914* (Philadelphia: Jewish Publication Society of America, 1984); Michael A. Meyer, *The Origins of the Modern Jew* (Detroit: Wayne State University, 1967); Jacob Katz, *Out of the Ghetto: The Social Background of Jewish Emancipation, 1770–1870* (Cambridge: Harvard University Press, 1973); John Murray Cuddihy, *The Ordeal of Civility: Freud, Marx, Lévi-Strauss, and the Jewish Struggle with Modernity* (Boston: Beacon Press, 1974).

2. Bach, *The German Jew;* Werner Mosse, *Jews in the German Economy: The German-Jewish Economic Elite, 1820–1935* (Oxford: Clarendon Press, 1987); George Mosse, *German Jews beyond Judaism* (Bloomington: Indiana University Press, 1985); Katz, *Out of the Ghetto;* Katz, *Jewish Emancipation and Self-Emancipation;* Jacob Toury, *Kavim Le-Heker Kenisath Ha-Yehudim Lahayim Ha-Ezrahim Be-Germania* (Tel Aviv: Diaspora Research Institute, University of Tel Aviv, 1972); Jehuda Reinharz and Walter Schatzenberg, eds., *The Jewish Response to German Culture: From the Enlightenment to the Second World War* (Hanover, N.H.: University Press of New England, 1985); Jacob Katz, *From Prejudice to Destruction: Anti-Semitism, 1700–1933* (Cambridge: Harvard University Press, 1980); Alfred D. Low, *Jews in the Eyes of the Germans: From the Enlightenment to Imperial Germany* (Philadelphia: Institute for the Study of Human Issues, 1979); Michael A. Meyer, *Response to Modernity: A History of the Reform Movement in Judaism* (New York: Oxford University Press, 1988); David Sorkin, *The Transformation of German Jewry, 1780–1840* (New York: Oxford University Press, 1987); Jacob Katz, *Jews and Freemasons in Europe, 1723–1939* (Cambridge: Harvard University Press, 1970); Werner Mosse, Arnold Paucker, and Reinhard Rürup, *Revolution and Evolution: 1848 in German-Jewish History* (Tübingen: J. C. B. Mohr, 1981); Todd M. Endelman, *Jews of Georgian England, 1714–1830: Tradition and Change in a Liberal Society* (Philadelphia: Jewish Publication Society of America, 1979); Marsha L. Rozenblit, *The Jews of Vienna: 1867–1914: Assimilation and Identity* (Albany: State

University of New York Press, 1983) represent just the tip of the iceberg of the scholarship that has appeared in book form. For a sense of the sweep of the journal literature, consult the *Yearbook* of the Leo Baeck Institute.

3. There is some disagreement within the literature on the timing of this phenomenon. While the conventional, and still widely shared assumption, has been that the process of Jewish urbanization had been completed by 1880, some recent historians disagree. Avraham Barkai has asserted that it did not happen until much later and he demonstrated that the 1920s was the appropriate date. See Avraham Barkai, "German-Jewish Migrations in the Nineteenth Century, 1830–1910," *Leo Baeck Institute Yearbook,* 30 (1985): 301–18.

4. Barkai, "German-Jewish Migrations," 301.

5. Steven M. Lowenstein, "The Rural Community and the Urbanization of German Jewry," *Central European Studies* 13, no. 3 (1980): 218–36; Alice Goldstein, "Urbanization in Baden, Germany: Focus on the Jews, 1825–1925," *Social Science History* 8, no. 1 (1984): 43–66; James F. Harris, "Bavarians and Jews in Conflict in 1866: Neighbors and Enemies," *Leo Baeck Institute Yearbook* 32 (1987): 103–117; Adolf Kober, "Jewish Emigration from Württemberg to the United States of America (1848–1855)," *Publications of the American Jewish Historical Society* 41, no. 3 (1952): 242.

6. Herman Schwab, *Jewish Rural Communities in Germany* (London: Cooper Books, 1957), 16; Harris, "Bavarians and Jews"; Monika Richarz, "Emancipation and Continuity: German Jews in the Rural Economy," in Mosse, Paucker, and Rürup, *Revolution and Evolution,* 95–115; Lowenstein, "Urbanization of German Jewry"; Barkai, "German-Jewish Migrations."

7. Richarz, "Emancipation and Continuity," 96; Goldstein, "Urbanization in Baden," 58; William Zvi Tannenbaum, "From Community to Citizenship: The Jews of Rural Franconia, 1801–1862" (Ph.D. diss., Stanford University, 1989); Steven Lowenstein, "Jewish Residential Concentration in Post-Emancipation Germany," *Leo Baeck Institute Yearbook* 28 (1983): 472; "Joseph Austrian's Autobiographical and Historical Sketches," American Jewish Archives (cited hereafter as AJA), box 2282.

8. Bernard D. Weinryb, "The Economic and Social Background of Modern Anti-Semitism," in *Essays on Antisemitism,* ed. Koppel S. Pinson (New York Conference on Jewish Relations, 1946), 28; W. Mosse, *Jews in the German Economy,* 30; Nachum Gross, ed., *Economic History of the Jews* (New York: Schocken Books, 1975), 61.

9. Tannenbaum, "From Community to Citizenship"; Schwab, *Jewish Rural Communities in Germany;* Richarz, "Emancipation and Continuity"; Arthur Ruppin, *The Jews in the Modern World* (London: Macmillan, 1934), 32; Gross, *Economic History of the Jews;* Goldstein, "Urbanization in Baden."

10. G. Mosse, *German Jews beyond Judaism,* 4; Goldstein, "Urbanization in Baden"; Avraham Barkai, "The German Jews at the Start of Industrialization: Structural Change and Mobility, 1835–1860," in Mosse, Paucker, and Rürup, *Revolution and Evolution,* 101; David L. Preston, "The German Jews in Secular Education, University Teaching, and Science: A Preliminary Inquiry," *Jewish Social Studies* 38, no. 2 (1976): 99–116.

11. Goldstein, "Urbanization in Baden"; Julius Carlebach, "Family Structure and the Position of Jewish Women," in Mosse, Paucker, and Rürup, *Revolution and Evolution,* 157–187; Marion Kaplan, "Family Structure and the Position of Jewish Women: A Comment," in Mosse, Paucker, and Rürup, *Revolution and Evolution,* 189–203; Leon Joseph Rosenberg, *Sangers': Pioneer Texas Merchants* (Austin: Texas State Historical Association, 1978), 1–3.

12. For an excellent statement of this phenomenon, see Katz, *Out of the Ghetto,* particularly chapter 11, "The Futile Flight from the Jewish Professions," 176–190; see also Bernard Weinryb, *Jewish Vocational Education: History and Appraisal of Training in Europe* (New York: J.T.S.P. University Press, 1948), 47; Eric E. Hirshler, *Jews from Germany in the United States* (New York: Farrar, Straus, and Cudahy, 1955).

13. Mark Wischnitzer, *A History of Jewish Crafts and Guilds* (New York: Jonathan David, 1965); Jacob Toury, "Jewish Manual Labour and Emigration: Records from Some Bavarian Districts (1830–1857)," *Leo Baeck Institute Yearbook* 16 (1971): 51.

14. Marion A. Kaplan, "Tradition and Transition: The Acculturation, Assimilation, and Integration of Jews in Imperial Germany: A Gender Analysis," *Leo Baeck Institute Yearbook* 27 (1982): 9; Mosse, *Jews in the German Economy;* Arcadius Kahan, *Essays in Jewish Social and Economic History* (Chicago: University of Chicago Press, 1986), 78.

15. Jacob Toury, "Types of Jewish Municipal Rights in German Townships: The Problem of Local Emancipation," *Leo Baeck Institute Yearbook* 22 (1974): 55–80.

16. Katz, *Out of the Ghetto,* 16–21; Selma Stern, *The Court Jew* (Philadelphia: Jewish Publication Society of America, 1950).

17. Katz, *Out of the Ghetto;* Katz, *Jewish Emancipation and Self-Emancipation;* Leon Poliakov, *The History of Anti-Semitism, from Voltaire to Wagner,* vol. 3 (New York: Vanguard Press, 1968); Gordon Mark, "German Nationalism and Jewish Assimilation: The Bismarck Period," *Leo Baeck Institute Yearbook* 22 (1977): 81–90; Michael A. Ruff, "The Government of Baden against Anti-Semitism: Political Expediency or Principle?" *Leo Baeck Institute Yearbook* 32 (1987): 119–34.

18. Steven M. Lowenstein, "Governmental Jewish Policies in Early Nineteenth Century Germany and Russia," *Jewish Social Studies* 46, 3–4 (1984): 303–20; Ismar Elbogen, *A Century of Jewish Life* (Philadelphia: Jewish Publication Society of America, 1944), xxx; Schwab, *Jewish Rural Communities,* 16; Katz, *Out of the Ghetto;* Harris, "Bavarians and Jews in Conflict," 104–5; quoted in Marc Lee Raphael, "Intra-Jewish Conflict in the United States, 1869–1915" (Ph.D. diss., University of California, Los Angeles, 1972), 15.

19. Ismar Schorsch, *Jewish Reactions to German Anti-Semitism 1870–1914* (New York: Columbia University Press, 1972), 2–3; Tannenbaum, "From Community to Citizenship"; Alfred Kober, "Emancipation's Impact on the Education and Vocational Training of German Jews," *Jewish Social Studies* 16, 2 (1954): 151–76; Sorkin, *The Transformation of German Jewry;* Katz, *Jewish Emancipation;* Richarz, "Emancipation and Continuity," 101.

20. Bach, *German Jew,* 93; George L. Mosse, "Jewish Emancipation: Between Bildung and Respectability," in Reinharz and Schatzenberg, eds., *The Jewish Response to German Culture,* 6; Gil Graff, *Separation of Church and State: Dina de-Malkhuta Dina in Jewish Law, 1750–1848* (University, Ala.: University of Alabama Press, 1985), 124; Sanford Rogins, *Jewish Responses to Anti-Semitism in Germany, 1870–1914* (Cincinnati: Hebrew University Press, 1980), 6; Katz, *Out of the Ghetto.*

21. Katz, *From Prejudice to Destruction;* Harris, "Bavarians and Jews," 104–195; Reinhard Rürup, "The European Revolutions of 1848 and Jewish Emancipation," in Mosse, Paucker, and Rürup, *Revolution and Evolution,* 42–43; Katz, *Jews and Freemasons in Europe,* 2; Steven E. Aschheim, "'The Jew Within': The Myth of 'Judaization' in Germany," in Reinharz and Schatzenberg, *Jewish Response,* 212–41; Poliakov, *The History of Anti-Semitism,* 380; Mark, "German Nationalism and Jewish Assimilation";

Rogins, *Jewish Response to Anti-Semitism,* 2; Peter G. Pulzer, *The Rise of Political Anti-Semitism in Germany and Austria* (New York: John Wiley and Son, 1964).

22. Salo Baron, "Civil versus Political Emancipation," in Siegfried Stein and Raphael Loewe, eds., *Studies in Jewish Religious and Intellectual History: Presented to Alexander Altmann on the Occasion of His Seventieth Birthday* (University, Ala.: University of Alabama Press, 1979), 33; Katz, *Out of the Ghetto,* 142; Heinz Moshe Graaupe, *The Rise of Modern Judaism: An Intellectual History of German Jewry, 1650–1942* (Huntington, N.Y.: Robert E. Krieger, 1978), 132; Harris, "Bavarians and Jews," 105.

23. Marjorie Lamberti, *Jewish Activism in Imperial Germany: The Struggle for Civil Equality* (New Haven: Yale University Press, 1978), 3; Schorsch, *Jewish Reactions to German Anti-Semitism,* 12; Harris, "Bavarians and Jews," 108.

24. Quoted in Mosse, *German Jews beyond Judaism,* 3; Mosse, "Jewish Emancipation," 5; Meyer, *The Origins of the Modern Jew,* 148.

25. Walter Cahn, "Moritz Oppenheim: Jewish Painting and Jewish History," *Orim* 1, no. 1 (1985): 77–85; Alfred Werner, "Jewish Artists of the Age of Emancipation," in Cecil Roth, ed., *Jewish Art: An Illustrated History* (New York: McGraw-Hill, 1961), 570; Karl Schwarz, *Jewish Artists of the 19th and 20th Centuries* (Freeport, N.Y.: Books for Libraries, 1949), 19; *Families and Feasts: Paintings by Oppenheim and Kaufman* (New York: Yeshiva University Museum, 1977); Moritz Daniel Oppenheim, *Pictures of Traditional Jewish Family Life* (New York: KTAV, 1976); Solomon Liptzin, *Germany's Step-Children* (Philadelphia: Jewish Publication Society of America, 1944), 92–94; Jeffrey L. Sammons, "Observations on Berthold Auerbach's Jewish Novels," *Orim* 1, no. 2 (1986): 61–74; Auerbach quote in Jacob Katz, "Berthold Auerbach's Anticipation of the German-Jewish Tragedy," *Hebrew Union College Annual* 53 (1982): 215–40.

26. Steven M. Lowenstein, "The Readership of Mendelssohn's Bible Translation," *Hebrew Union College Annual* 53 (1982): 179–213; Steven M. Lowenstein, "The Yiddish Written Word in Nineteenth Century Germany," *Leo Baeck Institute Yearbook* 24 (1979): 179–92; Peter Freimark, "Language Behaviour and Assimilation: The Situation of the Jews in Northern Germany in the First Half of the Nineteenth Century," *Leo Baeck Institute Yearbook* 24 (1979): 157–77; Tannenbaum, "From Community to Citizenship"; Joseph P. Schultz, "The 'Ze'enah U-Re'enah': Torah for the Folk," *Judaism* 36, no. 1 (1987); 90–91; Herman Pollack, *Jewish Folkways in Germanic Lands (1648–1806): Studies in Aspects of Daily Life* (Cambridge: MIT Press, 1971); Max Weinreich, *History of the Yiddish Language* (Chicago: University of Chicago Press, 1980) 104, 181, 241, 280, 722; Samuel Niger, "Yiddish Literature in the Past Two Hundred Years," in *The Jewish People Past and Present,* vol. 3 (New York: Jewish Encyclopedic Handbooks, 1952), 169; Barbara Kirshenblatt-Gimblett, "The Cut That Binds: The Western Ashkenazic Torah Binder as a Nexus Between Circumcision and Torah," in Victor Turner, ed., *Celebration: Studies in Festivity and Ritual* (Washington, D.C.: Smithsonian Institution Press, 1982), 136–46; David Biale, "Childhood, Marriage and the Family in the Eastern European Jewish Enlightenment," in Steven M. Cohen and Paula E. Hyman, eds., *The Jewish Family: Myths and Reality* (New York: Holmes and Meier, 1986), 54.

27. Alfred Rubens, *A History of Jewish Costume* (London: Peter Owen, 1967), 121; Preston, "The German Jews in Secular Education"; Marjorie Lamberti, "The Attempt to Form a Jewish Block: Jewish Notables and Politics in Wilhelmian Germany," *Central European History* 3, no. 1–2 (1970), 73.

28. Katz, *Jewish Emancipation and Self-Emancipation*, 71–73; Katz, *Jews and Free-masons in Europe*.

29. See Tannenbaum, "From Community to Citizenship," 187–200, for an in-depth analysis of the transformation of naming patterns in the Bavarian town of Zeilitzheim.

30. Steven M. Lowenstein, "Voluntary and Involuntary Limitation of Fertility in Nineteenth Century Bavarian Jewry," in Paul Ritterband, ed., *Modern Jewish Fertility* (Leiden: E. J. Brill, 1981).

31. Carlebach, "Position of Jewish Women"; John E. Knodel, *The Decline of Fertility in Germany, 1871–1939* (Princeton: Princeton University Press, 1974), 140; Kaplan, "Position of Jewish Women: A Comment"; Marion Kaplan, "Priestess and Hausfrau: Women and Tradition in the German Jewish Family," in Cohen and Hyman, eds., *The Jewish Family*, 62–81; Charlotte Baum, Paula Hyman, and Sonya Michel, *The Jewish Woman in America* (New York: New American Library, 1975), 18–24.

32. Deborah Hertz, *Jewish High Society in Old Regime Berlin* (New Haven: Yale University Press, 1988), 13.

33. There is a small but controversial body of literature about Jewish conversion to Christianity in nineteenth-century Germany. The usual assumption has been that the rates were very high and that for Jews who wanted the bounties of Germany, conversion was a logical step. According to David Sorkin in *The Transformation of German Jewry*, very few Jews took this step, and up to 1871, only eleven thousand had actually accepted Christianity. Deborah Hertz ("Seductive Conversion in Berlin, 1770–1809," in Todd M. Endelman, *Jewish Apostasy in the Modern World* [New York: Holmes and Meier, 1987]), claimed that women made up 60 percent of the converts in this early, preemancipation period. She found that women converted to marry Christian men who usually enjoyed higher status and higher income, while men converted for professional reasons. See also Todd M. Endelman, "The Social and Political Context of Conversion in Germany and England, 1870–1914," in *Jewish Apostasy*, 83–107. On Heine, see Hugo Bieber and Moses Hadas, *Heine: A Biographical Anthology* (Philadelphia: Jewish Publication Society of America, 1956); S. S. Prawer, *Heine's Jewish Comedy: A Study of His Portraits of Jews and Judaism* (Oxford: Clarendon Press, 1983).

34. Sorkin, *Transformation of German Jewry*; on Hess, see Jonathan Frankel, *Prophecy and Politics: Socialism, Nationalism and the Russian Jews, 1862–1917* (Cambridge: Cambridge University Press, 1981), 7–27.

35. Graff, *Separation of Church and State*, 39; David Novick, *The Image of the Non-Jew in Judaism: An Historical and Constructive Study of the Noahide Laws*, Studies in Theology, vol. 14 (Toronto: Edwin Mellen, 1983), 386; Lowenstein, "Mendelssohn's Bible Translation"; Katz, *Out of the Ghetto*, 51, 133, 143; David Biale, *Power and Powerlessness in Jewish History* (New York: Schocken Books, 1987), 109–17; quote in Meyer, *The Origins of the Modern Jew*, 46.

36. All references to the history of Reform Judaism need to take into account Michael A. Meyer's *Response to Modernity: A History of Reform Judaism* (New York: Oxford University Press, 1988)—see, for example, pp. 72, 80; Hyman G. Enelow, "A Biographical Essay," in Kaufmann Kohler, *The Origins of the Synagogue and the Church* (New York: Macmillan, 1929), viii–x; Ismar Schorsch, "Emancipation and the Crisis of Religious Authority: The Emergence of the Modern Rabbinate," in Mosse, Paucker, and Rürup, *Revolution and Evolution*, 205–47; Gershon Greenberg, "The Dimensions of Samuel Adler's Religious View of the World," *Hebrew Union College Annual* 46 (1975): 377–412.

37. Quoted in Baum, Hyman, and Michel, *The Jewish Woman,* 23; Steven M. Lowenstein, "The 1840s and the Creation of the German-Jewish Religious Reform Movement," in Mosse, Paucker, and Rürup, *Revolution and Evolution,* 255-97; Katz, *Out of the Ghetto;* Meyer, *Response to Modernity.* There is a general orientation in the literature to view Reform as an urban phenomenon, and most studies do focus on Berlin or Hamburg. Yet, there is tentative evidence that even in some of the small towns after 1860, reform-style innovations rather than full-blown Reform developed. See, for example, Lowenstein, "Urbanization of German Jewry," 224; Tannenbaum, "From Community to Citizenship," 151-53.

38. Meyer, *Response to Modernity,* 80-82.

39. While it is beyond the scope of this book, it is important to note that the very same impetus that gave rise to Reform also led to the creation of "positive-historical Judaism," which used the modern sciences of history, philosophy, philology, and biblical criticism to demonstrate that Judaism had always been influenced by the cultures in which it found itself and that the essence of Judaism was the national aspect, the Jewish people themselves. See, for example, Arnold Eisen, *Galut: Modern Jewish Reflection on Homelessness and Homecoming* (Bloomington: Indiana University Press, 1986), 65; Moshe Davis, *The Emergence of Conservative Judaism: The Historical School in 19th Century America* (Philadelphia: Jewish Publication Society of America, 1963), 13-15. Similarly, modern Orthodoxy, also a product of these same years because it, too, was a response to the strains of emancipation, sought to achieve a balance between Judaism and Germanism. See Robert Liberles, *Religious Conflict in Social Context: The Resurgence of Orthodox Judaism in Frankfurt am Main, 1838-1877* (Westport, Connecticut: Greenwood Press, 1985).

40. Sander L. Gilman, *Jewish Self-Hatred: Anti-Semitism and the Hidden Language of the Jews* (Baltimore: Johns Hopkins University Press, 1986); Peter Gay, *Freud, Jews and Other Germans: Masters and Victims in Modernist Culture* (New York: Oxford 1978), 179-230; Cuddihy, *The Ordeal of Civility.*

41. Jacob Katz, ed., *Toward Modernity: The European Jewish Model* (New Brunswick, N.J.: Transaction Books, 1987), 10; Leo Wiener, *The History of Yiddish Literature in the Nineteenth Century* (New York: Charles Scribners, 1899), 6; Niger, "Yiddish Literature," 169; Schultz, "The 'Ze'enah U-Re'enah,'" 90. The historical problem of positing German culture against eastern European culture can be seen in yet another way, one that needs much greater scholarly attention. German culture, particularly through the agency of the Haskalah, made itself felt well into the eastern European Jewish zone quite early in the nineteenth century. For example, Germanization seeped into Galicia, Volhyin, Lithuania, and Podolia, and many Jews in the small towns of Russia had some knowledge of and positive attitudes toward Germany and German culture in the nineteenth century. See, for example, Israel Bartal, "'The Heavenly City of German' and Absolutism à la Mode d'Autriche: The Rise of the Haskalah in Galicia," in Katz, *Towards Modernity,* 33-42.

42. Meyer, *Response to Modernity,* xi, 156-57, 197; Salo W. Baron, "Aspects of the Jewish Communal Crisis in 1848," *Jewish Social Studies* 14, no. 2 (1952); 102, 104, 111, 117, 123-24, 129, 141.

43. Emanuel Etkes, "Immanent Factors and Eternal Influences in the Development of the Haskalah Movement in Russia," in Katz, ed., *Towards Modernity,* 13-32; Mark Slobin, *Chosen Voices: The Story of the American Cantorate* (Urbana: University of

Illinois Press, 1989), 17–21; on Polish-born Reform rabbis, see, for example, Ella M. Mielziner, *Moses Mielziner: 1828–1903: A Biography with a Bibliography of His Writings* (New York: Ella McKenna Friend Mielziner, 1931).

44. Wiener, *The History of Yiddish Literature,* 16; Charlene A. Lea, *Emancipation, Assimilation and Stereotype: The Image of the Jew in German and Austrian Drama (1800–1850)* (Bonn: Bouvier Verlag Herbert Grundmann, 1978), 4–5; Bernard Drachman, *From the Heart of Israel: Jewish Tales and Types* (New York: J. Pott, 1905), 28; Schwab, *Jewish Rural Communities in Germany,* 35, 49, 59.

45. Werner J. Cahnman, "A Regional Approach to German Jewish History," *Jewish Social Studies* 5, no. 3 (1943): 211–24; Werner J. Cahnman, "The Three Regions of German-Jewish History," in *Jubilee Volume Dedicated to Curt C. Silver,* Herbert A. Strauss and Hans G. Reissner, eds. (New York: American Federation of Jews from Central Europe, 1969), 1–14.

46. Quoted in Mark, "German Nationalism and Jewish Assimilation," 83, 88.

47. Moses A. Shulvass, *From East to West: The Westward Migration of Jews from Eastern Europe during the Seventeenth and Eighteenth Centuries* (Detroit: Wayne State University Press, 1971); Lawrence Schofer, "Emancipation and Population Change," in Mosse, Paucker, and Rürup, *Revolution and Evolution,* 66; Jack Wertheimer, *Unwelcome Strangers: East European Jews in Imperial Germany* (New York: Oxford University Press, 1987), 11, 24, 78, 79, 93, 99; Lloyd P. Gartner, "Jewish Migrants en Route from Europe to North America," in Moses Rischin, ed., *The Jews of North America* (Detroit: Wayne State University Press, 1987), 25–26; Kahan, *Jewish Social and Economic History,* 78; Bernard Weinryb, *The Jews of Poland: A Social and Economic History of the Jewish Community in Poland from 1100 to 1800* (Philadelphia: Jewish Publication Society of America, 1973), vii, 115, 198, 202.

48. Gilman, *Jewish Self-Hatred;* Sander Gilman, "The Rediscovery of the Eastern Jews: German Jews in the East, 1890–1918," in David Bronsen, *Jews and Germans from 1860 to 1933* (Heidelberg: Carl Winter Universitats Verlag, 1979), 338–65; quoted in Steven E. Aschheim, *Brothers and Strangers: The East European Jew in German and German Jewish Consciousness, 1800–1923* (Madison: University of Wisconsin Press, 1982), 8.

49. Aschheim, *Brothers and Strangers,* 7; see also Prawer, *Heine's Jewish Comedy,* 59–63, on Heine's "Polish" problem.

50. Steven M. Lowenstein, "Governmental Jewish Policies," 316; Herbert Strauss, "Pre-Emancipation Prussian Policies toward the Jews, 1815–1847," *Leo Baeck Institute Yearbook* 11 (1966): 107–36; Herbert A. Strauss, "Liberalism and Conservatism in Prussian Legislation for Jewish Affairs, 1815–1847," in *Jubilee Volume Dedicated to Curt C. Silver,* 114–32; Mark J. Wischnitzer, "Jewish Communal Organization in Modern Times," in *Jewish People: Past and Present,* vol. 2, 202; Adolf Kober, "Emancipation's Impact on the Education and Vocational Training of German Jewry: Part I," *Jewish Social Studies* 16, no. 1 (1954), 21.

51. Barkai, "Jews at the Start of Industrialization," 135; Moses Kremer, "Jewish Artisans and Guilds in Former Poland, 16th–18th Centuries," *YIVO Annual of Jewish Social Science* 11 (1956–1957): 211–42; Julian Bartys, "Grand Duchy of Poznan under Prussian Rule: Changes in the Economic Position of the Jewish Population, 1815–1848," *Leo Baeck Institute Yearbook* 17 (1972): 194.

52. See Stefi Jersch-Wenzel, "German Jews in the Rural Economy: A Comment," in

Mosse, Paucker, and Rürup, *Revolution and Evolution,* 118, 120; Schwab, *Jewish Rural Communities,* 69–70.

53. Wischnitzer, *Jewish Crafts and Guilds,* 224–27; Rudolf Glanz, "Vanguard to the Russians: The Poseners in America," *YIVO Annual of Jewish Social Science* 18 (1983): 4–5; Michael M. Zarchin, *Jews in the Province of Posen: Studies in the Communal Records of the Eighteenth and Nineteenth Centuries* (Philadelphia: Dropsie College, 1939), 42–44; 74–77; see also Gross, *Economic History of the Jews,* 133–38, on Jews in the liquor industry in Russia and Lithuania, and on tailoring among eastern European Jews (p. 192).

54. On the different rates of mobility and poverty between German and Posnanian Jews, see Lowenstein, "Urbanization of German Jewry," 226–27; Bartys, "Grand Duchy of Poznan," 195; Schofer, "Emancipation and Population Change," 67–69.

55. Herbert Seelinger, "The Origin and Growth of the Berlin Jewish Community," *Leo Baeck Institute Yearbook* 3 (1958): 162; Werner J. Cahnman, "A Regional Approach to German Jewish History," *Jewish Social Science* 5, no. 3 (1943): 217; Lowenstein, "Jewish Residential Concentration," 472; Lowenstein, "Limitation of Fertility," 112; Rudolf Glanz, "Vanguard to the Russians," 3–4; Schofer, "Emancipation and Population Change," 64.

56. Cahnman, "German Jewish History," 217; Bernard D. Weinryb, "East European Jewry (Since the Partition of Poland, 1772–1795)," in Louis Finkelstein, ed., *The Jews: Their History, Culture, and Religion,* 3d ed. (New York: Harper, 1970–1971), 329–31; Glanz, "Vanguard to the Russians," 5; Rubens, *A History of Jewish Costume,* 132, 208; Zarchin, *Jews in the Province of Posen,* 12; Yehuda Rosenthal, "Perakim B'Toldot Ha-Yishuv Ha-Yehudi Ha-Mizrach-Airope B'Chicago," in Simon Ravidowicz, ed., *Pinkas Chicago* (Chicago: College of Jewish Studies, 1952), 11; Robert M. Seltzer, "From Graetz to Dubnow: The Impact of the Eastern European Millieu on the Writing of Jewish History," in David Berger, ed., *The Legacy of Jewish Immigration: 1881 and Its Impact* (New York: Atlantic Research and Publications, 1983), 50; Walter Hagen, "Poles, Germans and Jews: The Nationality Conflict in Prussian Poland in the Nineteenth and Early Twentieth Century" (Ph.D. diss., University of Chicago, 1971), vol. 1, 667.

57. On the conflict between Prussia and the Poles, and the impact of the conflict on the Jews, see Hagen, "Poles, Germans and Jews," 247; Elbogen, *A Century of Jewish Life,* 7; Richarz, "Emancipation and Continuity," 102; Jacob Toury, "Jewish Townships in the German-Speaking Parts of the Austrian Empire—before and after the Revolution of 1848/1849," *Leo Baeck Institute Yearbook* 26 (1981): 62; Piotr S. Wandycz, *The Lands of Partitioned Poland, 1795–1918* (Seattle: University of Washington Press, 1974); Walter Breslauer, "Jews of the City of Posen One Hundred Years Ago (Based on Family Tradition and Inherited Documents,)" *Leo Baeck Institute Yearbook* 8 (1963): 229–37; Stefan Kleniewicz, "Polish Society and the Jewish Problem in the Nineteenth Century," in Chimen Abramsky, Maciej Jachimczyk, and Antony Polonsky, eds., *The Jews in Poland* (London: Basil Blackwell, 1986), 70–77; Jersch-Wenzel, "German Jews in the Rural Economy," 130–31. It should be noted that mid-nineteenth-century Polish Jewish immigrants came to America from places other than Posen. In the late 1860s, for example, a significant number of Jews from Suwalki, a province in northeastern Poland, came to the United States. Suwalki had been part of Congress Poland but in the 1860s was annexed by czarist Russia. Only marginally connected to the Prussian sphere, Suwalki Jewish life resembled that in Russia and Lithuania. See Judah David Eisenstein, *Ozar*

Zikhronothai: Korat Toldoti V'Mikre Yom B'Yomo (New York: J. D. Eisenstein, 1929); Hannah S. Berry, "A Colorado Family History," *Western States Jewish Historical Quarterly* (cited hereafter as *WSJHQ*) 5, no. 3 (1973): 158-59; Victor R. Greene, *American Immigrant Leaders, 1800-1910: Marginality and Identity* (Baltimore: Johns Hopkins University Press, 1987), 89.

58. Paula E. Hyman, *The Emancipation of the Jews of Alsace: Acculturation and Tradition in the Nineteenth Century* (New Haven: Yale University Press, 1991); Paula E. Hyman, "Jewish Fertility in Nineteenth Century France," in Ritterband, *Modern Jewish Fertility,* 79, 84, 86; Michael Burns, "Emancipation and Reaction: The Rural Exodus of Alsatian Jews, 1791-1848," in Reinharz, *Living with Anti-Semitism,* 23; Phyllis C. Albert, *The Modernization of French Jewry: Consistory and Community in the Nineteenth Century* (Hanover, N.H.: University Press of New England, 1977), 20-21, 26; Vicki Caron, "The Social and Religious Transformation of Alsace-Lorraine Jewry, 1871-1914," *Leo Baeck Institute Yearbook* 30 (1985): 323; Vicki Caron, *Between France and Germany: The Jews of Alsace-Lorraine, 1871-1918* (Stanford: Stanford University Press, 1988).

59. Burns, "Emancipation and Reaction," 21, 28-29, 31; Albert, *Modernization of French Jewry,* 21.

60. Albert, *Modernization of French Jewry,* 243, 252; Joshua Fishman, *Yiddish in America: Socio-Linguistic Description and Analysis* (Bloomington: Indiana University Press, 1965), 3; Niger, "Yiddish Literature," 169; Weinreich, *History of the Yiddish Language,* 246.

61. Ernest Jones, *The Life and Work of Sigmund Freud* (London: Penguin Books, 1961), 31-33.

62. See, for example, Rebekah Kohut, *My Portion: An Autobiography* (New York: T. Seltzer, 1925), 12, for a description of her rabbi father's controversy with his "fanatic" congregants in a small town in Hungary; Nathaniel Katzburg, "Assimilation in Hungary during the Nineteenth Century: Orthodox Positions," in Bela Vago, ed., *Jewish Assimilation in Modern Times* (Boulder, Colo.: Westview Press, 1981), 49-55. Reform made only minor inroads into Jewish Prague but had a greater impact in Vienna and Budapest. See Gary B. Cohen, "Jews in German Society: Prague, 1860-1914," *Central European History* 10, no. 1 (1977): 39; Meyer, *Response to Modernity,* 57, 156-57; on Vienna, see Marsha L. Rozenblit, "The Struggle over Religious Reform in Nineteenth-Century Vienna," *AJS Review,* 14, no. 2 (1989), 179-221.

63. Hillel J. Kieval, "Caution's Progress: The Modernization of Jewish Life in Prague, 1780-1830," in Katz, *Toward Modernity,* 71-105; Robert S. Wistrich, "The Modernization of Viennese Jewry: The Impact of German Culture in a Multi-Ethnic State," in Katz, *Towards Modernity,* 43-70; Reinhard Rürup, "The European Revolutions of 1848 and Jewish Emancipation" in Mosse, Paucker, and Rürup, *Revolution and Evolution,* 9, 43; Cahnman, "Regions of German-Jewish History," 9-11; Carl E. Schorske, *Fin-De-Siecle Vienna: Politics and Culture* (New York: Alfred A. Knopf, 1980), 146-51; Cuddihy, *The Ordeal of Civility,* 17-103; Joshua Fishman, *Ideology, Society and Language: The Odyssey of Nathan Birnbaum* (Ann Arbor: Karoma Publishers, 1987); Hillel J. Kieval, "Nationalism and Anti-Semitism," in Reinharz, *Living with Anti-Semitism,* 210-33.

64. Gary B. Cohen, "Jews in German Society," 306-37; R. Kestenberg-Gladstein, "The Internal Migrations of the Jews of Bohemia in the 19th Century," in *Papers of the*

Fourth World Congress of Jewish Studies, vol. 2 (Jerusalem: World Union of Jewish Studies, 1968), 195; Guido Kisch, "A Voyage to America Ninety Years Ago: The Diary of a Bohemian Jew on His Voyage from Hamburg to New York, 1847," *Publications of the American Jewish Historical Society* 35 (1939): 65–113.

65. Guido Kisch, *In Search of Freedom: A History of Jews From Czechoslovakia* (London: Edward Goldston, 1949), 4; Guido Kisch, "Linguistic Conditions among Czechoslovak Jewry," *Historica Judaica,* 8, no. 1 (1946): 19–32; Bruno Blau, "Nationality among Czechoslovak Jewry," *Historica Judaica* 10, no. 2 (1948): 147–54; Hillel Kieval, *The Making of Czech Jewry: National Conflict and Jewish Society in Bohemia, 1870–1918* (New York: Oxford University Press, 1988). An example of a Bohemian Jew who had to learn German can be found in the linguistic experience of Isaac Mayer Wise, the luminary of American Reform Judaism: Wise had to learn German in order to receive rabbinical ordination, and according to one historian, he never learned it well enough to cover up his original Judeo-German (Yiddish). See Bernard Martin, "The Americanization of Reform Judaism," *Journal of Reform Judaism* 27, no. 1 (1980): 40; James G. Heller, *Isaac M. Wise: His Life, Work and Thought* (New York: Union of American Hebrew Congregations), 53, 70; Kieval, *The Making of Czech Jewry,* 3.

Chapter Two. "On to America"

First epigraph quoted in Prawer, *Heine's Jewish Comedy,* 29; second epigraph from Morris U. Schappes, *A Documentary History of the Jews in the United States: 1654–1875* (New York: Shocken Books, 1971), 159–60; third epigraph from Jacob Rader Marcus, *Memoirs of American Jews: 1775–1865,* vol. 1 (Philadelphia: Jewish Publication Society of America, 1955), 304.

1. Lothar Kahn, "Early German-Jewish Writers and the Image of America (1820–1840)," *Leo Baeck Institute Yearbook* 31 (1986): 407–39; Liptzin, *Germany's Stepchildren,* 88; Paul Carl Weber, *America in the Imaginative German Literature of the First Half of the Nineteenth Century* (New York: Columbia University Press, 1926), 98–101, 219, 233, 240; Albert M. Friedenberg, "A German Jewish Poet on America," *Publications of the American Jewish Historical Society* 13 (1905): 89–92.

2. S. Niger Charney, "America in the Works of I. M. Dick (1814–1893)," *YIVO Annual of Jewish Social Science* 9 (1954): 63–71; Jacob Lestschinsky, "Jewish Migrations, 1840–1956," in Louis Finkelstein, *The Jews,* vol. 2 (Westport, Conn.: Greenwood Press, 1979), 1548; Israel Zinberg, *Die Geshikhte Fun Der Literatur Bay Yidn,* vol. 7 (Vilna: Farlag Tamar 1929–1966), 269; Zalmen Reyzen, "Campes entdekung fun amerike," *YIVO Bleter,* 4 (1932): 442.

3. A detailed study of the attitude toward emigration in the European Jewish press, heavily centered in the mid-nineteenth-century in Germany, has yet to be written. The fragments that appear widely scattered in the literature on American Jewish history provide an interesting possibility that the newspapers not only endorsed the migration but used such articles as a means to criticize the enduring disabilities and rising anti-Semitism in Germany. At a time when Jews were supposedly apolitical and sought to prove their loyalty to Germany or Austria, the newspapers may have used articles about America to express their profound skepticism about the possibilities of integration in Europe. See Rudolf Glanz, *Studies in Judaica Americana* (New York: KTAV, 1970), 1–84, for an undigested string of quotes from the European Jewish press on American condi-

tions. See also Joseph L. Blau and Salo Baron, eds., *The Jews of the United States, 1790–1840: A Documentary History,* vol. 1 (New York: Columbia University Press, 1963), 809–11.

4. Blau and Baron, *The Jews in the United States,* vol. 3, 805; Liptzin, *Germany's Stepchildren,* 99.

5. Schappes, *A Documentary History,* 159–60; Kahn, "Early German-Jewish Writers," 417–22; Guido Kisch, "The Founders of 'Wissenschaft des Judenthums' and America," in Jacob R. Marcus, ed., *Essays in American Jewish History: To Commemorate the Tenth Anniversary of the Founding of the American Jewish Archives* (New York: KTAV, 1975), 152–53; Bernard D. Weinryb, "The German Jewish Immigrants to America (A Critical Evaluation)," in Eric E. Hirshler, *Jews from Germany in the United States* (New York: Farrar, Straus, and Cudahy, 1955), 104; Hans G. Reissner, "'Ganstown, U.S.A.'— A German-Jewish Dream," *American Jewish Archives* 14, no. 1 (1962): 20–31; Mark Wischnitzer, *To Dwell in Safety: The Story of Jewish Migration since 1800* (Philadelphia: Jewish Publication Society of America, 1948), 17–19.

6. Salo Baron, "The Revolution of 1848 and Jewish Scholarship," part 2, *Proceedings of the American Academy for Jewish Research* 20 (1951): 23–26; Guido Kisch, "The Revolution of 1848 and the Jewish 'On To America Movement,'" *Publications of the American Jewish Historical Society* 38 (March 1949): 185–208.

7. Albert, *Modernization of French Jewry,* 18, 127, 139; Zosa Szajkowski, "Emigration to America or Reconstruction in Europe," *Publications of the American Jewish Historical Society* 42, no. 2 (1952): 157–77.

8. Lloyd P. Gartner, "Rumania, America, and World Jewry: Consul Peixotto in Bucharest, 1870–1876," *American Jewish Historical Quarterly (AJHQ)* 58, no. 1 (1968): 25–117; Lloyd P. Gartner, "Rumania and America, 1873: Leon Horowitz' Rumanian Tour and Its Background," *PAJHS* 45 (September 1955–June 1956): 67–92; Szajkowski, "Emigration to America," 172–75.

9. Jonathan Sarna, *Jacksonian Jew: The Two Worlds of Mordecai Noah* (New York: Holmes and Meier, 1981), 61–75.

10. Hyman B. Grinstein, *The Rise of the Jewish Community of New York: 1654–1860* (Philadelphia: Jewish Publication Society of America, 1945), 119.

11. Oscar Fleishaker, "The Illinois-Iowa Jewish Community on the Banks of the Mississippi River" (Ph.D. diss., Yeshiva University, 1957), 7; Louis Wirth, *The Ghetto* (Chicago: University of Chicago Press, 1928), 156; "Trail Blazers of the Trans-Mississippi West," *AJA* 8, no. 2 (1956): 59.

12. Quoted in Glanz, *Studies in Judaica Americana,* 94.

13. Quoted in Rudolf Glanz, "The Immigration of German Jews up to 1880," in *Studies in Judaica Americana,* 89; on the small and insignificant group of Jewish political exiles, see general articles, such as Bertram W. Korn, "Jewish 48'ers in America," in Jacob R. Marcus, ed., *Critical Studies in American Jewish History,* vol. 1 (Cincinnati: American Jewish Archives, 1971), 74–89; Guido Kisch, "*Israels Herold:* The First Jewish Weekly in New York," *Historica Judaica* 2, no. 2 (1940): 65–84.

14. Barkai, "German-Jewish Migrations," 301–18.

15. Bartys, "Poznan under Prussian Rule," 191–204; Glanz, "Vanguard to the Russians," 9; quoted in Kisch, "The Revolution of 1848," 197.

16. Pamela S. Nadell, "The Journey to America by Steam: The Jews of Eastern Europe in Transition" (Ph.D. diss., Ohio State University, 1982), 15.

17. Weinryb, "German Jewish Immigrants," 104; Barkai, "Jews at the Start of

Industrialisation," 130–36; Steven M. Lowenstein, "The Rural Community and the Urbanization of German Jewry," *Central European History* 13, no. 3 (1980), 226–27; Bernard D. Weinryb, "Jewish Immigration and Accommodation to America: Research, Trends, Problems," *PAJHS* 46 (September 1956–June 1957): 385–86; Toury, "Jewish Manual Labor," 55–57; Tannenbaum, "From Community to Citizenship," 234–57; quoted in Glanz, *Studies in Judaica Americana*, 284.

18. Toury, "Jewish Manual Labor," 56–57.

19. Vincent P. Carosso, "A Financial Elite: New York's German-Jewish Investment Bankers," *AJHQ* 66, no. 1 (1976): 67–88.

20. Biographical data is available for scores of rabbis who immigrated in the 1820–80 period, either as full-length books and articles or as part of the voluminous literature on synagogue history. For a listing of the latter, see Alexandra Shecket Korros and Jonathan Sarna, *American Synagogue History: A Bibliography and State-of-the-Field Survey* (New York: Markus Wiener Publishing, 1988); for a very small listing of biographies of rabbis of this period, see Davis, *Emergence of Conservative Judaism*, 329–66.

21. V. D. Lipman, *Social History of the Jews in England, 1850–1950* (London: Watts and Co., 1954), 65, 85. The migration of Polish Jews to England and then to America is a theme in numerous biographies and community histories. For example, Rosenthal, "Perakim B'Toldoth Hayishuv," pointed out that the Polish-born founders of Congregation Anshe Emeth had all sojourned in England before coming to Chicago. Moses Shulvass, *From East to West,* also confirms this, as does Weinryb, "German Jewish Immigrants."

22. Kober, "Jewish Emigration," 225–73; Eleanor Gordon Mlotek, "America in East European Yiddish Folksong," in Uriel Weinreich, *The Field of Yiddish: Studies in Yiddish Language, Folklore and Literature* (New York: Linguistic Circle of New York, 1954), 181, 191; Boris Bogin, *Jewish Philanthropy: An Exposition of Principles and Methods of Jewish Social Service in the United States* (New York: Macmillan, 1917), 89.

23. Esther L. Panitz, "The Polarity of American Jewish Attitudes toward Immigration (1870–1891)," *AJHQ* 53, no. 2 (1963): 104; Mark Wischnitzer, "A Century of Organized Jewish Migration," *Jewish Social Service Quarterly* 25, no. 1 (1948): 38–41.

24. Tannenbaum, "From Community to Citizenship," 235–36; Barkai, "German Jewish Migration," 313. The literature on Jewish immigration of this period has posited strikingly different motives for men and for women, with men migrating for money and women for marriage. Rudolf Glanz, for example, in *The Jewish Woman in America,* vol. 2 (New York: KTAV, 1976), 9, wrote about "the great drawing power exerted on young Jewish women by the possibility of marriage." Similarly, Marc Lee Raphael in *Jews and Judaism in a Midwestern Community* (Columbus: Ohio Historical Society, 1979), 15, asserted that "young Jewesses emigrated almost exclusively to marry." This kind of thinking, which runs through most of immigration history in general, not only ignores the high rate of economic participation of immigrant women, married or single, inside or outside the family, but it ignores the fact that men—just like women—migrated so that they could marry. There is no reason to assume that men had any less interest in marriage than women.

25. Marion Kaplan, "For Love or Money: The Marriage Strategies of Jews in Imperial Germany," *Leo Baeck Institute Yearbook* 28 (1983): 263–300; Kaplan, "Tradition and Transition," 3–35. Helga Kaplan, "Century of Adjustment: A History of the

Akron Jewish Community, 1865–1975" (Ph.D. diss., University of Akron, 1978), 84, indicated that the pattern of sending back or going back to get a wife operated among the Bohemian Jews who first settled in Akron, Ohio.

26. Toury, "Jewish Manual Labor," 58–59; Tannenbaum, "From Community to Citizenship," 238; Glanz, *Jewish Woman*, 8–12.

27. Alice Goldstein, "Some Demographic Characteristics of Village Jews in Germany: Nonnweier, 1800–1931," in Ritterband, *Modern Jewish Fertility*, 125.

28. Barkai, "German-Jewish Migrations," 312; Rudolf Glanz, "The 'Bayer' and the 'Pollack' in America," *Studies in Judaica Americana*, 187–202; Rudolf Glanz, "The German Jewish Mass Emigration: 1820–1880," *AJA* 22, no. 1 (1970): 52; Lestschinsky, "Jewish Migrations," 1561–62; H. G. Reissner, "The German-American Jews (1800–1850)," *Leo Baeck Institute Yearbook* 10 (1965): 61; Stephen G. Mostov, "A 'Jerusalem on the Ohio': The Social and Economic History of Cincinnati's Jewish Community, 1840–1875," (Ph.D. diss., Brandeis University, 1981).

29. Wertheimer, *Unwelcome Strangers*, 77–78; Shulvass, *From East to West*, 123; Mark, "German Nationalism," 84.

30. See, for example, Cohen, *Encounter with Emancipation*.

31. Louis Hacker, and Mark D. Hirsch, *Proskauer: His Life and Times* (University, Ala.: University of Alabama Press, 1978), 1; Harriet Lane Levy, *920 O'Farrell Street* (Garden City, N.Y.: Doubleday, 1947), 210–11; Norton B. Stern and William M. Kramer, "What's the Matter with Warsaw?," *Western States Jewish History (WSJH)* 7, no. 3 (1985): 305–7.

32. Bernard Drachman, *The Unfailing Light: Memoirs of an American Rabbi* (New York: The Rabbinical Council of America, 1948), 9, 12.

33. Lestschinsky, "Jewish Migrations," 1559–61; the issue of ethnic variations in synagogue formation will be discussed in greater detail in chapter 5.

34. Isaac Markens, *The Hebrews in America: A Series of Historical and Biographical Sketches* (New York: Isaac Markens, 1888).

35. Jacob Pfeffer, *Distinguished Jews of America*, vol. 1, *A Collection of Biographical Sketches of Jews Who Have Made Their Mark in Business, the Professions, Politics, Science, Etc.* (New York: Distinguished Jews of America Publishing Company, 1917); Jacob Pfeffer, *Distinguished Jews of America*, vol. 2, *A Collection of Biographical Sketches of Jews Who Have Distinguished Themselves in Commerical, Professional and Religious Endeavour* (Toledo, Ohio: Distinguished Jews of America Publishing Company, 1918).

36. See *Notable American Women: 1607–1950* (Cambridge, Mass.: Belknap Press, 1971) on Julia Richmann, Ernestine Rose, Frances Stern, Lillian Wald, Martha Wallstein, Fannie Bloomfield Zeisler, Frances Wisebart Jacobs, Florence Prag Kahn, Claribel and Etta Cone, Hannah Bachman Einstein.

37. "Men of Distinction in Early Los Angeles," *WSJH* 7, no. 3 (1975): 225–33.

38. A very brief and unsystematic listing of biographies of some either German-born American Jews or the children of German Jewish immigrants would include: Cyrus Adler, *Jacob Henry Schiff, A Biographical Sketch* (New York: American Jewish Committee, 1929); Cyrus Adler, *Louis Marshall: A Biographical Sketch and Memorial Addresses* (New York: American Jewish Committee, 1931); Harry Barnard, *The Forging of an American Jew: The Life and Times of Judge Julian W. Mack* (New York: Herzl Press, 1974); Isaac Wolfe Bernheim, *The Story of the Bernheim Family* (Louisville, Ky.: John P. Morton, 1910); Max E. Berkowitz, *The Beloved Rabbi: An Account of the Life and*

Works of Henry Berkowitz (New York: Macmillan, 1932); Frank L. Byrne and Jean Powers Soman, *Your True Marcus: The Civil War Letters of a Jewish Colonel* (Kent, Ohio: Kent State University Press, 1985); Carosso, "A Financial Elite," 67–88; Naomi Cohen, *A Dual Heritage: The Public Career of Oscar Straus* (Philadelphia: Jewish Publication Society of America, 1969); Carl Dernburg, *Memoirs of an American Pioneer (1857–1943)* (Chicago: private printing, 1943); Albert B. Faust, *The German Element in the United States: With Special Reference to Its Political, Moral, Social and Educational Influence,* vol. 2 (Boston: Houghton Mifflin, 1909), 109, 111, 120, 461–62; Floyd S. Fierman, "The Spiegelbergs: Pioneer Merchants and Bankers in the Southwest," *AJHQ* 56, no. 4 (1967), 371–451; Albert H. Friedlander, "An Ethical Letter: Benjamin M. Roth to His Son Solomon, 1854," *AJA* 6, no. 1 (1954), 6–12; Israel M. Goldman, "Henry W. Schneeberger: His Role in American Judaism," *AJHQ* 57, no. 2 (1967), 153–90; Abram V. Goodman, "A Jewish Peddler's Diary," in Jacob R. Marcus, ed., *Critical Studies in American Jewish History,* vol. 2 (Cincinnati: American Jewish Archives, 1971); Victor L. Ludlow, "Bernhard Felsenthal: Quest for Zion" (Ph.D. diss., Brandeis University, 1984); Henry Morgenthau, *All in a Life-Time* (Garden City, N.Y.: Doubleday, Page, 1922).

39. Thomas D. Clark, "The Post-Civil War Economy in the South," in Leonard Dinnerstein and Mary Dale Palsson, *The Jews in the South* (Baton Rouge: Louisiana State University Press, 1973), 160; Albert, *Modernization of French Jewry,* 18, 127, 139; William Kramer and Norton B. Stern, "French Jews in the Early West: An Aristocratic Cousinhood," *WSJH* 13, no. 4): 322–50; Bennett H. Wall, "Leon Godchaux and the Godchaux Business Enterprise," *AJHQ* 66, no. 1 (1976), 50–66; Richard B. Goldberg, "Michael Wormser, Capitalist," *AJA* 25, no. 2 (1973): 161–206; "Aaron Hirsch," American Jewish Archives, Biographies File.

40. Leo Goldhammer, "Jewish Emigration from Austria-Hungary in 1848–1849," *YIVO Annual of the Jewish Social Sciences* 9 (1959): 332–62; Guido Kisch, *In Search of Freedom: A History of American Jews from Czechoslovakia* (London: Edward Goldston, 1949); Henry G. Baker, *Rich's of Atlanta: The Story of a Store since 1867* (Atlanta: Atlanta Division, University of Georgia, 1953), 6–12; "Abraham Klaubner—A Pioneer Merchant," *WSJHQ* 2, no. 2 (1970): 68–83; Drachman, *Unfailing Light,* 28; Adolf Kraus, *Reminiscences and Comments: The Immigrant, the Citizen, a Public Office, the Jew* (Chicago: private printing, 1925), 4–7; for a few other random biographical fragments of Jews from Bohemia, Moravia, and Slovakia, see Abraham J. Karp, "Simon Tuska Becomes a Rabbi," *AJHQ* 50, no. 2 (1960): 79–97; "An Oakland Pioneer," *WSJHQ* 16, no. 2 (1983): 82; Abraham Flexner, *I Remember: The Autobiography of Abraham Flexner* (New York: Simon and Schuster, 1940), 4–7; Kisch, "A Voyage to America," 65–113; James G. Heller, *Isaac M. Wise: His Life, Work and Thought* (New York: Union of American Hebrew Congregations, 1965), 3–90; Josephine Goldmark, *Pilgrims of '48: One Man's Part in the Austrian Revolution of 1848 and a Family Migration to America* (New Haven: Yale University Press, 1930); Thomas B. Littlewood, *Horner of Illinois* (Evanston: Northwestern University Press, 1969), 10; Martha Kransdorf, "Julia Richman's Years in the New York City Public Schools: 1872–1912" (Ph.D. diss., University of Michigan, 1979); Harry Schwartz, "The Levi Saga, Temecula, Julian, San Diego," *WSJHQ* 6, no. 3 (1974): 161–76; Jeffery S. Zucker, "Edward Stark: American Cantor-Composer at the Turn of the Century," *Journal of Synagogue Music* 13, no. 1 (1983): 14–28; "Diary of Beck, of Company D. Fifth Alabama Regiment, Confederate Army. Mr 1864-F, 1865," American Jewish Archives, Biographies; Ella F. Auerbach, "Jewish Settlement in Nebraska, 1927," American Jewish Archives, Small Collection.

41. *American Israelite,* 10 June 1861; Rudolf Glanz, "Source Material on the History of Jewish Immigration to the United States, 1800–1880," in *Studies in Judaica Americana,* 11, 48–49; Marc L. Raphael, "Intra-Jewish Conflict in the United States, 1869–1915," (Ph.D. diss., University of California, Los Angeles, 1972), 7, 32–37; Yehuda Rosenthal, "Perakim B'Toldoth Hayishuv," in Rawidowicz, *Pinkas Chicago,* 11; Jacob Lestschinsky, "Die Yiddishe Immigratzia In Die Fareinigten Shtaten," in Elias Tcherikower, ed., *Gehichte Fun Der Yiddisher Arbeter Bavegung In Die Fareinigte Shtaten,* vol. 1 (New York: YIVO, 1943), 59.

42. Stern and Kramer, "What's the Matter with Warsaw," 305; Norton B. Stern and William M. Kramer, "The Major Role of Polish Jews in the Pioneer West," *WSJHQ* 8, no. 4 (1976): 326–44; Ezekiel Lifschutz, "Die Russishe-Poylishe Immigranten in Amerika Bizn Yohr 1881," in Tcherikower, *Geshichte Fun Der Yiddisher Arbeter,* 62; Lipman, *Jews in England,* 85; Lestschinsky, "Jewish Migrations," 1560–63; see also Charles S. Bernheimer, *The Russian Jew in the United States: Studies of Social Conditions in New York, Philadelphia, and Chicago, with A Description of Rural Settlements* (Philadelphia: John C. Winston, 1905), 76; Bernard Weinstein, *Die Yiddishe Unions in America: Bletter Geshichte Un Erinerungen* (New York: Fareinigten Yiddishe Geverkshaftn, 1929), 39; Herz Burgin, *Die Geshichte Fun Der Yidisher Arbeiter Bavegung in America, Russland, Un England* (New York: United Hebrew Trades, 1915), 68. For some methodological problems with pinpointing the numbers of Russian Jews leaving Russia before 1880, see Simon Kuznets, "Immigration of Russian Jews to the United States: Background and Structure," *Perspectives in American History* 9 (1975): 38–39, 41, 43, 83; quote from *Ha-Melitz* in Wischnitzer, *To Dwell in Safety,* 28–29.

43. Lifschutz, "Die Russishe-Poylishe Immigranten," 64–65; Bernheimer, *Russian Jew,* 83, 174; Louis Wirth, *The Ghetto* (Chicago: University of Chicago Press, 1928), 160; Judah David Eisenstein, "The History of the First Russian-American Jewish Congregation," *PAJHS* 9 (1901): 63–74; Alfred A. Greenbaum, "The Early Russian Congregation in America and Its Ethnic and Religious Setting," *AJHQ* 62, no. 2 (1972): 162–70; Robert Rockaway, "Detroit's Yom Kippur Day Riot," *Michigan Jewish History* 9, no. 1 (1969), 21–23; Jacob I. Hartstein, "The Polonies Talmud Torah of New York," *PAJHS* 34 (1937): 123–41; Glanz, "The 'Bayer' and the 'Pollack' in America," 187–202. There are literally hundreds of biographies, either full or fragmentary, of Polish Jews coming to the United States in the mid-nineteenth century. *The Western States Jewish Historical Quarterly* provides a sizable number of these biographies—too numerous to be cited here. For more biographical material, see Arthur Goren, *Dissenter in Zion: From the Writings of Judah L. Magnes* (Cambridge: Harvard University Press, 1982); Eisenstein, *Ozar Zikhronothai: Korat Toldoti V'Mikre Yom B'Yomo;* Victoria Jacobs, *Diary of a San Diego Girl—1856* (Santa Monica: Norton B. Stern, 1974); Sol Bloom, *The Autobiography of Sol Bloom* (New York: G. P. Putnam's Sons, 1948); Harris I. Kempner, "My Memories of Father," *AJA* 19, no. 1 (1967): 41–59; Louis Schmier, ed., *Reflections of Southern Jewry: The Letters of Charles Wessolowsky, 1878–1879* (Macon, Ga.: Mercer University Press, 1982).

44. Jesse E. Pope, *The Clothing Industry in New York* (New York: Burt Franklin, 1905), 45; Gerald Stanley, "Merchandising in the Southwest: The Mark I. Jacobs Company of Tucson, 1867–1875," *AJA* 23, no. 1 (1971), 86–102; Richard L. Golden and Arlene A. Golden, "The Mark I. Jacobs Family: A Discursive Overview," *WSJHQ* 13, no. 2 (1981): 99–114; Philip Cowen, *Memories of an American Jew* (New York: International Press, 1932), 18–21; Olivia Rossetti Agresti, *David Lubin: A Study in Practical Idealism*

(Berkeley: University of California Press, 1941), 15–20; Carole Krucoff, *Rodfei Zedek: The First Hundred Years* (Chicago: Congregation Rodfei Zedek, 1976); see also Lifschutz, "Die Russishe-Poylishe Immigranten," 66; Bill Williams, *The Making of Manchester Jewry, 1740–1875* (Manchester: Manchester University Press, 1976), 119, 180; Samuel Gompers, *Seventy Years of Life and Labor: An Autobiography* (New York: E. P. Dutton, 1925), 17; Lipman, *Jews in England,* 65; on Yiddish as the language of English and Dutch Jews, see H. Beem, "Yiddish in Holland: Linguistic and Socio-Linguistic Notes," in Weinreich, *Field of Yiddish,* 122–33; Todd M. Endelman, *The Jews of Georgian England, 1714–1830* (Philadelphia: Jewish Publication Society of America, 1979), 120, 176, 123–24, 170–79.

45. Mlotek, "America in East European Yiddish Folksong," 181; Devera Steinberg Strocker, "The Lipsitz Families: Early Jewish Settlers in Detroit," *Michigan Jewish History* 22, no. 2 (1982); 6; Bernard Horwich, *My First Eighty Years* (Chicago: Argus Books, 1939), 38; Rosenthal, "Perakim B'Toldoth Hayishuv," 15; Della Rubenstein Adler, "Immigrants in Buffalo," *AJA* 28, no. 1 (1966): 20–27; Berry, "A Colorado Family History," 158–61; Philip Applebaum, "The Jews of Iosco County, Michigan," *Michigan Jewish History* 16, no. 1 (1976): 18–38; Seebert Goldowsky, "Bernard Manuel Goldowsky, 1864–1936," *Rhode Island Jewish History Notes* 6, no. 1 (1971): 83–101; Ed Cray, *Levi's* (Boston: Houghton Mifflin, 1978), 16.

46. On the differences between Jews who stayed and those who did not, a tremendous amount of close scholarship remains to be done, and any generalizations are suggestions only. On traditionalism among the immigrants, see Wischnitzer, *To Dwell in Safety,* 6; Weinryb, "German Jewish Immigrants," 119; Kisch, "The Revolution of 1848," 197; Weinryb, "Jewish Immigration," 385; quoted in Glanz, *Jewish Woman,* 7.

47. Barkai, "German-Jewish Migrations"; Barkai, "Jews at the Start of Industrialization"; Glanz, "The German Jewish Mass Emigration"; Lowenstein, "The Urbanization of German Jewry"; Bartys, "Grand Duchy of Poznan"; Tannenbaum, "From Community to Citizenship"; on the structure and patterns of the non-Jewish, particularly German, immigration, see Frank Trommler and Joseph McVeigh, eds., *America and the Germans: An Assessment of a Three-Hundred-Year History: Immigration, Language, Ethnicity,* vol. 1 (Philadelphia: University of Pennsylvania Press, 1985); Mack Walker, *Germany and the Emigration: 1816–1885* (Cambridge: Harvard University Press, 1964); Wolfgang Kollmann and Peter Marschalck, "German Emigration to the United States," *Perspectives in American History* 7 (1983): 499–554; Johann Chmelar, "The Austrian Emigration: 1900–1914," *Perspectives in American History* 7 (1983): 275–378; Klaus Bade, "German Emigration to the United States and Continental European Immigration to Germany in the Late Nineteenth and Early Twentieth Centuries," *Central European Studies* 13 (December 1980): 348–77; Gunter Moltmann, "American-German Return Migration in the Nineteenth and Early Twentieth Centuries," *Central European Studies* 13 (December 1980): 378–92; Kathleen Neils Conzen, *Immigrant Milwaukee, 1836–1860* (Cambridge: Harvard University Press, 1976).

48. Ruppin, *The Jews in the Modern World,* xviii; J. D. Oppenheim, "The Jewish Population of the United States," *American Jewish Yearbook* 19 (1918): 2; Ira Rosenwaike, *On the Edge of Greatness: A Portrait of American Jewry in the Early Nineteenth Century* (Cincinnati: American Jewish Archives, 1985), xvi–17; Ira Rosenwaike, "The Jewish Population of the United States as Estimated from the Census of 1820," *AJHQ* 53, no. 2 (1963), 131–78; Harry S. Linfield, *Statistics of Jews and Jewish Organizations:*

Historical Review of Ten Censuses, 1850–1937 (New York: American Jewish Committee, 1939).

49. Oppenheim, "The Jewish Population of the United States"; Rudolf Glanz, "Where the Jewish Press Was Distributed in Pre-Civil War America," *WSJHQ* 5, no. 1 (1972): 1–14; Rudolf Glanz, "German-Jewish Names in America," in *Studies in Judaica Americana*, 278–313; Salo and Jeannette Baron, "Palestinian Messengers in America, 1849–79: A Record of Four Journeys," *Jewish Social Studies* 5 (1943): 115–62, 225–92; "Prayerbook of L. Elsner, a Mohel, with a List of those Circumcized in Northern New York State, 1849–1863," American Jewish Archives, Miscellaneous Collection; I. J. Benjamin, *Three Years in America, 1859–1862* (Philadelphia: Jewish Publication Society of America, 1956); William Burder, *A History of All Religions: With Accounts of the Ceremonies and Customs, or the Forms of Worship Practised by the Several Nations of the Known World, from the Earliest Records to the Year of 1872, with a Full Account, Historical, Doctrinal and Statistical, of All the Religious Denominations* (Philadelphia: William W. Harding, 1872), 582.

50. Mississippi Historical Records Survey Project, Division of Professional and Service Projects, and Works Projects Administration, *Inventory of the Church and Synagogue Archives of Mississippi: Jewish Congregations and Organizations* (Jackson, Miss.: Mississippi State Conference, B'nai B'rith, 1940); Leo and Evelyn Turitz, *Jews in Early Mississippi* (Jackson: University of Mississippi Press, 1983); Fedora S. Frank, *Five Families and Eight Young Men* (Nashville: Tennessee Book Company, 1962); Fedora S. Frank, *Beginnings on Market Street (Nashville and Her Jewry 1861–1901)* (Nashville: private printing, 1976); Janice O. Rothschild, "Pre-1867 Atlanta Jewry," *AJHQ* 62, no. 3 (1973): 242–49; Janice O. Rothschild, *As But a Day: The First Hundred Years, 1867–1967* (Atlanta: Hebrew Benevolent Congregation, 1967); Steven Hertzberg, *Strangers within the Gate City: The Jews of Atlanta, 1845–1915* (Philadelphia: Jewish Publication Society of America, 1978); Morris Speizman, *The Jews of Charlotte (North Carolina): A Chronicle with Commentary and Conjectures* (Charlotte: McNally and Loften, 1978); Alfred G. Moses, "The History of the Jews of Montgomery," *PAJHS* 13 (1905): 83–88; Hacker and Hirsch, *Proskauer*, 1–12; "Description of, and List of Names in the Clairborne, Alabama, Jewish Cemetery, 1828–1862," American Jewish Archives, Histories Collection; Raphael Goldstein, *History and Activities of Congregation Anshe-Emeth, Pine Bluff, Arkansas: 1867–1917* (N.p. 1917); Barnett A. Elzas, *The Jews of South Carolina from the Earliest Times to the Present Day* (Philadelphia: J. B. Lippincott, 1905); Bertram W. Korn, *The Early Jews of New Orleans* (Waltham, Mass.: American Jewish Historical Society, 1969); Louisiana Historical Records Survey, Division of Community Service Programs, and Works Progress Administration, *Inventory of the Church and Synagogue Archives of Louisiana: Jewish Congregations and Organizations* (University, La.: Louisiana State University Press, 1941); Leo Shpall, *The Jews in Louisiana* (New Orleans: Steeg Printing and Publishing, 1936); Benjamin Kaplan, *The Eternal Stranger: A Study of Jewish Life in the Small Community* (New York: Bookman Associates, 1957); Julian B. Feibelman, "A Social and Economic Study of the New Orleans Jewish Community" (Ph.D. diss., University of Pennsylvania, 1941); Elliott Ashkenazi, "Creoles of Jerusalem: Jewish Businessmen in Louisiana, 1840–1875" (Ph.D. diss., George Washington University, 1983); Schmier, *Reflections of Southern Jewry;* Max Rosenberg and Arthur Marmor, *Temple Beth El: A Centennial History of Beth El Hebrew Congregation Serving Northern Virginia since 1859* (Alexandria, Va.: Beth El Hebrew Con-

gregation, 1962); Myron Berman, *Richmond's Jewry, 1769–1976: Shabbat in Shockoe* (Charlottesville: University Press of Virginia, 1979); Herbert Ezekiel and Gaston Lichtenstein, *The History of the Jews of Richmond from 1769 to 1917* (Richmond, Va.: private printing, 1917); Ruth Sinberg Baker, "The German Jews: Alexandria's New Ethnic Sub-Community," in James A. Braden, ed., *Proceedings of Northern Virginia Studies Conference, 1983: Alexandria: Empire to Commonwealth* (Alexandria: Northern Virginia Community Colleges, 1984); Dinnerstein and Palsson, *Jews in the South.*

51. Julius J. Nodel, *The Ties Between: A Century of Judaism on America's Last Frontier: The Human Story of Congregation Beth Israel, Portland, Oregon, the Oldest Jewish Congregation in the Pacific Northwest* (Portland, Oreg.: Temple Beth Israel, 1959); William Toll, *The Making of an Ethnic Middle Class: Portland Jewry over Four Generations* (Albany, N.Y.: State University of New York Press, 1982); Scott Cline, "Creation of an Ethnic Community: Portland's Jews, 1851–1866," *Pacific Northwest Quarterly* 76, no. 2 (1985), 52–60; Steven Lowenstein, *The Jews of Oregon: 1850–1960* (Portland: Jewish Historical Society of Oregon, 1987).

Chapter Three. The Ties of Work

First epigraph quoted in Blau and Baron, *Jews of the United States,* 811; second epigraph quoted in "Reminiscences of Jewish Life in Newark, N.J.," *YIVO Annual of Jewish Social Science* 6 (1951): 177; third epigraph is a quote from *Richmond Whig,* 1866, Hertzberg, *Strangers within the Gate City,* 34.

1. Grinstein, *Jewish Community of New York,* 142–43; Barbara M. Solomon, *Pioneers in Service: The History of the Associated Jewish Philanthropies of Boston* (Boston: Associated Jewish Philanthropies, 1956), 3; Yechiel Lander, "Jewish Religious Education in Cincinnati As Reflected in the Minutes of Talmud Yelodim Institute, 1849–1885," term paper, Hebrew Union College, American Jewish Archives, box 2542; Jacqueline Bernard, *The Children You Gave Us: A History of 150 Years of Service to Children* (New York: Bloch, 1972); I. M. Wise quote in Feibelman, "New Orleans Jewish Community" (Ph.D. diss., University of Pennsylvania, 1941), 76; Evelyn Bodek, "'Making Do': Jewish Women and Philanthropy," in Murray Friedman, ed., *Jewish Life in Philadelphia: 1830–1940* (Philadelphia: ISHI Publications, 1983), 143–62; David Philipson, *My Life as an American Jew: An Autobiography* (Cincinnati: John G. Kidd, 1941): 8; Gary E. Polster, "A Member of the Herd: Growing up in the Cleveland Jewish Orphan Asylum, 1868–1919" (Ph.D. diss., Case Western Reserve University, 1984).

2. Nurith Zmora, "The Baltimore Hebrew Orphan Asylum through the Lives of Its First Fifty Orphans," *American Jewish History (AJH)* 77, no. 3 (1988), 476–81; Max Vorspan and Lloyd P. Gartner, *History of the Jews of Los Angeles* (San Marino, Calif.: The Huntington Library, 1970), 9.

3. Donald I. Makovsky, *The Philipsons: The First Jewish Settlers in St. Louis* (St. Louis: Judaism Sesquicentennial Committee of St. Louis, 1958); Philipson, *My Life,* 1; David Philipson, "Personal Contacts with the Founders of the Hebrew Union College," *Hebrew Union College Annual,* 11 (1936): 1.

4. Sol Bloom, *The Autobiography of Sol Bloom* (New York: G. P. Putnam's, 1948), 10; Mary Fels, *The Life of Joseph Fels* (New York: Doubleday, Doran, 1940), 3; Jacob R. Marcus, "An Arizona Pioneer: Memoirs of Sam Aaron," *AJA* 10, no. 2 (1958): 95, 98–99.

5. Bodek, "Jewish Women and Philanthropy;" Zmora, "The Baltimore Hebrew Asylum;" Glanz, *The Jewish Woman in America,* 20; Edward J. Bristow, *Prostitution and Prejudice: The Jewish Fight against White Slavery, 1870–1939* (New York: Schocken Books, 1982), 151.

6. Moses Bruml, "From a Polish Town to Gold Rush California," *WSJHQ* 17, no. 1 (1984): 91–94; Audrey R. Karsh, "Mannasse Chico: Enlightened Merchant of San Diego," *WSJHQ* 8, no. 1 (1975): 45–54; Adler, "Immigrants in Buffalo," 20–27; see also Gartner, *Jews of Cleveland,* 13.

7. Leon Harris, *Merchant Princes: An Intimate History of Jewish Families Who Built Great Department Stores* (New York: Harper and Row, 1979).

8. Barry E. Supple, "A Business Elite: German-Jewish Financiers in Nineteenth Century New York," *Business History Review* 31, no. 2 (1957), 143–78; Carosso, "Financial Elite," 67–88.

9. John Shaw Billings, *Vital Statistics of the Jews in the United States,* 11th Census, Bulletin No. 19 (Washington, D.C.: United States Census Bureau, 1890).

10. On the links between transience and peddling, see Toll, *Portland Jewry;* Jacob S. Feldman, "The Pioneers of a Community: Regional Diversity among the Jews of Pittsburgh, 1845–1861," *AJA* 32, no. 2 (1980), 119–24; Ruth Sinberg Baker, "The German Jews: Alexandria's New Ethnic Sub-Community, 1850–1871," in James Allen Braden, ed., *Proceedings of Northern Virginia Studies Conference, 1983: Alexandria: Empire to Commonwealth* (1984); on peddling as a means of mobility, particularly in the West, see Berry, "A Colorado Family History," 158–61; Cohen, *Dual Heritage,* 5; Rudolf Glanz, "Notes on Early Jewish Peddling in America," in *Studies in Judaica Americana,* 105; Rudolf Glanz, "Jew and Yankee: A Historic Comparison," in *Studies in Judaica Americana,* 330–57; Fred Mitchell Jones, "Middlemen in the Domestic Trade of the United States, 1800–1860," *Illinois Studies in the Social Sciences* 21, no. 3 (1937): 62–63.

11. Gay Talese, *The Kingdom and the Power* (London: Calder and Bayars, 1966), 81; Abram Vossen Goodman, "A Jewish Peddler's Diary," in Jacob R. Marcus, ed., *Critical Studies in American Jewish History* (Cincinnati: American Jewish Archives, 1971), 1:45–73; Toll, *Portland Jewry,* 11; Lipman, *Jews in England;* Irena Narell, *Our City: The Jews of San Francisco* (San Diego: Howell-North, 1981), 17; Berman, *Richmond's Jewry, 1769–1976: Shabbat in Shockoe,* 134–35.

12. Schmier, *Reflections of Southern Jewry,* 14.

13. Naftali H. Rubinger, "Albany Jewry of the Nineteenth Century—Historic Roots and Communal Evolution" (D.H.L. diss., Yeshiva University, 1970), 146; Morris A. Gutstein, *A Priceless Heritage: The Epic Growth of Nineteenth Century Chicago Jewry* (New York: Bloch, 1953), 33.

14. Frank, *Beginnings on Market Street (Nashville and Her Jewry, 1861–1901)* 153; Stephen G. Mostov, "A Sociological Portrait of German Jewish Immigrants in Boston: 1845–1861," in *Association for Jewish Studies Review (AJS Review)* 3 (1978): 137; Joshua Trachtenberg, *Consider the Years: The Story of the Jewish Community of Easton, 1752–1942* (Easton, Pa: Centennial Committee of Temple Brith Shalom, 1944), 113; Reissner, "The German-American Jews," 73; Jonathan Mesinger, "The Jewish Community in Syracuse, 1850–1880: The Growth and Structure of an Urban Ethnic Region" (Ph.D. diss., Syracuse University, 1977), 99–100; S. Joshua Kohn, *The Jewish Community of Utica, New York, 1847–1948* (New York: American Jewish Historical Society,

1959), 15; for the universality of peddling among the most economically successful of nineteenth-century American Jews, see Carosso, "Financial Elite"; Supple, "Business Elite," 151; Harris, *Merchant Princes*.

15. Trachtenberg, *Consider the Years*, 153.

16. Stuart E. Rosenberg, *The Jewish Community in Rochester, 1843–1925* (New York: Columbia University Press, 1954), 5–6; Pink Horwitt, *Jews in Berkshire County* (private printing, 1972); Bernard Shuman, *A History of the Sioux City Jewish Community, 1869–1969* (Sioux City, Iowa: Jewish Federation of Sioux City, 1969); Rosaline Levenson, *Chico Jewish Pioneers: Adaptation to Small Town Life in Northern California*, WSJHQ 17, no. 3 (1985): 195–213; Wirth, *The Ghetto*, 153; Alan S. Pine, Jean C. Hershenov, and Aaron H. Lefkowitz, *Peddler to Suburbanite: The History of the Jews of Monmouth County, N.J.: From the Colonial Period to 1980* (Deal Park, N.J.: Monmouth Jewish Community Council, 1981); Stephen G. Mostov, "Migration Patterns of America's German Jews: Cincinnati, 1840–1875," in *Papers in Jewish Demography: 1981*, Jewish Population Studies Series (Jerusalem: Institute of Contemporary Jewry, Hebrew University, 1981), 96–97; David A. Brener, *Lancaster's Gates of Heaven: Portals to the Past: The 19th Century Jewish Community of Lancaster, Pennsylvania, and Congregation Shaarai Shomayim, 1856–1976* (Lancaster, Pa: private printing, 1976), 11; Hertzberg, *Strangers within the Gate City*, 16–18; see also the numerous references to peddlers as the first Jews in a town in Harriet and Fred Rochlin, *Pioneer Jews: A New Life in the Far West* (Boston: Houghton Mifflin, 1984).

17. Alice W. Heyneman, "A Backward Look at a Pioneer Grandfather, Sol Wagenheim," *WSJHQ* 3, no. 2 (1972): 89–90; Lee M. Friedman, "The Problems of Nineteenth Century American Jewish Peddlers," *PAJHS* 44, no. 1 (1954): 1–7; Kraus, *Reminiscences and Comments*, 13; Glanz, "Early Jewish Peddling in America," 104–21; Rosenthal, "Perakim B'Toldot Hayishuv," 19.

18. Mississippi Historical Records Survey Project, *Inventory of the Church and Synagogue Archives*, 3; Gutstein, *Priceless Heritage*, 266; Esther L. Panitz, *Simon Wolf: Private Conscience and Public Image* (Rutherford, N.J.: Farleigh Dickinson University Press, 1987), 13; Supple, "Business Elite," 151.

19. Norton Stern, ed., "Interesting Accounts of the Travels of Abraham Abrahamsohn to America and Especially to the Gold Mines of California and Australia," *WSJHQ* 1, no. 3 (1969): 133–34; "Translated Autobiography of William Frank," American Jewish Archives; Raphael, *Jews and Judaism*, 35; Henry and Lea Fine, "North Dakota Memories," *WSJHQ* 9, no. 4 (1977), 331; Solomon, *Pioneers in Service*, 8–9.

20. Examples of peddlers settling down and then bringing over parents and brothers and sisters include "Translation of Autobiography of William Frank," American Jewish Archives, 2; Barnard, *Forging of American Jew*, 7; Cray, *Levi's*, 2, 7; Aaron Hirsch, "Autobiography," American Jewish Archives, Biographies File; Wall, "Leon Godchaux," *AJHQ* 50–66; Friedlander, "Ethical Letter," 90–96; Frank Rosenthal, *The Jews of Des Moines: The First Century* (Des Moines, Iowa: Jewish Welfare Federation, 1957), 1; Carosso, "Financial Elite."

21. Cohen, *Dual Heritage*, 5; Norton B. Stern, "Myer Joseph Newmark—Los Angeles Civil Leader," *WSJHQ* 2, no. 3 (1970): 137–39; Devora Strocker, "When Grandfather Julius Came to Michigan," *Michigan Jewish History* 6, no. 1 (1965): 12; Rothschild, "Atlanta Jewry," 242–49.

22. Toll, *Portland Jewry*, 9, 11, 15, 44–46; Abraham Flexner, *I Remember: The*

Autobiography of Abraham Flexner (New York: Simon and Schuster, 1940), 12; Friedlander, "Ethical Letter"; Morris R. Werner, *Julius Rosenwald: The Life of a Practical Humanitarian* (New York: Harper and Brothers, 1939), 4; "Translated Autobiography of William Frank."

23. Hertzberg, *Strangers within the Gate City,* 15, 78; Adler, "Immigrants in Buffalo," 22; Selig Adler and Thomas E. Connolly, *From Ararat to Suburbia: The History of the Jewish Community of Buffalo* (Philadelphia: Jewish Publication Society of America, 1960), 31–34; Blake McKelvey, "The Jews of Rochester: A Contribution to their History during the Nineteenth Century," *PAJHS* 40, no. 1 (1950): 57–73; Bernard G. Rudolph, *From a Minyan to a Community: A History of the Jews of Syracuse* (Syracuse: Syracuse University Press, 1970), 29–31, 34–35; Kohn, *Jewish Community of Utica,* 9; Mesinger, "Jewish Community in Syracuse," 99–105, 115–17, 131; Benjamin Bond, *Portland Jewry: Its Growth and Development* (Portland, Maine: Jewish Historical Society, 1955), 11; Fleishaker, "Illinois-Iowa Jewish Community," 37; Irving I. Katz, *The Beth El Story with a History of the Jews in Michigan before 1850 and Three Hundred Years in America* (Detroit: Wayne State University Press, 1955); Nodel, *The Ties Between,* 12; Friedlander, "Ethical Letter"; "Population of the Jewish Community of Providence, 1877," *Rhode Island Jewish Historical News* 1, no. 1 (1954): 72–74; Joan Dash, *Summoned to Jerusalem: The Life of Henrietta Szold* (New York: Harper and Row, 1979), 7; Stephen F. Mostov, "Dun and Bradstreet Reports as a Source of Jewish Economic History: Cincinnati, 1840–1875," *AJH* 72, no. 3 (1983): 340, 342; Arthur Mann, *Growth and Achievement: Temple Israel, 1854–1954* (Cambridge: Riverside Press, 1954), 19; Hacker and Hirsch, *Proskauer,* 9; Marlene S. Gaines, "The Early Sacramento Jewish Community," *WSJHQ* 3, no. 2 (1971): 65–68; Mostov, "Jerusalem on the Ohio," 90, 121; Fine, "North Dakota Memories," 331; Pittsburgh Section, National Council of Jewish Women, *By Myself I'm A Book! An Oral History of the Immigrant Jewish Experience in Pittsburgh* (Waltham, Mass.: American Jewish Historical Society, 1972), 150; Robert Ernst, *Immigrant Life in New York City: 1825–1863* (New York: King's Crown Press, 1949), 84–85.

24. Isaac Mayer Wise, *Reminiscences of Isaac M. Wise* (Cincinnati: L. Wise and Co., 1901), 38; Wirth, *The Ghetto,* 154.

25. Kussy, "Reminiscences of Jewish Life," 177; Charles F. Goldsmith, "Lansburgh's: Three Brothers' Saga," *The Record of the Washington Jewish Historical Society* 7, no. 1 (1974): 5; Esther Sulman, *A Goodly Heritage: The Story of the Jewish Community in New London, 1860–1955* (New London: private printing, 1957), 5; Stanley Nadel, "Kleindeutschland: New York City's Germans, 1845–1880" (Ph.D. diss., Columbia University, 1981), 179; Bloom, *Autobiography,* 19; Arnold Wieder, *The Early Jewish Community of Boston's North End: A Sociologically Oriented Study of an Eastern European Jewish Immigrant Community in an American Big-City Neighborhood between 1870 and 1900* (Waltham, Mass.: Brandeis University, 1962), 66; Carole Krucoff, *Rodfei Zedek: The First Hundred Years* (Chicago: Congregation Rodfei Zedek, 1976), 2–9; Moshe Hazkani, "Itonut Yiddish B'Chicago (1877–1951)," in Rawidowicz, *Pinkas Chicago,* 70.

26. Nadel, "Kleindeutschland," 163–64, 211; Kohn, *Jewish Community of Utica,* 15–16; Kraus, *Reminiscences,* 14; Louis E. Lowenthal, "David Werner Amram," *AJYB* 42 (1941): 375; "A Memorial For a Blue-Collar, Bavarian-Born, San Francisco Forty-Niner," *WSJHQ* 14, no. 1 (1981): 42–44; "Jacob Lanzit, diary," American Jewish Archives, Biographies File; Ezekiel Lifschutz and Elias Tcherikower, "Die Pionere—T'kufah fun

Der Yiddisher Arbetter Bavegung Biz 1886," in Tcherikower, *Geshichte,* 241–42; Moshe Shtarkman, "Vichtige Momenten in der Geshichte fun der Yiddisher Presse in America," in Jacob Glatstein, Samuel Niger, and Hillel Rogoff, eds., *Finf un Zibitzik Yor Yiddishe Presse In America, 1870–1945* (New York: Y.L. Peretz Writers' Association, 1945), 11; quoted in Ezekiel Lifschutz, "The Jewish Labor Movement in the United States: Jewish and Non-Jewish Influences," *AJHQ* 52, no. 2 (1962): 134.

27. Judah David Eisenstein, "The History of the First Russian-American Jewish Congregation," *PAJHS* 9 (1901): 68; Ernst, *Immigrant Life,* 85; Lifschitz, "Die Russishe-Poylishe Immigranten" 70; Cowen, *Memoirs of an American Jew,* 23; Samuel P. Abelow, *History of Brooklyn Jewry* (Brooklyn: Scheba Publishing Company, 1937), 11; Toll, *Portland Jewry,* 26; see also Martha Kransdorf, "Julia Richman's Years in the New York City Public Schools: 1872–1912" (Ph.D. diss., University of Michigan, 1979), 59; Bruml, "Gold Rush California," 93.

28. Bernard Weinstein, *Die Yiddishe Unions in America,* 79, 82; Samuel Gompers, *Seventy Years of Life and Labor: An Autobiography* (New York: E. P. Dutton, 1925), 36; Kohn, *Jewish Community of Utica,* 15–16; Abraham Meyer, "Formative Years of the Jewish Labor Movement in the United States (1890–1900)" (Ph.D. diss., Columbia University, 1945), 4; Patricia A. Cooper, *Once a Cigar Maker: Men, Women and Work Culture in American Cigar Factories, 1900–1919* (Urbana: University of Illinois Press, 1987).

29. Burgin, *Yiddishe Arbeiter Bavegung,* 88; Ernst, *Immigrant Life,* 77; Rudolf Glanz, *Jew and Irish: Historic Group Relations and Immigration* (New York: Waldon Press, 1966), 144; Lifschitz and Tcherikower, "Die Pionere," 239.

30. See, for example, material on San Francisco's rabbi and editor, Julius Eckman, who, beginning in the 1850s, urged his fellow Jews to become agriculturalists: Reva Clar, "Agricultural Gleanings from San Francisco's Weekly Gleaner," *WSJHQ* 17, no. 1 (1984): 52–62; see also *American Israelite,* 10 June 1864.

31. Lorna J. Sass, "The Great Nosh: Some Landmark New York Delis," *Journal of Gastronomy* 4, no. 1 (1988) 38; Trachtenberg, *Consider the Years,* 127.

32. Selma Berrol, "Who Went to School in Mid-Nineteenth Century New York?" in Irving Yellowitz, *Essays in the History of New York City: A Memorial to Sidney Pomerantz* (Port Washington, N.Y.: Kennikat Press, 1978), 51–52.

33. Hundreds of articles can be found in journals, such as the *Western States Jewish Historical Quarterly,* as well as other publications, such as *Michigan Jewish History,* chronicling settlement patterns and overwhelming commercial concentration of Jews. Similarly, the American Jewish Archives contains a vast array of documents attesting to the penetration of Jewish merchants into almost every corner of America. See, for example, Henry Schwartz, "The Levi Saga, Temecula, Julian, San Diego," *WSJHQ* 6, no. 3 (1974): 161–76; "Dictation of Mr. Katz of San Bernardino, California, taken from the Hubert Howe Bancroft papers, housed at University of California, Berkeley," American Jewish Archives, Biographies; Blaine Peterson Lamb, "Jewish Pioneers in Arizona, 1850–1920" (Ph.D. diss., Arizona State University, 1982); Samuel P. Johnson, ed., *Alaska Commercial Company, 1868–1940* (n.p., n.d.), American Jewish Archives; Max Wolkow, "A History of the Jews of Wichita from 1870s to 1920," American Jewish Archives, Histories; Benjamin Kelson, "The Jews of Montana," *WSJHQ* 3, no. 3 (1971): 113–21; Rochlin, *Pioneer Jews;* Lowenstein, *Jews of Oregon.*

34. For examples of partnerships within the Jewish communities, see Walter Ehrlich, "Origins of the Jewish Community of St. Louis," *AJH* 77, no. 4 (1988): 513; Flexner, *Autobiography,* 6; Frank A. Adler, *Roots in a Moving Stream: The Centennial History of Congregation B'nai Jehuda of Kansas City, 1870–1970* (Kansas City, Mo.: The Temple, Congregation B'nai Jehuda, 1972), 8–10; Vorspan and Gartner, *Jews of Los Angeles,* 34–37; James L. Allen, "Marcus Schiller: San Diego's Jewish Horatio Alger," *WSJHQ* 3, no. 1 (1970): 28–29; Karsh, "Mannasse Chico," 46; Allan Tarshish, "The Economic Life of the American Jew in the Middle Nineteenth Century," in Jacob R. Marcus, ed., *Essays in American Jewish History* (New York: KTAV, 1975), 263–93; Rosenthal, *Jews of Des Moines,* 18; Heyneman, "Sol Wagenheim," 92–93.

35. Mostov, "Jewish Economic History," 333–53.

36. See, for example, Richard B. Goldberg, "Michael Wormser, Capitalist," *AJA* 25, no. 2 (1973): 163; Daniel Jacobson, "Lansing's Jewish Community: The Beginnings," *Michigan Jewish History* 16, no. 1 (1976): 6; Sulman, *Goodly Heritage,* 6; Toll, *Portland Jewry,* 11–18; Solomon, *Pioneers in Service,* 8–9.

37. Panitz, *Simon Wolf,* 19.

38. On Jews in small-town general stores, see Thomas D. Clark, *Pills, Petticoats, and Plows: The Southern Country Store* (Indianapolis: Bobbs Merrill, 1944), 22–23, 318, 319; Lewis A. Atherton, *A Southern Country Store: 1800–1860* (Baton Rouge: Louisiana State University Press, 1949), 190–91; Gerald Carson, *The Old Country Store* (New York: E. P. Dutton, 1965); Cyrus Adler, *I Have Considered the Days* (Philadelphia: Jewish Publication Society of America, 1941), 4–6; James A. Wax, "Isidor Bush, American Patriot and Abolitionist," *Historica Judaica* 5, no. 2 (1943): 184; Selig Adler, "Zebulon B. Vance and the 'Scattered Nation,'" *Journal of Southern History* 7, no. 3 (1941): 357–77; "Autobiography of Aaron Hirsch," American Jewish Archives, Biographies; references to the progress from dry-goods to department stores include Goldsmith, "Lansburgh's," 5; Harris, *Merchant Princes.*

39. Atherton, *Southern Country Store;* Samuel Broches, "A Chapter in the History of the Jews of Boston," *YIVO Annual of Jewish Social Science* 9 (1954): 205; Thomas B. Littlewood, *Horner of Illinois* (Evanston: Northwestern University Press, 1969), 11; *Cleveland Plain Dealer,* 30 January 1856, American Jewish Archives, Small Collection.

40. Adler, "Zebulon Vance," 358–59; Allan Nevins, *Herbert H. Lehman and His Era* (New York: Charles Scribner's Sons, 1963), 5; Hacker and Hirsch, *Proskauer,* 1; Supple, "Business Elite"; Carosso, "Financial Elite"; Neuman, "Cyrus Adler," 24; Walter Bean, *Boss Ruef's San Francisco: The Story of the Union Labor Party, Big Business and the Graft Prosecution* (Berkeley: University of California Press, 1952), 1.

41. Rochlin, *Pioneer Jews,* 141–68; and Toll, *Portland Jewry,* 87–88, are but two of hundreds of references to the participation of Jewish merchants in civic affairs across the United States.

42. Kisch, *In Search of Freedom,* 153; Friedlander, "Ethical Letter," 91; Irving I. Katz, *The Jewish Soldier from Michigan in the Civil War* (Detroit: Wayne State University Press, 1962), 15; David F. and Mary R. Hoexter, "Daniel Meyer: San Francisco Banker," *WSJHQ* 12, no. 3 (1980): 195; James A. Gelin, *Starting Over: The Formation of the Jewish Community of Springfield, Massachusetts, 1840–1905* (Lanham, Md: University Press of America, 1984), 26; Devera S. Strocker, "The Lipsitz Families: Early Jewish Settlers in Detroit," *Michigan Jewish History* 22, no. 2 (1982): 6; Rudolf Glanz, "Jews and Chinese in America," in *Studies in Judaica Americana,* 314–29.

43. Raphael, *Jews and Judaism,* 40–41; Judith Endelman, *The Jewish Community of Indianapolis: 1849 to the Present* (Bloomington: Indiana University Press, 1984), 25; Louis J. Swichkow, "The Jewish Community of Milwaukee, 1860–1870," *PAJHS* 47, no. 1 (1957): 36; Winograd, "The Horse Died at Windber," 32; Mostov, "'Jerusalem' on the Ohio," 109–14; Griffin, *Natives and Newcomers,* 121; numerous other community histories focusing on large cities and small towns confirm the high Jewish concentration in the making and selling of clothing.

44. Glanz, "Vanguard to the Russians," 16; Willet, *Employment of Women,* 34; Gutstein, *Priceless Heritage,* 366; Marsha L. Rozenblit, "Choosing a Synagogue: The Social Composition of Two German Congregations in Nineteenth-Century Baltimore," in Jack Wertheimer, ed., *American Synagogue* (Cambridge: Cambridge University Press, 1987), 329, 344–45; "The First Fund-Raisers for the Hebrew Union College in the Far West," *WSJHQ* 8, no. 1 (1975): 55–58; J. D. Eisenstein, "The History of the First Russian-American Jewish Congregation," *PAJHS* 9 (1901): 65.

45. Quoted in Rudolf Glanz, "German Jews in New York City in the 19th Century," in *Studies in Judaica Americana,* 127; Egal Feldman, "Jews in the Early Growth of New York City's Men's Clothing Trade," *AJA* 12, no. 1 (1960): 3–14; Ernst, *Immigrant Life,* 77; Bond, *Portland Jewry,* 11; Jesse E. Pope, *The Clothing Industry in New York* (New York: Burt Franklin, 1905), 7.

46. Pope, *Clothing Industry;* Willet, *Employment of Women,* 34–36; Sean Wilentz, *Chants Democratic: New York City and the Rise of the American Working Class, 1788–1850* (New York: Oxford University Press, 1984), 120–24; Christine Stansell, *City of Women: Sex and Class in New York, 1789–1860* (Urbana: University of Illinois Press, 1987), 107–16; Glanz, "Jews and Chinese," 316–18.

47. There are no statistics to draw upon, but biographical and autobiographical details lead to this as a tentative conclusion. Philipson, in *My Life,* 1, claimed that as of 1873, "No Jewish lad in Columbus up to that time had attended the high school."

48. Baum, Hyman, and Michel, *Jewish Woman in America,* 55.

49. Esther Levy, *Jewish Cookery Book on Principles of Economy, Adapted for Jewish Housekeepers with the Addition of Many Useful Medicinal Recipes, and Other Valuable Information, Relative to Housekeeping and Domestic Management* (Philadelphia: W. S. Turner, 1871); Reva Clar, "Women in the Weekly Gleaner," *WSJHQ* 18, no. 1 (1985): 47–57; Bertram W. Korn, *Jews and Negro Slavery in the Old South* (Elkins Park, Pennsylvania, 1961), 25; Toll, *Ethnic Middle Class,* 45; for biographic details of women as homemakers and removed from work, see also Fels, *The Life of Joseph Fels,* 2; Michael L. Lawson, "Flora Langermann Spiegelberg: Grand Lady of Santa Fe," *WSJHQ* 8, no. 4 (1976): 291–305.

50. Quoted in Glanz, *Jewish Woman in America,* 2:19.

51. Josephine Goldmark, *Pilgrims of '48: One Man's Part in the Austrian Revolution of 1848 and a Family Migration to America* (New Haven: Yale University Press, 1930), 189; Norman Bentwich, *For Zion's Sake: A Biography of Judah L. Magnes* (Philadelphia: Jewish Publication Society of America, 1954), 9.

52. Littlewood, *Horner of Illinois,* 11; Louise Sindler, "Westward Bound," *The Record* 2, no. 1 (1982): 10; Barnard, *Forging of American Jew,* 6.

53. Brener, *Lancaster's Gates of Heaven,* 20.

54. Adler, "Immigrants in Buffalo," 22; Morgenthau, *All in a Lifetime,* 13; Nodel, *The Ties Between,* 12; William M. Kramer, "The Emergence of Oakland Jewry,"

WSJHQ 10, no. 2 (1978): 100; Neil C. Sandberg, *Jewish Life in Los Angeles: A Window to Tomorrow* (New York: University Press of America, 1986), 27.

55. Early Manufacturer, San Francisco," *WSJHQ* 13, no. 4 (1981): 363; Gartner, "Immigrant Letters," 236; Laurence J. Stuppy, "Henry H. Lissner, M.D.: Los Angeles Physician," *WSJHQ* 8, no. 3 (1976): 210; Irene D. Neu, "The Jewish Businesswoman in America," *AJHQ* 66, no. 1 (1976): 144; William M. Kramer and Norton B. Stern, "Early California Associations of Michael Goldwater and His Family," *WSJHQ* 4, no. 4 (1972): 175.

56. On women learning a craft, particularly in the needle trades prior to migration, see Kussy, "Reminiscences of Jewish Life," 177; Glanz, *Jewish Woman*, 11–15.

57. For references on Jewish women sewing for a living, see, for example, Pope, *Clothing Industry*, 13–15; Flexner, *Autobiography*, 11; "The Editor's Page," *WSJHQ* 17, no. 1 (1984): 95.

58. For references on Jewish women as school teachers in this period, see *Weekly Gleaner*, 11 June 1859, 5; "Reminiscences, Chicago, Illinois, 1859–1934, Gerstley, Mrs. Henry," American Jewish Archives, box 2072; *Jewish Messenger*, 16 February 1863, 53; Benjamin, *Three Years in America*, 232; Kransdorf, "Julia Richman," 59–60.

59. Yechiel Lander, "Jewish Religious Education in Cincinnati as Reflected in the Minutes of Talmud Yelodim Institute, 1849–1885" (Term paper, Hebrew Union College, 1964), American Jewish Archives, box 2542; Polster, "Member of the Herd," 37–38; Zmora, "Orphan Asylum," 472; Bernard, *Children You Gave Us*, 29.

60. Arthur Bielfeld, "A Study of the Home for Widows and Orphans of New Orleans Taken from the Minutes of the Meetings of the Association, 1855–1884" (Term paper, Hebrew Union College, 1962), American Jewish Archives, box 236; Zmora, "Orphan Asylum," 470; Polster, "Member of the Herd," 38.

Chapter Four. The Links of Community

First epigraph quoted in Carol Gendler, "The Jews of Omaha—The First Sixty Years," *WSJHQ* 11, no. 4 (1979): 290; second epigraph quoted in Benjamin, *Three Years in America*, 80; third epigraph quoted from *The Chronicles of Emanu-El: Being an Account of the Rise and Progress of the Congregation Emanu-El Which Was Founded in July, 1850 and Will Celebrate Its Fiftieth Anniversary, December 23, 1900* (San Francisco: George Spaulding, 1900), 17.

1. Quoted in Lawrence A. Hoffman, *Beyond the Text: A Holistic Approach to Liturgy* (Bloomington: Indiana University Press, 1987), 165.

2. Salo W. Baron, "American Jewish History: Problems and Methods," *PAJHS* 39 (1950): 249–55; Naomi Cohen, *Encounter with Emancipation*, 42, 44–46; Deborah D. Moore, *B'nai B'rith and the Challenge of Ethnic Leadership* (Albany: State University of New York Press, 1987), 1.

3. Quoted in Marcus, *Memoirs of American Jews*, 2: 6.

4. Rudolph, *Jews of Syracuse*, 2.

5. Hannah G. Solomon, *Fabric of My Life* (New York: Bloch, 1946), 10; Mrs. Henry Gerstley, "Reminiscences, Chicago, Illinois, 1859–1934," American Jewish Archives, box 2072; Norton B. Stern, "The Location of Los Angeles Jewry at the Beginning of 1851," *WSJHQ* 5, no. 1 (1972): 25–26; Helen Aminoff, "The First Jews of Ann Arbor,"

Michigan Jewish History 23, no. 1 (1983): 5–6; W. Gunther Plaut, *The Jews in Minnesota: The First Seventy-Five Years* (New York: American Jewish Historical Society, 1959), 54; Frank, *Five Families and Eight Young Men, 121.*

6. Quoted in Isaac Fein, *The Making of an American Jewish Community: The History of Baltimore Jewry from 1773 to 1920* (Philadelphia: Jewish Publication Society of America, 1971), 78.

7. Jonathan S. Mesinger, "Reconstructing the Social Geography of the Nineteenth Century Jewish Community from Primary Sources," *AJH* 72, no. 3 (1983): 354–68; Glazer, *Jews of Iowa,* 238; Wirth, *The Ghetto,* 155, 157, 164; Rozenblit, "Choosing a Synagogue," 327–62; Fein, *American Jewish Community,* 77; Albert Ehrenfried, *A Chronicle of Boston Jewry: From the Colonial Settlement to 1900* (private printing, 1963), 328; Mostov, "Jewish Immigrants in Boston," 138–43; David A. Gerber, "Cutting Out Shylock: Elite Anti-Semitism and the Quest for Moral Order in the Mid-Nineteenth Century American Marketplace," in David A. Gerber, ed., *Anti-Semitism in American History* (Urbana: University of Illinois Press, 1986), 207; Hertzberg, *Strangers within the Gate City,* 19, 43–49.

8. Kenneth D. Roseman, "The United States Census of 1850: Philadelphia, Pennsylvania" (Term paper, Hebrew Union College, 1967), American Jewish Archives, box 2774; Rosenwaike, *On the Edge of Greatness,* 43–50; Robert Ernst, *Immigrant Life in New York City: 1825–1863* (New York: King's Crown Press, 1949), 46.

9. Ernst, *Immigrant Life,* 46.

10. Simon Glazer, *The Jews of Iowa: A Complete History and Accurate Account of Their Religious, Social, Economical and Educational Progress in Their State; A History of the Jews of Europe, North and South America in Modern Times and a Brief History of Iowa* (Des Moines: Koch Brothers, 1904), 235.

11. Cowen, *Memories of an American Jew,* 21; Ella F. Auerbach, "Jewish Settlement in Nebraska, 1927," American Jewish Archives, Small Collection.

12. Arthur Goren, "Traditional Institutions Transplanted: The Hevra Kadisha in Europe and America," in Moses Rischin, ed., *The Jews of North America* (Detroit: Wayne State University Press, 1987), 62–78; Jacob R. Marcus, *Communal Sick-Care in the German Ghetto* (Cincinnati: Hebrew Union College Press, 1947), 116.

13. Adler and Connally, *From Ararat to Suburbia,* 47; Goren, "Traditional Institutions"; James G. Heller, *Isaac M. Wise: His Life, Work and Thought* (New York: Union of American Hebrew Congregations, 1965), 169.

14. Sulman, *Goodly Heritage,* 7; Arthur Goldberg, "The Jew in Norwich, Connecticut: A Century of Jewish Life," *Rhode Island Jewish History Notes* 7, no. 1 (1975): 81; Hillel Marans, *Jews in Greater Washington: A Panoramic History of Washington Jewry for the Years 1795–1960* (Washington, D.C.: private printing, 1961), 142; Mesinger, "Jewish Community in Syracuse," 177.

15. While in California on an expedition with John C. Fremont, artist Solomon Nunes Carvalho, a Baltimorean, helped Jews in Los Angeles establish their Hebrew Benevolent Society, the first Jewish institution in southern California. See Solomon Nunes Carvalho, *Incidents of Travel and Adventures in the Far West* (Philadelphia: Jewish Publication Society of America, 1954), 34.

16. Norton B. Stern and William M. Kramer, "A Murder Victim's Burial in Los Angeles—1855," *WSJHQ* 9, no. 1 (1976): 46–48; *Chronicles of Emanu-El,* 29.

17. For some of the names of these benevolent associations, see Edwin Wolf and

Maxwell Whiteman, *The History of the Jews of Philadelphia from Colonial Times to the Age of Jackson* (Philadelphia: Jewish Publication Society of America, 1956), 267; Ruth Zweig, *The First Hundred and Twenty-Five Years* (Ft. Wayne, Ind.: Indiana Jewish Historical Society, 1973), 3; *Weekly Gleaner*, 20 February 1857, 45; Ehrenfried, *Chronicle of Boston Jewry*, 312; Alfred G. Moses, "The History of the Jews of Montgomery," *PAJHS* 13 (1905): 83–88; *Jewish Messenger*, 9 September 1870, 4; Katz, *Beth El Story*, 51; "Minute Books, 1853–1869, Chevra Gemiloth Chesed, Boston, Mass.," American Jewish Archives, box 1701; Edward H. Mazur, "Minyans for a Prairie City: The Politics of Chicago Jewry, 1850–1940" (Ph.D. diss., University of Chicago, 1974), 10; "Records of Ahafath Achim," American Jewish Archives, box X182.

18. "The Hebrew Society of Hebra Ahavat Ahim, July, 1859," American Jewish Archives, Small Collection.

19. "Constitution and By-Laws (1872)," Charlotte, N.C., Hebrew Benevolent Society, American Jewish Archives; Rothschild, *As But a Day*, 2; "The First Jewish Organization in Texas: Houston—1855," *WSJHQ* 11, no. 1 (1978): 55; Michael M. Zarchin, *Glimpses of Jewish Life in San Francisco (History of San Francisco Jewry)* (Berkeley: Willis E. Berg, 1952), 98; "Minute Books, Hebrew Benevolent Society—Charleston, South Carolina," American Jewish Archives; Kelson, "Jews of Montana," 228.

20. Jay Edelstein, "The Chevra Gemiloth Chesed of the City of Boston: December 25, 1853, to December 26, 1869" (Term paper, Hebrew Union College), American Jewish Archives, Miscellaneous File.

21. Norton B. Stern, "When the Franco-Prussian War Came to Los Angeles," *WSJHQ* 10, no. 1 (1977): 68–73; quoted in George J. Fogelson, "The Jews of Santa Cruz: The First Eighty Years, 1854–1934," *WSJHQ* 14, no. 2 (1982): 104.

22. No aspect of nineteenth-century American Jewish life is as unstudied as the role of benevolent associations and burial societies, and, even more so, the existence and structure of the women's societies. Even books written from a decidedly feminist perspective, such as Baum, Hyman, and Michel, *Jewish Woman in America*, ignore the existence of these groups that existed in every city and, instead, concentrate on women's associational life in the philanthropic sphere.

23. "The Ahavas Achos Constitution," *Jews in New Haven* 1 (1978): 17–20; see also "Minute Books, Hebrew Ladies Benevolent Society, Albany, Georgia," American Jewish Archives, box X166; David C. Adelman, "Montefiore Lodge, Ladies Hebrew Benevolent Association," *Rhode Island Jewish History Notes* 4, no. 1 (1963): 47–71; *American Israelite*, 15 January 1864, 22; ibid., 5 August 1863, 74; *Jewish Messenger*, 3 June 1864, 166; ibid., 24 October 1862, 122–23; Jack Wolfe, *A Century with Iowa Jewry: As Complete a History As Could Be Obtained of Iowa Jewry from 1833 through 1940* (Des Moines: Iowa Printing Company, 1941), 69; Rudolph, *Jews of Syracuse*, 33; Plaut, *Jews in Minnesota*, 57; Harold I. Sharfman, *Nothing Left to Commemorate: The Story of the Pioneer Jews of Jackson, Amador County, California* (Glendale, Calif.: Arthur H. Clark, 1969), 76; Abraham I. Shinedling, *West Virginia Jewry: Origins and History, 1850–1958* (Philadelphia: Maurice Jacobs, 1963), 1:xxviii; Brener, *Lancaster's Gates of Heaven*, 16; Nancy A. Hewitt, *Women's Activism and Social Change: Rochester, New York, 1822–1872* (Ithaca: Cornell University Press, 1984), 218.

24. Barnard, *Forging of American Jew*, 16; "Jacob Rich and Bride, San Francisco, 1853," *WSJHQ* 12, no. 3 (1980): 260.

25. Vorspan and Gartner, *Jews of Los Angeles,* 19.

26. Benjamin, *Three Years in America,* 70–73, 215–29.

27. "Constitution and Minutes, 1862 and 1863, Binghamton, New York—Hebrew Benevolent Society," American Jewish Archives, Histories File; "The News from Woodland and Oroville, California, in 1879," *WSJHQ* 11, no. 2 (1979): 162; Schmier, *Reflections of Southern Jewry,* 15; "Minute Book, 1872–1878," Hebrew Benevolent Association, Dallas, Texas," American Jewish Archives, box 1311; Edelstein, "Chevra Gemiloth Chesed."

28. See Raphael, *Jews and Judaism,* 57; Rosenberg, *Jewish Community in Rochester,* 21; Benjamin Kaplan, *The Eternal Stranger: A Study of Jewish Life in the Small Community* (New York: Bookman Associates, 1957), 95; Elaine S. Anderson, "The Jews of Toledo: 1845–1895" (Ph.D. diss., University of Toledo, 1974), 71.

29. Isidor Blum, *The Jews of Baltimore: An Historical Summary of Their Progress and Status as Citizens of Baltimore from Early Days to the Year Nineteen Hundred and Ten* (Baltimore: Historical Review Publishing Co., 1910), 7; Audrey D. Kariel, "The Jewish Story and Memories of Marshall, Texas," *WSJHQ* 14, no. 3 (1982): 197; Hynda Rudd, "The Mountain West as a Jewish Frontier," *WSJHQ* 13, no. 3 (1981): 249–51; Louisiana Historical Records Survey, Division of Community Service Programs, and Works Projects Administration, *Inventory of the Church and Synagogue Archives of Louisiana: Jewish Congregations and Organizations,* 2–9; Gendler, "Jews of Omaha," 289–90; *Jewish Messenger,* 13 February 1857, 29; Stephen D. Kinsey, "The Development of the Jewish Community of San Jose, California: 1850–1900," *WSJHQ* 7, no. 1 (1974): 71; Mississippi Historical Records Survey Project (MHRSP), Division of Professional Service Projects, and Works Projects Administration, *Inventory of the Church and Synagogue Archives of Mississippi: Jewish Congregations and Organizations,* 3, 16–17, 19; Rosenthal, *Jews of Des Moines,* 50; Bella Schultz, "The Highest Degree of Tzedakah: Jewish Philanthropy in Kansas City, 1870–1933," in Joseph Schultz, ed., *Mid-America's Promise: A Profile of Kansas City Jewry* (Waltham, Mass.: American Jewish Historical Society, 1982), 202; Ehrlich, "Jewish Community of St. Louis," 521.

30. Kinsey, "Jewish Community of San Jose," 71; Louisiana Historical Records Survey, *Inventory of the Church and Synagogue Archives,* 5; Pittsburgh Section, National Council of Jewish Women, *I'm a Book!* 149; Edward N. Calisch, *The Light Burns On: Centennial Anniversary Congregation Beth Ahabah* (Richmond: private printing, 1941), 13; Suzanne Somberg and Silvia G. Roffman, *Consider the Years: 1871–1971: Congregation of Temple Israel, Omaha, Nebraska* (Omaha: The Temple, 1971), 12.

31. *Die Deborah,* one of the few German-language newspapers written for American Jews, ran special articles deemed to be of interest to women. See Heller, *Isaac M. Wise,* 271.

32. Irving I. Katz, "Sister Love Society Existed in 1859," *Michigan Jewish History* 12, no. 1 (1972): 17–18; "Baton Rouge, La., Ladies Hebrew Association," American Jewish Archives, box 687.

33. Jacob R. Marcus, *Memoirs of American Jews: 1775–1865,* (Philadelphia: Jewish Publication Society of America, 1955), 2:283.

34. Maxwell Whiteman, "The Legacy of Isaac Leeser," in Friedman, *Jewish Life in Philadelphia,* 37–38; Lance J. Sussman, "The Life and Career of Isaac Leeser (1806–1868: A Study of American Judaism in Its Formative Period" (Ph.D. diss., Hebrew Union

College—Jewish Institute of Religion, 1987); Terry K. Fisher, "Lending as Philanthropy: The Philadelphia Jewish Experience, 1847–1954" (Ph.D. diss., Bryn Mawr College, 1987), 44–45; David Max Eichhorn, *Evangelizing the American Jew* (Middle Village, N.Y.: Jonathan David, 1978); Bogen, *Jewish Philanthropy,* 86; Bernard, *Children You Gave Us,* 8.

35. Burder, *History of All Religions,* 580–81.

36. Nathan M. Kaganoff, "Organized Jewish Welfare Activity in New York City (1848–1860)," *AJHQ* 56, no. 1 (1966): 27–49; for listings of Jewish charitable institutions, see also Homer Folks, *The Care of Destitute, Neglected, and Delinquent Children* (New York: J. B. Lyon, 1900), 61; James H. Connelly, *Charities of the Hebrew of New York: Comprehensive Benevolence beyond All Bounds of Race or Creeds* (New York: Stettiner, Lambert, and Co., 1888); Robert E. Cray, Jr., *Paupers and Poor Relief in New York City and Its Rural Environs, 1700–1830* (Philadelphia: Temple University Press, 1988), 179–80.

37. Dianne C. Ashton, "Rebecca Gratz and the Domestication of American Judaism" (Ph.D. diss., Temple University, 1986), 201–3.

38. Robert Bremner, *American Philanthropy* (Chicago: University of Chicago Press, 1960).

39. Grinstein, *Rise of the Jewish Community,* 135–61; Fisher, "Lending as Philanthropy"; Zmora, "Orphan Asylum," 475.

40. Morris Silverman, *Hartford Jews: 1659–1970* (Hartford: Connecticut Historical Society, 1970), 22; Allen A. Warsen, *Jewish Communal Institutions in Detroit* (Detroit: private printing, 1952), 25; Eleanor Horwitz, "The Years of the Jewish Woman," *Rhode Island Jewish Historical Notes* 7, no. 1 (1975): 152–70; Littlewood, *Horner of Illinois,* 11; Beth S. Wenger, "Jewish Women of the Club: The Changing Public Role of Atlanta's Jewish Women (1870–1930)," *AJH* 76, no. 3 (1987), 311–33; Kaganoff, "Jewish Welfare Activity," 30; Grinstein, *Rise of the Jewish Community,* 151–54; Lowenthal, "David Werner Amram," 375; Bernard, *Children You Gave Us,* 15–16; Toll, *Portland Jewry,* 42–51.

41. Philip Goodman, "The Purim Association of the City of New York (1862–1902)," *PAJHS* 40, no. 2 (1950): 135–72; Grinstein, *Rise of the Jewish Community,* 149–51; Feibelman, "New Orleans Jewish Community."

42. Ashton, "Rebecca Gratz," 215; Arthur A. Bielfeld, "A Study of the Home for Widows and Orphans of New Orleans Taken from the Minutes of the Meetings of the Association, 1855–1884" (Term paper, Hebrew Union College, 1962), American Jewish Archives, box 236.

43. Ashton, "Rebecca Gratz," 215; Bielfeld, "Widows and Orphans"; Fisher, "Lending as Philanthropy"; Grinstein, *Rise of the Jewish Community,* 158; Joseph Hirsh and Beka Doherty, *The First Hundred Years of the Mount Sinai Hospital of New York* (New York: Mt. Sinai Hospital, 1952).

44. Solomon, *Pioneers in Service,* 9.

45. Milton Doroshkin, *Yiddish in America: Social and Cultural Foundations* (Rutherford, N.J.: Farleigh Dickinson University Press, 1969), 137, 139, 230–31; Lamed Shapiro, "Immigratzia un Landsmanshaftn," in Works Progress Administration (WPA) in the City of New York, *Die Iddishe Landsmanshaftn Fun New York* (New York: Y. L. Peretz Writers' Union, 1938), 27–28; Baruch A. Weinrebe, "Die Sotziale Role Fun Der Landsmanshaftn," in WPA, *Die Iddishe Landsmanshaftn,* 70; Shlomo Gimplin, "A Lands-

manshaft Fun Der Elster Yiddisher Kehilla in New York," in WPA, *Die Iddishe Landsmanshaftn,* 113; Louis Levy, "Philanthropy: Philadelphia," in Charles S. Bernheimer, *The Russian Jew in the United States: Studies of Social Conditions in New York, Philadelphia, and Chicago, with a Description of Rural Settlements* (Philadelphia: John C. Winston, 1905), 83–84.

46. Nancy Moses Bloom, "The Inter-Relationship between American and Immigrant Jews in Washington, D.C., 1880–1915" (Master's thesis, George Washington University, 1970), 16; Rosenberg and Marmor, *Temple Beth El: A Centennial History of Beth El Hebrew Congregation,* 1.

47. Benjamin Rabinowitz, "The Young Men's Hebrew Associations (1854–1913)," *PAJHS* 37 (1947): 223.

48. Rabinowitz, "YMHA's" 232–33, 272.

49. Timothy Smith, *Revivalism and Social Reform in Mid-Nineteenth Century America* (New York: Abingdon Press, 1957).

50. Harvey Green, *Fit for America: Health, Fitness, Sport and American Society* (New York: Pantheon, 1986).

51. Rabinowitz, "YMHA's"; Alexander Dushkin, *Jewish Education in New York City* (New York: Board of Jewish Education, 1918), 60.

52. Burder, *History of All Religions,* 584; Michael N. Dobkowski, ed., *Jewish Voluntary Organizations* (New York: Greenwood, 1986), 118, 387.

53. Sadie S. Ratner, "United Order of True Sisters, New Haven, Number 4: 117 Years of Sisterhood and Beneficence," *Jews in New Haven* 3 (1981): 50–63.

54. Edward E. Grusd, *B'nai B'rith: The Story of a Covenant* (New York: Appleton-Century, 1966), 19.

55. Moore, *B'nai B'rith,* 7.

56. Edward M. Maline, "The Day to Day Activities of a Jewish Fraternity, 1870–1900" (Term paper, Hebrew Union College), American Jewish Archives, box 2270; see also "Record Book, Grand Prairie Lodge No. 281," American Jewish Archives, box 182.

57. "By-Laws of Grand Prairie Lodge No. 281, I.O.B.B. Champaign, Illinois, Adopted July 15, 1877," American Jewish Archives, box X182; "Applications for Membership, Grand Prairie Lodge, No. 281," ibid.

58. Grusd, *B'nai B'rith,* 13–24; Moore, *B'nai B'rith,* 13.

59. MHRSP, *Church and Synagogue Archives,* 18; Warsen, *Jewish Communal Institutions,* 25; "Proceedings of B'er Chayim Lodge No. 177 I.O.B.B., Cumberland, Maryland," American Jewish Archives, box 2235; Wax, "Isidor Bush," 186; Werner, *Julius Rosenwald,* 12; "Early Days of the Providence Jewish Community," *Rhode Island Jewish History Notes* 3, no. 3 (1960): 158.

60. Rubinger, "Albany Jewry," 286; "Record Book, Grand Prairie Lodge," 17 March, 1878; Silverman, *Hartford Jews,* 20.

61. "Proceedings of B'er Chayim Lodge," 20 October 1876, 19 November 1876; Grusd, *B'nai B'rith,* 17.

62. Phyllis Newman, "A San Bernardino Centennial: The Founding of Paradise Lodge No. 237, B'nai B'rith," *WSJHQ* 7, no. 4 (1975): 305.

63. Toll, *Portland Jewry,* 26.

64. Polster, "Member of the Herd"; Grusd, *B'nai B'rith,* 33–84.

Chapter Five. *Striving for the Sacred*

First epigraph from *The Hebrew*, 26 January 1872, 4; second epigraph quoted in Rose Greenberg, *The Chronicle of Baltimore Hebrew Congregation: 1830–1975* (Baltimore: Baltimore Hebrew Congregation, 1976), 17–18; third epigraph quoted in Ruth M. Patt, *The Jewish Scene in New Jersey's Raritan Valley* (New Brunswick: Jewish Historical Society of Raritan Valley, 1978), 34; fourth epigraph from *Occident* 14 (1856), quoted in Mostov, "Jewish Immigrants in Boston," 149.

1. The vast literature on American religion makes this point repeatedly. See, for example, Martin Marty, *Pilgrims in Their Own Land: 500 Years of Religion in America* (New York: Penguin Books, 1984); R. Laurence Moore, *Religious Outsiders and the Making of Americans* (New York: Oxford University Press, 1986).

2. Sidney Mead, "From Coercion to Persuasion: Another Look at the Rise of Religious Liberty and the Emergence of Denominationalism," *Church History* 25, no. 2 (1956): 317–37; H. Richard Niebuhr, *The Social Sources of Denominationalism* (New York: Henry Holt, 1929).

3. On Lutheranism, see, for example, "Immigration in the Nineteenth Century in Its Relation to the Lutheran Church in the United States," *Lutheran Church Review* 31, no. 2 (1912): 272–79; ibid., no. 3 (1912): 466–73; George M. Stephenson, *The Religious Aspects of Swedish Immigration: A Study of Immigrant Churches* (Minneapolis: University of Minnesota Press, 1932); Mead, *From Coercion to Persuasion*, 327; on Catholicism in the United States, see John Tracey Ellis, *American Catholicism* (Chicago: University of Chicago Press, 1955), 50; Edward Wakin and Joseph F. Scheuer, *The De-Romanization of the American Catholic Church* (New York: New American Library, 1966); see also Will Herberg, *Protestant, Catholic, Jew* (Garden City, New York: Doubleday, 1955).

4. Ann Douglas, *The Feminization of American Culture* (New York: Alfred A. Knopf, 1977).

5. *The Constitution of the Reformed Society of Israelites for Promoting True Principles of Judaism According to Its Purity and Spirit* (Charleston: B. Levy, 1825); Robert Liberles, "Conflict over Reform: The Case of Congregation Beth Elohim, Charlestown, South Carolina," in Wertheimer, *Sanctuary Transformed*, 274–96; Barnett Elzas, *The Jews of South Carolina from the Earliest Times to the Present Day* (Philadelphia: J. B. Lippincott, 1905), 151–64; Lou H. Silberman, "American Impact: Judaism in the United States in the Early Nineteenth Century," in A. Leland Jamison, ed., *Tradition and Change in Jewish Experience: The B. G. Rudolph Lectures in Judaic Studies* (Syracuse: Syracuse University, 1978), 89–105.

6. Leon Jick, *The Americanization of the Synagogue* (Hanover, N.H.: University Press of New England, 1976); Jerome W. Grollman, "The Emergence of Reform Judaism in the United States," *AJA* 2, no. 2 (1950): 3–14; Jonathan Sarna, "The Debate over Mixed Seating in the American Synagogue," in Wertheimer, *American Synagogue*, 363–94; Kay Kaufman Shelemay, "Music in the American Synagogue: A Case Study from Houston," in Wertheimer, *American Synagogue*, 395–415.

7. Lowenstein, "Religious Reform Movement"; Meyer, *Response to Modernity*.

8. Meyer, *Response to Modernity*; 248–50; 257–60.

9. See Hoffman, *Beyond the Text*, on the differences between *Minhag America* and *Olath Tamid*; Beryl Levy, *Reform Judaism in America: A Study in Religious Adaptation* (Menasha, Wis.: George Banta, 1933), 8.

10. Meyer, *Response to Modernity,* 233–63.

11. See, for example, Wirth, *The Ghetto,* 153–93; Judah David Eisenstein, "The History of the First Russian-American Jewish Congregation," *PAJHS* 9 (1901): 63–74.

12. Hardly a community study or congregational history lacks a discussion or story of the conflict between the rabbis and congregations, while biographies of individual rabbis are replete with the other side of the controversy.

13. At an annual banquet of New York's Shaare Zedek Congregation in 1844, the members decided to allow the women to watch the banquet from behind a curtain. This bold step was considered quite innovative and noteworthy. See Jacob Monsky, *Within the Gates: A Religious, Social and Cultural History: 1837–1962* (New York: Congregation Shaare Zedek, 1964), 46.

14. Philipson, *My Life,* 2.

15. Baton Rouge, Louisiana—Ladies Hebrew Association, *Constitution, January 29, 1871,* American Jewish Archives, box 687; Drachman, *Unfailing Light,* 25; Tom Owen, "The First Synagogue in Los Angeles," *WSJHQ* 1, no. 1 (1968): 9.

16. See, for example, Toll, *Portland Jewry,* 46.

17. Ashton, "Rebecca Gratz."

18. Sarna, "Mixed Seating."

19. I. Harold Sharfman, *The First Rabbi: Origins of Conflict between Orthodox and Reform: Jewish Polemic Warfare in pre-Civil War America: A Biographical History* (Malibu, Calif.: Pangloss Press, 1988); quoted in Max Heller, *Jubilee Souvenir of Temple Sinai, 1872–1922* (New Orleans, 1922), 43–44.

20. Sussman, "Isaac Leeser"; Lance J. Sussman, "Isaac Leeser and the Protestant-ization of American Judaism," *AJA* 38, no. 1 (1986): 1–21.

21. David Ellenson, "A Jewish Legal Decision by Rabbi Bernard Illowy of New Orleans and Its Discussion in Nineteenth Century Europe," *AJH* 69, no. 2 (1979): 174–95.

22. Jeffrey S. Gurock, *When Harlem Was Jewish: 1870–1930* (New York: Columbia University Press, 1979), 9.

23. Jick, *Americanization of the Synagogue,* 126–29.

24. Evelyn L. Greenberg, "Adas Israel 1869–1876: The Emergence of a Congregation," typescript; Rozenblit, "Choosing a Synagogue."

25. Ron Robin, "Jewish Architecture and Folk History in San Francisco," *Journal of the West* 26, no. 4 (1987): 67–73; Rachel B. Wischnitzer, *Synagogue Architecture in the United States* (Philadelphia: Jewish Publication Society of America, 1955), 5.

26. David Philipson, *The Oldest Jewish Congregation in the West (B'ne Israel, Cincinnati)* (Cincinnati: C. I. Krehbiel, 1984), 46.

27. Bruno Funaro, "American Synagogue Design: 1729–1939," *Architectural Record* 86, no. 5 (1939): 58–65; Wischnitzer, *Synagogue Architecture,* 6–7; Montgomery Schuyler, "A Great American Architect: Leopold Eidlitz," *Architectural Record* 24, no. 3 (1908): 164–79; Brian de Breffny, *The Synagogue* (New York: Macmillan, 1978); Rachel Wischnitzer, "Thomas U. Walter's Crown Street Synagogue, 1848–49," *Journal of the Society of Architectural Historians* 13, no. 4 (1954): 29–31.

28. Quoted in Heller, *Isaac M. Wise,* 58.

29. Many of the community and congregational histories allude to the first services in homes or commercial establishments. See, for example, "Memoirs of Zion Congregation," American Jewish Archives, Histories File.

30. Jonathan Sarna, *People Walk on Their Heads: Moses Weinberger's Jews and Judaism in New York* (New York: Holmes and Meier, 1981), 12; Glatstein, Niger, and Rogoff, *Finf Un Zibitzik Yor;* Greene, *American Immigrant Leaders,* 89–90; Abraham J. Karp, "New York Chooses a Chief Rabbi," *PAJHS* 44 (September 1954–June, 1955): 130–33; Glanz, "Vanguard to the Russians," 1–38; Krucoff, *Rodfei Zedek;* Israel Goldman, *Lifelong Learning among Jews: Adult Education in Judaism from Biblical Times to the Twentieth Century* (New York: KTAV, 1975), 252.

31. William M. Kramer and Norton B. Stern, "The Layman as Rabbinic Officiant in the Nineteenth Century," *WSJHQ* 16, no. 1 (1983): 49–53; Norton Stern, "Memoirs of Marcus Katz—San Bernadino Pioneer," *WSJHQ* 1, no. 1 (1968): 20–33.

32. "The First Jewish Sermon in the West: Yom Kippur, 1850, San Francisco," *WSJHQ* 10, no. 1 (1977): 3–5; Norton B. Stern, "Toward a Biography of Isaias W. Hellman—Pioneer Builder of California," *WSJHQ* 2, no. 1 (1969): 27–39; William M. Kramer, "David Solis-Cohen of Portland: Patriot, Pietist, Litterateur and Lawyer," *WSJHQ* 14, no. 1 (1981): 143; Gerald W. Johnson, *An Honorable Titan: A Biographical Study of Adolph S. Ochs* (New York: Harper and Brothers, 1946), 18; Bernard I. Nordlinger, "About my Grandfather, Bernard Nordlinger, Confederate Soldier and Unofficial Rabbi," *The Record* 3, no. 1 (1968): 26–27.

33. Emma Felsenthal, *Bernhard Felsenthal: Teacher in Israel: Selections from His Writings with Biographical Sketch and Bibliography* (New York: Oxford University Press, 1924), 20; Victor L. Ludlow, "Bernhard Felsenthal: Quest for Zion" (Ph.D. diss., Brandeis University, 1984); Joseph Gutmann, "Watchman on an American Rhine: New Light on Isaac M. Wise," *AJA* 10, no. 2 (1958): 135–43.

34. For the role of the cantor as religious functionary in the early communities, see Mark Slobin, *Chosen Voices: The Story of the American Cantorate* (Urbana: University of Illinois Press, 1989), 35–37; Beryl Segal, "Jewish Schools and Teachers in Metropolitan Providence—The First Century," *Rhode Island Jewish Historical Notes* 7, no. 3 (1977): 410.

35. Some references from traditionalists such as Isaac Leeser and Abraham Rice indicate that men who married non-Jewish women were not likely to circumcise their sons, and this practice raised problems when, for example, the father wanted to have the sons participate in the synagogue or, if they died, be buried according to the Jewish rite. See Sharfman, *First Rabbi,* 113–18.

36. Allen du Pont Breck, *The Centennial History of the Jews of Colorado* (Denver: University of Denver Press, 1960), 23; Charles Weiss, "A Worldwide Survey of the Current Practice of *Milha* (Ritual Circumcision)," *Jewish Social Studies* 24, no. 1 (1962): 32; Greenberg, "Perception of America," 318.

37. Comparative statements about levels of personal piety in Europe and the United States are riddled with evidentiary problems. While in small, traditional European Jewish communities everyone probably did conform to the code of kashrut, Sabbath, family purity, and other laws, Jews in Europe were also migrating to cities there as part of the process of modernization. Assertions about the level of personal observance in European cities are much more problematic, and it is not possible to claim that Jews in New York kept kosher more or less than Jews in Frankfurt, Posen, Budapest, or Prague.

38. Discussion of the degree to which American Jews observed kashrut in the nineteenth century are complicated by problems of evidence. First, no hard data is available as to how many Jews bought kosher meat, how many maintained separate

dairy and meat dishes, and the like, and therefore only conjectures can be made from the scattered sources. Secondly, we have no way of measuring the change from Europe to the United States. That is, no firm body of evidence can prove how rigorously or laxly the Jews in Europe at the same time, or before migration, adhered to kashrut either. What we have, however, are comments, often made by the traditionalists who harbored negative feelings about observance in America in general, that American Jews differed dramatically from their European coreligionists. On the structural problems of kashrut in America, see Harold P. Gastwirt, *Fraud, Corruption, and Holiness: The Controversy over the Supervision of Jewish Dietary Practice in New York City, 1881–1940* (Port Washington, N.Y.: Kennikat Press, 1974), 21–26; Samuel Krislov, "'Church,' State and *Kashrut*: Some Hidden Dimensions of Pluralism," *Jewish Social Studies* 25, no. 3 (1963): 174–85; Jeremiah Berman, *Shehita: A Study in the Cultural and Social Life of the Jewish People* (New York: Bloch, 1941), 273, 285–95, 350–65.

39. Levy, *Jewish Cookery Book,* 3.

40. Frank L. Byrne and Jean Powers Soman, *Your True Marcus: The Civil War Letters of a Jewish Colonel* (Kent, Ohio: Kent State University Press, 1985), 6; quoted in Hertzberg, *Strangers within the Gate City,* 67; W. Gunther Plaut, *Mount Zion: 1856–1956* (St. Paul, Minn.: Mt. Zion Hebrew Congregation, 1956), 23.

41. "Early Nevada City Jewry, A Picture Story," *WSJHQ* 16, no. 2 (1984): 160.

42. Drachman, *Unfailing Light,* 18.

43. See, for example, "Record of the Congregation Ahavat Achim Brotherly Love Bangor State of Maine, Pennobscot County (1850)," American Jewish Archives, box 1178; "History of Mizpah Congregation, Chattanooga, Tennessee," American Jewish Archives, Histories File; Kohn, *Jewish Community of Utica,* 17; Winograd, "The Horse Died at Windber," 116; Sam Shankman, *Baron Hirsch Congregation: From Ur to Memphis* (Jackson, Tenn.: Baron Hirsch Congregation, 1957), 19–20; *Weekly Gleaner,* 10 April 1857.

44. *American Israelite,* 15 September 1865; Rochlin, *Pioneer Jews,* 205; Paul Menitoff, "The Akron Jewish Community, 1865–1965, as Reflected in the Records Deposited in the American Jewish Archives," American Jewish Archives, box 1533; Benjamin Band, *Portland Jewry: Its Growth and Development* (Portland, Maine: Jewish Historical Society, 1955), 8; Martha B. Katz-Hyman, "A Note on Rabbi Moses Ziskind Finesilver, 1847–1922," *Rhode Island Jewish Historical Notes* 7, no. 3 (1977): 430; Zweig, *Hundred and Twenty-Five years,* 3; Schmier, *Reflections of Southern Jewry,* 40–41; Berman, "Jewish Religious Observance," 35–38.

45. See, for example, Biefeld, "Widows and Orphans."

46. Edgar M. Kahn, "The Saga of the First Fifty Years of Congregation Emanu-El, San Francisco," *WSJHQ* 3, no. 3 (1971): 135; Saul J. Rubin, *Third to None: The Saga of Savannah Jewry, 1733–1983* (Savannah, Ga.: Mickve Israel, 1983), 113; Auerbach, "Jewish Settlement in Nebraska," 33; Fein, *American Jewish Community,* 52; Adler and Connolly, *From Ararat to Suburbia,* 50.

47. Kaplan, "Century of Adjustment," 126; "Columbus, Ohio. Temple Israel. Condensed Minutes of the Congregation from 1868 to 1939," American Jewish Archives, Histories Collection; Raphael, *Jews and Judaism,* 64; Adler, *Roots in Moving Stream,* xiii; see also Trachtenberg, *Consider the Days,* 155.

48. Bloom, *Autobiography,* 12.

49. Auerbach, "Jewish Settlement in Nebraska," 33; Marans, *Jews in Greater Washington,* 11. Abraham A. Neuman, "Cyrus Adler: A Biographical Sketch," *American*

Jewish Yearbook: 5701, 42: 25; Aminoff, "Jews of Ann Arbor," 5; Rochlin, *Pioneer Jews,* 205; see also, Ehrlich, "Jewish Community of St. Louis," 509; David Philipson, "The Cincinnati Community in 1825," *PAJHS* 10 (1902): 98.

50. Mann, *Growth and Achievement;* Hoffman, *Beyond the Text,* 165.

51. Richard Gottheil, *The Life of Gustav Gottheil: Memoir of a Priest in Israel* (Williamsport, Pa.: Bayard Press, 1936), 16; Berman, "Jewish Religious Observance," 31–53; Leon Jick, "The Reform Synagogue," in Wertheimer, *American Synagogue,* 91; *History of Congregation Adath Israel, Louisville, Kentucky and Addresses Delivered at the Dedication of Its New Temple: September 7, 8, and 9, 1906* (Louisville, n.p., 1906), 14; Kerr Olitzky, "The Sunday-Sabbath Movement in American Reform Judaism: Strategy or Evolution?," *AJA* 34, no. 1 (1982): 75–88; Kerr Olitzky, "Sundays at Chicago Sinai Congregation: Paradigm for a Movement," *AJH* 74, no. 4 (1985): 356–68.

52. William M. Kramer, "The Western Journal of Isaac Mayer Wise," *WSJHQ* 5, no. 1 (1972): 51; ibid. no. 2 (1973): 131; Hoffman, *Beyond the Text,* 165; Kussy, "Reminiscences of Jewish Life," 182.

53. Robert Shosteck and Samuel H. Holland, "Adolphus Simeon Solomons: His Washington Years," *The Record* 5, no. 1 (1970): 15, 23; Solomon, *Fabric of My Life,* 16; Gerstley, "Reminiscences"; Adler, *Jacob H. Schiff,* 4–5; Victoria Jacobs, *Diary of a San Diego Girl—1856* (Santa Monica, Calif.: Norton B. Stern, 1974); *Jewish Messenger,* 2, no. 2 (1857): 13.

54. Patt, *Jewish Scene,* 16–17; Berman, "Jewish Religious Observance," 44–46.

55. Berman, "Jewish Religious Observance," 47–49; Kussy, "Reminiscences of Jewish Life," 182–83.

56. Hyman B. Grinstein, "In the Course of the Nineteenth Century," in Judah Pilch, ed., *A History of Jewish Education in America* (New York: American Association for Jewish Education, 1969), 28.

57. *Occident,* 7 (1848): 431–35; Walter Ackerman, "Some Uses of Justification in Jewish Education," *AJS Review* 2 (1977): 9.

58. William Chomsky, "Beginnings of Jewish Education in America," *Gratz College Annual of Jewish Studies* 5 (1976): 7; Jeremiah Berman, "Jewish Education in New York City, 1860–1900," *YIVO Annual of Jewish Social Science* (1954): 247–75; Israel Friedlaender, *The Problem of Jewish Education in America and the Bureau of Jewish Education of the Jewish Community of New York City,* Report of the Commissioner of Education for the Year Ending June 30, 1913 (Washington, D.C.: Department of the Interior, 1913), 365–93; Dushkin, *Jewish Education,* 33, 42–62.

59. Zevi Scharfstein, *Haheder Behayei Ameinu* (Tel Aviv: Newman Publishing, 1951), 51.

60. Sussman, "Isaac Leeser," 13; Jonathan Sarna, *JPS: The Americanization of Jewish Culture, 1888–1988* (Philadelphia: Jewish Publication Society of America, 1989), 1–4; Bernard Wishy, *The Child and the Republic: The Dawn of Modern American Child Nurture* (Philadelphia: University of Pennsylvania Press, 1967).

61. The education of Jewish girls in America has received even less attention than that of boys. Yet, the congregational and communal histories provide at least the outlines of the emergence of Jewish coeducation in America.

62. Eduard L. Rauch, "Jewish Education in the United States: 1840–1920" (Ph.D. diss., Harvard University, 1978), 30; Ackerman, "Jewish Education," 1–44; Grinstein, "Nineteenth Century," 32; Lander, "Jewish Religious Education."

63. Berman, "Jewish Education," 254.

64. Ackerman, "Jewish Education," 5

65. Rothschild, "Atlanta Jewry," 242–49; *AJHQ* 62, no. 3. (March, 1973): 242–49; Louis Ginsberg, *History of the Jews of Petersburg: 1789–1950* (Petersburg, Va.: Williams Printing Company, 1954), 25; *Occident*, 15 (1857): 45–46; *Jewish Messenger*, 1 (1857): 4; "The News from Woodland and Oroville, California, in 1879," *WSJHQ* 11, no. 2 (1979): 162–63; "Calvert, Texas: Two Views—1880," *WSJHQ* 14, no. 1 (1981): 119.

66. Julia Richman, "The Jewish Sunday School Movement in the United States," *Jewish Quarterly Review* 12 (July 1900): 563–92; Uriah Z. Engelman, "Jewish Education in Charleston, South Carolina, during the Eighteenth and Nineteenth Centuries," *PAJHS* 42, no. 1 (1952): 43–70; Joseph R. Rosenbloom, "Rebecca Gratz and the Jewish Sunday School Movement in Philadelphia," *PAJHS* 48, no. 1–4 (September 1958—June 1959): 71–77; on the cultural meaning of the Christian Sunday school movement, see Anne M. Boylan, *Sunday School: The Formation of an American Institution, 1790–1880* (New Haven: Yale University Press, 1987).

67. The meaning of the existence of mikvaot is a thorny problem for historical analysis. Since a mikvah was used for several purposes, including fulfillment of the commandments of family purity, making dishes kosher, conversion ceremonies, and possibly also just for the purposes of male bathing, it is not always possible to find out why a community built and maintained one.

68. *Weekly Gleaner*, 10 April 1857.

69. Sharfman, *First Rabbi*, 144–46; Fein, *American Jewish Community*, 52; Trachtenberg, *Consider the Years*, 130; Adler and Connolly, *From Ararat to Suburbia*, 68, 98, 154; Joseph Gutmann, "Religious Life in the Old Northwest, on the Eve of the Civil War, As Reflected in the Minutes of Congregation Tifereth Israel, 1850–1860" (Term paper, Hebrew Union College), American Jewish Archives, Miscellaneous File; Beryl Segal, "Congregation Sons of Zion, Providence, Rhode Island: The Orms Street Synagogue," *Rhode Island Jewish Historical Notes* 4, no. 3 (1965): 274; Gerstley, "Reminiscences"; Abraham Feldman, *Remember the Days of Old: An Outline History of the Congregation Beth Israel, 1843–1943* (Hartford, Conn.: n.p. 1943), 25.

70. J. Goldner, "A Gold Rush Community in 1873," *WSJHQ* 9, no. 3 (1977): 216; almost every study of Jewish communities outside of the pre-1820s settlements indicates that the first time that Jews got together for worship was during the high holidays; those same studies catalog the yearly newspaper references to the holidays and to the Jewish business closures.

71. "Yom Kippur, San Francisco, 1858," *WSJHQ* 18, no. 1 (1985): 76; Zweig, *Hundred and Twenty-Five Years*, 8.

72. Rudolf Glanz, *The Jews in American Alaska (1867–1880)* (New York: private printing, 1953), 24; Frank, *Five Families*, 123; Kaplan, *Eternal Stranger*, 40; Adler, "Zebulon B. Vance," 359; Sulman, *Goodly Heritage*, 7; Kohn, *Jewish Community of Utica*, 17; on other elements in American Passover observance, see Jonathan Sarna, "Passover Raisin Wine, The American Temperance Movement, and Mordecai Noah: The Origins, Meaning, and Wider Significance of a Nineteenth-Century American Jewish Religious Practice," *Hebrew Union College Annual* 59 (1988): 269–88.

73. Fein, *American Jewish Community*, 150, is just one of many references to charitable Purim balls among nineteenth-century American Jews.

74. Hertz, *Jewish High Society*, 204–50.

75. Grinstein, *Jewish Community of New York*, 340, 346, 369, 372–87; Malcolm

H. Stern, "Jewish Marriage and Intermarriage in the Federal Period (1776–1840)," manuscript, American Jewish Archives; Rosenwaike, *On the Edge of Greatness*, 53.

76. Rochlin, *Pioneer Jews*, 90.

77. Jack Steinberg, *United for Worship and Charity: A History of Congregation Children of Israel* (Augusta, Ga.: Phoenix Commercial Printers, 1983), 2.

78. Flexner, *I Remember*, 13; Rochlin, *Pioneer Jews*, 83–89; Korn, *Early Jews of New Orleans*, 203.

79. Moses Mielziner, "Upon the Intermarriage Question," *American Israelite*, 28 May 1880; S. H. Sonneschein, "Should a Rabbi Perform the Ceremonies at the Intermarriage between Jew and Gentile?" *American Israelite*, 7 and 14 May 1880; Diane M. Lichtenstein, "On Whose Native Ground? Nineteenth Century Myths of American Womanhood and Jewish Women Writers" (Ph.D. diss., University of Pennsylvania, 1985); Grusd, *B'nai B'rith*, 73; on congregations, see, for example, *History of Congregation Adath Israel*, 13; Paul R. Spickard, *Mixed Blood: Intermarriage and Ethnic Identity in Twentieth Century America* (Madison: University of Wisconsin Press, 1989), 170–72.

80. The absence of statistical data poses a problem on the issue of conversions to Judaism. Yet it seems possible to say that they were more common in the United States than in Europe. Conversion to Judaism was, for example, forbidden by Prussian law until the 1830s. European rabbis, such as Akiba Eger, supported this ban. See David Max Eichhorn, ed., *Conversion to Judaism: A History and Analysis* (New York: KTAV, 1965), 137; on Christian conversion to Judaism in Vienna, see Rozenblit, *Jews of Vienna*, 140.

81. Eichhorn, *Conversion to Judaism*, 141; Esther E. Rawidowicz, "I. L. Chronik and His *Zeichen Der Zeit*," in Rawidowicz, *Chicago Pinkas*, 163.

82. Byrne and Soman, *Your True Marcus*, 6; Ashkenazi, "Creoles of Jerusalem," 45, 62; George J. Fogelson, "A Conversion At Santa Cruz, California, 1877," *WSJHQ* 11, no. 2 (1979): 138–44.

Chapter Six. Looking Outward

First epigraph from Benjamin, *Three Years in America*, 235; second epigraph quoted in Joakim Isaacs, "Candidate Grant and the Jews," *AJA* 17, no. 1 (1965): 12–13; third epigraph from *Savannah Republican*, 17 September 1862.

1. Quoted in Lawrence H. Fuchs, ed., *American Ethnic Politics* (New York: Harper and Row, 1968), 12; Waldo Edward Emerson and Waldo Emerson Forbes, *Journals of Ralph Waldo Emerson* (Boston: Houghton Mifflin, 1900–1914), 7:115–16.

2. Lawrence A. Cremin, ed., *The Republic and the School: Horace Mann "On the Education of Free Men"* (New York: Teachers College Press, 1957), 87.

3. See biographical sketches of Jewish merchants who participated in nineteenth-century politics, such as Goodman, "Jewish Peddler's Diary," 45–73; Hacker and Hirsch, *Proskauer: His Life and Times*, 13; Norton B. Stern, "Louis Phillips and the Pomona Valley: Rancher and Real Estate Investor," *WSJHQ* 16, no. 1 (1983): 54–81; Karsh, "Mannasse Chico," 45–54; Fleishaker, "Illinois-Iowa Jewish Community," 21–22; Louis J. Swichkow and Lloyd P. Gartner, *The History of the Jews of Milwaukee* (Philadelphia: Jewish Publication Society of America, 1963), 19; Byrne and Soman, *Your True Marcus*, 8; Bertram Wallace Korn, "The Jews of Mobile, Alabama, Prior to the Organization of

the First Congregation in 1841," *HUC Annual* 40–41 (1969–1970): p. 495; Adler, *Roots in Moving Stream,* 7; Toll, *Portland Jewry,* 79–80.

4. On nineteenth-century localism, see Robert Wiebe, *The Search for Order: 1877–1920* (New York: Hill and Wang, 1967); for some names of Jewish officeholders in the Western region, see Rudd, "Jewish Frontier," 252–54.

5. Mazur, "Chicago Jewry," 96.

6. Vorspan and Gartner, *Jews of Los Angeles,* 17; Swichkow, "Jewish Community of Milwaukee," 46.

7. Arthur M. Silver, "Jews in the Political Life of New York City, 1865–1897," (Ph.D. diss., Yeshiva University, 1954); Lawrence H. Fuchs, *The Political Behavior of American Jews* (Glencoe, Ill.: Free Press, 1956), 29–43.

8. Silver, "Jews in Political Life," 13; Mazur, "Chicago Jewry," 89–90.

9. *Occident* 12 (February 1855): 561–63; *Occident* 7 (November 1879): 1.

10. Nodel, *The Ties Between,* 11; Lowenstein, *Jews of Oregon,* 66–67.

11. Sandberg, *Jewish Life in Los Angeles,* 27; Barry E. Herman, "Maier Zunder: New Haven's First Jewish School Board Member," *Jews in New Haven* 1 (1978): 12; Goodman, "Jewish Peddler's Diary," 45; Stern, "Marcus Katz," 31; Silver, "Jews in Political Life," 30; Toll, *Portland Jewry,* 80; for a listing of Jews in Congress, see *American Jewish Yearbook: 1900–1901,* (Philadelphia: Jewish Publication Society of America, 1901), 517–24.

12. Irena P. Narell, "Bernhard Marks: Retailer, Miner, Educator and Land Developer," *WSJHQ* 8, no. 1 (1975): 30–31; Robert Rockaway, "Anti-Semitism in an American City: Detroit, 1850–1914," *AJHQ* 64, no. 1 (1974): 42–54; Robert Rockaway, *The Jews of Detroit from the Beginning, 1762–1914* (Detroit: Wayne State University Press, 1986), 23; Wolf and Whiteman, *Jews of Philadelphia,* 299.

13. Liberles, "Conflict over Reform," 274–96.

14. Israel Goldstein, *A Century of Judaism in New York: B'nai Jeshurun, 1825–1925* (New York: Congregation B'nai Jeshurun, 1930), 120; Heller, *Isaac M. Wise,* 321–59; "Letters in Cincinnati, Ohio, Newspapers from Several Cincinnati Jews Condemning Wise, re: Dred Scott," American Jewish Archives, Miscellaneous File; Morris B. Margolies, "The American Career of Rabbi Henry Vidaver," *WSJHQ* 16, no. 1 (1983): 30–32; Fein, *American Jewish Community,* 96–98; Benny Kraut, *From Reform Judaism to Ethical Culture: The Religious Evolution of Felix Adler* (Cincinnati: Hebrew Union College Press, 1979), 17.

15. Bielfeld, "Widows and Orphans"; Bernard, *Children You Gave Us,* 9.

16. Abram Simon, *A History of the Washington Hebrew Congregation: In Commemoration of Its Jubilee* (Washington, D.C.: Lippman Printing, 1905), 19; U.S. Congress, *Report of the Committee on District of Columbia on the Memorial of the Washington Hebrew Congregation,* 34th Cong., Dept. 58.

17. See, for example, Breck, *Centennial History,* 10.

18. Berman, *Shehita,* 285–87; Krislov, "'Church,' State and *Kashrut,*" 174–85.

19. Fein, *American Jewish Community,* 114–17; Liberles, "Conflict over Reform," 290–91; Eisenstein, *Ozar Zikhronothai,* 248.

20. E. Milton Altfeld, *The Jew's Stand for Religious and Civil Liberty in Maryland* (Baltimore: M. Curlander, 1924); Morton Borden, *Jews, Turks, and Infidels* (Chapel Hill: University of North Carolina Press, 1984), 37–42; Fein, *American Jewish Community,* 25–44; *Worthington's Speech on the Maryland Test Act, 1824* (Baltimore: William Wooddy, 1824).

21. Borden, *Jews, Turks, and Infidels*, 36–42.

22. Simon Wolf, *The Presidents I Have Known from 1860–1918* (Washington, D.C.: Byron S. Adams, 1918), 205.

23. Sol M. Stroock, "Switzerland and the American Jews," in Abraham J. Karp, ed., *The Jewish Experience in America*, vol. 3 (Waltham, Mass.: American Jewish Historical Society, 1969), 78–81; "Article: *Cincinnati Commercial*, 25 February 1851," American Jewish Archives, Miscellaneous File.

24. Albert M. Friedenberg, "The Jews and the American Sunday Laws," *PAJHS* 11 (1903): 101–15; Borden, *Jews, Turks, and Infidels*, 11–125.

25. "Anti-Jewish Sentiment in California, 1855," *AJA* 12, no. 1 (1960): 15–33; Stern, "Los Angeles Jewry," 312–22.

26. For some scattered reference to Jewish public school attendance, see David Philipson, "Personal Contacts with the Founder of the Hebrew Union College," *HUC Annual* 11 (1936): 2; Morgenthau, *All in a Life-Time*, 6; Drachman, *Unfailing Light*, 2, 7; Adler, *Louis Marshall*, 6; Simon Litman, *Ray Frank Litman: A Memoir* (New York: American Jewish Historical Society, 1957), 4; Goldowsky Seebert, "Bernard Manuel Goldowsky, 1864-1936," *Rhode Island Jewish Historical Notes* 6, no. 1 (1971): 85; Selma Berrol, "Who Went to School in Mid-Nineteenth Century New York? An Essay in the New Urban History," in Irwin Yellowitz, ed., *Essays in the History of New York City: A Memorial to Sidney Pomerantz* (Port Washington, New York: Kennikat Press, 1978), 43–60; Ida Cohen Selavan, "The Education of Jewish Immigrants in Pittsburgh, 1862–1932," *YIVO Annual of Jewish Social Science* 15 (1974): 126–44.

27. Selavan, "Education of Jewish Immigrants"; Gerstley, "Reminiscences"; Mesinger, "Jewish Community in Syracuse," 208; Goldstein, *Congregation Anshe-Emeth*, 28.

28. Ackerman, "Jewish Education," 12.

29. Cohen, *Encounter with Emancipation*, 92; Diane Ravitch, *The Great School Wars: New York City, 1805-1973: A History of the Public Schools as a Battlefield of Social Change* (New York: Basic Books, 1974), 52–53.

30. "Condensed Minutes of the Congregation from 1868 to 1939," Columbus, Ohio, Temple Israel, American Jewish Archives, Histories File; Michael Perka, "The Building Up of Zion: Religion and Education in Nineteenth Century Cincinnati," *Cincinnati Historical Society Bulletin* 38 (1980): 97–114; Robert Michaelson, *Piety in the Public School: Trends and Issues in the Relationship between Religion and the Public School in the United States* (New York: Macmillan, 1970), 89; Heller, *Isaac Mayer Wise*, 620.

31. Jonathan D. Sarna, *Jacksonian Jew: The Two Worlds of Mordecai Noah* (New York: Holmes and Meier, 1981), 61–75.

32. Joseph Jacobs, "The Damascus Affair of 1840 and the Jews of America," *PAJHS* 10 (1902): 119–28; *Persecutions of The Jews in The East. Containing The Proceedings of a Meeting Held At The Synagogue Mikveh Israel, Philadelphia, On Thursday Evening, the 28th of Ab, 5600. Corresponding with the 27th of August, 1840* (Philadelphia: C. Sherman and Company, 1840).

33. Bertram W. Korn, *The American Reaction to the Mortara Case: 1858-1859* (Cincinnati: American Jewish Archives, 1957).

34. Gartner, "Consul Peixotto," 25–117; Wolf, *Presidents I Have Known*, 76.

35. Wolf, *Presidents I Have Known*, 86–87; Gary Dean Best, *To Free a People: Jewish Leaders and the Jewish Problem in Eastern Europe, 1890-1914* (Westport, Conn.: Greenwood Press, 1982), 8–10; Evelyn Levow Greenberg, "An 1869 Petition on Behalf of Russian Jews," *AJHQ* 54, no. 3 (1965): 278–95.

36. Gartner, "Consul Peixotto," 33.

37. Max J. Kohler, "The Board of Delegates of American Israelites, 1859–1878," *PAJHS* 29 (1925): 75–131; Allan Tarshish, "The Board of Delegates of American Israelites (1859–1878)," *PAJHS* 49, no. 1 (1959): 16–32; on the relationship between the Board of Delegates and its European counterpart, the Alliance Israelite Universelle, see Zosa Szajkowski, "The Alliance Israelite Universelle in the United States, 1860–1949," *PAJHS* 39, no. 4 (1950): 389–443.

38. Shosteck and Holland, "Adolphus Simeon Solomons," 13–23; Abram V. Goodman, "Adolphus S. Solomons and Clara Barton: A Forgotten Chapter in the Early Years of the American Red Cross," *AJHQ* 59, no. 3 (1970): 331–56.

39. David H. and Esther L. Panitz, "Simon Wolf as United States Consul to Egypt," *PAJHS* 47, no. 2 (1957): 76–100; Samuel Reznick, "Simon Wolf—Public Servant and Spokesman for the Oppressed," *The Record* 9, no. 1 (1978): 31–33; Panitz, *Simon Wolf;* Wolf, *Presidents I Have Known.*

40. On Jews as supporters of slavery, see Korn, *Jews and Negro Slavery;* on Jews as abolitionists, see Louis Ruchames, "The Abolitionists and the Jews," *PAJHS* 42, no. 2 (1952): 131–56; Max J. Kohler, "The Jews and the American Anti-Slavery Movement," *PAJHS* 5 (1897): 137–55; Jayme A. Sokolow, "Revolution and Reform: The Antebellum Jewish Abolitionists," *Journal of Ethnic Studies* 9, no. 1 (1981): 28–41.

41. Bertram W. Korn, *American Jewry and the Civil War* (Philadelphia: Jewish Publication Society of America, 1961); Simon Wolf, *The American Jew as Patriot, Soldier and Citizen* (Philadelphia: Levytype Company, 1895).

42. On the involvement of Jewish women in civilian support efforts for both sides, see Stanley R. Brav, "The Jewish Woman, 1861–1865," *AJA* 17, no. 1 (1965): 55–65.

43. Gutstein, *Priceless Heritage,* 33.

44. John Hope Franklin, *From Slavery to Freedom: A History of Negro Americans* (New York: Alfred A. Knopf, 1967), 263.

45. Grusd, *B'nai B'rith,* 58.

46. Audrey Daniels Kariel, "The Jewish Story and Memories of Marshall, Texas," *WSJHQ* 14, no. 3 (1982): 196.

47. Bertram W. Korn, "Jewish Chaplains during the Civil War," *AJA* 1, no. 1 (1948): 6–7.

48. Louis Barish, "The American Jewish Chaplaincy," *AJHQ* 52, no. 1 (1962): 9–11; Tarshish, "Board of Delegates," 22; "Petitions Contained in the U.S. Senate Files Treating with the Subject of Jewish Chaplains," American Jewish Archives, Documents Collection.

49. Stanley F. Chyet, "Ohio Valley Jewry during the Civil War," *Bulletin of the Historical and Philosophical Society of Ohio* 21, no. 3 (1963): 180, 187.

50. Louis Schmier, "Notes and Documents on the 1862 Expulsion of Jews from Thomasville, Georgia," *AJA* 32, no. 1 (1980): 9–22; Bertram Wallace Korn, "American Judaeophobia: Confederate Version," in Leonard Dinnerstein and Mary Dale Palsson, eds., *Jews in the South* (Baton Rouge: Louisiana State University Press, 1973), 137–55.

51. Stephen V. Ash, "Civil War Exodus: The Jews and Grant's General Order No. 11," *The Historian* 44, no. 4 (1982): 505–23; "Petition of Protest to Pres. Lincoln by Missouri Lodge B'nai B'rith, St. Louis," American Jewish Archives, Documents Collection.

52. Edmund Wilson, *Patriotic Gore: Studies in the Literature of the American Civil War* (New York: Oxford University Press, 1966).

53. Dean Sprague, *Freedom under Lincoln* (Boston: Houghton Mifflin, 1965).

54. Isaacs, "Candidate Grant," 3–16; Norton B. Stern, "Mayor Strauss of Tucson," *WSJHQ* 12, no. 3 (1980): 348–49; Norton B. Stern, "Los Angeles Jewish Voters during Grant's First Presidential Race," *WSJHQ* 13, no. 2 (1981): 179–85; Panitz, *Simon Wolf,* 32–34.

55. Katz, *Jews and Freemasons;* Dorothy Ann Lipson, *Freemasonry in Federalist Connecticut* (Princeton: Princeton University Press, 1977), 3–9, 112, 143–45, 163–67, 253; Lynn Dumenil, *Freemasonry and American Culture, 1880–1930* (Princeton: Princeton University Press, 1984), 54–55, 69–70; Allen E. Roberts, *Freemasonry in American History* (Richmond, Va.: Macoy Publishing and Masonic Supply Company, 1985).

56. On Masonic use of Hebrew and Jewish symbols, see *Mackey's Symbolism of Freemasonry: Its Science, Philosophy, Legends, Myths and Symbols* (1869, reprint Chicago: Masonic History Company, 1945); Albert G. Mackey, *A Text-Book of Masonic Jurisprudence; Illustrating the Written and Unwritten Laws of Freemasonry* (New York: Macoy and Sickels, 1865); "Masonic Certificate, F 20, 1860, Given to Lewis Beekman," American Jewish Archives, Documents File. Numerous references document the widespread Jewish membership in Masonic lodges in America. See, for example, Albert M. Friedenberg, "A List of Jews Who Were Grand Masters of Masons in Various States of This Country," *PAJHS* 19 (1910): 95–100; Joseph Friedman, "Jewish Participation in California Gold Rush Era Freemasonry," *WSJHQ* 176, no. 4 (1984): 294–95; Kaplan, "Century of Adjustment," 217; Cowen, *Memories of American Jew,* 22; David C. Adelman, "Congregation of the Sons of Israel and David (Temple Beth El), The Early Years," *Rhode Island Jewish Historical Notes* 3, no. 4 (1960): 196.

57. Ehrlich, "Jewish Community of St. Louis," 519.

58. Menitoff, "Akron Jewish Community," Heller, *Jubilee Souvenir,* 55; Morris Sherman, *Hartford Jews: 1659–1970* (Hartford: Connecticut Historical Society, 1970), 11; Rubin, *Savannah Jewry,* 65; Rothschild, *As But a Day,* 10; "Petersburg Lodge No. 15, A.F. and A.M.," American Jewish Archives, Histories File.

59. Alice Greenwald, "The Masonic Mizrah and Lamp: Jewish Ritual Art as a Reflection of Cultural Assimilation," *Journal of Jewish Art* 10 (1984): 87–101; Norman L. Kleeblatt and Gerard C. Wertkin, *The Jewish Heritage in American Folk Art* (New York: Universe Books, 1984), 52, 60.

60. C. A. Rubenstein, *History of Har Sinai Congregation of the City of Baltimore* (Baltimore: Kohn and Pollock, 1918), 7.

61. "Problems of a Nevada Jewish Community in 1875," *WSJHQ* 8, no. 2 (1976): 160–62.

62. Quoted in Greenwald, "Masonic Mizrah and Lamp," 95.

63. Norton B. Stern and William M. Kramer, "Jewish Padre to the Pueblo: Pioneer Los Angeles Rabbi Abraham Wolf Edelman," *WSJHQ* 3, no. 4 (1971): 198.

64. Roberts, *Freemasonry,* 85; Tony Fels, "Religious Assimilation in a Fraternal Organization: Jews and Freemasonry in Gilded-Age San Francisco," *American Jewish History* 74, no. 4 (1985): 369–403.

65. Winograd, "The Horse Died at Windber," 38.

66. For some references on Jews and the Odd Fellows, see Mesinger, "Jewish Community in Syracuse," 207; Sulman, *Goodly Heritage,* 63; Reva Clar, "Early Stockton Jewry and Its Cantor-Rabbi Herman Davidson," *WSJHQ* 5, no. 2 (1933): 67; "Goodman and Rimpau, Anaheim," *WSJHQ* 16, no. 2 (1983): 83; Francine Landau,

"Solomon Lazard of Los Angeles," *WSJHQ* 5, no. 3 (1973): 153; Samuel Reznick, "Early Jews of Riverside," *WSJHQ* 12, no. 2 (1980): 102; on Jewish membership in the Knights of Pythias, see Walter P. Zand, "The Jews of Port Chester" (Ph.D. diss., Yeshiva University, 1956), 19–20; Clyde and Sally Griffen, *Natives and Newcomers: The Ordering of Opportunity in Mid-Nineteenth Century Poughkeepsie* (Cambridge: Harvard University Press, 1978), 30; Blum, *Jews of Baltimore*, 203.

67. Anderson, "Jews of Toledo," 94; "A Memorial for a Blue-Collar Bavarian-Born, San Francisco Forty-Niner," *WSJHQ* 14, no. 1 (1981): 43; Rosenberg, *Pioneer Texas Merchants*, 35; Gendler, "Jews of Omaha," 209; Aminoff, "Jews of Ann Arbor," 6; Ruth S. Baker, "Henry Strauss: An Alexandrian Leader," *The Record* 7, no. 1 (1974): 16.

68. There is no literature on the Order of the Eastern Star comparable to that about Masonry, and, therefore, generalization about Jewish women's membership is tentative at best. Furthermore, few histories of Jewish communities make reference to Jewish women's membership in non-Jewish organizations. It is, however, not clear if that is because they did not belong or because their activities were unrecorded or if the historians just did not consider this an important element in the development of the community. For two exceptions, see Bloom, "American and Immigrant Jews," 12; Fogelson, "Jews of Santa Cruz," 101.

69. See, for example, Ashton, "Rebecca Gratz."

70. Herman Eliassof, *German-American Jews* (Chicago: German-American Historical Society of Illinois, 1915), 5.

71. Michele Helene Pavin, "Sports and Leisure of the American Jewish Community: 1848 to 1976" (Ph.D. diss., Ohio State University, 1981), 166; Toll, *Portland Jewry*, 54.

72. William M. Kramer and Norton B. Stern, "The Turnverein: A German Experience for Western Jewry," *WSJHQ* 16, no. 3 (1984): 227–29; "America's Top Sharpshooter," *WSJHQ* 9, no. 1 (1976): 43–45; Pavin, "Sports and Leisure," 163; Swichkow and Gartner, *Jews of Milwaukee*, 54.

73. Stanley Nadel, "Jewish Race and German Soul in Nineteenth Century America," *AJH* 77, no. 1 (1987): 12–15; Carl Wittke, *Refugees of Revolution: The German Forty-Eighters in America* (Philadelphia: University of Pennsylvania Press, 1952), 293.

74. Nadel, "Jewish Race," 12.

75. Nadel, "Jewish Race," 15–20; Swichkow, "Jewish Community of Milwaukee," 49; Ruth S. Baker, "Victorian Wedding in Olde Town," *The Record* 10, no. 1 (1979): 10; Justin G. Turner, "The First Decade of Los Angeles Jewry: A Pioneer History (1850–1860)," *AJHQ* 54, no. 2 (1964): 130; Swichkow and Gartner, *Jews of Milwaukee*, 54.

76. Nadel, "Jewish Race," 13–15; Max J. Kohler, "The German-Jewish Migration to America," *PAJHS* 9 (1901): 102.

77. Rudolph Glanz, *Jews in Relation to the Cultural Milieu of the Germans in America up to the Eighteen Eighties* (New York: YIVO, 1948), 33.

78. Hans L. Trefousse, *Carl Schurz: A Biography* (Knoxville: University of Tennessee Press, 1982), 255; Kathleen Neils Conzen, *Immigrant Milwaukee, 1836–1860* (Cambridge: Harvard University Press, 1976), 211–12.

79. Nadel, "Kleindeutschland," 211.

80. Quoted in Hirshler, *Jews from Germany*, 50; quoted in Panitz, "Simon Wolf," 76–77; see also Glanz, *Jews in Relation to the Cultural Milieu*.

81. Toll, *Portland Jewry*, 54.

82. Nadel, "Kleindeutschland," 209.

83. Drachman, *Unfailing Light*, 12.

84. Alan N. Bernstein, "Immigrants and Residential Mobility: The Irish and Germans in Philadelphia, 1850–1880," in Theodore Hershberg, *Philadelphia: Work, Space, Family, and Group Experience in the Nineteenth Century: Essays toward an Interdisciplinary History of the City* (New York: Oxford University Press, 1981), 180; Mesinger, "Jewish Community in Syracuse," 54; Mesinger, "Social Geography," 361; Mostov, "'Jerusalem' on the Ohio," 199; Plaut, *Jews in Minnesota*, 54, 59.

85. Kussy, "Reminiscences of Jewish Life," 180.

86. Sarna, *Jacksonian Jew*; Charles P. Daly, *The Settlement of the Jews in North America* (New York: Philip Cowen, 1893), 102–3, 139–40; David Grimstead, *Melodrama Unveiled: American Theater and Culture, 1800–1850* (Chicago: University of Chicago Press, 1968), 151, 217; Sol Liptzin, *The Jew in American Literature* (New York: Bloch, 1966), 264–69; *Solomon Nunes Carvalho: Painter, Photographer, and Prophet in Nineteenth Century America* (Baltimore: Jewish Historical Society of Maryland, 1989); Gay Talese, *The Kingdom and the Power* (London: Colder and Bayars, 1966); William M. Kramer and Norton B. Stern, "Sir Henry Heyman: San Francisco's Noble Musician," *WSJHQ* 18, no. 4 (1986): 310–13.

87. Joseph Gutmann, "Jewish Participation in the Visual Arts of Eighteenth- and Nineteenth-Century America," *AJA* 15, no. 1 (1963): 24–46.

88. Jonathan D. Sarna, "A Jewish Student in Nineteenth Century America: The Diary of Louis Ehrich—Yale '69," *Jews in New Haven* 1 (1978): 70; Eli Evans, *Judah P. Benjamin, The Jewish Confederate* (New York: Free Press, 1988); Dan Oren, *Joining the Club: A History of Jews and Yale* (New Haven: Yale University Press, 1985), 5–13; E. Digby Baltzell, Allen Glicksman and Jacquelyn Litt, "The Jewish Communities of Philadelphia and Boston: A Tale of Two Cities," in Friedman, *Jewish Life in Philadelphia*, 308.

89. Quoted in Cohen, *Dual Heritage*, 10; see also *Memorial Volume: Leo N. Levi: I.O.B.B., 1905* (Chicago: Homburger Printing, 1905), 13, on a Jewish student at the University of Virginia.

90. Sarna, "Jewish Student"; Allon Gal, *Brandeis of Boston* (Cambridge: Harvard University Press, 1980).

91. Goldman, "Henry W. Schneeberger," 153; Karp, "Simon Tuska," 79–97.

92. Lewis S. Feuer, "America's First Jewish Professor: James Jacob Sylvester at the University of Virginia," *AJA* 36, no. 2 (1984): 152–56.

93. Oren, *Jews and Yale*, 10–11; Guido Kisch, "Two American Jewish Pioneeers of New Haven," *Historica Judaica* 4, no. 1 (1942): 19.

94. Trachtenberg, *Consider the Years*, 110; Paul Ritterband and Harold S. Wechsler, "Jewish Studies: Origins and Early Conflicts," *Jewish Studies Network* 3, no. 1 (1989): 1; Harold S. Wechsler, "Community and Academy: Jewish Learning at the University of California, 1870–1920," *WSJHQ* 18, no. 2 (1986): 131–33.

95. Karp, "Simon Tuska."

96. Quoted in Oscar Handlin, ed., *This Was America: As Recorded by European Travellers in the Eighteenth, Nineteenth, and Twentieth Centuries* (New York: Harper and Row, 1949), 319.

97. "A Tree Is Planted at Mount Vernon," *The Record* 7, no. 1 (1974): 37–40.

98. Isaac Markens, "Lincoln and the Jews," *PAJHS* 17 (1909): 109–65; William M. Kramer, "'They Have Killed Our Man But Not Our Cause': The California Jewish Mourners of Abraham Lincoln," *WSJHQ* 2, no. 4 (1970): 187–216.

99. *Jewish Messenger* 2, no. 1 (1857): 4.
100. Ibid.

Chapter Seven. In the Eyes of Others

First epigraph from *Atlanta Daily Herald,* quoted in Hertzberg, *Strangers in the Gate City,* 34; second epigraph quoted in Mostov, "'Jerusalem' on the Ohio," 95; third epigraph from Winograd, "The Horse Died at Windber," 41.

1. Daly, *Jews in North America,* 92–95.
2. Wechsler, "Community and Academy," 132.
3. Adler, "Zebulon B. Vance," 357–77.
4. For a classic statement about the near absence of American anti-Semitism, see Oscar Handlin, *Adventures in Freedom: 300 Years of Jewish Life in America* (New York: McGraw-Hill, 1954); for a harsher view, which, however, still located anti-Semitism at the margins of respectability, see John Higham, "Anti-Semitism in the Gilded Age," *Mississippi Valley Historical Review* 43, no. 3 (1957): 559–78; John Higham, "American Anti-Semitism Historically Reconsidered," in Charles H. Stember, ed., *Jews in the Mind of America* (New York: Basic Books, 1966), 237–58; John Higham, "Social Discrimination against Jews in America," *PAJHS* 47, no. 1 (1957): 1–33; a more recent and more negative assessment of American anti-Semitism, which sees Americans by and large sharing in the western European tradition, is Michael Dobkowski, *The Tarnished Dream: The Basis of American Anti-Semitism* (Westport, Conn.: Greenwood Press, 1979).
5. The term "anti-Semitism" is in itself a matter of historical concern. The word was coined in 1879 by a German agitator, Wilhelm Marr. Marr used the term to refer to organized political campaigns against the Jews. It assumed that Jews constituted a separate and inferior race that stood out as defective and unassimilable into German society. It attributed the Jews' alien culture (and religion) to their biological inferiority. Scholars, social analysts, and others concerned with issues of Jewish history have also used the terms "anti-Semitism," "anti-Semitic," and "anti-Semite" to indicate more broadly any action, policy, sentiment, or analysis that seems hostile to Jews and Judaism. Depending on usage, the term may or may not reflect the concerns of Marr and his contemporaries with racial typologies. In this book, I try to distinguish American views of Judaism and Jews based on race from those based on other kinds of analysis.
6. On the ways in which Americans, particularly in the nineteenth century, used these other groups as vehicles by which they expressed concerns about their own national identity, see Robert Berkhofer, *The White Man's Indian: Images of the American Indian from Columbus to the Present* (New York: Random House, 1978); Winthrop Jordan, *White over Black: American Attitudes toward the Negro, 1550–1812* (Baltimore: Penguin, 1968); Dale T. Knobel, *Paddy and the Republic: Ethnicity and Nationality in Antebellum America* (Middletown, Conn.: Wesleyan University Press, 1986).
7. Michael Kammen, *People of Paradox: An Inquiry Concerning the Origins of American Civilization* (New York: Oxford University Press, 1972); Frederick Jackson Turner, *The Frontier in American History* (New York: Holt, Rinehart and Winston, 1962); Daniel Boorstin, *The Image, or What Happened to the American Dream* (New York: Atheneum, 1962); Margaret Mead, *And Keep Your Powder Dry: An Anthropolo-*

gist Looks at America (New York: W. Morrow, 1942); David Potter, *People of Plenty: Economic Abundance and the American Character* (Chicago: University of Chicago Press, 1954).

8. Alexis De Tocqueville, *Democracy in America,* 2d ed. (New York: G. Adlard, 1838).

9. John Higham, *Strangers in the Land: Patterns of American Nativism 1860–1925* (New Brunswick, N.J.: Rutgers University Press, 1955).

10. Richard Hofstadter, *The Age of Reform: From Bryan to F.D.R.* (New York: Random House, 1955), 23–59.

11. George W. Pierson, *The Moving American* (New York: Alfred A. Knopf, 1973); Louis B. Wright, *Culture on the Moving Frontier* (New York: Harper and Row, 1955).

12. Berkhofer, *White Man's Indian;* Jordan, *White over Black;* Joel Williamson, *A Rage for Order: Black-White Relations in the American South since Emancipation* (New York: Oxford University Press, 1986); George M. Fredrickson, *White Supremacy: A Comparative Study on American and South African History* (New York: Oxford University Press, 1981).

13. Sidney Mead, *The Lively Experiment: The Shaping of Christianity in America* (New York: Harper and Row, 1963); Martin Marty, *Righteous Empire: The Protestant Experience in America* (New York: Dial, 1970).

14. Ray Allen Billington, *The Protestant Crusade: 1800–1860: A Study in the Origins of American Nativism* (Chicago: Quadrangle, 1938): Higham, *Strangers in Land.*

15. Quoted in Borden, *Jews, Turks, and Infidels,* 126; for an example of linking Sunday closing laws with anti-Semitism, see Naomi Cohen, "Anti-Semitism in the Gilded Age: The Jewish View," *Jewish Social Studies* 41, no. 3–4 (1979): 190–91; Friedenberg, "American Sunday Laws," 101–15.

16. Henry F. May, *Protestant Churches in Industrial America* (New York: Harper, 1949); *Proceedings of the National Convention to Secure the Religious Amendment of the Constitution of the United States* (n.p., 1872); Jerry W. Brown, *The Rise of Biblical Criticism in America* (Middletown, Conn.: Wesleyan University Press, 1969); Robert Cross, *The Church and the City* (Indianapolis: Bobbs-Merrill, 1967).

17. Borden, *Jews, Turks, and Infidels.*

18. Ibid., 42.

19. Kraut, *Felix Adler,* 101.

20. Frank Fox, "Quaker, Shaker, Rabbi: Warder Cresson, The Story of a Philadelphia Mystic," *Pennsylvania Magazine of History and Biography* 95, no. 2 (1971): 147–94.

21. Felsenthal, *Teacher In Israel,* 42–43.

22. Mazur, "Minyans for a Prairie City," 12.

23. Greenberg, *Baltimore Hebrew Congregation,* 5–6; Broches, "Jews of Boston," 206.

24. Bertram Wallace Korn, *American Jewry and the Civil War* (Philadelphia: Jewish Publication Society of America, 1951) 168; Ruchames, "Abolitionists and Jews," 139; Lewis Wallace, *Ben-Hur, A Tale of the Christ* (New York: Harper and Brothers, 1880), 534.

25. Alan Tarshish, *Dawn in the West* (Lanham, Md.: University Press of America, 1985), 105.

26. Louise Mayo, *Ambivalent Image: Nineteenth Century America's Perception of the Jew* (Rutherford, N.J.: Fairleigh Dickinson University Press, 1988), 29.

27. Thomas Wentworth Higginson, "Negro Spirituals," *Atlantic Monthly* 19 (June 1867): 688.

28. Quoted in Martin I. Cohen, "Jews in New Haven: 1840–1860: The Americanization of a Community," *Jews in New Haven* 4 (March 1968): 66.

29. Jonathan Sarna, "American Christian Opposition to Missions to the Jews: 1816–1900," *Journal of Ecumenical Studies* 23, no. 2 (1986): 225–38; Mayo, *Ambivalent Image*, 25; on opposition within the Masonic order to evangelizing the Jews, see Lipson, *Freemasonry in Connecticut*, 181–82.

30. David A. Rausch, *Louis Meyer's Eminent Hebrew Christians of the Nineteenth Century: Brief Biographical Sketches* (New York: Edwin Mellen, 1983); Eichhorn, *Evangelizing the American Jew;* Lorman Ratner, "Conversion of the Jews and Pre-Civil War Reform," *American Quarterly* 13, no. 1 (1961): 43–54; Bernard, *Children You Gave Us,* 6, 8.

31. Ashton, "Rebecca Gratz," 149.

32. *Ladies Literary Cabinet* 4 (6 October 1821): 173–74; for more general discussions of conversionism in nineteenth-century American literature, see Mayo, *Ambivalent Image*, 23–26; Louis Harap, *The Image of the Jew in American Literature: From Early Republic to Mass Immigration* (Philadelphia: Jewish Publication Society, 1974), 74–77, 135–38, 145–88.

33. Jonathan D. Sarna, "Jewish-Christian Hostility in the United States: Perceptions from a Jewish Point of View," in Robert Bellah and Frederick E. Greenspahn, eds., *Uncivil Religion: Interreligious Hostility in America* (New York: Crossroads, 1987), 7.

34. Charles Rosenberg, *The Cholera Years: The United States in 1832, 1849 and 1866* (Chicago: University of Chicago Press, 1962), 140.

35. Peter Amann, "Prophet in Zion: The Saga of George J. Adams," *New England Quarterly* 37, no. 4 (1964): 477–500; David A. Rausch, *Zionism within Early American Fundamentalism, 1878–1918* (New York: Edwin Mellen, 1979), 84–88; Michael J. Pragai, *Faith and Fulfilment: Christians and the Return to the Promised Land* (London: Valentine, Michael, 1985); David H. Finnie, *Pioneers East: The Early American Experience in the Middle East* (Cambridge: Harvard University Press, 1967); Lawrence Epstein, *Zion's Call: Christian Contributions to the Origins and Development of Israel* (Lanham, Md.: University Press of America, 1984), 7–25; Moshe Davis, "The Holy Land Idea in American Spiritual History," in Moshe Davis, ed., *With Eyes toward Zion: Scholars Colloquium on America-Holy Land Studies* (New York: Arno Press, 1977), 3–33; Robert T. Handy, "Sources for Understanding American Christian Attitudes towards the Holy Land, 1800–1950," in Davis, *With Eyes Toward Zion,* 34–56; Louis Ruchames, "Mordecai Manuel Noah and Early American Zionism," *AJHQ* 64, no. 3 (1975): 195–223.

36. Quoted in Davis, "Holy Land Idea," 18.

37. Rosenberg and Marmor, *Temple Beth El,* 2.

38. Friedman, "Visit to a New York Synagogue," 181.

39. Mostov, "German Jewish Immigrants," 129.

40. On the state of Protestantism in the nineteenth century, see Ann Douglas, *The Feminization of American Religion* (New York: Doubleday, 1988).

41. *The Poetical Works of Longfellow* (Cambridge: Houghton Mifflin, 1975), 191–92.

42. Ibid., 113–64.

43. Sarna, "Mixed Seating," 363–94.

44. Quoted in Polster, "Member of the Herd," 22.

45. Gendler, "Jews of Omaha," 297.

46. Rubinger, "Albany Jewry," 336; Fogelson, "Jews of Santa Cruz," 107–8.

47. Robert E. Levinson, *Jews in the California Gold Rush* (New York: KTAV, 1978), 113.

48. Clipping, Baer Family Papers, American Jewish Archives, Documents Collection; "A Jewish Wedding," *Rhode Island Jewish Historical Notes* 2, no. 2 (1975): 208–9.

49. Baker, "Victorian Wedding," 11.

50. Owen, "First Synagogue," 12.

51. Moses, *Jews of Mobile*, 121–22.

52. *The Chronicles of Emanu-El*, 30.

53. Hanover *Spectator* 1872, clippings, American Jewish Archives, Miscellaneous File.

54. Fleishaker, "Illinois-Iowa Jewish Community," 324; Breck, *Centennial History*, 24; Stern, "Jewish Community," 52.

55. Quoted in Hertzberg, *Strangers within the Gate City*, 34.

56. Quoted in Norton B. Stern and William M. Kramer, "Anti-Semitism and the Jewish Image in the Early West," 76, no. 2 (1974): 138–39; quoted in Higham, "American Anti-Semitism," 247.

57. Barrington Moore, *Social Origins of Dictatorship and Democracy: Lord and Peasant in the Making of the Modern World* (Boston: Beacon Press, 1966), 11–155; George Frederickson, *The Inner Civil War: Northern Intellectuals and the Crisis of Union* (New York: Harper, 1965); Eric Foner, *Free Soil, Free Labor, Free Men: The Ideology of the Republican Party* (New York: Oxford University Press, 1970).

58. Rubin, *Savannah Jewry*, 137; J. George Fredman and Louis A. Falk, *Jews in American Wars* (New York: Jewish War Veterans of the United States, 1942), 24; Schmier, "Expulsion of Jews," 9–22.

59. Quoted in Rockaway, "Anti-Semitism in Detroit," 44.

60. Greenberg, "Adas Israel"; Wolf, *Presidents I Have Known*, 73–74.

61. Quoted in Lowenstein, *Jews of Oregon*, 67.

62. Ashkenazi, "Creoles of Jerusalem," 237.

63. Gerber, "Cutting Out Shylock," 219; Griffen, *Natives and Newcomers*, 122–23; Peter Decker, *Fortunes and Failures: White-Collar Mobility in Nineteenth Century San Francisco* (Cambridge: Harvard University Press, 1978), 100.

64. Mostov, "Jewish Economic History," 333–53; Cline, "Portland Jews," 56.

65. Quoted in Leon Huhner, *The Life of Judah Touro (1775–1854)* (Philadelphia: Jewish Publication Society of America, 1946), 109.

66. Quoted in Levinson, *California Gold Rush*, 7.

67. Harap, *Jew in American Literature*; Liptzin, *Jew in American Literature*; Dobkowski, *Tarnished Dream*; Mayo, *Ambivalent Image*; Ellen Schiff, "Shylock's Mishpocheh: Anti-Semitism on the American Stage," in Gerber, *Anti-Semitism in America*, 79–83.

68. Quoted in Harap, *Jew in American Literature*, 47.

69. Albert Aiken, *The California Detective, or the Witches of New York* (New

York: Beadle and Adam, 1878); Edward Z. C. Judson, *Morgan or the Knight of the Black Flag, A Strange Story of By-Gone Times* (New York: E. A. Brady, 1860); Albert Aiken, *The Phantom Hand: or, the Heiress on Fifth Avenue, a Story of New York* (New York: Beadle and Adams, 1877); George Lippard, *The Quaker City; or, the Monks of Monks Hall, a Romance of Philadelphia, Life, Mystery, and Crime* (Philadelphia: 1849); Liptzin, *Jew in American Literature,* 33; Carole Kessner, "More Devils Than Hell Can Hold: Anti-Semitism in American Literature," in Herbert Hirsch and Jack D. Spiro, eds., *Persistent Prejudice: Perspectives on Anti-Semitism* (Fairfax, Va.: George Mason University Press, 1988), 83–97.

70. Matthew Hale Smith, *Sunshine and Shadow in New York* (Hartford: J. B. Burr, 1868), 453; Pine, Hershenov, and Lefkowitz, *Peddler to Suburbanite,* 31.

71. William J. Day to his sister, 23 August 1868, American Jewish Archives, Correspondence File.

72. E. Digby Baltzell, *The Protestant Establishment: Aristocracy and Caste in America* (New York: Vintage Books, 1964), 56, 119; Mayo, *Ambivalent Image,* 94–96.

73. *Coney Island and the Jews: A History of the Development and Success of This Famous Seaside Resort, Together with a Full Account of the Recent Jewish Controversy* (New York: G. W. Carleton and Company, 1879); Mayo, *Ambivalent Image,* 100–103.

74. Lowenstein, *Jews of Oregon,* 67.

75. John Kasson, *Amusing the Millions: Coney Island at the Turn of the Century* (New York: Hill and Wang, 1978), 29–33; Kathy Peiss, *Cheap Amusements: Working Women and Leisure in Turn-of-the-Century New York* (Philadelphia: Temple University Press, 1986), 100, 122–38;

76. *Coney Island and Jews,* 21.

77. Ibid.

78. On the rise of biological determinism toward the end of the century, see Thomas F. Gossett, *Race: The History of an Idea* (New York: Schocken Books, 1963); Stephen Jay Gould, *The Mismeasure of Man* (New York: W. W. Norton, 1981); see also Knobel, *Paddy and the Republic,* as an example of how the early and mid-nineteenth century rhetoric on the Irish assumed the changeability of nature and the adaptive capacity of human beings, while later in the century, the public discourse saw the Irish "personality" as fixed by nature and immutable.

79. Friedman, "Visit to a New York Synagogue," 181.

80. John Beddoe, "On the Physical Characteristics of the Jews," *Transactions of the Ethnological Society of London,* vol. 1 (London: Ethnological Society 1861), 222–37; Josiah C. Nott, *The Physical History of the Jewish Race* (Charleston, S. C.: Walker and James, 1850), 4–6.

81. Quoted in Glanz, *Jewish Woman in America,* 146.

82. John J. Appel, "Jews in American Caricature: 1820–1914," *AJH* 71, no. 1 (1981): 103–33.

83. Luke Shortfield [John Beauchamp Jones], *The Western Merchant, a narrative containing useful instruction for the Western man of business who makes his purchases in the East; also, information for the Eastern man whose customers are in the West: Otherwise, hints for those who design emigrating to the West; deduced from actual experience* (Philadelphia: n.p., 1849), 128; George G. Foster, *New York by Gas-light;*

with Here and There a Streak of Sunshine (New York: Dewitt and Davenport, 1950), 58–59.

84. Quoted in Liptzin, *Jew in American Literature,* 40.

85. For examples of this kind of pro-Jewish stereotyping, see Norton B. Stern and William M. Kramer, "An 1869 Jewish Standard for Gentile Behavior," *WSJHQ* 9, no. 3 (1977): 282–85; "A Case of Pro-Semitism," *WSJHQ* 16, no. 3 (1984): 242–43; Feibelman, "New Orleans Jewish Community," 73; Stern, "Myer Joseph Newmark," 154; Moses, *Jews of Mobile,* 121–22; Cray, *Paupers and Poor Relief,* 180.

86. Stern, "First Jew," 251.

87. Quoted in Arnold Shankman, *The Ambivalent Friends: Afro-Americans View the Immigrant* (Westport, Conn.: Greenwood Press, 1982), 115.

88. Wolf, *Presidents I Have Known,* 72.

89. Levenson, "Chico Jewish Pioneers," 211; on an incident in 1861, also in California, involving anti-Jewish rhetoric during a political campaign, see Narell, "Bernhard Marks," 30–31.

90. Swichkow and Gartner, *Jews of Milwaukee,* 23–24

91. Drachman, *Unfailing Light,* 7; Morgenthau, *All in a Life-Time,* 8; *Memorial Volume: Leo N. Levi: I.O.B.B.,* 1905 (Chicago: Hamburger Printing Company, 1905), 13.

92. Jonathan D. Sarna, "The Pork on the Fork: A Nineteenth Century Anti-Jewish Ditty," *Jewish Social Studies* 45, no. 2 (1982): 169–72.

93. Ehrlich, "Jewish Community of St. Louis," 519; Rosenberg, *Pioneer Texas Merchants,* 10–11.

94. Cohen, "Antisemitism," 189–90.

95. Newspaper clipping, *Army and Navy Journal,* 19 March 1864, American Jewish Archives, Miscellaneous Collection.

96. See, for example, *American Israelite,* 1 April 1859, 306; Bret Harte, "That Ebrew Jew," *AJA* 6, no. 2 (1954): 148–50; Altfeld, *Religious and Civil Liberty,* 21; Fredman and Falk, *Jews in American Wars,* 25; Markens, "Lincoln and Jews," 117–23.

Chapter Eight. Inside/Outside

First epigraph from Burder, *History of All Religions,* 587; second epigraph from *Weekly Gleaner,* 2 March 1860, 2.

1. Due to insufficient funds and disputes between the B'nai B'rith and the artist, Moses Ezekiel, the statue could not be unveiled on July 4, 1876, and the dedication had to wait until Thanksgiving of that year. See Grusd, *B'nai B'rith,* 81.

2. Moses Jacob Ezekiel, *Memoirs from the Baths of Diocletian* (Detroit: Wayne State University Press, 1975).

3. *American Israelite,* 16 February 1877, 3, 5; 4 May 1877, 4.

4. "Israelites Centennial Monument," B'nai B'rith Archives, box 14.

5. Malcolm Stern, "The First Triplets Born in the West—1867," *WSJHQ* 19, no. 4 (1987): 299–305.

6. Cohen, *Encounter with Emancipation,* 132; Jonathan Sarna, *JPS: The Americanization of Jewish Culture* (Philadelphia: Jewish Publication Society of America, 1989), 1; Benny Kraut, *From Reform Judaism to Ethical Culture* (Cincinnati: He-

brew Union College Press, 1979), 215; Arthur Hertzberg, *The Jews of America: Four Centuries of an Uneasy Encounter: A History* (New York: Simon and Schuster, 1989), 90–151.

7. Clifford Geertz, *The Interpretation of Cultures* (New York: Basic Books, 1973), 5.

8. Lee M. Friedman, *Early American Jews* (Cambridge: Harvard University Press, 1934); Rosenwaike, *On the Edge of Greatness.*

9. Wischnitzer, *Synagogue Architecture,* 5–7, 32; Robin, "Jewish Architecture," 67–73; de Breffny, *Synagogue,* 140, 149–59, 166–69; Funaro, "American Synagogue Design," 58–65; Frank J. Roos, Jr., "The Egyptian Style: Notes on Early American Taste," *Magazine of Art* 33, no. 4 (1940): 218–23.

10. For one listing of nineteenth-century names of congregations, see Jacques J. Lyons and Abraham De Sola, *A Jewish Calendar for Fifty Years* (Montreal: John Lovell, 1854), 148–73; see also *American Jewish Yearbook: 1900–1901,* 2:499–501; Simon, *Washington Hebrew Congregation,* 24.

11. Alfred Werner, "Jewish Artists of the Age of Emancipation," in Cecil Roth, ed., *Jewish Art: An Illustrated History* (New York: McGraw Hill, 1961), 541–74; Gutmann, "Visual Arts," 21–24.

12. Carvalho, *Incidents of Travel,* 13–52; Bertram W. Korn, "Introduction," in Carvalho, *Incidents of Travel,* 13–52; *Solomon Nunes Carvalho: Painter, Photographer, and Prophet in Nineteenth Century America* (Baltimore: Jewish Historical Society of Maryland, 1989).

13. Ezekiel, *Baths of Diocletian,* 18, 20–23.

14. Greenwald, "Masonic Mizrah and Lamp," 87–101; Kleeblatt and Wertkin, *Jewish Heritage ,* 14, 25, 43–44, 52–54, 57–60, 68.

15. J. Goldner, "A Gold Rush Community in 1873," *WSJHQ* 9, no. 3 (1977): 216–17; "The Rise and Fall of the Jewish Community of Austin, Nevada," *WSJHQ* 9, no. 1 (1976): 87.

16. Miller, *Pioneers in Service,* 87.

17. Minute Books, Hebrew Ladies' Benevolent Society of Albany, Georgia, American Jewish Archives, box X166.

18. *The Jew* 1 (1823): 1.

19. Bertram Wallace Korn, *Eventful Years and Experiences: Studies in Nineteenth Century American Jewish History* (Cincinnati: American Jewish Archives, 1954), 39.

20. Board of Delegates of American Israelites and Union of American Hebrew Congregations, *Statistics of the Jews of the United States* (Philadelphia: Union of American Hebrew Congregations, 1880), 59.

21. Sussman, "Isaac Leeser."

22. Heller, *Isaac M. Wise*; Joseph Gutmann, "Watchman on an American Rhine: New Light on Isaac M. Wise," *AJA* 10, no. 2 (1958): 135–43.

23. Yechiel Simon, "Samuel Myer Isaacs: 19th Century Jewish Minister in New York City" (D.H.L. diss., Yeshiva University, New York, 1974).

24. Patt, *Jewish Scene,* 35.

25. Fleishaker, "Illinois-Iowa Jewish Community," 24.

26. "A San Francisco Rabbi Reports on a Visit to Sacramento in 1858," *WSJHQ* 11, no. 1 (1978): 60–63.

27. William M. Kramer, "Pioneer Lawyer of California and Texas: Henry J. Labatt (1832–1900)," *WSJHQ* 15, no. 1 (1982): 9–11; "The First Jewish Newspaper in the West—1856," *WSJHQ* 4, no. 1 (1973): 224.

28. Hertzberg, *Strangers within the Gate City,* 63.

29. See, for example, Maxine Seller, "Isaac Leeser's View on the Restoration of a Jewish Palestine," *AJHQ* 58, no. 1 (1968): 118–35; "Stockton Aids Morocco Jewry—1860," *WSJHQ* 13, no. 1 (1980): 75; Panitz, "Jewish Attitudes towards Immigration," 99–103; Joseph Buchler, "The Struggle for Unity: Attempts at Union in American Jewish Life: 1854–1868," in Marcus, *American Jewish History,* 97–121; Ernst, *Immigrant Life,* 138; Jonathan Sarna, "The Spectrum of Jewish Leadership in Ante-Bellum America," *Journal of American Ethnic History* 1, no. 2 (1982): 59–67.

30. Kisch, "Israels Herold," 65–85; Wax, "Isidor Bush," 183–203.

31. *The Asmonean* 1, 1849, clipping, American Jewish Archives, Miscellaneous Collection.

32. Rudolf Glanz, "Where the Jewish Press Was Distributed in Pre-Civil War America," *WSJHQ* 5, no. 1 (1972): 1–14.

33. *Jewish Messenger,* 30 January 1857, 18; see also Joan Dash, *Summoned to Jerusalem: The Life of Henrietta Szold* (New York: Harper and Row, 1979), on Szold's early writings in the *Messenger* under the name Shulamith.

34. Martin, "Yiddish Literature," 184–209; *American Jewish Yearbook: 5660; September 5, 1899, to September 23, 1900* (Philadelphia: Jewish Publication Society of America, 1899), 277–82; Jacob Kabakoff, "New Light on Arnold Bogomil Ehrlich," *AJA* 36, no. 2 (1984): 202–24; Abraham Meyer Rogoff, *Formative Years of the Jewish Labor Movement in the United States (1890–1900)* (Ann Arbor, Mich.: Edwards Brothers, 1945); Leo Wiener, *The History of Yiddish Literature in the Nineteenth Century* (New York: Charles Scribners, 1899), 216; Shtarkman, "Vichtige Momenten," in Glatstein, Niger, and Rogoff, *Finf un Zibitzik Yor,* 11–19; Lifschutz and Tcherikower, "Die Pionere," 240–43; Greene, *American Immigrant Leaders,* 89–90; Ezekiel Lifschutz, *"Die Yiddishe Gazeten* (1874–1928)," *Yiddish* 2, no. 2–3 (1976): 32–38; Moshe Hazkani, "Itonut Yiddish B'Chicago (1877–1951)," in Rawidowicz, *Pinkas Chicago,* 69–72; Rawidowicz, "I. L. Chronik," 137–76.

35. Jacob Kabakoff, *Ha'lvrit Ha'Safrut Ha'lvirt B'America* (Tel Aviv: Yavneh, 1966), 13; Eisenstein, *Ozar Zikhronothai,* 11; Shtarkman, "Vichtige Momenten," 17; Fannie M. Brody, "The Hebrew Press in America, 1871–1931: A Bibliographical Survey," *PAJHS* 33 (1934): 127–70; Haim Rothblatt, "Ha'Itonut Ha'Ivrit B'Chicago," in *Pinkas Chicago,* 35–36; Gartner, "Rumania and America," 70–75.

36. *Occident,* January 1853, 511.

37. Harap, *Jew in American Literature,* 261–69; N. Bryllion Fagin, "Isaac Harby and the Early American Theater," *AJA* 8, no. 1 (1956): 3–13.

38. Harap, *Jew in American Literature,* 259–99; Liptzin, *Jew in American Literature,* 53–67; Diane Lichtenstein, "Fannie Hurst and Her Nineteenth-Century Predecessors," *Studies in American Jewish Literature* 7 (Spring 1988): 26–39; Lichtenstein, "On Whose Native Ground"; Solomon Breibart, "Penina Moise, Southern Jewish Poetess," in Samuel Proctor, Louise Schmier, and Malcom Stern, eds., *Jews of the South: Selected Essays from the Southern Jewish Historical Society* (Macon, Ga.: Mercer University Press, 1984), 31–43.

39. Joseph Mersand, *Traditions in American Literature: A Study of Jewish Characters and Authors* (New York: Modern Chapbooks, 1939), 119; Penina Moise, *Secular and Religious Works of Penina Moise with a Brief Sketch of Her Life* (Charleston, S.C.: N. G. Duffy, 1911), 177; Emma Lazarus, *Songs of a Semite* (New York: American Hebrew, 1882), 56.

40. Lev Raphael, "'The Pen and the Pulpit': Isaac Mayer Wise's Fiction in the *Israelite"* (Ph.D. diss., Michigan State University, 1986), 2; Heller, *Isaac M. Wise,* 661.

41. Harap, *Jew in American Literature,* 272–74; Raphael, "Pen and Pulpit"; Isaac M. Wise, *The Combat of the People; or, Hillel and Herod, a Historical Romance of the Time of Herod I* (Cincinnati: Bloch and Company, 1859); Isaac M. Wise, *The First of the Maccabees* (Cincinnati: Bloch Publishing Co., 1860).

42. Mersand, *American Literature,* 83; Harap, *Jew in American Literature,* 276–79; Abraham H. Steinberg, "Jewish Characters in the American Novel to 1900" (Ph.D. diss., New York University, 1956), 259; Nathan Mayer, *Differences* (Cincinnati: Bloch Publishing Co., 1867).

43. Harap, *Jew in American Literature,* 274.

44. Martin, "Yiddish Literature," 184–87; Hazkani, "Itonut B'Iddish B'Chicago," 72–73.

45. Kabakoff, *Halutzei Hasafrut,* 25–41.

46. Ibid., 12, 38–40, 79.

47. Abraham J. Karp, *Beginnings: Early American Judaica* (Philadelphia: Jewish Publication Society of America, 1975), 37–40.

48. Korn, "Isaac Leeser," 127–41; Whiteman, "Legacy of Isaac Leeser," 26–47.

49. Eisenstein, *Ozar Zikhronothai,* 31–33; Allan E. Levine, *An American Jewish Bibliography: A List of Books and Pamphlets by Jews Printed in the United States from 1851 to 1875* (Cincinnati: American Jewish Archives, 1959); Eric L. Friedland, "Hebrew Liturgical Creativity in Nineteenth-Century America," *Modern Judaism* 1, no. 3 (1981): 323–36.

50. Eisenstein, *Ozar Zikhronothai,* 11.

51. Stephen S. Wise, "Charles E. Bloch," *American Jewish Yearbook:* 5702 (Philadelphia: Jewish Publication Society of America, 1941), 43: 381; Solomon Grayzel, "A Hundred Years of the Bloch Publishing Company," *Jewish Book Annual* 12 (1953–54): 72–76; Samuel Niger, "Yiddish Culture," in *Jewish People: Past and Present* 4: 269–70.

52. Wiener, *Yiddish Literature,* 216.

53. Kisch, *"Israels Herold,"* 69–70.

54. Simon, "Samuel Myer Isaacs," 13–14.

55. "Two Letters to Harriet Choynski," *WSJHQ* 7, no. 1 (1974): 44; Niger, "Yiddish Culture," 271; Sarna, *Judaism in New York,* 72.

56. Grayzel, "Bloch Publishing Company."

57. Quoted in Sarna, *JPS,* 8.

58. Sarna, *JPS,* 7–12.

59. Kaplan, "Akron Jewish Community," 202–3.

60. Ackerman, "Jewish Education," 5.

61. Rubin, *Savannah Jewry,* 159; "Two Letters to Harriet Choynski," 44; Rothschild, *As But a Day,* 5; Norton B. Stern and William M. Kramer, "The San Bernadino Hebrew and English Academy, 1868–1972," *WSJHQ* 8, no. 2 (1976): 102–17.

62. For one example, Washington, D.C., see Nathan M. Kaganoff, "The Education of the Jewish Child in the District of Columbia" (M.A. thesis, The American University, 1956).

63. Adler, *I Have Considered the Days,* 11; Ezekiel and Lichtenstein, *Jews of Richmond,* 225; Kohut, *Autobiography,* 12.

64. Berman, "Jewish Education," 247–62.

65. Philipson, *Autobiography*, 2.

66. Sussman, "Isaac Leeser," 113; see, for example, *The Teachers' and Parents' Assistant; or, Thirteen Lessons Conveying to Uninformed Minds the First Ideas of God and His Attributes. By an American Jewess* (Philadelphia: C. Sherman, 1855).

67. *American Israelite* 1 (December 1854): 197–98.

68. Heller, *Isaac M. Wise*, 254; Michael Meyer, "A Centennial History," in Samuel E. Karff, *Hebrew Union College-Jewish Institute of Religion at One Hundred Years* (Cincinnati: Hebrew Union College Press, 1976), 3–83.

69. "Letter from San Francisco in 1854," *WSJHQ* 5, no. 4 (1973): 54.

70. See, for example, Gartner, *Jews of Cleveland*, 15–16.

71. Heller, *Isaac M. Wise*, 92–93.

72. Kohut, *Autobiography*, 13.

73. On the mid-nineteenth century "New Germany" idea to preserve intact German language and culture in America, see John A. Hawgood, *The Tragedy of German America: The Germans in the United States of America during the Nineteenth Century and After* (New York: G. P. Putnam, 1940), 93–224; Richard O'Connor, *The German Americans* (Boston: Little Brown, 1968), 767–97.

74. Simon, "Samuel Myer Isaacs," 4.

75. *Solomon Nunes Carvalho*, 16.

76. Gerstley, "Reminiscences."

77. Bernhard Cohn, "Early German Preaching in America," *Historica Judaica* 15, no. 2 (1953): 86–134; Cohen, *Encounter with Emancipation*, 58–60; Nadel, "Jewish Race," 6–26.

78. Polster, "Member of the Herd," 45–46.

79. Moore, *B'nai B'rith*, 20.

80. Morton Berman, *Our First Century: Temple Isaiah Israel, 1852–1952* (Chicago: n.p., 1952), 14.

81. Reissner, "German-American Jews," 92–93.

82. Isaac Wolfe Bernheim, *The Story of the Bernheim Family* (Louisville: John P. Morton, 1910), 44.

83. "The Beginning of Organized Jewish Life in Kansas—1858," *WSJHQ* 13, no. 4 (1980): 304; Jacobs, *San Diego Girl*, 46, 57.

84. Rosenberg, *Jewish Community in Rochester*, 87.

85. Zmora, "Orphan Asylum," 463; Grinstein, "Nineteenth Century," 48.

86. Margolies, "Henry Vidaver," 28–29.

87. Quoted in Heller, *Isaac M. Wise*, 392; Gutstein, *Priceless Heritage*, 226.

88. Emanuel Hertz, *Lincoln's Contacts: Delivered at the Jewish Club October 1, 1929* (Tarrytown, N.Y.: Magazine of History with Notes and Queries, 1930), 4–5.

89. Trachtenberg, *Consider the Years*, 113.

90. Heller, *Isaac M. Wise*, 583, 586; Mielziner, *Moses Mielziner*, 4.

91. Ashkenazi, "Creoles of Jerusalem," 55; Bentwich, *For Zion's Sake*, 14; Drachman, *Unfailing Light*, 12.

92. Niger, "Yiddish Culture," 271.

93. *Jewish Messenger* 1, 2 January 1857, 4.

94. Quoted in Dena Wilansky, *Sinai to Chicago: Lay Views on the Writings of Isaac M. Wise, Founder of Reform Judaism in America* (New York: Renaissance, 1937), 27–28.

95. Bernheim, *Bernheim Family*, 34–35.

96. Werner, *Julius Rosenwald,* 11.
97. Swichkow and Gartner, *Jews of Milwaukee,* 23.
98. Cohen, *Dual Heritage,* 7.
99. Plaut, *Mount Zion,* 35.
100. Karp, "Simon Tuska," 79–97.
101. David Einhorn Hirsch, *Rabbi Emil G. Hirsch: The Reform Advocate* (Chicago: Whitehall, 1968), 6.

A NOTE ON SOURCES

THE SOURCES for the study of mid-nineteenth-century American Jews are extraordinarily rich, providing a veritable gold mine for historians willing to sift through vast amounts of published and unpublished data. Because so many American Jewish communities and institutions owe their existence to the efforts of the "pioneers" of the middle decades of the nineteenth century, Jews in communities across America have tried to record the experiences of these years.

Most historians sneer at commissioned, celebratory volumes, extolling as they do the great achievements of a particular synagogue, the noble altruism of a charity, or the boastful listing of eminent sons and daughters of a specific community. Yet those "fileopietistic" records of the past contain valuable material to scholars willing to dig, to interpret, and to wring out of such often amateur writings important patterns of social and cultural development. The vast records and published histories of numerous synagogues, benevolent associations, and charitable societies provide a detailed trove of data on the social history of individual communities. Memoirs and family recollections, autobiographies and portraits of community founders provide useful insights into the myriad details of community life and kinship networks despite their uncritical tone. Buttressed by the wide-ranging commentary and reportage in such available newspapers as the *Occident,* the *American Israelite,* the *Jewish Messenger,* the *Weekly Gleaner,* and others, one can reconstruct the interconnected processes of migration and community development, and the intersection of family, work, ethnicity, and religion.

Local and regional Jewish historical societies have played an important role in the collection and publication of many of these sources. Their archives are rich in primary materials. Moreover, the Jewish Historical Societies of Rhode Island, Michigan, Washington, D.C., and New Haven have also published large amounts of material. While such articles and books may not quite match a standard of professional scholarship, they are an important and immensely rich basis for reasearch and interpretation. The *Western States Jewish Historical Quarterly* is probably the best example of popular history serving multiple purposes and demonstrating the inextricable link between the "professional" scholar and the "amateur" buff.

There is also a large corpus of secondary work that I have drawn upon to produce this book. The sections of this book that detail Jewish life in Europe were informed by the work of such historians as Jacob Katz, Michael Meyer, Avraham Barkai, Alice Goldstein, Zvi William Tennenbaum, Marsha Rozenblit, Marion Kaplan, and many others. In general, the social and cultural history of European Jewry in the nineteenth century seems to be much more closely allied and conceptually interwoven with intellectual trends in the study of "host" society history than the American material.

This does not mean that American Jewish history has not been informed by developments in American history in general. Certainly, there are many books in the field that have been terribly useful to me. First, I benefitted greatly from the work of the first generation of American Jewish community biographers: Isaac Fein, Hyman Grinstein, Selig Adler, Bertram Korn, Morris Silverman, and scores upon scores of others who labored to present books and articles chronicling the histories of Baltimore, New York, Buffalo, Mobile, Hartford, and many other Jewish communities. These were writers who certainly had a sense of the political and social developments in America against which they set the evolution of Jewish communities. Their interest, however, was first and foremost in detailing the latter, with the American scene creating a kind of hazy backdrop. More recent students of American Jewish history, practitioners of the "new social history" —William Toll, writing about Portland; Steven Mostov on Boston; Peter Decker on San Francisco; Steven Hertzberg for Atlanta—have correctly asserted that in order to understand the development of Jewish life and institutions in a particular place, the historian must have a thorough understanding of the city or region in which Jews settled. The Jewish communities that emerged in America, after all, represented a creative fusion of traditional Jewish life with the conditions of life in American cities and towns.

In the main, the available scholarship on nineteenth-century American Jewry focuses on individual communities. This is certainly appropriate since it was in their local settings that Jews worked, created families, worshipped, helped each other out, voted, and rubbed shoulders with the other Americans. I have therefore learned much from those who painstakingly studied one community after another, and I have drawn deeply from the details of Jewish life that they painted.

Other historians before me have attempted to synthesize this entire sweep of time in American Jewish history. I am certainly indebted to the labors of such eminent writers as Rudolf Glanz, Bertram Korn, and Jacob Rader Marcus, the founders of American Jewish history as a recognized field within both the American and Jewish scholarly contexts. More recent scholars, Jonathan Sarna, Benny Kraut, and Deborah Dash Moore, have made significant contributions to our understanding of nineteenth-century American Jewry. However, since its publication in 1984, Naomi Cohen's *Encounter With Emancipation* has stood out as the premier book to tackle the nature of Jewish adjustment to America in the nineteenth century. While my book begins with some different premises, asks some different questions, and consequently deals with the material in a very different way, her work still stands without question as an important marker in the development of the field.

INDEX

ABOUT THE AMERICAN
JEWISH HISTORICAL SOCIETY

THE TWENTIETH CENTURY has been a period of change for the American Jewish community, bringing growth in numbers and in status and, most important, a new perception of itself as part of the history of the United States. The American Jewish Historical Society has also grown over the century, emerging as a professional historical association with a depth of scholarship that enables it to redefine what is *American* and what is *Jewish* in the American saga. To record and examine this saga and to honor its own centennial, the society has published this five-volume series, *The Jewish People in America.*

The society was founded on 7 June 1892 in New York City, where it was housed in two crowded rooms in the Jewish Theological Seminary. At the first meeting, its president Cyrus Adler declared that it was the patriotic duty of every ethnic group in America to record its contributions to the country. Another founding father emphasized the need to popularize such studies "in order to stem the growing anti-Semitism in this country." As late as the 1950s, the society was encouraging young doctoral students in history to research and publish material of Jewish interest, even though such research, according to Rabbi Isidore Meyer, then the society's librarian, would impede the writers' advancement in academia. In this climate, the early writings in the society's journal, *Publications of the American Jewish Historical Society,* were primarily the work of amateurs; they were narrowly focused, often simply a recounting of the deeds of the writers' ancestors. However, these studies did bring to light original data of great importance to subsequent historians and constitute an invaluable corpus of American Jewish historiography.

The situation has changed materially. One hundred years later, the society has its own building on the campus of Brandeis University; the building houses the society's office space, exhibit area, and library. The Academic Council of the society includes sixty-three professors of American history whose primary interest is American Jewish history. Articles in the society's publication, now called *American Jewish History,* meet the highest professional standards and are often presented at the annual meeting of the American Historical Association. The society has also published an extensive series of monographs, which culminates in the publication of these volumes. The purpose of *The Jewish People in America* series is to provide a comprehensive historical study of the American Jewish experience from the age of discovery to the present time that both satisfies the standards of the historical profession and holds the interest of the intelligent lay reader.

Dr. Abram Kanof
Past President
American Jewish Historical Society
and Chairman
The Jewish People in America Project